GERMAN POLITICS UNDER
SOVIET OCCUPATION

GERMAN POLITICS
under
SOVIET OCCUPATION

HENRY KRISCH

1974

Columbia University Press

new york and london

Library of Congress Cataloging in Publication Data

Krisch, Henry.
  German politics under Soviet occupation.

  Bibliography: p.
  1. Germany (Territory under Allied occupation, 1945–
1955. Russian Zone). 2. Sozialistische Einheitspartei
Deutschlands—History. 3. Kommunistische Partei Deut-
schlands—History. 4. Sozialdemokratische Partei
Deutschlands—History. 1. Title.
DD257.4.K75   329.9′43   74-3288
ISBN 0-231-03835-6

FOR JUNE

Studies of the Russian Institute, Columbia University

The Russian Institute of Columbia University sponsors the Studies of the Russian Institute in the belief that their publication contributes to scholarly research and public understanding. In this way the Institute, while not necessarily endorsing their conclusions, is pleased to make available the results of some of the research conducted under its auspices. A list of the Studies of the Russian Institute appears at the back of the book.

Acknowledgments

I am grateful for help given me by numerous persons both here and abroad. I wish especially to thank those individuals who consented to be interviewed or to grant me access to their private papers; their names are indicated in the Bibliography.

Like every author, I am indebted to many librarians, especially those of the Columbia University Libraries, the Library of Congress, and librarians and archivists in Bonn, Berlin, and elsewhere.

The Ford Foundation, Barnard College, the University of Connecticut Research Foundation, and the Deutsche Akademischer Austauschdienst (DAAD) helped me financially.

Colleagues at several universities were generous in giving me useful criticism and friendly advice; of the many who gave of their time I should like to mention my dissertation sponsor, Alexander Dallin, and Loren R. Graham. The Columbia University Press and especially its Chief Copy Editor, Joan McQuary, have saved a neophyte author from many errors. My wife, June, knows better than even I how essential her support has been. Full responsibility for the errors remaining in this work is solely my own.

June, 1974   H. K.

Contents

Abbreviations

ACC   Allied Control Council—formally, the Control Council for
           Germany
AKB   Allied Kommandatura Berlin (Allied Command in Berlin)
BL   Bezirksleitung ([KPD] district leadership)--in the Soviet Zone
BV   Bezirksvorstand—([SPD] district leadership)—in the Soviet Zone
CDU   Christlich-Demokratische Union (Christian Democratic Union)
DDR   Deutsche Demokratische Republik (German Democratic Republic
           [East Germany])
EAC   European Advisory Commission—American British Soviet com-
           mittee for postwar agrangements on German and Austrian occu-
           pation, 1943–1945
KPD   Kommunistische Partei Deutschlands (Communist Party of
           Germany)
LDP[D]   Liberal-Demokratische Partei [Deutschlands] (Liberal Democratic
           Party [of Germany])
LL   Landesleitung ([KPD]*Land* leadership)—provincial leadership in
           the Soviet Zone
LV   Landesvorstand ([SPD] provincial leadership)—in the Soviet Zone
NK "FD"   National-Komitee "Freies Deutschland" (National Committee
           "Free Germany")—1943–1945
OMGUS   Office of Military Government—United States
PV   Parteivorstand ([SPD] national leadership)—before 1933
SBZ   Sowjetische Besatzungzone (Soviet Zone of Occupation)
SED   Sozialistische Einheitspartei Deutschlands (Socialist Unity Party of
           Germany)—after April 1946
SMA[D]   Soviet Military Administration [in Germany])
SOPADE   Sozialdemokratische Partei Deutschlands (Social Democratic Party
           of Germany)—exile leadership after 1933

SPD Sozialdemokratische Partei Deutschlands (Social Democratic Party of Germany)—after April 1946 in Berlin and Western Zones only

ZA Zentralausschuss ([SPD] central leadership)—in the Soviet Zone

ZK Zentral Komitee ([KPD] Central Committee)

ZS Zentralsekretariat ([SED] Central Secretariat)

GERMAN POLITICS UNDER
SOVIET OCCUPATION

Introduction

Stalin presented his views on the distinctive nature of the war that was being waged: "This war is not as in the past; whoever occupies a territory also imposes on it his own social system. Everyone imposes his own system as far as his army can reach. It cannot be otherwise."

—Milovan Djilas

Occupation in our time represents for the Occupant an arena in which the crusading power of internal political values meets the rational reckoning of foreign policy.

—Leonard Krieger

With the passing of more than a quarter century since the closing years of World War II and its immediate postwar aftermath, the policies of the major powers at that time have become the objects of extensive study. The events of that era are now seen as having shaped our present world, and the search for explanations of general or particular developments is thus also a search for understanding of our times.

In the process of reconsideration of the origins of our immediate past, a major focus of scholarship has been on American policy. The comparative neglect of Soviet policy in those years is due in part to the inaccessibility of sources,[1] and in perhaps larger part to the "revisionist" convictions of scholars in this field. The official American view of the early Cold War involved the assumption of Soviet culpability for the breakdown of the wartime alliance; those taking a fresh look at this period therefore tended to concentrate on Western actions, assuming Soviet policy to be basically responsive in nature.

The nature and timing of Soviet actions nevertheless remain crucial aspects of the history of the postwar period. While Soviet policy undoubtedly was shaped in part by actual or anticipated American action,[2] the question as to an active and purposeful Soviet policy can only be answered by detailed examination of specific Soviet behavior.

John Gimbel has noted that reconsiderations of policies relating to Germany have been surprisingly scanty in view of the importance of Germany as both the chief problem to be dealt with and the "chief prize to be won in Europe."[3] Indeed, such studies as have been done on the German question rarely focus on Soviet policy in the field during the early period of occupation, and still less frequently on political affairs (as opposed to, say, reparations).[4] This neglect of Soviet attitudes and actions in political matters may reflect the conviction that Germany initiatives in such matters would be of little importance for some time to come. Such a view overlooks the considerations that long-range Soviet expectations of European developments may be more readily adduced from policy on political questions—that is, on questions of gaining and wielding state power—than on any other matter.

This study is a detailed examination of Soviet policy in the immediate postwar period in Germany as that policy affected German political life. Specifically, it focuses on the process by which the Communist and Social Democratic parties were first separately established and then merged in the Soviet Zone between April 1945 and May 1946.

This concentration on a narrow topic and a limited time span will be justified if it results in increased understanding of Soviet policy and international politics in the postwar era by providing some of the missing empirical data without which analyses of Soviet behavior must remain abstract and arid constructs for scholars' convenience.

In seeking to illuminate Soviet policy toward German politics, we will also suggest that it was a particular example of Soviet policy toward European political movements more generally. It is our contention that Soviet policy was shaped with deliberate reference to the prewar cleavages of European politics, and that Soviet intentions in the postwar era are an outgrowth of Soviet judgments as to the nature and future of various political tendencies.[5]

Moreover, in the context of the Marxist tradition in European politics, Soviet intervention in the conduct of Communist and Social

Democratic politics was decisive in securing (in the Soviet Zone) a climactic party unification after three decades of intense rivalry. This particular outcome has been for over a quarter century the foundation of the claim to legitimate political leadership by the ruling party of the German Democratic Republic. Hence Soviet policy in this matter is an essential component of any evaluation of the policies of that party, of its leadership in the Walter Ulbricht era, and of its views on questions of German nationhood and politics.

Soviet policy in Germany is also of special interest because here the confrontation and political competition of the former wartime allies was most direct. The Soviet Union, as a participant in the four-power occupation of the defeated Germany enemy, could deal directly with the leading "bourgeois" power of the day, while as sovereign in its zone, it could directly shape a part of the German future.[6] In addition, the Soviet Zone formed the westernmost portion of an extended area of Soviet influence in Eastern and Central Europe. In its area of occupation, Soviet techniques for manipulating political forces and consolidating political control, techniques later applied elsewhere, could be tested.

While Soviet policy toward politics in the Soviet Zone can thus be subjected to comparison and generalization, the subject matter and context of that policy were firmly set in a framework of historical antecedents, national peculiarities, ideological speculation, and personal reactions. In no other Soviet-occupied area was Soviet influence so qualified by Four-Power influence; nowhere else was the Great Power confrontation so continuous and immediate. Yet, nowhere else (not, for example, in the other former "Axis" nations such as Hungary or Rumania) was Soviet control as absolute as in the Zone of Occupation in Germany. Finally, in Germany, both the Social Democrats and Communists possessed powerful and famous traditions, which was not equally true in other countries.

In Germany, Soviet dealings with European Social Democracy faced the marginal test of an ancient and honorable movement, with deep roots in parts of the Soviet Zone, such as Saxony. Here the Soviet Union could act directly and on its own overt initiative. Any policy that included in its calculations an anticipated American or British reaction would receive an almost daily test. Indeed, Soviet policy in this area is significant for later implication precisely because it represents an extreme or marginal instance of policies followed elsewhere in more obscure and indirect fashion. This policy, focused on the unification of Marxist parties, not only was consummated here at an earlier date than elsewhere in Europe, but it may be investigated as to whether it also was intended to be the start of a wider development in countries of preponderant Soviet influence. On the scene of the greatest Soviet victory, at the place of greatest opportunity and most direct challenge, the political strategy of Soviet foreign policy may surely be studied with profit.

CHAPTER 1

The German Communist and Social Democratic Parties

Their Relations to 1945

When, after World War II, German Communists and Social Democrats considered the possible unification of their parties, they found little in their mutual histories to support such a policy. Indeed, they found it necessary to overcome a record of bitter rivalry and a legacy of mistrust and recrimination, and to explain why and how the SPD and KPD might have changed between 1933 and 1945 so as to make unity possible.

The ideal of a united working class party had always had a high place in the socialist hierarchy of values. In 1945–1946 there was little opposition among East German Socialists and Communists to "unity" in the abstract. The controversy over unification between KPD and SPD and within the SPD centered rather on the scope and content of that unity, for one aspect of the urge to unity had been the insistence in both parties on an ideologically correct basis for organizational consolidation. The central questions always were: which groups (classes, parties, factions) are to be united? Shall socialist unity take the form of unity between Social Democrats and Communists, or of a concentration of democratic socialists, perhaps on a British or Scandinavian model? Will there be an agreed-on theoretical analysis of the social and political situation as a basis for the unification? In 1945–1946, specifically, the concrete organizational problems were accompanied and influenced by a program of "ideological clarification." These two parallel processes of organizational and ideological relations sometimes complemented one another, and sometimes were in opposition; it proved difficult to agree on the pace, timing, and precedence of the one or the other, as well as on the degree of ideological consensus needed for consummation of the unification process.

In searching for suitable precedents for unity, the postwar SPD and KPD naturally looked back to the classical period of German Social Democracy, the period of the strongly Marxist Erfurt Program of 1891, and to the leadership of the SPD by August Bebel in the years around the turn of the century.[1] This "mother party," which had been founded in an historic act of unification at Gotha in 1875, was still vivid in the memories of older Communists and Social Democrats alike.[2] Although factional struggles on ideological and organizational grounds were not unknown in the "Bebel party," they had failed to shake its formal cohesion and had, indeed, strengthened the hold of the ideal of unity on the party's members. The SPD of that era was a safe model to inspire latter-day heirs of its traditions, and the leader who incorporated these traditions, August Bebel, was paraded as a patron saint of unity at every possible occasion.[3]

For those who believed that unity was a worthwhile end in itself, the question of responsibility for this split was a vital political matter. The search for the date on which the old German Social Democracy fell from united grace into divided sin involved the participants in complicated and ironic exercises, and provides the observer with an interesting clue as to the state of interparty relations.

The ideal of organizational unity usually implied agreement as to unity of content. Most calls for party unity, therefore, had the effect of implicitly excluding some potential party members. In 1945–1946 it was the Communists who were clearest about such implications, although they disguised their convictions for tactical purposes. The Social Democrats seemed more tolerant of a variety of views, but in fact for many of them the chief difficulty about unity with the KPD was the latter's history of opposition to democratic political forms. Indeed, all groups contending on the unity issue in 1945–1946 represented some strand of German Marxist history that had been involved in divisive activities in the past; this applied equally to "Majority" Social Democrats, "Independents," Communists, and members of the myriad splinter groups of the 1920s and 1930s.

In selecting some particular date or action as the occasion of disunity, the partisans of 1945–1946 strove to show that the blame for the generally deplored lack of unity rested with their sometime opponents and anticipated future comrades. A good example of such a contrast is to be found in the opening statements of Wilhelm Pieck and Otto Grotewohl at the joint conference of KPD and SPD leaderships in December 1945. Pieck identified the rise of "reformism" around 1900, culminating in the approval of war-credits on August 4, 1914, as the source of disunion; Grotewohl stressed the Bolshevik Revolution and the emergence of a Communist party tightly bound to a centralized International as the crucial factor. Generally, the more a given Social Democrat favored a pro-Communist stance, the more likely he was to stress that the behavior of the great mass of the pre-1914 SPD was responsible for the split, thus justifying the 1918–1919 Communist breakaway.[4]

While the antecedents of the KPD can be traced back into German Social Democracy—the KPD was only quasi-Leninist at its founding— the most important fact about German Communism in the Weimar era, for our purposes, is its progressive Bolshevization.[5] Here was the fundamental obstacle to any reunification with the SPD. The other issues that divided the parties were real enough; they include such questions as the choice between a parliamentary republic and a Soviet dictatorship, the Leninist party structure, Eastern versus Western orientation in German foreign policy, and many others. Nevertheless, these issues might all have been resolved, or at least postponed, under the pressure of changed circumstances or some overwhelming common danger, such as the rise of Hitler. Any compromise was ruled out by the KPD's increasing dependence on Soviet control and direction, which led the Communists to undertake a radical assault on the SPD. When, in the Popular Front era, it did propose the sort of tactical compromise mentioned above, the SPD rejected its proposals because of the well-founded suspicion that the KPD's new reasonableness was simply a consequence of a change in Soviet attitudes.

In the closing years of the Weimar Republic, the question of Communist-Social Democratic cooperation (let alone unification) seemed rather academic.[6] The hostility of the SPD to Leninist theory and practice was further buttressed by the party's opposition to Soviet cooperation with conservative German circles in foreign policy and military matters. As for the KPD, 1928–1933 were the years of the notorious "third period" of Comintern policy. Added to the party's long-standing hostility to the Weimar Republic was the doctrine first enunciated at the 6th Comintern Congress that a new and decisive crisis in the capitalist world had begun. In Germany (and other capitalist countries) the crisis was characterized by the rise of fascism and the growing danger of an armed attack on the USSR. Fortunately, a truly revolutionary, "Bolshevik," Communist Party stood ready to lead the radicalized proletariat in victorious revolution.[7]

The crucial aspect of this dogma was the claim that German "fascism" meant not Hitler but Brüning, i.e., that Hitler's rise signified only a shift within the constellation of an already existing German fascism. Of the fascist forces arrayed against the proletariat, the most dangerous, because the most misleading, element was the SPD, the party of (as the Communist phrase had it) "social fascism."[8] Up to the very moment of the Nazi accession to power, and indeed for many months thereafter, the Communists officially described the SPD as the chief enemy to be fought in the interest of mobilizing a class-conscious proletariat. To this end, the KPD pursued an aggressive policy toward the SPD and the major trade union organization (the ADGB) allied to it. In regard to the Social Democrats, the Communist policy was "united front from below," that is, recruitment of individual SPD members into the KPD; in regard to the trade unions, it was formation of a rival Communist union organization (RGO) which engaged in a series of bitter jurisdictional struggles with the larger ADGB.

For the most part, then, the last months of pre-Hitler Germany saw the SPD and KPD engaged in their separate struggles. Gestures toward cooperation against Hitler were spasmodic and ineffectual.[9] The SPD's effort to invoke Soviet authority came to naught;[10] sporadic KPD offers of "united action" went unheeded by the SPD in view of years of defamation.[11] In the spring of 1933, both parties met their common fate at Hitler's hands, unresisting and disunited.

With both parties accepting the assertion that their disunity had brought about the Hitler regime,[12] it remained only to assign the blame. While naturally each side indulged both in criticism and self-criticism, it was soon noticeable that the KPD's postwar analysis consistently limited its self-criticism to avowal of tactical errors in its estimation of the Nazi danger and unwarranted rebuffs of the SPD membership. The Weimar Republic was criticized and the SPD was charged with a fundamental miscalculation of social and political realities. The SPD for its part acknowledged far deeper errors of calculation and action; its leadership in the Soviet Zone believed in the retroactive validation of unity with an almost guilty fervor.

At the time of the Nazi seizure of power, however, and for many months thereafter, SPD and KPD attitudes toward these questions remained what they had been prior to 1933. In its stubborn adherence to its previous positions, the KPD was echoing the statements of its Soviet mentors. The significance of Hitler's assumption of power seems to have been misunderstood in Moscow; indeed, seen in the context of German-Soviet relations in the 1920s, the defeat of the Weimar coalition and its replacement by ultraconservative forces may have seemed desirable from the standpoint of Soviet foreign policy.[13] In any case, the Communists argued, the proletarian cause in Germany had not been defeated, but rather advanced by the elimination of the "Social Fascists." Eleven months after Hitler became Chancellor, *Bol'shevik* could still claim that

> In Germany the proletarian revolution is nearer to realization than in any other country; and the victory of the proletariat in Germany means victory of proletarian revolution throughout Europe. . . . He who does not understand the German question does not understand the path of development of proletarian revolution in Europe.[14]

The chief culprit was, naturally, the SPD; that the Nazis purged the "Social Fascists" from public life did not change anything in the SPD's role as a "chief prop" of fascism.[15] However, now that the SPD (and the illusions about democracy that it fostered among the workers) had been crushed, the KPD stood ready to harvest the fruits of the inevitable collapse of the Nazi regime. According to the KPD leadership, only "philistines [and] . . . idiotic and ignorant people" could believe that the jailing of thousands of Communists could have smashed a party with millions of followers.[16]

In a recent Soviet study of this period that criticizes the continued stress on the SPD as the chief enemy, the authors quote from a statement of an ECCI staff worker to the 13th ECCI Plenum in December 1933, as follows: "The main enemy is the bourgeoisie, which bases itself on the forces of fascism. But in order to accomplish the overthrow of fascism it is necessary, for the immediate future, to direct the main blow against the Social Democratic parties."[17] Even in this context the Social Democrats cannot escape censure; although it was a mistake for the Communists still to be fighting "Social Fascism" in mid-1934, "greater harm was done to the mutual relations" of the Communist and Socialist parties by the anti-Communist views of right-wing Socialist leaders.

Nevertheless, the overwhelming facts of the Nazi triumph and especially of the new regime's seeming permanence demanded some KPD response beyond repetition of inadequate dogmas. It seems clear that at least by the fall of 1934, a minority of the KPD's Central Committee, including Pieck and Ulbricht, advocated a change of policy. At this time, and at a Central Committee meeting of January 1935,[18] the partisans of the old line still retained their positions. The decisive shift in the KPD line came after, and as a result of the 7th Congress of the Comintern in the summer of 1935.

The sluggishness of the exiled KPD leadership in reconsidering its policies toward the Hitler regime and toward the SPD was due to despair with the mass of German workers in the wake of the defeat, factional struggles within the party's leadership, uncertainty regarding the ultimate decision of the Soviet leadership regarding the new line, and, perhaps, an all too human failing, shared with the SPD leadership, of seeking to avoid the blame that would follow an admission of incorrect policy.[19]

However, as early as June 1934, Dimitrov, in outlining his proposed speech to the organizers of the 7th Comintern Congress, made clear that the new line would amount to a reversal of the major injunctions of the old, especially regarding Communist attitudes toward the Social Democrats.[20] In his major speech to that Comintern Congress, Dimitrov made it clear that the new tactics would not be a disguised recruitment campaign designed to capture individual Social Democrats. He also stressed that united front and Popular Front tactics did not mean abandonment of ultimate Communist aims—but neither did they mean harnessing non-Communist parties to those aims. The Communists were ready to cooperate for the limited goal of defeating fascism. While he assigned "great historical responsibility" for the rise of fascism to the

Social Democratic leadership, he also indicted the Communists for "an impermissible underestimation of the Fascist danger," and he was able to provide many examples of this error.[21]

Among the first to grasp the implications of the new line was Walter Ulbricht. In the fall of 1934 he publicly called on the left Social Democrats to free themselves from the SPD leadership and join the Communists in a united struggle against fascism.[22] In speaking to the Comintern Congress, he again criticized the indecision of the left Social Democrats but called for unity of action against Hitler and blamed, "sectarianism" in helping to block this. Following Dimitrov, he declared the KPD's ultimate goal to be a Soviet Germany but acknowledged that the current balance of forces was sufficient only for the creation of an "anti-Fascist Popular Front."[23]

Further progress toward a genuine offer of collaboration to the SPD *as such* had to await the reorganization of the KPD leadership in the wake of the 7th Comintern Congress. The German congress took place soon after the Comintern sessions, on October 3 to 15, 1935, at Rublevo, a town near Moscow; for reasons of anti-Nazi security this conference was referred to as the "Brussels Conference."[24] The unusual length of the congress was a tribute to the gravity of the changes in policy and leadership consummated there;[25] and the importance the Comintern placed on bringing the KPD into line is attested to by the participation of Comintern leaders Palmiro Togliatti and Dmitry Manuilski in the proceedings.[26]

As a result of the leadership changes made at the conference, several opponents of a new relationship with the SPD were removed from the leadership, proponents of the new policy added, and some former "sectarians" were elected after a change in their positions. The leadership of the party lay more clearly than ever with Pieck and Ulbricht.[27]

The changes in policy effected at the conference generally followed the line of the 7th Comintern Congress and may be conveniently summarized through the main speech of the conference, given by Wilhelm Pieck. The style in which Pieck handles the delicate task of abandoning the party's previous position is cool and unruffled and was employed in the KPD analyses in 1945–1946. A new line is needed, says Pieck, because the world situation has changed. The conference should concern itself with past events only insofar as it needs to correct past mistakes.[28] These mistakes were chiefly that "We still directed our main attack against Social Democracy at a time when we should have directed our main attack against the Fascist movement."[29] (It is true that Pieck ascribed these KPD errors to faulty Marxist-Leninist analysis, but he did not suggest how the process that had produced the faulty analysis might be improved.)

Basic to the new line was a new approach to the SPD. Pieck stressed that the SPD must have explicit assurances that the KPD would recognize its coordinate status in any united front arrangement, which would not be seen as an opportunity to recruit rank-and-file Social Democrats or to unmask SPD leaders. The proper basis on which to create a united front is the realization that the two parties have a "common foe, a common goal, and a common fight."[30]

To buttress the new approach to the SPD theoretically, Pieck declared that the SPD had changed under the impact of fascist rule; the party (and especially its left wing) had been forced into a stance of miltant confrontation with the Hitler regime. This provided a real if limited basis for genuine KPD-SPD cooperation. Political differences still exist between the parties; the SPD's "reformism" must still be discussed and countered, but not in a hostile or "schoolmasterish" manner.[31]

This new line toward the SPD was undoubtedly difficult for many Communists to accept. Especially those leaders who had opposed the change in policy most strenuously could not resist stressing the need to create the united front by struggle against the SPD leadership, if need be.[32] However, any thought of serious resistance to the new Comintern line could hardly have survived the devastating review of the Communist record by the ECCI's representative, "Ercoli" (Palmiro Togliatti).[33]

The conference's final resolution followed the changed line described above. Although it laid primary blame for Hitler on the SPD, it admitted that the experience of Nazi dictatorship had substantially transformed the position of the SPD. Despite the unevenness of the "radicalization" of the SPD, a "new relationship" between the two parties, and a united front were now possible. Significantly, the resolution stressed that the united front would have to be created through an agreement of the party leaderships, who had a special obligation to foster the anti-Hitler struggle. In this struggle, members and functionaries of the

SPD and KPD would be "fully equal comrades." Further, the united front experience would lead to the creation of a "united political mass party of the German working class," but only on the basis of a revolutionary overthrow of the bourgeoisie and the erection of a proletarian dictatorship of Soviets.[34]

Promptly after the Brussels Conference, the KPD "extended a hand" (in Ulbricht's phrase) to the exiled leadership (PV) of the SPD (SOPADE). On several occasions during 1935, the KPD had addressed letters to the SOPADE processing joint action, but these had not met a positive response.[35] Now, following upon a letter of November 10, a meeting was arranged for November 23, 1935 in Prague (the SOPADE's location) between Hans Vogel and Friedrich Stampfer of the SPD and Walter Ulbricht and Franz Dahlem of the KPD. The Communists proposed publication by the party leaderships of a joint statement and joint guidelines for the underground struggle within Germany. The SPD delegates rejected these proposals.[36]

The difference in approach of the two sides is instructive. The SPD spokesmen insisted that the KPD offered no evidence of a fundamental change of heart regarding the questions of democracy, the SPD, and the future of Germany. Insofar as the new Communist position reflected a new attitude in Moscow in the first instance, it could not remove the SPD's basic objection to close cooperation: the KPD's dependence on the Soviet leadership. To the Social Democrats, the slogan of a united front recalled past Communist tactics that aimed at conquest of the SPD organization. They felt that Communist-Social Democratic collaboration would make the anti-Hitler fight more difficult, for it would make plausible the Nazi charge that "Bolshevism" was their only foe. Moreover, a united front would scare away anti-Hitler elements in the middle class, army, etc.[37]

Speaking for the KPD, Ulbricht insisted that the conferees should focus on immediate practical tasks; since both parties desired Hitler's overthrow, it should be possible to achieve a minimal common position. The anti-Nazi masses in Germany favored united action, would be encouraged by a party agreement, and indeed expected it of the exile leaderships. To soothe SPD fears, he declared explicitly that the KPD was "in favor of equal responsibility and complete equality of both organizations. . . . In connection with an agreement for unity of action we are prepared to agree to a cessation of mutual warfare between SPD and KPD. Up to now our press has not attacked anyone who favored the United Front."

Furthermore, Ulbricht continued, charges at the 7th Comintern Congress by Dimitrov and others that the SPD was to blame for Hitler should no longer bother the SPD, since the latter had "objectively" changed under pressure of circumstances. As for the effect of a united front on possible bourgeois anti-Hitler allies, did not the SPD prefer a united front with "antifascist fighters inside Germany" to one with bourgeois groups?[38]

This exchange foreshadowed many similar arguments within Germany after the war. The KPD expected other parties and groups to be satisfied with the explanation that, no matter what had been said in the past, Bolshevik wisdom now prescribed a different course. The recipients of such advice were presumably not to wonder what might happen if objective circumstances changed. As for the SPD, many of its members, and especially many of its leaders had been wounded beyond healing by the KPD charges of the past. Moreover, their antipathy to Leninist political principles and practice was real and profound. While specific and limited joint undertakings might be feasible, no general collaboration was possible.

This was the dominant attitude of the SPD leadership throughout the years of exile. It saw in such later events as the Moscow Trials and the Hitler-Stalin Pact ample justification for its position. Even during the war, and while lauding the heroic fighting qualities of the Red Army, it continued to regard the KPD as an "abject tool of Soviet totalitarianism."[39] It consistently refused to associate with the various offshoots of the Moscow-based National Committee "Free Germany."[40]

If the official SPD leadership refused to help in establishing a united front, the reaction of left-wing Social Democrats to the KPD seemed more hopeful.[41] Their advocacy, in 1934–1936, of interparty cooperation was responsible for whatever consideration the SOPADE gave the question. In response to repeated Communist urging that they act without SOPADE approval in entering a united front, however, the various left-wing groups always drew back, insisting that they could more usefully work within the SPD to effect a united front. Here the Moscow Trials also had a discouraging effect, but after the Munich agreement, a loose coalition of left-wing German and Austrian Socialist groups (exluding the SOPADE) joined with the KPD (and Austrian Communists, then acting together) to protest the German occupation of Bohemia-Moravia in March 1939 and pledge joint efforts toward a socialist revolution in Germany.[42] These contacts were, in turn, negated by the Hitler-Stalin Pact.

Somewhat greater success was achieved by the Communists in relations with a number of Social Democrats who were acting on their own responsibility. In February 1935 a "preparatory commission" for the German Popular Front (*Deutsche Volksfront*) was established in Paris; Heinrich Mann was president, a number of other notable anti-Hitler intellectuals were members, the KPD was officially represented, and several prominent Social Democrats, including Rudolph Breitscheid and Max Braun,[43] among others, participated as individuals. After some months, Ulbricht became chief KPD representative; the results were unfortunate. In a series of mean controversies that embittered Mann against Ulbricht personally and led him to direct an official complaint against Ulbricht to the KPD Central Committee, the *Volksfront* enterprise petered out without having any significant effect on the underground struggle in Germany or on the creation of a United Front. Ironically, in view of Ulbricht's charges against him in 1936–1937, Breitscheid's participation in this effort earned him an honorable mention in postwar propaganda. Having tragically failed to escape from France in 1940, Breitscheid died at Buchenwald in 1944; this coincidence of fate with that of Thälmann led to the frequent coupling of their names in postwar memorial observances.[44]

Thus, by the outbreak of the war, the German Communists' efforts to place their relations with the SPD on a new basis of anti-Hitler cooperation had had little success. While in part this was due to continued "sectarian" feeling within the KPD (especially within Germany),[45] the chief reason was clearly the hostile attitude of the Social Democrats. German Social Democracy did not emerge from the Hitler period with any sort of commitment to or tradition of collaboration (let alone anything closer) with the KPD. It must be added that by 1939 an organized SPD no longer existed. The various underground groups in Germany had been dispersed. Those party officials still at large had withdrawn to private life and political passivity, and the exile leadership, politically, personally, and geographically splintered, was impotent. Many of the most prominent leaders had died either in exile or as a result of Nazi persecution in Germany.[46]

For the KPD the situation in this respect was quite different. Despite severe personnel losses, a coherent leadership maintained itself in being (after 1940 largely in Soviet exile) and emerged after the war with an elaborate program for political action in Germany, a program that included specific provisions concerning relations with the Social Democrats.[47]

Earlier, on the eve of the war, the KPD had met to assess the results of its united front activity. The Berne Conference of the KPD was held on January 30–31 and February 1, 1939,[48] in the French town of Draveil, south of Paris. In materials prepared for the conference, the Central Committee admitted that Communist-Social Democratic cooperation had made little progress. Many members of *both* parties had resigned themselves to the belief that only defeat in war could topple Hitler; the "mutual trust" of KPD and SPD members limited itself to "hatred of Hitler."[49] The fault for the lack of progress in increasing cooperation was ascribed to the exiled SPD leaders with their belief in a military revolt or a "revolution from above."[50] In the KPD's view, "The situation does not permit the leaders of the Social Democratic emigration, in contradiction to the growing will to unity of the workers in Germany, to reject outright or smother with objections the United Front proposals of the KPD." All in all, as Pieck admitted, the KPD was still "far from the goal" of a united front.[51]

To a far greater extent than at the Brussels Conference, the KPD now stressed the future unity party that was to emerge from a united front. The Berne documents refer to Social Democratic insistence that this fundamental question be raised;[52] Duhnke has suggested that this was a Communist effort to forestall plans for a "socialist cartel" (not including the KPD) sponsored by left-wing Social Democrats that was entered into by a variety of socialist groups but rejected by the SOPADE.[53]

As early as May 1938, the KPD had called for a "united revolutionary party of the German working class."[54] Now at Berne, the Central Committee raised

the question of the creation of a unity party for discussion by the whole Germany working class, and demands especially of Communists and Social

Democrats that they state their views, reach understandings, and, where a Communist organization and a Social Democratic organization (factory, locality, etc.) have reached a mutual understanding, a united organization of the future united party of the German working class be created.

This must have sounded to many Social Democrats like a reversion to the old "united front from below" tactic, but it must be added in the KPD's defense that in 1939 a coherent SPD with which to unite hardly existed.

Speaking at the Berne Conference, Pieck warned that the creation of a unity party was not "just an organizational step" but a political one requiring patient preparation on the basis of joint programs for the post-Hitler future and joint struggle in the interim.[55] A 1940 report of Central Committee member Anton Ackermann suggested that this premature emphasis on a unity party not only led to neglect of efforts to arrange more limited forms of cooperation, but also caused Communists to rely on "only a small portion of the more progressive Social Democratic workers,"[56]—in short, most Social Democrats were no readier than their leaders to unite immediately with the KPD.

If there was one group of Communists and Social Democrats who might have been thought to be enthusiastically in favor of unity, it was that composed of members of either party active in underground work in Germany and, especially, those joined by suffering in Nazi jails and concentration camps. It was and has remained a Communist dogma that the underground activists of both parties were more ready than their leaders (especially in the case of the SPD) for genuine cooperation. It is not clear how this is to be reconciled with the frequent KPD assertions, after the war, that unity had to be postponed pending ideological clarification, especially for the benefit of those comrades who had been unable, in the underground or in camps, to acquaint themselves with the post-1935 line. These assertions must also be read against the frequent complaints, before 1945, of sectarian influences among the KPD rank and file in Germany.

Information on the political attitudes and activities of either group is hard to obtain.[57] It is generally agreed that the Communists formed the best organized group among the political prisoners, that they used this advantage to secure influence over the life of the camps, and that they used this influence in part for partisan purposes. Before 1941 most of the

Communist prisoners, who represented the most activist elements in the KPD of the early 1930s, retained and even strengthened their hostile attitude toward the Social Democrats. After the Soviet entry into the war, with the increasing stress in Soviet propaganda on joint anti-Hitler action, the attitude of Communist prisoners toward the Social Democrats softened. Yet there was little activity pointing toward a unification of political organizations, and although individuals sometimes crossed over from one group to another, and although some prisoners undoubtedly gained the conviction that there must not be a resumption of KPD-SPD hostility after the war, the available evidence seems to show that at the war's end the political prisoners in each camp continued to be divided between Social Democratic and Communist organizations. This was certainly the picture at the Buchenwald camp of whose inmates' political activity we know the most.[58]

Whatever the effects of the concentration camp experience may have been on the political views of the inmates, it is important to bear in mind that almost none of the postwar leaders of the KPD or Soviet Zone SPD actually underwent this experience. Of the Communists prominent in 1945, only Franz Dahlem had served a concentration camp sentence (at Dachau), although some former camp inmates (such as Ottomar Geschke) were active in secondary roles in the Soviet Zone. Pieck, Ulbricht, Ackermann, Matern, and the members of the groups of German Communists who returned with the Red Army in 1945, had spent almost all of the Hitler years in exile. Several of the Soviet Zone SPD leaders had been arrested and jailed for short periods of time (especially during a wave of arrests in the late 1930s and after the 1944 attempt on Hitler's life), but none (with the exception of Dahrendorf) had undergone lengthy incarceration.[59] It is striking that two of the most prominent SPD concentration camp prisoners, Kurt Schumacher and Herman Brill, were hostile to KPD plans. In general, there seems to have been little correspondence between the personal experiences of a given Communist or Social Democrat (insofar as underground, prison, or concentration camp experience is concerned), and his views on unity.

One of the most common claims made by East German and Soviet historians is that the postwar policy of the KPD/SED leadership in relation to the SPD was a logical elaboration of the policy followed by the KPD after 1935.[60] Without excluding possible inconsistencies in policy, many Western students have come to a basically similar conclusion about Soviet policy in Eastern Europe. Thus Horst Duhnke: "The Seventh Congress of the Comintern and the new tactical line which it introduced was to become the blueprint for the "non-violent" seizure of power by the Communist parties of Eastern Europe after World War II."[61] Kermit McKenzie refers to the "meticulous" fashion in which the 1935 line was carried out in post-1944 Eastern Europe.[62]

The thesis of a certain continuity in Soviet and Communist strategy between the time of the Popular Front and the postwar period has been challenged on the ground that the earlier policy was in fact a defensive effort which did not look to the establishment of Communist power in the various lands where the Popular Front was fostered.[63] It is true that the earlier of these policies reflected a situation of Soviet weakness both in relation to the rising power of fascist states, as well as the domestic rivals of the Communist parties, whereas the postwar policy was set in a context of a great relative increase in Soviet power on both levels. Nevertheless, the similarities between the two policies tend to justify Richard Lowenthal's observation that the Popular Front was "the first great experiment in using totalitarian Communist parties to gain influence within the state machine of Western democracies by parliamentary means."[64] The Popular Front strategy was in part a trial run of the strategy of acquiring power through Communist influence over a broadly based, nationally oriented coalition. Within this strategy, the elimination of significant competition from the Socialist movement underlay the united front tactic whose implementation in postwar Germany is the subject of this case study.

The basis of the change in the KPD (and general Communist) line in the 1930s was a recognition of the inability of the Communists to gain power or even influence its exercise in an important way by a narrow policy of class revolution. The new line after 1935 tried to organize around the Communist core ever wider circles of political strength, with a goal appropriate to each. The only historically viable political forces, those of the proletariat, were to be captured through seduction rather than by bold assault. The demonstrated strength of national sentiment was, at the least, to be neutralized. Rather than challenging the existing society from a position of proud isolation, the Communists would strive to isolate their main and immediate foes by alliances with what may be called their "postponed" foes (and rivals).

All of these elements were present in KPD policy after 1935 and again after 1945. At neither time was this strategy entirely successful. In the earlier phase, certain important elements, later added to the political repertoire of the KPD, were missing. For one thing, the KPD in the 1930s still adhered to its goal of a "Soviet Germany," as well as to a proletarian dictatorship. Moreover, only after Soviet participation in the war could "Fascist" be finally adopted as description of the Communists' enemies. The concept of "anti-Fascism" not only possessed an immediate resonance in the world of 1945, but it constituted an extension of the "Popular Front" idea to even wider nationalist circles.

Any study of the postwar relationship of the KPD and SPD must take into account the legacy of mutual hostility of the SPD and the KPD. The actual measure of cooperation between KPD and SPD attained in the 1935–1945 period was very small—much less, in fact, than in such countries as France or Spain. It may be noted especially that there was little formal, organizational cooperation between the two parties. However, the catastrophic events of the Hitler era imbued a number of Communists and Social Democrats with the conviction that the unification of their forces would have prevented Hitler's triumph and was needed in the post-Hitler era to insure against any revival of those German economic, social, and political forces that had made Hitler possible. Thus, in the postwar period, the notion of collaboration, or even unification, rested more on hopes, slogans, and programs than on any record of accomplishment.

CHAPTER 2

The Occupation Regime

German politics in the Soviet Zone took place within a framework of Allied agreements for the occupation of Germany that had been worked out between 1943 and 1945. These agreements were intended to set general policies to guide each of the occupying powers. As will be shown below, decisions as to political activity in each zone were left largely to the particular occupying power. Of greater importance for SPD and KPD activity, therefore, were the structures, policies, personnel, and attitudes of the Soviet military government.

The formal structure of the four-power occupation of Germany, including demarcation of the zonal borders (and Berlin sector lines), as well as establishment of a coordinating Allied "Control Council for Germany," had been worked out by the three-power European Advisory Commission established by decision of the Moscow Conference in November 1943. The relevant agreements were ready by September 1944; formal ratification by the governments concerned was secured in time for the texts to be included in the decisions of the Yalta Conference (February 1945). (French acceptance was negotiated separately in November–December 1944.)

At the time of the German surrender, however, the Control Council had not yet been established, nor had specific agreements on German political activity been reached. These items were left for the next heads-of-government meeting, which was the Potsdam (Berlin) Conference of July–August 1945. In the interim, military governmental control was established by the advancing armies in the areas they occupied.

Detailed Allied planning for common policy on political activity did not resume in any meaningful way until early April 1945 and, judging from its content, was not likely to cause any Soviet concern.[1] The draft agreement that emerged from these deliberations of the European Advisory Commission in London (later ratified at the Potsdam Conference), while providing in a general way for "democratic" political parties, did not place any obstacles in the way of Soviet policy. The Declaration of June 5, 1945,[2] by which the zonal commanders separately and jointly assumed sovereign powers in Germany, completed the process by which Soviet freedom of action was assured. On June 10 the SMA's Order No. 2 was issued; it allowed for the establishment of "anti-fascist," democratic parties.[3]

Although formal Allied agreement on the nature and scope of future German political activity was to be decided at the Potsdam Conference, the SMA's initiative in June had in effect preempted the Conference's decision-making power; no objections were raised by the other occupying powers. The Soviet decree seemed to correspond to current Allied thinking; in any case, each occupying power was taking immediate steps to organize its own zone—hopefully, in line with future joint policy.[4]

Between June 10 and the opening of the Potsdam Conference on July 17, 1945, American military government sources did comment on the resumption of political activity in the Soviet Zone. These comments indicated suspicions of Soviet intentions but not a sense of urgency regarding possible countermeasures nor any feeling that the Soviet initiative was an illegitimate one.[5] Robert Murphy (the political advisor to OMGUS), surveying the political situation at the end of June, reported to the State Department that Soviet policy indicated a trend toward one-party rule as in Eastern Europe and the possibility that the KPD would be supported by "one" of the occupying powers. Both this report and one sent together with General Lucius D. Clay (deputy American commander) on July 5, 1945, stressed the greater initial activity of the Communists among political groups, and noted "paradoxical feelings of envy" aroused in the rest of Germany by reports of political activity in the Soviet Zone.[6] Curiously, another Murphy memorandum, which presented current Communist activity against a background of events since 1919, made no mention of German developments; nor did it list any German names among those Communist leaders (such as Bierut, Tito, Togliatti,

Pauker, and Dimitrov) who were being "publicized as logical leaders of their countries when liberated."[7] The official U.S. military government comment on the resumption of German politics in the Soviet Zone was quite restrained. In describing the positions taken by the four parties of the Bloc, the report stressed the parties having acknowledged the "need of the German people to pay for the evil deeds of the Hitler Government. . . ."[8]

In the actual course of American preparations for the Potsdam Conference, a paper sent from the Political Affairs Section of the United States Group at the Control Council to Murphy raised the question of

> How far shall we accept those political parties already permitted by the Soviets to exist in our sector of Berlin, or those formed in the Soviet Zone on a "national" basis? . . . It would seem that the problem of policy toward political activities must be worked out by the Control Council at the national level, as otherwise there may be such divergencies of attitude as to create a serious divisive factor.[9]

The discussion at Potsdam concerning political parties was rather cursory and based on United States draft proposals. Working from the materials prepared in the EAC,[10] the American delegation drafted a section of the final statement on political parties that, with minor modification, found its way into the Protocol of the Conference. It was agreed that "all democratic political parties with rights of assembly and public discussion shall be allowed and encouraged throughout Germany."[11]

On Soviet initiative, the American draft's reference to "non-Nazi" parties was changed to "democratic." Although the Western delegations did not take this matter very seriously, it is interesting that Vyshinsky bothered to argue that the most democratic party was the one most opposed to Nazism.[12] Subsequently, in the political life of the Soviet Zone, it became very difficult to challenge the KPD's "anti-Nazism"; by dint of convenient self-definition, the KPD became Germany's most democratic political party.

Although Truman and Byrnes may have come to Potsdam eager to have German political activities regulated on a joint four-power basis,[13] they had their own reasons for stressing the unilateral prerogatives of each occupying power. Byrnes told the first meeting of the foreign ministers at the Conference that "no administering authority should be precluded from starting the democratic process if it thought the communities in question were ready."[14] Mosely has argued that the American delegation was concerned lest Soviet procrastination make the holding of local elections in the American Zone difficult.[15] Whatever the motive, this American position precluded objecting to the unilateral Soviet move of June 10.

Thus the Potsdam Conference implicitly sanctioned the earlier Soviet actions in the area of political party activity. The Conference's stipulations on this question were deliberately framed so broadly as to allow each occupying power latitude in its actions; in the circumstances, the ready agreement on the basis of the EAC's preparatory work is not surprising.[16] Soviet comment was understandably favorable. *Bol'shevik* declared editorially that "As is well known, up to the present time the existence of democratic parties was permitted only in the Soviet Zone of Occupation, where a bloc of four parties was created. . . . Now democratic parties can operate in all territories of Germany."[17]

The importance of the "political party question" was stressed by another Soviet writer who compared the record of the Western Zone unfavorably with developments in the Soviet Zone.[18] The Western ban on political activity was stigmatized as "this . . . peculiar policy of 'non-interference' in German affairs"; encouraging political activity on democratic lines was considered the converse of fighting Nazism. In this view, therefore, the Potsdam decisions were a "decisive blow" at the plans of "international reaction" for Germany.

The situation at the close of the Potsdam Conference in August 1945 with respect to German political parties was thus as follows: In the Soviet Zone parties had been in existence for between four and six weeks and were in the process of spreading their organizational network throughout the Zone; each had a daily party newspaper, and through press and radio could appeal to Germans beyond the zonal borders. This Soviet Zone priority had been retroactively sanctioned by the meetings at Potsdam.[19] In the Western Zones, party activity was just beginning. Whatever policy the Soviet Union chose to follow in this field, it possessed selected instruments and a clear advantage in time, as well as a seemingly greater purposefulness, as compared with the other occupying powers.

Although there was to be no common Allied policy regarding party activity, for the remainder of the period from the summer of 1945 to

April 1946 the Soviet Union continued to press for the adoption of such a policy. Allied joint decisions had not thus far worked against Soviet interests in Berlin and Germany generally, and the Soviet authorities may have expected that a common policy would not hinder them in the area of political parties either.

Speaking to the Council of Foreign Ministers on March 13, 1947, Molotov claimed that "Ever since October 1945, the Soviet representatives in the Control Council have been vainly urging the adoption of a law which would at last recognize the right of German democratic parties and trade unions to unite on an all-German scale."[20]

The lack of such an agreement worked to the disadvantage of the power which could most easily rely on an indigenous nationwide political instrument; thus the presumptive all-German advantages of the formation of the SED were denied to the Soviet Union. By March 1946, the discussions in the Control Council had gotten to the point of a "Draft Directive Concerning National Political Parties";[21] the Soviet representative on the Control Council, Marshal Sokolovskii, favored the proposal,[22] as did the British and American delegates. However, as was common in this period, the French were vigilant in blocking any move toward German unity—and did so effectively.[23]

Meanwhile, the Soviet occupation regime for Berlin had been established on April 28, 1945, with the proclamation of General N. E. Berzarin as Commandant of the city, while the formal establishment of military government waited on further decisions. The shift from mere military occupation to military government was accomplished through the inter-Allied agreements of June 5, 1945, which provided (in the absence of decisions at the governmental level) for the Allied commands to assume "supreme authority" in Germany, exercise that authority through a Control Council, and direct the administration of Berlin through an inter-Allied body subordinate to the Control Council. Subsequently, after the entry of British and American troops into Berlin on July 7, 1945, and their concurrent withdrawal from the western portions of the Soviet Zone during the first weeks of July, an Allied Military Kommandatura was formally set up for joint administration of Berlin.[24]

Following the proclamation of June 5, the Soviet Military Administration (SMA) was established for the Soviet Zone of Occupation.[25] It was the SMA that implemented the Soviet policy on political parties.

Unfortunately, the lack of detailed information about the SMA's routine makes it necessary to rely largely on peripheral sources in discussing the activity of the Soviet military government.[26]

The SMA was formally established on June 5, 1945, as the central organization of military government for the Soviet Zone by Marshal G. K. Zhukov's Order No. 1 of June 9; the provincial SMA commands were established by Order No. 5 one month later on July 9, 1945, (after Western and Soviet troops had shifted to the agreed-on zonal borders).[27] The central and provincial SMA commanders were largely the Soviet commanders in place at the war's end. At zonal headquarters the commander was Marshal Zhukov, with Colonel General V. V. Kurasov as his Chief of Staff, Colonel General I. A. Serov as civil affairs deputy, and Army General V. D. Sokolovskii as military affairs deputy (and eventual successor).

On the provincial level, the five deputies for civil affairs were directly involved in the affairs of the political parties. Notable among them were Major General A. G. Kotikov at Halle and Major General [?] Kolesnichenko in Weimar. The important post of Berlin Commandant was first filled by Colonel General N. E. Berzarin until his ceath in an automobile crash on June 16, 1945. From then until October 18, 1945, the post was held by Colonel General A. V. Gorbatov, who was succeeded by his former deputy, Lieutenant General A. [?] Smirnov. Smirnov served until April 2, 1946; his deputy (briefly) and successor was the politically active civil affairs chief from Halle, General Kotikov.[28]

Of great importance for this study were the political officers attached to each Soviet command.[29] While subordinate in the military hierarchy, these officers reported upward through their own "chain of command" to SMA headquarters, and specifically to Colonel Sergei Ivanovich Tiul'panov who was Chief of the Information and Propaganda Department of the SMA and concurrently head of the Party organization in the SMA. Tiul'panov was, by every available account, the most important Soviet official dealing with German politics during the period under consideration and as such deserves a closer examination.[30]

Tiul'panov's career was closely associated with Leningrad and Germany.[31] Following service in the Civil War, he may have received engineering training in Leningrad and remained there to teach and to work in the Leningrad party organization. He may also have traveled in

Germany in the 1920s, and it is clear that he was thoroughly familiar with German cultural and political affairs. During the war, Tiul'panov did political work with German war prisoners. In October 1943 he was head of the 7th department of the Main Political Administration in Tolbukhin's 4th Ukrainian Front.[32] After his withdrawal from German affairs in the early 1950s, he returned to Leningrad, where he remains as a teacher, author, and vice-rector at the university there.

Tiul'panov made a vivid impression on everyone he met because of his striking physical appearance, his controlled but intense manner, and for his keen intelligence and knowledge of German affairs. Whether chiding a German prisoner for being poorly acquainted with both Russian and German literature or lecturing to the SED's highest party school on the nature of "People's Democracy," he has generally[33] been widely remembered.[34]

Above all, he quickly impressed the Social Democrats as the man with whom they would have to deal. While Zhukov was telling SPD leaders that the advent of the other occupying powers in Berlin need have no effect on their continued residence in the western sectors of the city, Tiul'panov was indicating that "certain differences" in political thinking had arisen between the USSR and its Western allies, and it might be better to move into the Soviet Sector.[35] As one Social Democrat summed up, "He took part in all important discussions which we had with the generals of the [Soviet Military] Administration, as well as conducting talks with us himself. He would come to us and we would go to see him."[36] Throughout the year between war's end and party unification, Tiul'panov was to "go to the SPD and have them come to him"—sometimes chiding, sometimes cajoling, and sometimes informing, as when he tipped them off in January 1946 to Zhukov's forthcoming replacement.[37]

The political officers at provincial and *Kreis* levels played a part analogous to that of Tiul'panov at the zonal level. They were the pace setters for political actions; they controlled the approval of meetings, influenced the censorship of newspapers, and interfered in personnel matters. In short, they were an ever-present element in the detailed political life of the SPD; although, if it became necessary, the political officers' actions could be more or less sincerely disowned by their superiors. In many cases, local Social Democrats felt them as a suffocating presence transforming German political life.[38]

Tiul'panov has recently revealed one aspect of the process by which the SMA's political officers were briefed as to the correct political line on German party affairs. After a major meeting of SPD and KPD leaders in December 1945, Tiul'panov held a special meeting of political officers in inform them to the latest developments in the campaign to unite the two parties, as well as to gather information on local differences in the progress of the campaign. A decision was taken at the meeting to conduct an informational campaign among the Soviet occupation officers, stressing, among other things, that unity of the parties would be in the interests of the Soviet state.[39]

In the early phases of the Soviet occupation, local Soviet commanders were under fairly loose control by military government personnel. This was due partly to the hectic atmosphere of the war's closing days and partly to the fact that, until sometime in mid-summer 1945, most of the SMA's work was carried on by men who were primarily military commanders rather than occupation specialists.[40] Somewhat surprisingly, this irregular execution was also true of political affairs, although there is little evidence that any idiosyncratic deviations were tolerated for long.[41] In the first weeks, however, the tasks confronting the Soviet commanders were many, their political training sometimes meager, and the number of Soviet or KPD helpers small.

Even prior to the end of the fighting, Soviet commanders had been instructed to find and install "responsible German administrators."[42] Two examples will show the sometimes naïvely direct (but not necessarily harmful) fashion in which this task was carried out. The Berlin actor, Walter Frank, related how his selection as Deputy Borough Mayor of Berlin-Schmargendorf resulted from a Red Army interpreter seeing in Frank's library books that had been banned under Hitler. Josef Orlopp, a Social Democrat who served in the first Berlin *magistrat,* owned his selection in the first instance to having been "discovered" on May 4, 1945, by Walter Ulbricht. Apparently acting on this recommendation, a Soviet officer appeared on the following day and, desiring "democratic" legitimization, routed out some fifty men and women from nearby houses and asked them whether they agreed to Orlopp's appointment. They did. Orlopp was, in this fashion, confirmed in office.[43]

An element of uncertainty remained as part of all SPD and KPD dealings with local Soviet commanders who, even as they attempted to carry out the SMA's line, sometimes managed to impart individualistic features to it.[44] However, the impression gained from reading numerous accounts of confrontations between commanders and Social Democrats (especially) is that rugged character was not allowed to interfere for long with the plans of higher authorities. Indeed, sometimes the excesses of lower commanders allowed SMA personnel to pose as reasonable and moderating influences—until the next SPD complaint.[45]

Gradually "professional occupiers" replaced purely military men and saw to steady policy execution. Wolfgang Friedmann noted the presence of "a number of specialized and highly qualified officers at the top level, as well as political intelligence officers dispersed throughout the Zone."[46] Nettl notes the influx in July 1945 of "men specially picked for the job, in some cases long before the end of the war" to act as experts on German politics and other matters for the SMA.[47] According to Tiul'panov, the political officers were not "occupation experts," but had usually served as political officers with military units during the war. These men tended not to be regular army officers but recruits from the universities (again like Tiul'panov himself and like many American personnel).[48] As we have already noted, the best of such men impressed the Germans with whom they came into contact as men of keen under-standing and ample information concerning German political life.[49]

Soviet policy was carried out in the context of inherited attitudes, both German and Soviet, that influenced behavior in 1945–1946. Above all, it must be remembered that a major and brutal military struggle between Soviet and German forces had just ended and the attitudes of that period was ever present.[50]

One may begin with Stalin, whose reactions to Germany and Germans (especially those of the KPD and the SPD) were such as to suggest an image of Germany as a powerful instrument which the SPD and KPD had failed to master—a task that Stalin would now attempt. Many of his *obiter dicta* have become well known, as, "Socialism fits the Germans as does a saddle a cow."[51] Djilas was there when Stalin declared of the Germans that

> They are queer people, like sheep. I remember from my childhood: wherever the ram went, all the rest followed. I remember also when I was in Germany before the revolution: a group of German Social Democrats came late to the Congress because they had to wait to have their tickets con-firmed or something of that sort. When would Russians ever do that?

> Someone has said well: "In Germany you cannot have a revolution because you would have to step on the lawns."[52]

German Communists were not much better; Stalin's opinions of them did not seem to have improved since the early 1930s.[53] On the other hand, Germany itself was "a highly developed industrial country with extremely well qualified and numerous working class and intelligentsia. Give them twelve to fifteen years and they'll be on their feet again."[54] During the war, Stalin was concerned to establish a record of not being the bloodthirsty destroyer of the Germans. Thus as early as his first wartime broadcast to the Soviet people on July 3, 1941, he maintained that the "best part" of the German people supported the Allied effort against Hitler.[55] In February 1942 he made his famous assertion that while Hitler would have to go: "It would be silly to identify Hitler's clique with the German people, with the German state. The experience of history shows that Hitlers come and go, but the German people, the German state remain."[56]

In his victory statement Stalin explicitly renounced any Soviet intention to "dismember or destroy Germany."[57] A year later, Soviet policy still maintained the line of severe, aloof understanding. At a Council of Foreign Ministers meeting of July 10, 1946, Molotov declared that it would be wrong to "identify Hitler Germany with the German people, although the German people cannot divest themselves of responsibility for Germany's aggression and for its dire consequences."[58] (After the war, Stalin's reassuring statements were collected in an untitled booklet and distributed in the Soviet Zone by the Soviet Zone by the Soviet authorities.)[59]

A different idea of Russo-German relations may have had more effect on the behavior of the Red Army in Germany, if not on the policies of the SMA and its political officers. That theme was the one of hostility to all things German, notoriously exemplified by the articles of Ilya Ehrenburg.[60] A policy that differentiated among Germans would be difficult to implement through a military force trained to hate all things German; hence, an ostentatious signal for such a differentiation was forthcoming shortly before the end of the war. The occasion was Ehrenburg's article "Enough!" in *Krasnaia Zvezda*.[61] In it Ehrenburg wrote, among other things, that "Germany is dying pitifully—without honor." The Germans' guilty instincts made them fight harder against the Soviet forces than in the West.

It may be accurate that, as Ehrenburg insists,[62] this article was no worse than others he had written and that, in any case, he had never forgotten to differentiate between some Germans and others. The article provoked a reply in *Pravda,* the article "Comrade Ehrenburg Oversimplifies" on April 14, 1945, by G. F. Alexandrov.[63] In it, Alexandrov denied that all Germans were one "colossal gang" and quoted Stalin to support his case that some Germans were anti-Hitler; statements that the Germans were fighting harder in the East were an attempt to sow mistrust among the Allies.

At least among the Soviet officers, the signal was clearly understood.[64] Its reception among the troops was another matter, and led to political complications for the SMA and KPD. The behavior of the invading Red Army troops was an important factor in shaping German attitudes toward the SMA regime, as were Red Army aid to the civilian population and dismantling of industrial facilities.

The subject of offenses committed by Red Army soldiers against German civilians, especially against women was a touchy one. It is neither the precise extent of these acts nor their possible justification that is relevant here, but rather the political consequences of their behavior and of the reactions to it of SMA and KPD. That there was enough of a problem to cause political difficulties can hardly be denied. Whatever Stalin's instructions to his Red Army commanders may have been, his comments to outsiders reflect an attitutde of casual dismissal of this problem.[65] It has been widely attested that Soviet commanders were generally sincere if not always effective in their attempts to curb these excesses.[66] Indeed, the official SMA attitude was one of frosty nonfraternization.[67]

The SMA did not, and perhaps could not, make any political pronouncements on this question. But for the one party most closely identified with the Soviet occupiers, the KPD, a clear stance seemed imperative. None was forthcoming. Wolfgang Leonhard has described how an attempt at a KPD meeting to discuss abortions for impregnated rape victims soon turned into a discussion of possible KPD moves publicly to disassociate the party from such deeds, and how all discussion of this issue was suppressed by the meeting's chairman, Walter Ulbricht.[68] Only a few cautious references to this question could be found in KPD materials from 1945–1946; for example, an attack on those who "exaggerated certain war-time phenomena."[69]

Ulbricht himself made one of the most explicit references to this theme in his speech of October 12, 1945, in which he remarked that

> Had those people, who today are always talking about all sorts of aftereffects of the war, fought as hard against the Hitlerite war as did our party, then . . . [we] would now have no territorial losses or other unpleasantnesses. If there are those . . . who feel compelled to seek political advantage in the unpleasantnesses which are bound up here or there with the occupation, I can only say to them: Such maneuvering signifies nothing so much as support for fascist forces of disruption (*Zersetzungskräfte*).[70]

A search through the SED literature of the past twenty-odd years has turned up equally little mention of this topic.[71]

Judging the matter in terms of human emotions, and considering that a bitter, brutal war had just ended, it may be understandable that Soviet policy permitted no concessions on this issue. Nevertheless, the effects of the Soviet troops' actions and, even more, of the KPD's silence, were clearly harmful to Soviet political interests, and nothing was done to remedy the situation.[72]

Against this must be set the Soviet record of help to the German population in the first postwar weeks. This took the form of providing food supplies, restoring transportation and sanitation facilities, restoring utilities, and clearing away rubble and other war damage. Such activity was vital in preventing a catastrophic decimation of the urban population, particularly in Berlin and Dresden.[73] That such metropolitan areas were the likeliest sources of support for Soviet policy does not change the fact that they were also the centers of the greatest need. As far as can be judged, the political effects of this aspect of the occupation were greatest for a small number of politically concerned individuals.[74]

The Soviet action with the most directly negative political consequences was the policy of dismantling factories. To the extent that the Soviet Union hoped to win adherents among German workers, it was engaging in self-defeating actions of uncertain economic value and definite political liabilities. This continued to be the case well after the period considered here.[75]

Relations between Social Democrats and Soviet occupation personnel were affected by a sense of psychological distance. For individuals from both sides there was often an uneasy feeling that the other, behind his familiar facade of Marxist phrases, was essentially foreign in outlook, perceptions, and style. Thus, for instance, Gniffke repeatedly noted the tendency of Soviet officers to lecture interminably on basic Marxist analyses of basic problems.[76]

On the other hand, personal relations between Social Democrats and Soviet officers were often quite good,[77] and for many Social Democrats the times called for an open-minded willingness to reconsider their traditional views toward the Soviet Union. Gniffke put it this way: "We had long doubted that the traditional SPD view of the Soviet Union was correct. After all, what did we really know of the Soviet Union? Now we were faced with the necessity of rapidly informing ourselves and possibly changing our opinions."[78] The implicit confession of error in that last remark was typical of and fateful for the Social Democrats of the Soviet Zone.

For many Soviet officers, the German Social Democrats were presumably equally exotic. Long denounced as foes of Lenin and the Soviet Union, how were they to be regarded now? When a Social Democratic delegation was ushered into a Karlshorst anteroom in which he was present, the Soviet diplomat V. V. Semenev at first refrained from giving his name. His motive, he later explained, was to "have a look" at these German Social Democrats.[79] Much later, Tiul'panov recalled: "It was not easy for us Soviet comrades to get used to this new situation and find the right line to take, for we had few concrete notions as to just what Social Democrats were and what role they had played during the war."[80]

Little material can be found on which to base a discussion of relations between KPD and SMA in 1945–1946. That they were close at both the zonal and local levels seems clear. Apart from their direction and obvious political and material connections, what were their attitudes toward each other? For some Communists, such as Walter Ulbricht or other members of the Ulbricht Group, the Soviet authorities were the "Friends," whose views were self-evidently to be heeded.[81] As Leonhard's account of the Ulbricht Group's first days in Germany makes clear, only a select few of the German Communists had frequent and regular contacts with the SMA.[82] Soviet utilization of the KPD for Soviet purposes was too firmly fixed as a feature of Soviet policy to be much affected by personal relations in any case. Certainly, for the average Commandant and political officer, the local KPD organization was the obvious ally; the local SPD organization was at best a dubious quantity.[83]

In guiding political developments in the Soviet Zone the SMA did not differ from the occupation regimes of the other zones, although the SMA acted more directly and purposefully.[84] While perhaps lacking an "elaborated 'theory of occupation administration,'"[85] the SMA did effectively supervise and direct the political life of the Soviet Zone, with the result that it achieved the immediate purposes in this area.

Soviet and German Communist evaluations of the SMA's role in 1945–1946 have shifted over the years. At first, emphasis was put on Soviet magnanimity in allowing the Germans to "work their passage back" to civilized humanity; this sentiment was as common among Social Democrats as among Communists.[86] In later years the usual description of SMA policy stressed the Soviet role in providing the German working class with protection from Western influence, material support, ideological guidance, but not direct interference.[87] As late as 1964, Siegfried Thomas could write that "In contrast to the Western powers, the Soviet Union respected the German people's right of self-determination, and . . . [the Soviet] authorities denied themselves any interference in the internal affairs of the two parties in question, or in the process of unification."[88]

After about 1962, however, the Communist interpretation of this same period has shifted. In 1962 Ulbricht declared that GDR historians had placed too much stress on the "objectively favorable" conditions of 1945 while overlooking the long struggle of the KPD for unity on a revolutionary basis."[89] In 1960 (in a speech first published in 1965) Ulbricht, while paying tribute to the "protecting hand" of the SMA, stressed that the "essential" lesson to be learned from the unity struggle involved the revolutionary leadership of the KPD and SED.[90] Since Ulbricht's replacement in 1971, however, the central role of the Soviet occupation command has received new emphasis.[91]

The Soviet view of the role played by the SMA has remained constant. The most prominent exponent of that role, S. I. Tiul'panov, has maintained that the SMA simply fulfilled "its international duty" in making it possible for the German working class to overcome its divisions. As he had previously pointed out:

> We Soviet personnel need not fear that, in playing our progressive role in Germany, we were interfering in the internal life of Germany. Unlike the imperialist occupation powers, we did not interfere in the inner affairs of

the German people. Basically, all we did was to foster . . . the necessary [*gesetzmässige*] political developments of the working class and not interfere with the elemental urge toward unity. In doing so we fulfilled our international duty.[92]

Eighteen years earlier, Tiul'panov had been franker about the role of the SMA. Leonhard cites him as stating that "the Soviet occupation authorities in Germany had made an unbelievable number of serious mistakes, which can be rectified only with difficulty. The only excuse that I can offer for this is that we previously never concerned ourselves with a socialist occupation."[93] Tantalizingly, he did not specify just what these errors had been, nor who had made them.

CHAPTER 3

Communist and Social Democratic Postwar Plans

1944–1945

While the revival of German political parties in 1945 took place within limits set by the occupying powers, this revival was not merely a response to external initiatives. Each party faced problems of organization leadership; furthermore, each party prepared itself in its own fashion for the post-Hitler era by elaborating certain programmatic guidelines. The programs of the KPD and SPD in the last months of the war and in the immediate postwar period centered on such vital issues as the responsibility for the split in the German working class and the relationship of that split to the rise of Hitler, the future relations of the two parties, the nature of the future German state, the attainment of socialism, and, finally, relations with the Soviet Union.

One important difference between the postwar planning of the two groups was that the KPD leadership determined the party's outlook for all parts of Germany. Although the KPD later had to wage a campaign against "sectarian" doubters in its ranks, the programs discussed below were clearly intended for an all-German party.[1] By contrast, various groups of Social Democrats, while hopeful that their ideas would be accepted by the entire party, were essentially speaking for themselves. Pronouncements by the SPD leadership in the Soviet Zone, for example, derived their basic force from *Soviet* endorsement of that leadership. This distinction was to prove significant when, in the winter of 1945–1946, not all German Social Democrats shared, or could be made to share, the same views on unification of the SPD and the KPD.

It is characteristic of the two parties that one begins the study of German Communist thinking with documents prepared in Moscow, while for Social Democratic views one turns largely to materials prepared in the Nazi concentration camps. Although it is possible to see in Soviet and KPD policy an extension and elaboration of the line laid down in the 1935–1939 period—especially in the materials of the Brussels and Berne conferences of the KPD—in fact, meaningful KPD preparations had to wait until inter-Allied discussions in the winter of 1944–1945 had clarified the conditions of German occupation.

Although Walter Ulbricht has cited mid-January as the time when the KPD drew up its plans for postwar activity in Germany,[2] the party leadership had already formulated a program for a broadly based political grouping; this was an "Action Program for a Bloc of Militant Democracy" dating to the last weeks of 1944.[3] The presumptive author of this document was Anton Ackermann, the KPD's chief ideologue in this period.[4] Insofar as the *Aktionsprogramm* discusses the KPD and the SPD, it only mentions working class unity as needed to give proper weight to working class views within a democratic bloc.[5] On the issue of responsibility for the weakness of the working class in opposing Hitler, however, a major share of the blame is assigned to the SPD while nothing is said to KPD mistakes (in this respect it is unlike other KPD documents of this period). The mistakes of 1918—failure to purge the state apparatus, and failure to destroy the power positions of reactionary warmongers—were the fault of the Social Democracy that "blocked the formation of working class unity in the fight against Imperialism and Fascism."

The Bloc was to be a mass anti-Fascist organization, but the *Aktionsprogramm* is unclear on the important question of whether this is to be a coalition of organizations or an organization that will itself mobilize individuals. The key paragraph reads: "development of a mass movement for the creation of a Bloc of Militant Democracy [*Block der kämpferischen Demokratie*] which will encompass all organizations, groups, parties, and persons, who wish to rescue Germany by destroying fascist-imperialist Reaction and erecting of a democratic people's regime.[6]

The "democratic people's regime" called for was to have people's control groups to supervise the administration and increase mass participation in government, as well as election by proportional representation. This regime, in cooperation with the trade unions and factory councils (*Betriebsräte*) would "guide and control" the economy; a free peasant economy and a democratic land reform were called for; the new state would see to German restitution of damage done to other peoples, especially to the Soviet people.[7]

Something like this program outline was most likely the basis for the lectures to German Communists in Moscow, in early 1945, described by Wolfgang Leonhard.[8] His account helps to clarify the later Soviet decision to sponsor the formation of political parties. As he remarks, a great deal was made of the various "Fronts" in the East European countries, while the activities of the Communist parites were understated.[9] These countries had active Communist parties that, characteristically in this period, acted within the framework of a broad coalition directed against a "Fascist" minority.

A document of April 5, 1945, presumably issued by the Political Administration in Zhukov's Command, entitled "Guidelines for the Work of German Anti-fascists in the Areas Occupied by the Red Army," was of relevance for the resumption of Communist activity in Germany.[10] The stress here is on activity, clearly Communist in substance but non-partisan in form, to organize the population in the manner desired by the Soviet occupation authorities, rather than as in the *Aktionsprogramm* on German initiatives. There is to be a newspaper[11] in which "anti-fascist, progressive forces . . . [shall] express themselves, so as to establish the unity on a new anti-fascist foundation, of progressive forces from all strata of the toiling people, of Communists, Social Democrats, bourgeois democrats, and Christians."[12]

Leadership in agitation, propaganda, and education[13] was to be in the hands of "groups of leading comrades" attached to the staffs of the appropriate Red Army Front Commands. "The Personnel Office is responsible for the selection and registration of functionaries. As a rule, the leadership of this office should be in the hands of a comrade who has worked outside of Germany as an anti-fascist functionary during the past few years."[14]

For administrative jobs of other sorts, anti-Hitler personnel from within Germany might be utilized. (By contrast, SPD views—whether those of a Brill in Weimar, a Dahrendorf in Berlin, or a Schumacher in Hanover—stressed the priority of leadership aspirants who had remained within Germany during the Hitler years.)

The next important KPD pronouncement on these issues was the party's *Aufruf* (Appeal) to the people of June 11, 1945.[15] This proclamation contained the ideas with which the KPD wished to be identified in all parts of Germany and was accepted as such by the other parties; it has been cited by SED historians ever since as a crucial document for Germany's postwar development.[16]

Who was responsible for Hitler? Far more than was true of the SPD, the KPD was careful to place a large share of the blame on the Nazis' "imperialist taskmasters," the "gentlemen" of the great banks and trusts. The KPD, despite the sacrifices of its best fighters and its record of having never wavered in the struggle, had to share in the blame for having failed to cement the anti-Fascist unity of workers, peasants, and intellectuals and to lead that coalition in successful opposition to Hitler. The SPD was spared even less: "Social Democratic workers will have to acknowledge the correctness" of the Communist position that the growth of Fascism in Germany was made possible by the failures of the Weimar leadership to create a "true democracy" after 1918; these failures (ascribed typically to the SPD, although not by name) include "the anti-Soviet agitation of some democratic leaders . . . and the rejection of the anti-Fascist United Front."

Not unexpectedly, the KPD branded as Hitler's greatest crime his "treacherous attack, in violation of his pledged word, on the Soviet Union, which had never wanted war with Germany."

What was to become of Germany? In the KPD's view, it was now time to complete the democratization of Germany begun in 1848. It was in this connection that the KPD officially abandoned its call for a "Soviet Germany."

> We hold the view that it would be wrong to force the Soviet system on Germany, for this system does not correspond to present-day conditions for the development of Germany.
> We believe rather that in the present situation the vital interests of the German people demand a different system for Germany, to wit, *the creation of an antifascist, democratic regime, a parliamentary-democratic republic*

with full democratic rights and freedoms for the people.[17] (Italics in original.)

This state was to have a reformed administrative structure, and to play a dominant role in the economy. While the Appeal contained no mention of socialism, it did call for local authorities to take over transportation and utilities as well as "abandoned" factories, and it demanded the confiscation of property of Nazi big shots (*Nazibonzen*) and war criminals; it called for a land reform striking at the landowning aristocracy, while promising protection for all peasants, rich peasants (*Grossbauern*) included.

Most notable was its silence on SPD-KPD unity. Instead, the KPD demanded unity of the people against reactionaries and Nazis, a democratic unity on the basis of a "Bloc of antifascist democratic parties": KPD, SPD, "*Zentrum* party and others."[18]

Thus, in its most formal statement, the KPD eschewed both an immediate merger with the SPD and the struggle for socialism, concentrating instead on the formation of a broadly based coalition having the establishment of a democratic state as its goal. Despite an explicit disavowal of the Weimar regime, the type of republic envisaged in the Appeal, judging by the specific demands that were made, would not have differed radically from the old republic, except perhaps in the explicit adoption of a pro-Soviet foreign policy.[19]

These ideas were further expounded by Walter Ulbricht in a series of speeches in Berlin in June 1945. Whereas on June 10 and June 12 he concentrated on the new role of the KPD as a party concerned with administrative work, and with the ideas of an anti-Fascist bloc, his speech to the first Berlin functionaries' conference on June 25, 1945, once more turned to the issues taken up in the party's Appeal.[20] The responsibility for Hitler's accession to power had to be shared by the whole German people; the German working class was not exempt from blame, having failed "historically" in 1932. The German people had allowed Hitler to plunge their country into a war with the Soviet Union, which had defeated Germany thanks to the superiority of its ideology and its social system; now that the consequences of defeat were upon them, the German people would have to accept their share of those consequences, including the Oder-Neisse border. The Polish and Soviet peoples had earned the right to guarantees for their security; the Germans had followed Hitler in gambling for high stakes—and lost.[21]

The KPD was for parliamentary democracy: Ulbricht quoted Lenin to show that it was the Communists' duty to further the development of a democratic state. Such a state allows the working class to overcome its disunity and to gain administrative experience; furthermore, by providing a broad minimum program for a variety of social groups, its aids national unity. The KPD could not ignore particular national conditions: "It would be a mistake to think that all countries develop in the identical way. In Germany we must follow the path dictated by the conditions of development in Germany, and this will not be just exactly the same path as in other countries."

"Some workers" had called for the immediate introduction of socialism. How is this possible, Ulbricht asked, as long as the workers are ideologically devastated and organizationally disunited? "It is high time to put a full stop to all attempts or maneuvers to represent capitalist institutions as constituting socialism. [Rather] we must turn to teaching the working class and the toilers scientific socialism as developed by Marx, Engels, Lenin, and Stalin."[22]

Ulbricht also touched on the unity question in reporting on a meeting with SPD representatives on June 19. An interparty agreement on cooperation was hailed as a step forward, but the SPD request to proceed with the formation of a united party was turned down with the argument that the agreed-upon collaboration of the two parties would provide the foundation for unity.[23] On the other hand, Ulbricht strongly endorsed the anti-Fascist bloc of democratic parties as an immediate measure, arguing that various groups in German society were able to cooperate in and through such a bloc.[24] The task of the KPD was to bring such people into "active anti-fascist work."

For this a new KPD was needed, a KPD that was a "truly national party, a party of the people, of construction," a party that could unite the toiling masses on the basis of the KPD's Appeal, "a party of peace, and the only [sic] party of scientific socialism." Party membership should not be denied to an "anti-fascist" who belongs to the Catholic, Evangelical [Protestant], or Jewish religious community.[25]

Despite the effort to extend the KPD's influence to broader social circles, the need to shape the party itself into a reliable and disciplined instrument was not forgotten. In terms of the party's ideological stance, it is revealing that internal (albeit not secret) publications for intraparty educational work stressed the KPD's political superiority, especially in comparison to the SPD, far more than did the materials addressed to the public at large.

The vehicle for this ideological stiffening was the intensive campaign of political education (*Parteischulung*) undertaken at the start of July 1945 under Fred Oelssner's direction.[26] How did Fascism come to Germany?[27] Not as a historically necessary phase but as the result of errors. Had the working class not been split by the Social Democratic policy of coalitions with the bourgeoisie, the other forces favoring Hitler (economic crises, demagoguery, right-wing complicity, bourgeois acquiescence) would have been blocked: "Social Democracy bears the historical blame for the failure of the German working class; through its policy of close co-operation with the bourgeoisie and its rejection of a united front it deepened the split (in the working class) and left the working class defenseless."

The KPD had made tactical sectarian errors. These included the failure to defend democratic rights against Nazi attack, underestimation of the Nazi danger, directing its chief attack against the SPD, and, generally, making the organization of a broad mass movement against fascism difficult. It is characteristic of the KPD that no real analysis of the reasons for these errors is provided, and each is explained by means of an appropriate quotation from Dimitrov's and Pieck's writings of 1934–1936.[28]

Despite these tactial slips, the KPD may be proud of its record: "The Communist Party [was] . . . the only one to fight resolutely and boldly against the Hitler dictatorship. Of all the German parties, our party is the only one to have kept its banners unspotted." After making this audacious claim, the document went on to extract the lesson from this history: the party must follow the policies outlined in the Appeal of June 11, 1945, and the speeches of Walter Ulbricht.

The KPD based its claim to leadership in Germany (insofar as ideological justification was concerned) on the correctness of its historical analysis, or, if that analysis had once been mistaken, on the quality of the corrections. The "self-criticism" of the KPD does not seem equal to the advertisements for it. Furthermore, if an examination of the party's record was to aid in the process of ideological clarification and the drawing together of KPD and SPD, the stress on the iniquities of the SPD was not to hopeful omen.

The most striking feature of the ideological materials pertaining to the resumption of activity by the SPD in the Soviet Zone is that so much original thinking was done prior to be war's end in the concentration camp at Buchenwald. The materials that emerged from the camp, authored largely by the later head of the SPD in Thuringia, Hermann Louis Brill, reveal interesting differences from the positions taken by both the KPD and SPD leadership groups in Berlin.[29] Although the Buchenwald materials were not a major influence on the politics of the SPD in the Soviet Zone, the SMA bent every effort, in an extraordinary sensitivity to independent political and ideological initiatives, to keep the Social Democrats from following the ideas developed in Buchenwald. Nevertheless, these materials show that there were alternatives to the pattern of Social Democratic politics represented in the SPD by the leadership in Berlin.

The so-called *Buchenwalder Plattform* of May 1, 1944, a document signed by German and foreign Socialists and Communists, included demands for the creation of a "German People's Republic" and for nationalization of heavy industry.[30] This document was issued by a "Popular Front Committee" that had met under Brill's leadership since February 1944.[31] The main point of this document was the notion of a new German political-administrative system arising out of a mass movement encompassing all antifascist groups.[32]

> An anti-nazi policy cannot be the work of single organizations but only the outgrowth of an anti-nazi movement of all the toiling masses both urban and rural. It is therefore necessary to direct such a movement toward concrete goals. The instrument for such a policy must be popular front committees (*Volksfront-Komitee*) including all anti-fascist groups. These committees are to be formed at every level throughout the nation and then combined into a German People's Congress, which will elect the representative body of the people and the government.

Under Brill's vision of Germany's future, separate political parties would dissolve themselves into this broad popular movement for Germany's regeneration. Industry was to be partly nationalized; peasant property was not. There were to be close relations between Germany and the USSR. Not only was economic and political collaboration stressed, but the maintenance of German unity was hopefully seen as being in the Soviet Union's own best interest.

Significant for subsequent political activity in the Soviet Zone was the Buchenwald Manifesto of April 13, 1945.[33] Whereas earlier pronouncements had had the unofficial agreement of Communists in the camp, this Manifesto was solely a Social Democratic document. That this was not Brill's desire is shown by his bitter comments afterwards:

> We had hoped that a great, united, socialist, and democratic organization would emerge from the *Volksfront.* That is why, after the liberation, we refrained from constituting ourselves as the [SPD]. As early as the second day after the liberation, however, we had to recognize that the KPD was the same old KPD. [The Communists] desired the *Volksfront* only as a bridge to non-Communist circles.[34]

Brill's disappointment may be understandable but, in view of the position taken on these questions by the KPD leadership in Berlin, it is hardly surprising that Communist agreement with Brill's ideas should have been repudiated by the KPD.[35]

According to the Manifesto, the new Germany is to be a People's Republic (*Volksrepublik*) based on a hierarchy of People's Committees (*Volksausschüsse*) from which a government is to emerge. Germany's foreign policy is to be closely coordinated with that of the USSR. Germany, together with all European socialist states, will work for a socialist Europe. The "realization of socialism" is a current task. Therefore, a united socialist movement must arise out of the "unity of practical action, of proletarian action." All "honest" socialists were to be united under the slogan "Freedom in discussion, discipline in execution"—a piece of neo-Leninism that reflected the radicalism of dissatisfied Social Democrats as much as a bid to the KPD. However, since parties were to be reestablished, "We expect that those parties and trade unions which base themselves on the class struggle will, once essential preliminary discussions have taken place, set up an organizational committee which will convoke a constituent congress [*Gründungskongress*] [for unification]."

Thus the Buchenwald program provided for a radical reform of state and society, socialist unity on the basis of a new, fraternal, disciplined organization dedicated to an immediate and elitist introduction of socialism. Such a program hardly matched that of Water Ulbricht; nor did it correspond to that of Berlin Social Democrats.

This may not be entirely fair to the men who reactivated the SPD in Berlin, for such leaders as Karl Germer wanted a new type of party (albeit a reformist and not, like Brill, a radical one), while Gustav Dahrendorf certainly wanted the immediate formation of a united party to replace both SPD and KPD. Germer found no response among the Social Democrats and Dahrendorf none among the Communists. What in effect guided the SPD in Berlin were the ideas contained in the party's first public proclamation, June 15, 1945.[36]

Who, in the Social Democratic view, was responsible for the Nazi era? Although the "criminal greed of German imperialism" was not forgotten, more stress was put on "dishonorable gamblers, witless power politicians, and political adventurers." What lies ahead for Germany? "Democracy in State and Localities, Socialism in the Economy and the Society!" The German working class is the only force capable of effecting this; it must not be distracted by selfish party squabbling. Hence the SPD welcomes the KPD's statement of June 11, which declared that Germany's future must be determined according to German conditions, and supported a parliamentary democratic republic. The SPD would go further:

> Above all, we wish to conduct the *struggle for a reformed [Germany]* on *the basis of the organizational unity of the German working class!* We see this as moral restitution for the political errors of the past, in order that we may hand on to the next generation a unified political organization of struggle. (Italics in original.)

Having offered their "fraternal hand" to all those willing to fight for democracy and socialism, knowing that the KPD had already refused to shake it, the leadership (in what was a practical step but a non sequitur) called on all Social Democrats to build up their own party.[37]

Summing up the views of the parties as they resumed political activity in postwar Germany, we find that on the question of the split in the working class movement, the KPD tended to blame the policies of the SPD leadership in 1918 (during the following months this was pushed back to August 1914) and in the Weimar period generally. In effect, this was to restate that Soviet and KPD critique of the 1920's against the SPD: what had gone wrong was the failure of German Social Democrats to follow the Bolshevik path! The SPD tended to stress the mutual hostility of the parties in the last years of the Weimar republic, while blaming itself for having allowed the "enemies of democracy" to enjoy democratic liberties. (In 1945, naturally, the "enemies of democracy" no longer included the KPD.)

In assessing responsibility for the rise of Hitler, the KPD placed major blame on German "monopoly capital" and the right-wing leadership of the trade unions. The KPD was franker than the SPD in blaming the Germans as a people for Hitler; Communist errors, compared with those of the SPD, were of a lesser, "tactical" nature, due to sectarianism within the party. Communist offers for united action had therefore lacked credibility. The KPD or, at any rate, its leadership had been free from such errors since at least 1935. In the view of the SPD, blame for Hitler's rise rested more on reactionaries and on the Nazis themselves than on the German people as such. What is striking is that, while the KPD criticized the SPD's policies in 1930–1933, the SPD did not respond with a candid examination of the KPD's record in those years (or in 1939–1941). This inhibition may have been due, in part, to a reluctance to stir up animosities, but as a general phenomenon it owned more to the significant differences in the relationship of the two parties to the Soviet occupation. (SPD criticism of the Communists was much freer in the Western Zones.)

When it came to Germany's future, both parties advocated a democratic, parliamentary republic (although not one as radical as proposed by Brill) with increased power for the working class and its organizations. The SPD had traditionally advocated such a state; the KPD advocated it as "necessary" to the stage of historical development that Germany had reached by 1945.

The KPD would go no further than to present a program of social-economic reform that would be acceptable to "progressive" bourgeois elements. The SPD, on the other hand, insisted that socialist parties should present socialist programs.[38] It is among the ironic features of the German occupation that socialist demands were as unpopular and impossible of fulfillment (in 1945–1946) under Soviet as under American occupation; the promulgation of socialist slogans aroused the opposition of the SMA.

Finally, the Social Democrats, convinced that "socialist disunity" had led directly to Hitler's seizure of power, wanted a new and unified socialist party to direct post-Hitler German politics into new and more hopeful channels. The KPD insisted on the reestablishment of the old party structures, which, in that case, meant the transfer to Germany of the party organization preserved in exile.

Regarding relations to the Soviet Union, the KPD was concerned to stress its autonomous "German" standing, although it always emphasized the enormity of Hitler's attack on the USSR and boldly accepted the Oder-Neisse border.[39] The SPD, whose Weimar record was notoriously anti-Soviet, called for close political and economic relations with the Soviet Union.

Broadly speaking, the Social Democrats felt that 1945 was a "Year Zero" (as the popular phrase had it) in political as well as material life. Germany could, and should, start afresh, mindful of the errors of the past in building a better future. The KPD, while no less concerned with gaining the power to transform Germany, was committed to a detailed analysis of Germany's situation and a strategy for realizing the consequences of that analysis. In its views, not radicalism but respectability, not elitism but broad coalition, were called for in postwar Germany.

Thus, in a sense, each party was adopting features of the other's pre-1933 stance. The SPD now advocated more purposeful and radical action, and close relations to the USSR, while the KPD wished to mobilize large (and largely bourgeois) sections of the German populuation and stressed the "German" nature of the party. The SPD assumed that the KPD shared its own desire for a clean break with the past, and that united action only awaited the will to have it. The KPD's understanding of united action, however, adhered faithfully to the Leninist notion of Communist manipulation of less decisive political groups. As Leonhard was told in Moscow in 1945, it is not with whom you collaborate, but how and why that counts.[41]

CHAPTER 4

The Formation of the KPD and SPD
in the Soviet Zone
April to June 1945

A crucial step in the development of Soviet policy toward German politics was the decision to allow the formation of political parties. Seen in a larger perspective, this decision reflected a trend toward greater emphasis on the postwar role of Communist parties everywhere.[1] In the narrower German context, it was a bold early move toward possible mobilization of German political life under Soviet auspices. Not only did it anticipate by many months similar grants of permission in the Western Zones (where party activity on other than a *local* basis came even later); it also paralleled Soviet permission to undertake the formation of trade unions, cultural associations, and a four-party bloc (of KPD, SPD, CDU and LDP).[2]

For the KPD, finally, it meant a change from two earlier possible alternative forms of political activity. One of these was participation in a nationalist-conservative bloc (through the National Committee "Free Germany"); the other was participation in a democratic-radical "Bloc of Fighting Democracy." Both of these alternatives would have had the Communists submerging their organizational identity in larger political structures. Instead, Soviet policy provided for the resumption of the more traditional pattern of party activity, beginning with the rebuilding of the KPD; this KPD, however, as will be shown below, would not be the insurrectionary party of Weimar memory.

It would not be germane to consider here the detailed history of the National Committee "Free Germany" (*National-Komitee "Freies Deutschland"*).[3] Founded on July 12/13, 1943, with a mixed leadership of Communist emigres and captured officers, it was augmented in September 1943 through the formation of a subsidiary League of German Officers (*Bund deutscher Offiziere, BdO*). The work of the NK"FD" was directed partly at the German civilian population via radio propaganda, but primarily at the German toops fighting on the Eastern front. In this work it was a lamentable failure. It neither inspired German commanders to withdraw their forces from Soviet territory, nor did it inspire surrenders of encircled German troops; indeed, it hardly inspired many deserters.[4]

Two other developments further weakened the position of the Committee. One was the failure of the attempted revolt in Germany on July 20, 1944. More significantly, the growing inter-Allied agreement that marked the Moscow and Teheran Conferences lessened the importance for the Soviet Union of a potentially pro-Soviet German leadership group. Although the NK"FD" was allowed to linger on until its dissolution in November 1945, it played no important role after mid-1944.[5]

Despite the efforts of Soviet and German Communist historians to give the KPD a major role in the founding of the NK"FD", it is clear that the Committee was formed on Soviet initiative. The best evidence for this lies in the fact that the most distinctive aspect of the Committee, its stress on German nationalism in its work and its symbolism, was due to Soviet initiatives.[6] Along with the still rather obscure Soviet gestures toward separate peace negotiations with Germany in 1943,[7] the NK"FD" served the USSR as the basis of a possible alternative to alliance with the United States and Great Britain.

From the standpoint of the role of the KPD, the NK"FD" episode demonstrates that the KPD might have played a part in postwar German politics as the ally of military conservatives rather than of Social Democrats. Moreover, it helped the KPD to assimilate the notion of striking for power by utilizing positions within the structure of the state. It showed that even if the Soviet Union were to rely on conservative elements in German life for political support, it might well wish to use the KPD as a reliable controlling element.

The other alternative was the formation of a nonparty democratic bloc within which the German Communists would operate while concentrating on working in local administrations and generally supporting the occupation regime. Recalling the special lectures given in Moscow in early 1945 to German Communists selected to return to their homeland for political work, Wolfgang Leonhard has stated that these lectures did not prescribe the reestablishment of political parties. Rather, the German Communists were told to expect a lengthy period of occupation and, possibly, participation in a "democratic," antifascist mass organization with some title such as "Bloc of Fighting Democracy" (*Block der kämpferischen Demokratie*). Leonhard consequently described the subsequent announcement in early June of the formation of the KPD and other political parties as a "new line."[8]

However, the instructions Leonhard received did not preclude the formation of political parties. The KPD generally upheld the propriety of a lengthy occupation, and a postwar German political party could hardly have avoided supporting (the local) occupying power. Nor did party activity hamper working in and with local government. It is true that the returning Communists at first concentrated their efforts on building up local administrative agencies rather than party structure, but the later organization of provincial administrations was concurrent with the creation of party organizations. Moreover, a disciplined party organization not only helped to direct those party members active in public administration, but in fact was a political necessity. The first Communist returnees were too few in number to provide the personnel needed for staffing local administration, and those recruits who had spent the Hitler years in Western exile or German confinement were not considered by the SMA or the KPD leadership to be politically reliable. In addition, while former Social Democrats naturally graviated toward administrative work, especially on the communal level, the German Communists first had to be weaned away from their traditional hostility toward all "authorities."

It is clear from Leonhard's own account that the projected German "Bloc" was analogous to the various "National," "Patriotic," and other "Fronts" in existence in the various East European states and to the central wartime resistance organizations in such countries as France and Italy. This analogy suggests that the formation of a "Bloc" in Germany did not necessarily exclude the formation of political parties. Indeed, it is more than likely that Soviet policy makers planned on the establishment of both forms of political activity.[9]

The formation of political parties in the Soviet Zone took place almost as soon as two important prerequisites had been secured. First, the immediate physical aftermath of the last bitter fighting in Eastern Germany was dealt with. Secondly, on June 5, 1945, the juridical basis of the Soviet Occupation was established by the four-power declaration on assumption of sovereign rights in Germany. Within a week of this declaration, the KPD had resumed public activity in the Soviet Zone; active preparation for this step had begun at least two weeks earlier. Thus it cannot be argued that the resumption of party activity was preceded by a delay that must be explained.

It seems clear that in sponsoring "democratic" German political parties the SMA had some definite notions as to which type of parties were to be permitted. In addition to a Communist party and a Social Democratic party, there was to be a "liberal bourgeois" party and a Catholic one. In short, the Left and Center of the Weimar party spectrum were to be represented, although individuals further to the right might be utilized in the administration. Three general "rules" seem to have been applied: there was to be no "premature" fusion of the KPD and the SPD; a Social Democratic "opening to the right" to include Catholic and liberal groups (perhaps along Labour Party lines) was to be avoided; and a multiplicity of party formations was to be discouraged.

That Soviet policy in this area was based on a serious analysis of the indigenous political forces of German society is suggested by the fact that there was no attempt to have non-Communist parties organized directly by the Soviet authorities.[10] A prime example of this was the expansion of the "Catholic" party foreseen by the SMA into the inter-Confessional CDU. Given the largely Protestant population of the Soviet Zone, this was a development favorable to Soviet plans, but it does not seem to have been inspired by the SMA.[11]

Thus the formation of German political parties represented a conjunction of German and Soviet purposes. The result was the establishment of a limited number of centrally organized parties coordinated in a multiparty Bloc, supervised at every level by Soviet political officers, capable of extending their influence into the other zones, and encompassing all the politically "legitimate" non-Nazi social forces in postwar Germany.

Some striking and revealing differences between the Communist and Social Democrat parties involved the process of their reemergence on the German political scene. As a consequence of their contrasting destinies during the Hitler era, their reentry into German politics differed in that the KPD *resumed* its activities with centralized leadership and firm ideological guidance, whereas the SPD was, in Albrecht Kaden's term, "refounded." The SPD leadership comprised scattered and unofficial groups and persons, and the party's existence was more a tribute to its former members' sense of history than to the immediate postwar situation. These contrasting descriptions of the KPD and SPD, sharpened by the circumstances of 1945, involved the basic nature as well as the future of each party.

Thanks to the differing policies of the occupying powers, party organizations were established first in the Soviet Zone. The KPD leaders never wavered in either the belief in or the intention of heading an all-German party. That their efforts in this direction ultimately failed was due to the obstacles created by the policies of the Western occupation authorities.[12] The Social Democrats certainly intended to re-create a united all-German party, but none of their zonal leadership could reasonably assume that it did, in fact, represent an all-German party. The early notion of the Soviet Zone leadership, that it constituted one of a number of autonomous but roughly parallel provisional leaderships that would merge into a united party as soon as possible, gave way to the reality of independent and competing party centers with divergent views.

The Revival of the KPD

The core of the KPD's postwar leadership consisted of a group of party functionaries who had increasingly dominated the party's affairs since 1935 and whose chief common characteristic was their dependence on the Soviet Union. This dependence expressed itself in personal terms, for some of the members of this leading group had had lengthy party careers while in the Soviet Union; it showed in their subordination in matters of policy; it was demonstrated by the use made of them by the Soviet authorities in the earliest days of the occupation.

This continuity of leadership by Moscow emigres may be illustrated by comparing the membership of the KPD Central Committees of 1935 and 1939 with the list of signers of the KPD's 1945 Appeal and of KPD members elected at large to the Socialist Unity Party (SED) *Zentralsekretariat* in 1946. Of the sixteen members of the 1939 Central Committee, four "Muscovites" (Pieck, Ulbricht, Ackermann, and Elli Schmidt, under her pseudonym of "Irene Gartner") signed the 1945 statement.[13] A fifth Central Committee member, Franz Dahlem, had been jailed in France and later at Dachau, from whence he made his way to Moscow in 1945, just in time to have his name added to the Appeal.[14] These men were to be five of the seven KPD members of the unity party's *Zentralsekretariat* when it was set up in 1946. The two additions were Hermann Matern, who had risen to prominence in Soviet emigration, and Paul Merker, a Central Committee member of 1935 and 1939 who returned from Mexican exile in 1946 and was elected *in absentia*.[15]

Six of these seven (excluding Merker) were also signers of the 1945 Appeal. Of the remaining ten signatories, eight had spent the war years in Moscow; only two, Hans Jendretzky and Ottomar Geschke, had remained in Germany.[16] Only four of these fourteen "Muscovites" had been Central Committee members in 1939; but at least six of the fourteen were active in the unofficial groups of Communists sent to Germany at the end of April 1945.[17]

However, the KPD leadership in 1945–1946 was not identical with these *Initiativsgruppen*.[18] The less important members of these groups were not involved in policy-making, while some of the party's leaders remained in Moscow until July 1945, chief among them Wilhelm Pieck. Members of the *Initiativsgruppen* of sufficient importance (Ulbricht, Ackermann, Matern) were involved in the formulation of important party declarations and in setting party policy; whether they actually returned briefly to Moscow for these purposes is not clear. Both Dahlem and Ackermann, in their retrospective accounts, tell of Ulbricht, Dahlem, and Sobottka meeting with Pieck in Moscow to discuss the contents of the KPD Appeal.[19]

In short, during the first postwar weeks, the KPD's leadership consisted mainly of party functionaries who had spent the war years in Moscow, and of whom some were already at work in Germany. During the twelve months following the war's end, while the KPD made great efforts to present itself as a distinctly German party, the direction of its affairs was securely in the hands of a Moscow-oriented leadership.[20]

In contrast to the SPD, no challenge was raised within the KPD to the leadership of the Moscow group by either of the two conceivable alternative party centers: the emigres in the West, or the Communists who had remained in Germany itself. Nor did the Communists who had remained in Germany, to emerge in 1945, many of them from jails and concentration camps, put forward a political line of their own, based on their unique perspectives. Although many individual Communists may have felt a certain special respect for such comrades, the leaders of the party did not;[21] the moral force that Schumacher and other Social Democrats derived from this aspect of their experiences was not a decisive factor within the KPD.[22]

It is in this connection that the *Initiativsgruppen* played a crucial role in intraparty affairs. Not only did they direct the KPD's relationships with other political parties and Communist recruitment into the administrative machinery of the Soviet Zone, but through their presence and activity they asserted the party leadership's authority over the KPD membership. By the sheer symbolism of their presence, as well as by the concrete activities of their members—especially those of the Ulbricht Group—the *Initiativsgruppen* inhibited the development of possible competitors within the KPD.

The chief of these *Initiativsgruppen,* and the one about which most is known, was the one that was headed by Walter Ulbricht.[23] It left Moscow by air on April 30, 1945, arriving late that day at Zhukov's field headquarters at Bruchmühle near Berlin.[24] A similar group headed by Anton Ackermann and Hermann Matern left Moscow on the same date for Dresden.[25] On May 6, 1945, a mixed group of Communists and graduates of a Soviet "Antifascist School" for German war prisoners left Moscow for the general area of Mecklenburg-Vorpommern.[26]

Ulbricht's party position and the importance of Berlin marked out the Ulbricht Group as the pace-setting one. Important new developments in KPD policy were begun by the Group and it supervised party activities elsewhere in the Soviet Zone.[27] The recollections of Leonhard, Maron, and Gyptner gave a strikingly similar picture of the Group's activities. The first weeks in Berlin, of which Leonhard has given an excellent description,[28] were spent in setting up borough and citywide administrations; at the same time party cadres were gathered and organized, so that public party activity, when it was permitted by the SMA, proceeded without delay.[29]

Government administrations in the Soviet Zone were staffed in a manner that was typical for Soviet procedures in Eastern Europe in this period: great care was taken to give government a "coalition appearance"; but Communists were installed in crucial positions.[30] In Berlin, the post of First Deputy Lord Mayor, plus those of "Commissioners" (*Stadträte*) for Personnel and Education were among the positions assigned to Communits.[31] (A similar pattern could be observed in the staffing of the five *Länder* administrations.)[32] This emphasis on securing a firm hold on the administrative structure was not immediately accepted by all of the party's rank and file; undoubtedly, years of Leninist teaching concerning the need to smash the state machinery through revolutionary action were not to be denied simply by a command, even if it came from an Ulbricht just returned from Moscow. Many German Communists had deep prejudices against the "Establishment"; on one occasion they balked at setting up a borough administration with the cry. "We don't want to become big shots."[33]

The position of the Ulbricht Group within the party may be judged by the nature of the occasions when erring local Communists had to be brought back to the new path. In the Berlin district of Wedding, old anticlerical prejudices remained; in Steglitz and Schöneberg the Communists were reluctant to share administrative posts with "anti-fascists" in general; in Neukölln the Communists were reluctant to acknowledge pre-1933 errors; in Friedrichshain an "improper" personnel policy was being executed.[34] Errors of this type—one and all labeled "Sectarianism"—were to be found in leadership positions of the KPD as well as among ordinary members.[35] The Ulbricht Group's domain included the organization of the nearby *Land* Brandenburg at Potsdam, and the policies of that party organization had to be corrected.[36]

This spontaneous revival of the repressed activism of German Communism was quickly and rather easily quashed by the Ulbricht Group.[37]

One weapon was the promulgation of the new orthodoxy at a series of meetings of party cadres prior to the resumption of formal party activity.[38] Often more direct and forceful forms of intervention than mere admonitions were needed to assert the authority of the KPD leadership over the uncontrolled formation of political action groups.[39] In Berlin, as elsewhere in the Soviet Zone, Communists came together voluntarily and had to be "regulated" be the Ulbricht Group. In addition to would-be party groups, however, there was also a conglomeration of Committees and Bureaus, "Antifascist," "Free Germany," and whatnot. In many of these, individual Communists were important if not dominant (and very active) members. They all were closed down by the Ulbricht leadership. Leonhard has described this process in detail as he was involved with it in Berlin.[40] The reasons for this action seem to be clear. These "unofficial" organizations prevented the KPD leadership from harnessing all the available energies so that the work of reconstruction could be carried out under its central leadership through the new administrative bodies,[41] and—presumably the more compelling motive—it was more difficult to bring the members of these groups to follow a common political line.

A classic statement of the "official" Communist fear of independent political thinking is cited by Siegfried Thomas, quoting from his interview with the KPD Chairman of Berlin-Neukölln, Gertrud Rosenmeyer: "Still other comrades had had their "own" thoughts, thanks to the lack of central [party] discipline; this had led to divergent opinions and could be overcome only as the party's political life gradually resumed." Thomas lists, as subjects likely to inspire unwanted initiatives in thinking, the bourgeois-democratic revolution, the anti-fascist-democratic order, and cooperation with bourgeois elements in postwar reconstruction.[42] Frequently mentioned, in addition, was the question of founding one united workers' party.[43] In short, all the main elements of the new policy that Ulbricht had brought back for the KPD from the Soviet Union were called into question. Elements of the Ulbricht program were rejected both by those who adhered to old, pre-1933 ("Sectarian") opinions, as well as those who wished for a new departure in collaboration with other socialist and democratic elements, primarily with the Social Democrats.[44] There is thus little reason to wonder at Ulbricht's harsh insistence that all such groups must cease to exist.

The centralizing and controlling ambitions of the KPD leadership were not restricted to internal party affairs and small nonparty groups. In a model demonstration of the possibilities for political action opened up for the KPD by its participation in the operation of the state machinery, the *Magistrat* of Berlin was moved to decree *one day* after the issuance of SMA Order No. 2 that registration of new parties was to be strictly limited.[45] A letter to all officials of the city administration, Borough Mayors, and district police chiefs sent out over the signature of the Deputy Lord Mayor, Karl Maron, (of the KPD) declared:

> The order . . . of June 10, 1945, which permitted the formation and activity of antifascist parties, has resulted in an increasing number of individuals and small groups coming to the . . . *Berlin Magistrat* to secure the registration of the most varied new parties and organizations, hoping thereby to secure the right to public activity. To accede to these requests would mean to permit the splintering and dispersion of the very forces needed to perform the urgent tasks of reconstruction and of the removal of the heritage of Hitler's rule.
>
> The *Magistrat* . . . has therfore resolved, in its session of June 11, that until further notice and except for a free united trade union, *only the known, large, former democratic-antifascist parties will be allowed to register* and thus to appear before the public. No other new party foundings will be permitted. Evidence of one-time existence will not (apart from the aforementioned parties) be considered grounds for an exception to this rule.[46] (Italics added.)

After warning of attempts to register at only the borough level to avoid this ban, the letter lists the three organizations registered as of June 17, 1945: KPD, SPD, and the local organizing committee of the trade union federation.

This attitude served to buttress, in the Soviet Zone, the application of the general Soviet policy of the period: the harnessing of the permitted parties into a supraparty bloc designed to present a united front, thus preventing the public espousal of undesired opinions that might have followed from interparty competition. According to the East German historian Horst Schützler, the four parties of the bloc "expressed all the important democratic currents of the immediate postwar period in Berlin. The *Magistrat* therefore took the position that no further parties would be allowed to organize in Berlin, and turned down the applications of a number of dubious little groups."[47]

As we have seen, however, this determination was made before "too many" parties had applied for registration; in fact, it was official policy to discourage just such a flowering of political forms.

Meanwhile, the Ulbricht Group pursued the task of preparing for the public appearance of the KPD. Special attention was paid to those boroughs of Berlin that would soon become Western occupation sectors.[48] Meetings were held to acquaint the party members with the forthcoming legalization of party activity and the Appeal which the KPD would thereupon issue. Ulbricht later wrote that a major purpose of these Sunday meetings was to combat "sectarianism" within the ranks of the KPD.[49]

The climax to this series of meetings came on Sunday, June 10, at a meeting held before an audience of some eighty KPD officials. The party, he declared was the party of those who worked the hardest, as well as the party that put forward concrete slogans concerning immediate tasks, unlike those parties that issued "declarations full of vague phrases."[50] Ulbricht criticized insincere execution of this policy. This was in connection with his emphatic disavowal of any KPD ambition to get up a Soviet power in Germany: "We declare openly that *in the present circumstances* we oppose any attempt to force a Soviet system on the people; we consider the situation wholly unsuitable for raising the question of Soviet power." (Italics added.) This change of goals for the immediate future was closely tied up with two other considerations: relations with the Social Democrats and, beyond them, with other democratic forces, and the immediate tasks of the Communist Party.

In one of the frankest statements made by a Communist leader on this topic, Ulbricht explained the connection between KPD-SPD relations and working for a democratic-parliamentary republic; failure to understand this had been the KPD's major strategic blunder in the early 1930's: "Obviously, unification is possible only in terms of a democratic republic as the goals. Another goal would mean making joint struggle impossible. . . . But it is for this purpose that agreements are to be reached with all organizations [of the SPD]."[51]

This policy of reaching out into broader circles of the population would have to be applied to the KPD organization itself. In a statement that must have startled his listeners,[52] Ulbricht waived adherence to "dialectial materialism" as a membership qualification; good Catholics were to be welcomed as members.[53] Did his listeners know that in 1932 50 percent of the KPD members in the Rheinland were Catholics? The KPD was not fighting against the Good Lord, but rather with the Good Lord against Nazism.[54]

The KPD itself would have to adopt new styles of work. The party needed a new emphasis on constructive effort in administrative and economic fields.

> We Communists, too, must learn to be good administrators. No longer should we, as happened in the past, content ourselves with loud propaganda while *standing aside from the actual organs of power* [italics added]. . . .
> We must learn to lead the millions, we must learn to lead the masses, step by step. . . . Too many [of us] believed one could establish a Soviet system with submachine guns.

For such tasks the KPD must be strengthened and transformed:

> It is necessary . . . in the first place that our KPD strengthens itself and fortifies itself ideologically. Renewed legalization of the party does not mean roaring through the streets in trucks in recruiting campaigns. It is necessary for Communists to prove themselves the best representatives of the population through their work in responsible positions in the local administration.

The party must learn to represent Germany's national interests. Only through such responsible behavior in the fulfillment of concrete tasks could it hope to achieve the leadership of an antifascist block with the cooperation of the leaders of parties of differing views.[55]

Promptly on schedule on June 11, 1945, the KPD announced its formal return to German political life with its Appeal to (characteristically for the new period) the "working (*schaffendes*)[56] people in town and country, men and women, German youth."[57] Two days later, on June 13, 1945 the party's central daily newspaper, the *Deutsche Volkszeitung* (*DVZ*) (German People's Newspaper), appeared. In its first issue it addressed itself to its readers, offering its aid to all "progressive forces willing to work in reconstruction."[58]

On June 12, 1945, at a nonpartisan meeting Ulbricht elucidated the Communist position and Gustav Dahrendorf spoke on behalf of the Social Democrats (then striving to organize an SPD in Berlin).[59] Ulbricht's speech was in the same vein as his prior comments, and made

clear the new role that was envisaged for the KPD. Turning to interparty relations, he said

> I am convinced that I speak your minds when I declare that the granting
> of permission for the organization of antifascist parties must not lead to par-
> tisan strife. . . .
> We all know that a deep urge to unity is sweeping the Berlin workers.
> We are convinced that we are responding to this will to unification when we
> propose a *strong democratic unity* for the definitive liquidation of Nazism
> and the building of a new democratic Germany.
> We propose to the representatives of the antifascist parties that a *Bloc of
> the KPD, and SPD, the Zentrum, and other antifascist democratic parties*
> be created.[60] (Italics in original.)

The KPD's program was then read; it was to serve, explicitly, as the
basis for a common program of the just-proposed multiparty bloc.

Thus by June 13, 1945, one month after the war's end, the KPD had
reappeared on the German scene equipped with a set leadership, a close
relation to the local occupying authority, a newspaper (the third to appear in Berlin since the end of the fighting and the first party organ),
and a carefully thought out program. It was a program designed to appeal to broad strata of society, specifically including "progressive"
bourgeois groups, the peasantry, and the "people" at large, as well as
the proletariat; in the circumstances of 1945, the groups appealed to
were in practice all those with the potential for influencing German life.
At the price of subduing its previous character (and of dealing with some
rank-and-file resentment and confusion), it boldly claimed for itself the
leadership of those forces. On the narrower plane of party activity, the
KPD set out to avoid the perils of direct party competition through its
proposed Bloc. Organization, policy, and program were in place. The
party now awaited the response of a still comatose Germany.

Popular reaction, as the party may have expected, was weak and slow.
Leonhard tells the amusing story of how he attempted to gather "man-
in-the-street" reactions to the KPD Appeal, only to meet with scorn and
indifference.[61] The results, as reported in the DVZ, were nonetheless
splendid.[62]

More important was the reaction from the minority of Germans able
and willing to resume political action; in the first instance, the Social
Democrats, to whose early stirrings in Berlin we now turn.

The Emergence of the SPD

The KPD of 1945 was neither a new party nor the reestablished version of an old party;[63] the SPD of 1945 found itself in a strikingly different position.[64] What remained of its emigré leadership consisted of scattered groups and individuals, most of whom could not return to Germany until after the first crucial postwar months had passed.

The SPD had long ceased to possess any organized leadership within Germany; after the unsuccessful attempt on Hitler's life in July 1944, many of its leading personalities within Germany were either arrested or executed. Where the party was reestablished after Germany's defeat, this was due to the tenacious initiatives of small numbers of dedicated individuals.[65]

This *ad hoc* character of the SPD revival is well illustrated by the establishment of the *Zentralausschuss* (ZA) in Berlin in May–June 1945.[66] Here was an organization that came to speak for the Social Democrats of the Soviet Zone, ostensibly on a par with the KPD's *Zentralkomitee* (and the leading organs of the other two parties); the ZA, however, was an irregular body composed of individuals brought together by accidents of personal acquaintance and wartime dislocation, possessing no mandate from either the membership at large or from some prior legitimate organ of the party. Ironically, the major political activity of its leading members just prior to forming the ZA was to make proposals to the KPD that would have rendered the whole question of SPD leadership superfluous by establishing a new, united Socialist Party in Germany.

Under some circumstances, of course, this lack of legitimization need not have been a serious problem. Had there been a firm intention to make a new beginning, or had there been an elitist conviction of the need to act regardless of membership approval, this issue would have been of small importance. In fact, however, the ZA constantly looked for some source of legitimization, citing now the one and now the other, without ever choosing one firm basis for its activities.[67]

What made this indecision so serious was that the membership of the ZA could never admit that the one firm foundation for its activity was its recognition as the leadership of the SPD by the Soviet occupation authorities and, to a lesser extent, by their treatment as such in negotiations for mutual action by the KPD leaders. An open avowal of this situation as an unavoidable fact of Soviet Zone life would have been better for the ZA's public standing than the carefully nurtured thesis of independence.[68] The relationship between ZA and SMA was marked by two basic facts: the Social Democrats who came together to form the ZA were *self-selected* and *not* chosen by Soviet authorities; on the other hand, it was Soviet recognition and support, especially vis-à-vis the provincial and other lower party bodies that gave the *Zentralausschuss* its authoritative position. A more modest claim would have made it unnecessary for the ZA to be evasive about the sources of its authority; on the other hand, party tradition called for a more centrally organized movement than such a claim would have provided (the rapid coalescence around the authority of Schumacher in the Western Zones is instructive in this regard). It is doubtful, in any case, whether the SMA would not have insisted—successfully, under the circumstances—on an "official" leadership to deal with.

One of the groups that later formed the ZA was the circle around Erich W. Gniffke and Otto Grotewohl.[69] Gniffke and Grotewohl had been associated in party and governmental affairs before 1933 in the small North German state of Brunswick, where Grotewohl had been a cabinet minister, and they retained personal and business relationships all through the Hitler era. The war's end found them in Berlin; Gniffke's heating-equipment shop served as a center at which former Social Democrats gathered.

When the composition of the new Berlin municipal administration was announced, Gniffke, Grotewohl, and Engelbert Graf, who had joined them, recognized two of the members by name: Josef Orlopp, a former SPD member, and Arthur Pieck (whose family Graf knew).[70] On May 14, 1945, therefore, the three Social Democrats went to Orlopp to see about an appointment with Pieck.

Having met Orlopp, Karl Maron, and Otto Winzer, they were taken to see Pieck, and repeated to him what they had told the others:

> We offered . . . the co-operation of the Social Democracy and asked for a conference with members of the Central Committee [of the KPD], at which conference the question of *the organizational unity of the political workers' movement* would be clarified.[71] Arthur Pieck agreed to transmit our request to the members of the Central Committee of the KPD in charge of these

matters; he also agreed to arrange for Communist representatives to appear at our Action Bureau, Bülow Street No. 17, at noon on May 17, 1945, to engage in mutual discussions.[72] (Italics added.)

However, no KPD representative appeared at the appointed time and place; nor were there replies to several further overtures. Soon thereafter came the official licensing of parties, whereupon these difficulties became more understandable in retrospect.

By this time many other Social Democrats had made their way to the Bülowstrasse shop, including the future editor of the party newspaper, Otto Meier, future ZA staff members August Karsten and Toni Wohlgemuth, and the influential "political-economic secretary" of the ZA and Grotwohl's chief speechwriter in the fall and winter of 1945, Gustav Klingelhöfer. Among them was the former Reichstag deputy from Hamburg, Gustav Dahrendorf, who was to play a leading part both in cooperation with the KPD and resistance to it.[73]

Dahrendorf had been liberated by the Red Army from Brandenburg Prison in Potsdam on April 27, 1945.[74] Eleven days later, he and his fellow prisoners had reached a barracks in the western part of Berlin.[75] Here their Soviet guides asked them to wait, since they might be needed for the planned city administration. On May 12, 1945, Walter Ulbricht, Karl Maron, and Arthur Pieck appeared there; Maron approached Dahrendorf, who was standing amid a group of Social Democrats, and called out: "At last I meet some Social Democrats here in Berlin. For days we've looked high and low for Social Democrats, without finding any. And now here I find no less than two *Reichstag* deputies and one *Landtag* deputy. We need you!"[876] Dahrendorf's comment on this: "We weren't needed. We went home."[77] Dahrendorf soon made his way to Gniffke, Grotewohl and the others; together "[we] went ahead and arranged for a provisional party center."[78]

Whereas Gniffke and Grotewohl had been cooperative but uncertain as to the future of the SPD and its relations with the Communists, Dahrendorf was at first enthusiastically in favor of a new party, formed jointly by Communists and Social Democrats and dedicated to democracy and the rule of the working class.[79]

A new beginning of a different sort was in the minds of still another group that came to the growing Social Democratic center.[80] This group was to contribute to the *Zentralausschuss* Richard Weimann, Fritz

Neubecker, the trade unionists Hermann Schlimme and Bernard Göring, and its youngest member, Karl J. Germer, Jr. They had all been part of a group that met at the Germer home on May 15, 1945,[81] decided on separate party and trade union organizations, presumed that the SMA would allow the SPD to organize, and planned to have personnel prepared in the various Berlin districts.[82] Germer's draft program for this meeting made no mention of the Soviet Occupation or of the KPD, but merely promised cooperation with all antifascist parties to build democracy in Germany.[83] His ideas were expressed more clearly in a letter of May 18, 1945, to Hermann Schlimme (a leading pre-1933 trade unionist), reporting with approval a talk he had had with the former Catholic trade unionist, Jacob Kaiser. Kaiser, who was involved in the organization of a nonpartisan, nonsectarian trade union federation as well as of the CDU of the Soviet Zone, asked that "the SPD organize itself on so broad a basis that the establishment of a *Zentrum,* for example, would be superfluous . . . [the British Labour Party might serve as an example.]" The attitude of the Communists toward this notion remained unclear, Kaiser added.[84] It has since become clearer that it was one of hostility, since Germer's initiative was seen as an alternative to unity with the Communists, and Thomas is correct in stating that this idea found little response among Berlin Social Democrats in 1945.[85] Nevertheless, it is important to bear in mind that for many Social Democrats the goal of a concentration of socialist forces in a "united"party did not mean the simple merger of an organized KPD with the SPD.

Loosely connected with the Germer group through its trade union members was Max Fechner, who represented another of the elements that came together to form the *Zentralausschuss.* Fechner, a controversial figure heartily disliked by some of his fellow Social Democrats,[86] was welcome to the Social Democratic groups in May 1945 because of his connections to the local Berlin functionaries of the pre-Hitler SPD. His role has special significance in relation to two obscure developments: his letter to Ulbricht of April 28, 1945, and his claim to possess a special mandate from the SPD *Parteivorstand* in 1933.

The letter to Ulbricht was first mentioned publicly by Otto Grotewohl eight months later, during the discussions of the conference of the SPD and KPD representatives on December 20–21, 1945. Our knowledge of its contents stems from the Protocol of that meeting.[87] On that occasion, Grotewohl, seeking to establish SPD priority in sponsorship of the unity idea, outlined not only the attempts of Gniffke, Graf, and himself to see Arthur Pieck, but also mentioned a letter supposedly sent by Fechner to Ulbricht, in which he wrote

> I have heard from several political friends that you have returned to the homeland with the victorious Red Army and, if I am correctly informed, have immediately resumed political activity.[88] Allow me first of all (in the name of my political friends as well as myself) to offer you our socialist greetings. . . . I would like to speak to you about how the desired united organization of the German working class might be established. My political friends and I believe that at the first opportunity for political activity, we must follow a new path, sweeping aside the past to make the new path one of joint action by SPD and KPD. I would venture that it would be easier, at the very beginning of political activity, to achieve unity than it will be when we have to deal with the consequences of the war.[89]

Whether or not Ulbricht ever got this particular letter, one may speculate about the effects of the expression of such sentiments (and those expressed to Pieck and Maron as well) on the KPD leadership. Throughout the thirties they had argued—and, perhaps, believed more than the evidence warranted—that the Social Democrats in Germany were more inclined for cooperation with the Communists than were their exiled leaders. Now, upon their return to Germany, various Social Democrats who had remained in the country came to them and, apparently quite independently of each other, offered not only cooperation, but unity! Well might the KPD have believed that a sentiment so seemingly widespread could be harvested at the politically most advantageous season. Although they doubtless expected some Social Democratic hostility, these proposals may have induced excessive optimism in the Communist leaders about the ease of securing party unification, when they desired it. For the present, however, the KPD's task was to fend off Social Democratic importuning and establish a more detached relationship.

The letter shows that Fechner was apparently quite prepared, as the war drew to its close, to forego reestablishment of an independent SPD,[90] despite his claim to possess a valid mandate from the exiled *Parteivorstand* (PV) of 1933 that entitled him to reorganize the party.[91]

Was this claim of Fechner's ever accepted? Neither the SPD of the Western zones, nor the emigrés in London under Erich Ollenhauer's leadership (after Hans Vogel's death in October 1945) ever recognized it.[92] It had little significance for most of the SPD leaders of the Soviet Zone; members of the *Zentralausschuss,* although they heard of this claim from Fechner in May 1945, do not seem to have very much impressed by it.[93] The one PV member on the ZA, Karl Litke, remained silent on this question. Few Western writers have ever accepted Fechner's claim,[94] although SED historians have subsequently been pleased to feature it.[95] In 1945–1946, however, Communist spokesmen rarely mentioned it.

Furthermore, during the controversies over unification of the parties in 1945–1946, Fechner, although he sometimes put forth proposals running counter to the KPD's position on the unity question, never tried to use his "mandate" as an argument in any discussions with the SMA or KPD.[96] It was brought up from time to time as a weapon in the ZA's competition with other Social Democratic groups seeking to become the focal point for a reestablished SPD. It seems odd that a man who could passionately proclaim his "obligations" under such a "trust" would also willingly offer to negotiate the disappearance of the party with whose fate he had supposedly been "entrusted."

Surveying the groups and individuals who come together to form the *Zentralausschuss,* one may note, first, that they did not represent the top level of party leadership in the Weimar era. On the other hand, they were not "new men," having typically been active before 1933 in the second rank of the party or of associated organizations.[97] A common characteristic, and one that sharply differentiates them from the KPD leaders, was that they had spent all the Hitler years inside Germany. (While many of them had suffered arrest or other harassment, few had served lengthy prison or concentration camp terms.) The fact that all of the ZA members had remained in Germany in 1933–1945 was an important factor in forming their attitudes. Long years of enforced political inactivity, filled with brooding over the defeat of 1933 and punctuated by arrest or persecution (often together with local Communists) tended to fix in their minds the idea that "working class disunity" had led directly to Hitler's triumph. The experience left many of them with their thinking firmly anchored in Marxist verities of class struggle and proletarian unity—albeit without losing that typical Social Democratic ambiguity of insisting simultaneously on absolute values such as "freedom" and "democracy."[98] Their view of the Soviet Union was shaped by lack of knowledge of the Stalin era (quite aside from the problem of developing a critical view of the USSR while living under Soviet censorship); at the same time they noted hopefully the seemingly new posture of the USSR as a member of the Allied coalition.[99] Such qualities of thought helped shape the ideas that guided the *Zentralausschuss* and the Soviet Zone SPD in their first months.

The organizers of the SPD in Berlin, having been rebuffed by the Communists in May in their attempts to form "one big workers' party," now responded to Order No. 2, and to the appearance of the KPD by applying for permission to organize the SPD, and by preparing a program that they might issue to match that of the KPD. They presented their party and program to the public at a meeting of June 17, 1945, that brought together, on a Sunday morning and under rather hurried conditions, over a thousand former members and functionaries of the SPD.[100] As was the case at so many KPD and SPD meetings in the early summer of 1945, the dominant tone was one of relief at having survived, joy in reunion, and pride in the durability of the organization.[101] The call for the meeting, sent out from Gniffke's shop (hastily dubbed *Zentralbüro* for the occasion) and signed by Fechner, Weimann, Gniffke, Grotewohl, Hermann Harnisch, and Otto Meier, announced that SPD functionaries (who would have to identify themselves at the meeting) would "gather" at the meeting place.[102] In keeping with their tenacious loyalty to the old party, large numbers came; not only did local Berlin functionaries come, but also transients from other parts of Germany, many of them recently freed from nearby prisons and concentration camps. No precise check was even made of who attended and where they were from; nor was there any attempt to organize the meeting in a formal way. The audience "approved"[103] the formation and composition of the *Zentralausschuss* (as that body had been presented to the SMA on the license application)[104] and its Appeal of June 15, 1945.[105]

Subsequently, this meeting of June 17 became the chief prop of the ZA's claim of legitimacy. Invoked time and again in speeches and articles, the details of its composition seemed to grow clearer as time went on. Thus, at the Soviet Zone SPD party congress in April 1946, Grotewohl could declare that "thanks to the trust in us shown by the [SMA] we [could] proceed with the founding of our party on June 17, 1945." The audience count was now put at 1,700, of whom 300 were from parts of Germany since included in the Western Zones.[106]

From the standpoint of political reality, both the claims of the ZA and the strictures of those who later rejected the validity of a "June 17 legitimization" are somewhat irrelevant.[107] Few SPD gatherings in Germany in 1945 had much formal legitimacy; this is especially applicable to the crucial "founding" meetings, such as this one of June 17, or the meeting at Wennigsen-Hannover in October 1945. While it is true that the various provincial *Parteitage* in the Soviet Zone were composed of delegates elected by local party organizations, these organizations in their turn had varied and self-determined standards. Insofar as they conformed to the ZA's standards, they simply returned the problem of legitimacy to the zonal level.

The major event at the meeting of June 17 was the speech of Otto Grotewohl. Public oratory was one of this strengths, and he soon won over the audience, as he was to do often in the months to come. For Grotewohl it was a particularly useful achievement, since it enabled him, a stranger to most of the local Social Democrats, to win considerable support among the party membership in Berlin.[108]

The speech contained what were to become typical Grotewohl elements.[109] There was a little dash of nationalism,[110] some antifascist unity on the basis of the bitter experiences of the past twelve years, unity of action with the KPD growing out of common efforts to meet pressing needs rather than from "declamations," and the then-standard pledge of cooperation with the occupying powers.

When it came to the unity of the working class movement, he expressed readiness to work with any like-minded persons or parties toward "organizational unity of the working class." Narrow-minded concern for one's own party must not stand in the way. As was his wont, Grotewohl here included an emotional, fervent passage: "Unity is the greatest treasure of the working class. We want to be able some day to hand it on, untarnished, to the generation that will follow us, so that they will not be able to say, 'You were petty in a great hour!'"[111] He thereupon announced that the *Zentralausschuss* and the ZK of the KPD had formed a joint working committee to settle on an equal basis both problems of practical work and those of conflicting ideologies.[112] Thus the parties would render the barriers between them obsolete.

Finally, Grotewohl showed that his understanding of democracy, like the KPD's, also involved prior determination of what form of expression the people needed. The Soviet expression of trust in the German people—the decision to allow political activity—must not be misused: "We will know how to prevent dozens of parties and little groups, which seek to pursue their selfish interests at the expense of the people's needs, from establishing themselves in our [future] republic." Freedom of expression would have to be limited by the needs of the state for self-preservation and of the individual for honor and respect.[113]

The leaders who formed the ZA were, for the Soviet authorities, an unknown quantity; the leaders of the KPD had undergone the rigorous selection process of survival in Stalin's Moscow. There is no evidence that the ZA members were known beforehand to the SMA or had been sought out by it to organize the SPD. On the other hand, the SMA presumably received information or at least opinion about the Social Democrats from the KPD. As far as is known, no objection was raised by the SMA to any of the members of the ZA. (This may have been related to the acceptability of their program, for it stands in sharp contrast to the Soviet reaction to the leader of the SPD in Thuringia, Hermann Brill).

The *Zentralausschuss* based its leadership on three factors: the traditional SPD impulse toward organizational discipline, the continuing importance of the old capital city, Berlin, and recognition by the SMA. In June 1945 it was hardly unreasonable to assume that an organizational center that was first in the field, had the backing of one of the occupying powers, and was exerting its influence from Berlin, would be of great importance for German political life.

In the early summer of 1945 Berlin still meant the political and social center of their nation to most Germans, especially to a traditionally centralizing group such as the Social Democrats.[114] It was a reasonable hope that an organizing impulse emanating from Berlin might, in the absence of visible competition, fix many of the future features of the reemerging party. Nevertheless, such hopes were not realized. The KPD, of course, needed no "Berlin model," while the reestablishment of the SPD was clearly a spontaneous process in various parts of Germany.

To argue that the organization of the *Zentralausschuss* was the "starting point" for setting up the SPD in the other zones is to ignore the evidence.[115] Nor is it true that Soviet Zone developments were influential on party life in Western Germany by example if not through direct stimulation.[116] The seeming similarity of Communist, Social Democratic, Christian, and Liberal parties in all four zones overlooks the fact that in the last years of the Hitler era Germany had been unified through administrative measures and internal migration as never before. In 1945 Germany was still a single nation, responding politically in similar fashion in all of its parts.

What ruined the chances for a "Berlin model" was the division of Germany into occupation zones. As far as the SMA was concerned, any hope of extending Soviet influence outward from Berlin through the *Zentralausschuss* rested on the ZA's obtaining the voluntary allegiance of Social Democratic groups; this it could not get, due in large part to Soviet policies. Ironically, in the disputes between Kurt Schumacher and spokesmen for the ZA, the latter constantly insisted upon the reality (apart from the ideal) of German unity; Schumacher's "shocking" insistence on the reality of the zonal division proved to be the more prophetic contention.

During the fall and winter of 1945–1946, the ZA failed either to establish a fruitful, cooperative relationship with West German Social Democratic leadership groups or (despite some tentative gestures in that direction in November and December 1945) to supplant the SPD leadership in the Western zones. Both approaches ran into the effective resistance of the Schumacher leadership. Thus, in 1945–1946, the SPD of the Soviet Zone was to be severely limited as to the influence that the programmatic ideas or organizational initiatives could have on the party in the other parts of Germany.

For the SPD to exert influence on the Western zones from Berlin involved manipulating autonomous Social Democratic organizations; the KPD leadership in Berlin faced no such problems. In 1945–1946 the all-German leadership of the Berlin-based KPD Central Committee was unchallenged both in program and organization. The earlier start of the KPD in the Soviet Zone presumably eased the Berlin Central Committee's task in exerting this all-German leadership; there is little doubt, however, that the decisive factor in this regard was the nature and history of the KPD before 1945.

The position of the Berlin KPD leadership was best illustrated by the fact that the KPD alone, of all German parties, was able to hold all-German party meetings during the first postwar years. When the West German KPD organizations were established in 1945–1946, they unfailingly supported the Central Committee's posititition on such issues as cooperation and, later, merger with the SPD, establishment of a multiparty "antifascist" bloc, and support for a parliamentary republic.

By contrast, the SPD's *Zentralausschuss* was largely ignorant of party affairs in the West—until August 1945 it knew little even of party activities in other parts of the Soviet Zone—and had no authority outside of areas under Soviet control.[117] To profit from an SPD center in Berlin, the Soviet authorities would have to pursue policies allowing the ZA to win the voluntary support of Social Democrats elsewhere in Germany— or else attempt to swallow the SPD whole. The latter course involved fewer changes in Soviet policies and outlook and was the one chosen. However, the Soviet Union proved unable to achieve the contradictory goals of obtaining a voluntary following and a reliable tool.

Party Formation at the Provincial Level

The formation of the SPD and KPD throughout the Soviet Zone generally resembled the events in Berlin. This uniformity may be traced to two factors. First, both the SMA and the leadership of the KPD actively intervened in the formation of provincial and local party organizations in the Soviet Zone. (The role of the ZA in this connection was minimal.) On the other hand, spontaneous political activity by local groups of Communists and Social Democrats tended to be similar throughout the Soviet Zone and to show that the revival of political parties was not solely dependent on the initiatives of Soviet commanders or of central party leadership. Indeed, there is similar evidence regarding both the formation of political parties in the other occupation zones, as well as of the "non-Marxist" parties of the Soviet Zone, which points to the continuing vitality of Germany's suppressed political forces.[118]

There were, however, two important differences between Berlin and the provinces. Thanks to their prior start, the party leaderships in Berlin had an important influence on provincial developments, although this was true less for the SPD than for the KPD. In addition, the Soviet Zone consisted of two portions—that which had been occupied by the Red

Army from the start, and that portion, including Thuringia and western Saxony, that was under Anglo-American control until the early days of July 1945. Ironically, Western policy aided the Soviet program of political tutelage, for most overt political activity had been banned by the Western armies. Thus the Soviet occupation authorities found little by way of existing political organizations in these territories; this allowed them to assume the role of promoters of democratic politics. Nevertheless, in these areas—especially in Thuringia—there had been semilegal political activity that presented the SMA with special problems of control and coordination of party life. The Soviet response to these problems casts some light on Soviet conceptions and tactics in this field.

In the western portion of Saxony (*Land Sachsen*), which included such centers of SPD-KPD activity as Leipzig, Chemnitz (now Karl Marx Stadt), and Zwickau, the parties began with semilegal activity under the American occupation.[119] For the Communists, the controlling factor was the nearby presence, in Dresden, of the SMA for Saxony with Major General D. G. Dubrovskii as Deputy for Civil Affairs, and of the *Initiativsgruppe* of Anton Ackermann and Hermann Matern.[120] Working with characteristic energy and purposefulness, the KPD was ready to extend its party organization into the rest of Saxony almost immediately upon American withdrawal in early July. The Matern-Ackermann group has not received the same attention subsequently given the Ulbricht Group in Berlin, but it appears to have worked along similar lines: putting into effect plans previously worked out for building up the Dresden municipal administration, seeing to the organization of the Party, and gradually extending both operations into the surrounding Saxon countryside (all in close cooperation with the SMA in Dresden).[121] In one vital aspect the policies of the two groups were identical: the prominent role of Communists returning from Moscow. Matern has explained, in retrospect, that, "The leadership of the party was, naturally, in the hands of those comrades who had been trained in Moscow to assume the responsibility for the building of a new Germany after the collapse of the Hitler regime."[122] This control was exercised by placing reliable men in crucial positions. Like Arthur Pieck in Berlin, Hermann Matern in Dresden was in charge of personnel policy as the Municipal Councillor for Personnel Policy.[123]

The brief American interlude in Leipzig was apparently sufficient to allow the formation of a Communist organization autonomous of the KPD leadership. According to the scant sources available, the Communist survivors of one of the more successful anti-Nazi organizations came together under the American regime and formed an autonomous KPD organization.[124] When a leading pre-1933 Leipzig KPD leader, Fritz Selbmann, returned from Nazi captivity, he promptly took part in the work of this group.[125] Matern, true to KPD and SMA policies, effected its dissolution in the summer of 1945 by arresting two of its more prominent members and shunting Selbmann (against whom charges were also brought) into an administrative position in Dresden. The Leipzig KPD was reorganized on the standard Soviet Zone model.[126]

By contrast with the KPD, the reestablishment of the SPD in Saxony was the outcome of a spontaneous process among the surviving functionaries of the Party. As in Berlin, some of the individuals who became local leaders were there as a consequence of the whirlpool of Germany's destruction. This was most notable in the case of Otto Buchwitz, the Chairman of the SPD in Saxony, whose home in Silesia was perforce barred to him. Buchwitz was an unwavering proponent of unity with the KPD at whatever time the Communists would have it, and an effective speaker with a good anti-Hitler record; according to his own retrospective account, he was encouraged to participate in SPD affairs by the Dresden KPD.[127] Meanwhile, the work of organization had been effectively done. In Leipzig, for instance, 150 "shadow" local organizations of the SPD had been set up before the arrival of the Red Army.[128] Under Soviet occupation, the Dresden organization assumed the provisional leadership of the SPD in Saxony (it was later confirmed in office at the first Saxon SPD party congress in October 1945).[129] Typically, the Saxon SPD leaders were required by the Soviet authorities to obtain approval from the ZA in Berlin. That this ZA approval was somewhat *pro forma* is indicated by Buchwitz's admission that the local SPD was unable to obtain a full copy of the SPD's Appeal.[130] The first ZA representative, Gniffke, did not arrive until September 1945.[131]

Thuringia had no nearby *Initiativsgruppe* and so it received a visit from Walter Ulbricht at the time of the arrival of the Soviet troops.[132] Little is known of what he did on this occasion, but the consequences seem clear—and typical. He "helped" two officers of the SMA from Berlin to set up new administrations in Weimar, Jena, and Erfurt; he discussed the future of the university of Jena with the faculty there; he attended a session of the local KPD organization (*Ortsleitung*) in Jena.[133] The *Anti-Nazi Komitee, Thüringen-Ausschuss*, whose statement welcoming the Red Army had been reprinted in the first issue of the provincial KPD newspaper, the *Thüringer Volks-Zeitung*, on July 3, 1945, vanished from the political scene. The resolutions adopted then days after his visit by the first Conference of Thuringian KPD Functionaries were consistent with the new KPD party line.[134]

Indirect evidence of other KPD activity in Thuringia was provided in November 1945 by the Social Democratic leader Heinrich Hoffmann.[135] Inasmuch as Hoffman's purpose was to impress his fellow Social Democrats with the Communists' power, his account may be somewhat exaggerated; it sufficiently resembles what else we know of this activity, however, to be taken as close to fact.[136] According to Hoffman, the KPD had pursued from the start a policy designed to make it a "power in the emerging state," securing its influence in the major industrial plants of the province, as well as the provincial trade union leadership. Through its administration of the land-reform program, it built its influence in a number of rural districts (Weissensee, Langensalza, Saalfeld). Moreover, it dominated municipal (and especially police) administrations in a number of cities.

Nevertheless, the Social Democrats of Thuringia presented the SMA with a serious obstacle to its plans for the controlled and centralized organization of political parties in the Soviet Zone. The source of the difficulty lay largely in the activities of a single individual: the leader of the province's Social Democrats, Herman L. Brill.[137] His position rested on three factors: preparation, ideas, and opportunity. The first two have already been discussed in connection with the Buchenwald Manifesto. The last was provided by the two months of American occupation. At the time of Soviet entry into Thuringia, Brill not only was head of the provincial administration but, much more important, had organized the Social Democrats of Thuringia in a fashion deviating from the general SPD pattern, not only of the Soviet Zone, but of Germany generally. The notions that Brill had developed prior to the war's end he tried to incorporate in a "new style" socialist party: the "League of Democratic Socialists" (*Bund demokratischer Sozialisten*, or BdS), which had been provided with a "Program" that reflected those ideas first propounded in Buchenwald.

Promptly on July 5, 1945, the *Bund demokratischer Sozialisten – SPD – Landesberband Gross-Thuringen* had, basing itself on Order No. 2 of the SMA, convoked a first *Landeskonferenz* for July 8 in Weimar.[138] Brill had presumably prepared the guidelines (*Richtlinien*) for this occasion.[139] It was a document marked by that combination of activist elitism and faith in mass action characteristic of his writing, but not consistent with the SMA outlook. The subsequent gathering of 250 Social Democrats on July 8, with Heinrich Hoffmann presiding, was more "respectable." Cooperation with the KPD was termed "self-evident" and the "correct behavior" of the SMA was lauded.[140]

The July 8 meeting did produce a document, however, that probably helped fix Soviet suspicions on Brill and any organization influenced by him. It was a letter sent by the SPD to the Thuringia KPD leadership.[141] It began by reproducing in Thuringia that unwelcome SPD embrace of the KPD that Ulbricht already had had to fend off in Berlin:

> We consider it essential that, as soon as possible concrete steps be taken toward the complete merging of the socialist workers' movement. . . . The need to overcome the partisan split in the socialist workers' movement is so deep and fundamental, that nothing must take place which might weaken this [unity] sentiment of the working class.

More disturbing yet to the SMA was the conclusion immediately drawn in the letter from this "yearning for unity": the Thuringian SPD was to call upon the *Zentralausschuss* to consider steps toward unification. The ZA, incidentally, was characterized as an irregular, self-constituted body not authorized by Party Statutes, to which the Weimar SPD granted only conditional recognition so that it might convoke some form of all-German party gathering.

Having triply diverged from the policy favored by the KPD—by proposing immediate merger of the parties, challenging the ZA, and insisting on all-German SPD authority—the SPD careened on to suggest a number of measures designed to implement ideas already suggested in the Buchenwald Manifesto, such as "Socialization of the economy" and a closer form of detailed interparty cooperation. On the other hand, it was suggested (as part of a pro-atheist, pro"scientific," anti-Catholic program) that, for their part, the political parties should refrain from exercising any influence on ideological thought or feeling. As a parting shot, the letter contained the lofty suggestion that, if the local KPD was unable to participate in implementing these ideas due to its party's "centralized organization," the two provincial organizations might make a joint presentation to their zonal leaderships on these subjects.[142]

The KPD answered this letter on July 21, 1945.[143] It rejected all the controversial portions of the SPD proposals, using arguments that are familiar from the earlier events in Berlin. All this SPD initiative aroused the SMA's concern. The ZA in Berlin learned of this on June 21, when its leaders had an interview with military and political personnel of the SMA. The Soviet spokesman said that the SMA would regret having to place a "bourgeois" at the head of the Thuringian administration; Thuringia was known as a Social Democratic stronghold, a fact that the Americans had recognized in appointing a pre-1933 SPD leader, Brill, as provisional administrative head. After a brief whispered exchange with Tiul'panov, he declared that Brill was sponsoring a new party in Thuringia. "Are you familiar with the Buchenwald Manifesto?" he asked his visitors. Receiving a negative answer, he continued that it was the "program" of Brill's new party.[144]

Meanwhile, the harried Social Democrats had done their best to allay Soviet suspicions—but their efforts had not succeeded. The letter of July 10 to the KPD had marked the end, not the start, of autonomous policies. On several occasions Brill withdrew from direct participation in party affairs, although refusing to bow to Soviet pressure to resign altogether. This created a situation quite satisfactory to the Soviet command: it could deal with the less independently minded vice-chairman of the SPD in Thuringia, Heinrich Hoffmann.[145] (Later, Hoffmann's ambitions would be used by the SMA to bring the SPD of Thuringia into line with its policies.) The pressure on Brill grew to the point of his arrest by the NKVD on August 4, 1945.[146] Although he was released (and avoided a second summons to NKVD headquarters), it was falsely reported to Grotewohl and Meier, when they visited Weimar at the end of August, that Brill had been replaced by Hoffmann.[147] Yet Brill had never resigned, although he later claimed that the ZA had "hinted" to him at the end of August that he (Brill) might profitably take a vacation from politics.[148] This Brill did not do, and finally, when Gniffke arrived at the end of September, he not only accepted on behalf of the ZA Brill's continued stay in office, but accompanied Brill and Hans Freiburg,[149] of the *Landesvorstand,* to see the Soviet officer in charge of political affairs, Major General Kolesnichenko.[150]

However, this meeting had been preceded by a series of attempts by Brill and the *Landesvorstand* to placate the SMA. On July 12 the Thuringia SMA received a letter from Hoffmann on behalf of the LV, containging an SPD resolution of July 10, that stated that while the SPD continued to support Brill for the post of chief of government, it would accept another Social Democrat for the job. In the light of the pre-1933 Thuringia voting record, however, the LV held that a Social Democrat should have this position.[151] (It was given to a "bourgeois" politician, Rudolf Paul, who joined the SED in 1946.)[152] The aforementioned resolution had been adopted *after* consultation between the SPD, KPD, Democratic Party, and an SMA officer (i.e., it presumably took Soviet wishes into account) and transmitted by courier to the KPD (which never replied).[153]

On July 16, 1945, Brill, Hoffmann, and the party's organization secretary, Adolf Bremer, had been to see Kolesnichenko to plead fruitlessly for an SPD daily newspaper. They were met with complaints: the name *Bund demokratischer Sozialisten* was inadmissible, as was continued reference to the Buchenwald Manifesto. Brill replied that the party would stop using rubber stamps and stationery with the unwanted name, and would henceforth regard the Manifesto simply as a historical document.[154]

How little these assurances satisfied the SMA may be judged from the report of a meeting between Hoffmann and a group of Soviet officers, including Kolesnichenko, on July 24, 1945.[155] Kolesnichenko began by asking Hoffmann whether he had signed the application for a newspaper license and whether he stood by the Buchenwald Manifesto? Hoffmann twice answered, "Yes." The general than began to read from a Russian translation of the Manifesto, pausing when he reached Point 4, "Socialization of the economy." Hoffmann was asked how he understood this and answered—in the same way as Lenin had in Russia in 1917. He was told that this was an invalid comparison, inasmuch as Germany had no government and hence no state power to carry out socialization. Hoffmann replied that at the time the Manifesto was issued, no one could foresee that Germany would be without a central government.

Kolesnichenko brushed this aside, saying that Thuringia's small size and the German situation made socialization impossible.[156] He asked for comment on the apparent contradictions between the Buchenwald Manifesto and the Declarations of the ZA and ZK. Hoffmann replied that there had always been various schools of thought in the SPD; clarification could come only after a national party congress. Thereupon Kolesnichenko declared the SMA could not allow "that the German people's spiritual confusion" be increased through a multiplicity of programs; the German people must first recover its spiritual health and free itself from Nazi ideology. Hoffmann promptly asked for more freedom of speech, more meeting permits, and approval to publish a newspaper. He was corrected by Kolesnichenko: "No, before our ideas can be discussed, there must spiritual clarification. We must realize that, at the present time, a demand for socialization would be out of place."[157]

In many ways this "discussion" typified the contacts between the Social Democrats of the Soviet Zone and the SMA officers. What seemed to concern the latter most was the ideological correctness of presumptive party leaders not their pre-Hitler stance or their wartime record or even their personal capabilities. Again and again, the functionaries of the SPD would try to obtain relief from practical pressures of material shortages or occupation regulations, only to find that the Soviet officers wished to discuss ideological questions. Then the discussion would frequently consist of stubborn repetition of certain set formulas. (In fairness to the Soviet commanders, it must be remembered that, of course, they did not originate this line; their duty was merely to expound it.) Finally, and especially in the Thuringian context here, we must note the obsessive concentration on the Buchenwald Manifesto. Its presence seemed to infect the Thuringian SPD with an almost ineradicable taint of deviation from the desired pattern of politics in the Soviet Zone.

Brill and the SPD in Weimar found an unexpected source of strength in the ZA in Berlin.[158] At the beginning of August Brill visited the ZA in Berlin, and upon his return he reported his sudden enlightenment as to the source of the ZA's legitimization: nothing other than the legend of the Weimann-Fechner group "entrusted" with the SPD's continuity.[159] His recital of his Weimar comrades was true to the myth in all details. Since at this time no one in the ZA took this matter very seriously, how can Brill's sudden conversion be explained? Brill must have felt that he could blunt the continuing Soviet hostility by sheltering behind the authority of that party group that the Soviet authorities repeatedly cite as a desired model: the *Zentralauschuss*. At a special meeting of the Weimar

LV (*Gesamt-Erweitertenlandesvorstand*) on August 11, 1945, Hoffmann (in Brill's absence) put the matter this way: "Only those whom the *Zentralausschuss* has recognized may work for the party on the district level. This authorization must be shown the Russian Commandants."[160]

Furthermore, Hoffmann specifically withdrew the earlier assertion that Weimar regarded the ZA as "extra-legal": "Contrary to our assumption that the *Zentralausschuss* was formed contrary to party statues, we learned in the Berlin negotiations[161] that the *Zentralausschuss* is the legal successor to the *Parteivorstand* which emigated in 1933."

As long as it was the policy of the SMA to encourage formation of SPD provincial and local organizations subordinate to the ZA, affiliation with the ZA provided protection from Soviet criticism (at the price of sharing the ZA's own limitations). The tactical nature of this acknowledgment of the ZA's authority is indicated by the continued references to the need for the earliest possible convocation of an all-German party congress,[162] as well as the observation (especially important for Brill personally) that the ZA's members had either engaged in anti-Nazi activities or had served in jails and concentration camps.[163]

Helped by this connection with the ZA, Brill was able to establish better relations with the Soviet command. Sometime during the month of August 1945, the SMA received a memorandum from Hoffmann on behalf of the *Landesvorstand* in which he listed the factors that would determine the "political line" of the projected SPD Thuringian newspaper. The six items were notable for what was excluded: the Buchenwald Manifesto.[164] When Brill returned from his "vacation" at the beginning of September, he had an interview with Kolesnichenko in which the Buchenwald Manifesto came up once again. This time Brill was categorically reassuring: "I renounced the *Buchenwald Manifesto* as a basis for our work and declared that henceforth only the Appeal of the *Zentralausschuss* would have relevance for us. Kolesnichenko seemed to be satisfied."[165]

Thus when Gniffke accompanied Brill to the Thuringian SMA on October 1, 1945, all seemed well. Brill later recounted that "Comrade Gniffke took the opportunity to ask if there were any doubts about me. Kolesnichenko said there were none and added that, if Dr. Brill had the trust of the SPD, he also had his."[166]

In adjusting itself to Soviet Zone norms, the SPD under Brill also gave up (for the time being) its distinctive attitude towards the KPD. On August 8, 1945, representatives of the two parties' provincial leaderships agreed on a program of cooperation that echoed the agreement reached in June at the zonal level.[167] There would be cooperation in antifascist work, in building up the four-party bloc, in consultation on ideological clarification, and in joint representation of the interests of the urban and rural toilers.

To make sure that the local KPD was fully prepared for its tasks, Walter Ulbricht spoke at the Second KPD *Landesfunktionärskonferenz* in Weimar on August 5, 1945.[168] He made two important points. The KPD must stop being just an opposition party; it now shared responsibility for carrying out the tasks of the state power at all levels of government. On a more ominous note, he proclaimed that the chief factor underlying Germany's defeat was the failure of the German working class, despite the best educational efforts of the KPD to fully understand the historical significance of the October Revolution in Russia. It may have occurred to some Social Democrats that, since in the Weimar period the SPD had been the major factor in leading the German proletariat in a direction other than that indicated by the October Revolution, the SPD would have to undergo a major transformation if it was to participate in the building of a new Germany.

SPD and KPD: June 1945

Even before it existed officially as a party,[169] the SPD had begun to deal with the KPD. Although they had met with scant success in individual approaches, the SPD leaders apparently authorized Dahrendorf to speak for the party at the Communists' meeting of June 12.[170] He declared:

> I speak in the name of the newly resurrected Social Democratic Party; since June 11, 1945, it has arisen anew. Let me stay at once, that this new Social Democratic Party has no ties to the political practice of the last phase of the old Social Democratic Party (Bravo!) . . . Nor is it tied . . . to emigré politics. No one abroad is entitled to speak for the new Social Democratic party.

This new party, he continued, had a new line: it advocated the "political and if possible organizational unity of the toilers, of all antifascists." Turning to the KPD in particular, Dahrendorf made a concrete offer: "We are prepared to discuss all questions of unity with our Communist friends and ask when decisive discussions can take place."

Finally, he also "unreservedly" supported the KPD's "action program." Thus the ZA attempted once again to bring about the formation of a united socialist party; once again, the Communists were evasive. Ulbricht answered Dahrendorf by suggesting that talks about a program of joint action among *all antifascist parties* take place throughout the Soviet Zone.[171]

At the SPD's first meeting five days later Grotewohl knowingly repeated Dahrendorf's phrase about reconstructing Germany on the basis of the "organizational unity of the working class."[172] At a ZA meeting on June 17 Dahrendorf insisted that the SPD and the KPD must not be reestablished as separate organizations. He requested negotiating authority from the ZA so that he might present these views to the KPD's representatives. After a lively discussion, and against one negative vote (Germer's), the authorization was granted.[173]

The KPD's answer was to engage the SPD in a two-party arrangement that involved close and continous contact, with an assumed correspondence of goals, while at the same time championing the goal of uniting the two parties. The latter tactic was exemplified in a *DVZ* editorial that pictured the German people as wondering whether the antifascist parties would fall into a fateful disunity. With great relief the editorial announced that "comradely discussions" had taken place between SPD and KPD, and the resulting agreement "broke the ice" and "cleared the way" for Germany's future.[174]

What had happened? On June 19, 1945, five representatives of the SPD and five of the KPD had met to discuss mutual relations.[175] Many of them met each other for the first time; according to Gniffke the results were not entirely happy.[176] Ulbricht lectured the group on the inadvisability of an immediate party unification. If we do this without prior ideological clarification, he said, the newly united party will soon break apart. (Otto Meier's question, as to why such clarification had to take place in two parties, went unanswered.) Furthermore, Ulbricht continued, not socialism but democracy is the immediate problem. Grotewohl ventured to say that the Soviet Union had been less well prepared for socialism in 1917 than Germany was now, but Ackermann replied that the Soviet authorities had therefore moved slowly.[177] After further desultory discussion, described by the *DVZ* as having been marked by "mutual trust," an agreement embodying the Communist position was approved.[178]

It provided for a joint committee consisting of five representatives of each party center (formation of similar committee was recommended to lower party organizations). This committee had five areas of responsibility. One was to coordinate activities relating to reconstruction and eradication of Nazism. In this connection, the parties accepted the goal of a democratic-parliamentary republic, "which would avoid the weaknesses of the past and guarantee the working people all their democratic. liberties." Further points were: formation of a bloc with other antifascist parties; acting as joint spokesmen for the interests of urban and rural workers; arranging for joint meetings; seeking joint clarification of ideological questions.[179]

The first SPD-KPD meeting was in many ways typical of all that followed. The Communists came prepared with a detailed position that was hard to object to on general grounds.[180] The Social Democrats had doubts and defenses but no coherent plan of their own or any prepared refutation of the Communists' position. The KPD spokesmen presented their proposals for immediate action, not for consideration; somehow the SPD never simply refused. An agreement very close to the Communist proposals was reached, and it was then presented to the public as the fruit of comradely unanimity. Thus it was made harder for the SPD to disagree at a later date: why had they gone along in the first place? Every such agreement eased the way for the KPD in following sessions.

Nevertheless, it would be false to imagine that this agreement, or the many others like it, was somehow obtained from the SPD by force or trickery. Unity, cooperation, a fresh attack on Germany's ills—these were precious ideas to most Social Democrats in 1945. Ideology and hope combined to make "unity of action" attractive to the SPD. Many Social Democrats believed that close collaboration in dealing with immediate practical problems would sweep away the remaining resentments between members of the two parties. They held fast to such hopes, but in a realistic spirit; they were aware of the difficulties in party relations but convinced that Germany's plight made it necessary to create a united, democratic, socialist force. It was in such a spirit that Dahrendorf wrote to a party comrade in Rostock late in July 1945.[181] The atmosphere among the top leaders is distinctly favorable fo cooperation he reported, but the practical consequences remain to be seen. Aware of the KPD's advantages in terms of greater pre-1945 preparation and a privileged relationship to the SMA,[182] he nevertheless insisted on a sincere effort at cooperation:

> On the district level—above all in Berlin—our joint activity is not going well everywhere. There are some model districts in which the readiness on both sides to have genuine cooperation has resulted in practical arrangements. . . . You must also try to work according to these good examples, and freely discuss all doubts and question.[183]

The coming months would reveal what the results of such efforts at cooperation would be, and, more importantly, what practical cooperation could achieve in settling the political and ideological differences between the parties.

CHAPTER 5

Party Activity
July to October 1945

During the latter half of 1945 a large part of the KPD's political work consisted of defending and explaining its new political line, suggesting that the party was having some difficulty both in convincing its own members of the correctness of that policy, and in persuading Social Democrats of the KPD's "sincerity" in this regard. As early as June 14, 1945, Anton Ackermann, denouncing as "hidden foes of unity" those who questioned the KPD's moderate line, wrote that "Our demand for the creation of an antifascist, democratic republic, which will grant to the people full rights and freedom, is no tricky tactic, no diplomatic maneuver, no camouflage, but rather a sincere orientation toward the only goal which is a realistic one in the present situation."[1]

One month later Fred Oelssner, writing for internal party schooling, also attacked critics on two fronts: those on the right who doubted the KPD's commitment to the new line and those on the left who feared it.[2] For the former, Oelssner pointed to the record of the KPD since the war's end: Communists were the most consistent opponents of the remnants of Nazism in German life; they had taken the initiative in forming a bloc of antifascist parties without compromising the independence of those parties; they had not abused their positions in local administrations. The Social Democrats, however, despite their avowed disappointment with the weaknesses of the Weimar regime, still were committed to a democratic political order. They wondered about the extent to which the KPD's acceptance of a democratic regime represented merely a temporary tactic.

On this point, Oelssner made a telling argument by explaining why the KPD had been justified in opposing the Weimar Republic. Weimar had been a wretched regime, supported by reactionaries and one from which Hitlerite fascism had sprung. The post-Hitler German republic would not be a repetition of Weimar (a proposition that had wide support in 1945), and the KPD was for *that*, wholeheartedly.

There were other voices—identified as those either of "concerned Communists" or of "slanderous foes"—that claimed that the KPD had given up the goals of socialism and Soviet power. Not so, answered Oelssner, but for the moment there was no majority in Germany in favor of socialism, and "Soviet power cannot be forced on a people."

In keeping with this analysis, the Communists (unlike the SPD) concentrated on advocating a general, multiparty, multiclass coalition against fascism and for democracy. Although the proletariat was hailed as the "backbone" of the national unity of the toiling people, the KPD's emphasis was on the unity of all "democratic" forces in working for a new Germany. All democratic and antifascist forces were summoned to work with the KPD for Germany's future. The range of this invitation was revealing. Writing of the significance of concentration camp experiences, Franz Dahlem hailed the growing closeness of anti-Nazi men of various views: not only Communists, Social Democrats, and *Zentrum* members, but also Jehovah's Witnesses, anti-Nazi bourgeois, men from the foreign and the air force ministries, as well as officers of the July 20th movement![3] Nor was the closer collaboration of SPD and KPD any obstacle to the larger democratic "concentration."[4]

The KPD appealed to non-Socialist and nonproletarian elements by advocating actions that could be agreed to by a variety of groups and organizations. A striking example of this line is provided by the Berlin KPD's "Open Letter" to the city's inhabitants, in which the party called for action to alleviate the hardships feared for the coming winter.[5] Addressed to such varied audiences as factory councils, youth groups, and entrepreneurs, it avoided all political and social demands while suggesting practical measures for the improvement of daily life.

The intent of such a policy was clearly to mobilize large numbers of non-Communists in campaigns of social and political activity aimed at securing widely approved goals. The policy thus reflected, at the tactical level, the basic strategic concept of Communist activity during this period. By securing "unity of action" under Communist leadership in pursuit of immediate ends, the Communist parties would later be able to lead these new recruits in pursuit of more distant, and more Communist, goals. Essential to the success of this policy was the proposition that, at the proper moment, the Communists would be able to transfer their following from one goal to another. In the case of the KPD and SPD, such a transfer proved to be a difficult task whose partial accomplishment in the Soviet Zone compromised similar efforts on a wider scale.

Party organization and recruitment during this period also reflected this policy. The focus of recruitment was explicitly widened to include nonproletarian elements. An editorial in the KPD newspaper asked

> Who belongs in the ranks of our party? The most clear-sighted, self-sacrificing, and progressive antifascist fighters [do]; those who come to us of their own free will, who have decided, after weighing the issues carefully in their minds and consciences, that they henceforth wish to be known as "Communists". . . .

Only "sectarians" thought to limit new membership to workers; the KPD must represent the "unity of democratic forces." Every party unit would be judged by how well it recruited among nonproletarian elements, because

> The workers can never fulfill their tasks if they are separated from the other strata of the toiling masses (the white-collar workers [*Angestellte*], toiling peasants, artisans, and working intellectuals). Nor can the Communist Party fulfill its obligations to the people and the nation at the high levels demanded of it, unless it aligns itself, not only with the most progressive workers, but also with the most clear-sighted and progressive individuals from all strata of the toiling people. *As the representative of the workers' interests, the people's interests, and the true interests of the nation, the party must firmly anchor itself in all sections of the toiling people.*[6] (Italics in original.)

Detailed information concerning the organizational development of the KPD in these months is not available. There seems to have been some difficulty in the party's organizational drive, at least in Berlin.[7] It cannot be determined to what extent such difficulties resulted from popular identification of the party with the occupation forces or from the reluctance of older party members to accept the KPD's postwar line. Certainly the material requirements for effective recruiting were not lacking, especially in comparison with the means available to the SPD.

By November, according to Franz Dahlem, the KPD was gaining steadily in influence and support among the German people thanks to its role in reconstruction, democratization and the maintenance of German unity.[8] Given "free democratic development," he boasted, the KPD would become the "largest mass party in Germany." Already it was the only party covering all Germany with a rigid ideological and organizational structure. No longer an outlawed opposition party as in the Weimar days, the KPD was now a recognized party, supporting and building the new democratic Germany. For its part, the KPD sought out all "progressively thinking" men and women. Except for Nazis and "profascists," anyone could become a party member who—"regardless of former party membership or political beliefs—accepts the KPD's Action Program of June 1945 . . . with the condition that he accepts party discipline, joins a street or factory group of the KPD and is active with it."

An interesting sidelight on the KPD's organizational efforts was the campaign to make its chairman, Wilhelm Pieck, a paternal and national figure, a "grand old man" above partisan strife. The political significance of this tactic for the unity question became clearer when this campaign accelerated in January 1946, but it was already characteristic of SPD-KPD relations that in the summer of 1945 the SPD's Otto Grotewohl had a prominent part in this effort. On the occasion of the 50th anniversary of Pieck's political career, the SPD newspaper ran an article far more laudatory than anything it ever ran about an SPD leader.[9] The Communist DVZ was not slow to follow, as it showed with a lush description of Pieck's entrance at the KPD's public rally of July 20, 1945. Grotewohl, speaking for the SPD on this occasion, declared that Pieck belonged "not only to the KPD but to the entire German working class."[10] In fact, while Ulbricht aroused immediate hostility among Social Democrats, Pieck made a rather jolly impression on them; both reactions were unjustifiably exaggerated.[11]

The result of this party activity was to produce a KPD membership total of approximately 270,000 by November 1945; 500,000 to 600,000 in the Soviet Zone by early 1946, of which Berlin accounted for some 60, 000–70,000.[12] As many as half of these members may not have belonged to the party prior to 1933; by contrast, the party cadre consisted overwhelmingly of pre-Hitler KPD members. The situation in this regard was similar in both parties.[13] Inasmuch as the KPD had no experience in staffing trade union and governmental administrations, finding suitable personnel become a problem.[14]

The organizational development of the SPD in the Soviet Zone in the six months after the formation of the *Zentralauschuss* in Berlin was marked by substantial growth in the face of material difficulties.[15] The party's relation with the SMA were confused, with encouragement alternating with hindrance; Soviet approval of the "new" line of the ZA was mingled with suspicion of the SPD's ancestral anti-Soviet proclivities. Relations with the KPD were officially regulated by the agreement for mutual cooperation of June 19, but they actually grew worse in practice and more distant in their theoretical formulation as time went on. Finally, the SPD in these months (June–December 1945) continued the development of its ideas, its relation to the KPD, and its future role in German politics, ideas that played a part in shaping the SPD's response to the crisis over the unity question that came at the year's end.

Whereas the KPD leadership was in personal contact with the provincial organizations of their party from the start of party activity, representatives of the ZA could not travel to the major cities of the Soviet Zone until late August, when Grotewohl toured the zone.[16] Gniffke, who was in charge of organizational questions for the ZA, managed to make his first trip (of "inspection," but in fact more for purposes of acquaintance) in September 1945.[17]

The party leadership lacked adequate means of transportation (which at this time meant automobiles); what galled especially was the knowledge that transportation was available to the KPD.[18] The ZA's only recourse in such predicaments was to complain to the SMA; the Soviet officers were then in the fortunate position of being able to promise redress for conditions that Soviet actions had brought about.[19] It cannot be determined to what extent the obstacles encountered by the SPD reflected the poor performance of subordinate Soviet officials, or the generally disorganized conditions of occupied Germany. Nevertheless, what presumably was not accidental—and certainly struck the ZA as anything but accidental—was the favored position of the KPD in similar circumstances. In any case, the SPD leaders were painfully aware of their utter dependence on the SMA for even minimal logistic support.[20]

The SPD also suffered from a shortage of paid full-time party personnel. For example, the Soviet dismissal of Brill from his administrative position in Thuringia caused a financial crisis both for Brill and for the Thuringian party that was not settled satisfactorily while Brill remained in Weimar. Grotewohl was lost to party administrative work for several months after June 1945 because he had to take a paid position with the borough administration of Berlin-Schöneberg.[21] At lower levels of the party, in communities where the party was being organized in direct competition with KPD, the lack of full-time personnel was keenly felt.[22] Gniffke's report to the ZA on his inspection trip of September 1945 contains this description of the relative state of organization:

> There exists a substantial organizational disproportion between the KPD and the SPD. In every small town the KPD has a first secretary, a second secretary, an *Agitprop*-man, and an *Org*-man. In medium-sized cities there is a [KPD] apparatus with twenty or more paid staff employees; in the larger cities there is a party organization in every borough.
>
> Our party cannnot match this number of full-time party personnel. If we do nothing to overcome this discrepancy, we will be steamrollered by an *apparat* of this sort.
>
> Money is also a problem. The KPD is swimming in money; it has no worries along this line.[23]

Despite the ZA's efforts, which included frequent complaints to the SMA, a satisfactory organization was not created. The political effect this could have in a crisis situation became apparent in January 1946 when the ZA's connections with its provincial and local organizations proved to be inadequate to rally the party for political action.

Perhaps the most critical area in which the SPD suffered from lack of support in comparison to the KPD was that of the party press. The first party newspaper to appear was the *Deutsche Volkszeitung*,[24] the daily newspaper of the KPD Central Committee, beginning publication on June 13, 1945.[25] Its SPD equivalent, *Das Volk*, appeared on July 7,

1945, (three weeks after the party had been established) as the first non-Soviet or non-Communist newspaper in postwar Berlin.

In comparing the KPD and SPD newspapers throughout the Soviet Zone, one finds that generally the former appeared sooner, were published more frequently, and were allotted larger press runs. In Thuringia, the KPD's *Thüringer Volkszeitung* appeared as early as July 3, 1945, whereas the SPD's *Tribüne* began publishing on September 15, 1945. In *Land* Saxony, the KPD's *Sächsische Volkszeitung* first appeared sometime in July while the SPD's *Volksstimme* dates from September 11, 1945.[26] In the important Saxon provincial center of Zwickau, a Communist newspaper was published from the summer of 1945 on; the SPD newspaper appeared only in January 1946. In Brandenburg the KPD's *Volkswille* dates from September 15, 1945, the SPD's *Der Märker* from October 20, 1945.[27]

It was sometimes difficult to obtain the SMA's approval for publication of SPD newspapers, although granting such permission would seem to have been in the Soviet interest, once the SPD itself had been allowed to form. The needed approval was not always readily forthcoming, however, although application for a license to publish was usually the first SPD request to the SMA, both at the zonal and provincial levels. Reporting on Otto Meier's efforts on behalf of the ZA, Gniffke wrote that, "Otto Meier gave a report on the organization of a Social Democratic press. His report was largely a recital of the difficulties in the way of such an effort."[28]

Circulation figures for the party press were more indicative of paper allotments, and thus of political Soviet decisions, than of reader interest. Setting figures for printing runs and increasing them required negotiations with the SMA. Soviet policy in this regard is difficult to judge. Paper stocks were in short supply—and editors everywhere wished to increase their circulations. Presumably, SPD newspapers had a lower priority for the SMA than did its own newspapers, or the KPD's newspapers, or so Social Democrats believed. (Unfortunately, while the circulations of the SPD newspapers may be determined approximately, only scanty figures are available for KPD newspapers.)[29] In Berlin, at the end of October 1945, newspaper circulations were as follows: *Tägliche Rundschau,* (official SMA newspaper), 600,000; *Deutsche Volkszeitung,* 350,000; *Berliner Zeitung,* 300,000; *Das Volk,* 150,000.[30]

The SPD's *Volkswille* in Dresden and the *Tribüne* in Weimar both began with approximately 50,000 copies;[31] the *Tribüne* did not pass 100,000 in circulation, or become a daily, until February 1946 (when its policy had become pro-unity).[32]

Soviet controls were not limited to indirect means such as paper allocations. The press in the Soviet Zone, as in the other zones, was closely and overtly controlled by the occupying power. The contents of the press, both by direction and through anticipation, reflected the particular occupying power in type and content of story.[33] Soviet censorship was strict and politically purposeful; certain words or phrases were politically offensive; thus it was difficult for the SPD press to talk of Socialism in connection with specific economic problems. Censorship took the form of precensorship; articles had to be submitted, in advance, to local press officers.[34]

In several important instances, major events went unreported in the party press due to specific acts of Soviet censorship. Among them may be mentioned Grotewohl's speech of November 11 and the ZA resolution of January 15, 1946; neither of these important events were reported in the SPD press!

The experience of four to six months of SPD press activity was summed up afterwards by an embittered Gustav Dahrendorf as follows: "This was the situation at the turn of the year: the [SPD] had seven daily newspapers, whose combined total circulation was less than one million; according to reliable estimates, the Communist press had a circulation of about four million."[35] Paper supplies for other party publications (pamphlets, placards, etc.) were also available to the KPD in larger amounts.

Despite organizational difficulties such as these, the period of the summer and fall of 1945 was one of steady growth for the SPD in the Soviet Zone.[36] The party succeeded in establishing itself in all portions of the Soviet Zone, exceeding 1932 membership totals in a number of districts.[37] This growth of the party continued steadily throughout the first postwar year, but it is significant that the major portion of it often took place in the first months, when it owed less to organizational efforts than to a spontaneous rallying to the old party by its former members. By April 1946 the SPD in the Soviet Zone counted approximately 700,000 members, perhaps 60,000 of them in Berlin. A breakdown of the zonal figures into totals for Berlin, Thuringia, Saxony, and Brandenburg (as well as smaller districts for which data is available) shows that this growth took place in all parts of the Soviet Zone, and that this produced an SPD slightly larger than the KPD.[38]

This growth of the party was reflected in the holding of provincial party congresses in the fall of 1945. Such congresses took place in *Land* Saxony (October 7–9, 1945), Thuringia (October 28, 1945), Brandenburg (November 3–4, 1945), and in Berlin (November 25, 1945).[39] It was these congresses that provided the SPD in the provinces with postwar democratic legitimization.[40] At these provincial congresses, despite surface friendliness, there were clear signs of continuing disagreement with the KPD. As might be expected, the most striking dissents came from the party congress in Thuringia, but examples may be found elsewhere as well.

At the Saxon congress, for instance, Arno Hennig[41] told the delegates that in early May "We all [had] the hope that the war's end would see a socialist united front. We tried to do justice to this fundamental desire of the workers. We were forced, however, to found the Social Democratic Party, after the Communist fraternal party had preceded us by a week."[42]

The representative at the congress of the aforementioned "fraternal party" still spoke of unity only in general terms; Hermann Matern declared that the working class could master the tasks ahead only if it were united; Communists and Social Democrats should cooperate as members-to-be of the coming unity party. Equally as characteristic as his vagueness on the question of a merger of SPD and KPD was Matern's insistence that an end must be made of "anti-Bolshevism," for which "there is no room in our ranks. Even the usually compliant Otto Buchwitz, in his address to the congress, delivered some gentle rebukes to the Communists. In the postwar era both parties were breaking new ground; the KPD now knows what it means to share administrative responsibility, rather than simply to oppose. The "new SPD" is filled with the spirit of the Erfurt Program and is ready to unite unconditionally with the KPD. However, the SPD's strength entitled it to an equal voice in decision-making;it should not be a "fifth wheel" in political affairs.[43]

At the congress of his own Thuringian organization, Brill was even more outspoken than he had been as a guest at the Saxony meeting.[44] In a commentary on the congress he wrote that neither the KPD nor the SPD could simply resume its Weimar style. What was needed was "a completely new type of party, one which would find its permanent form in the course of future work."[45] The "primarily . . . moral question" of uniting the parties would not be solved "from one day to the next."[46]

> It will not be brought about by the impatient switch of individuals from one party to another, and not by joint meetings on the local level; the unity of the working class can only result from a lengthy process of education, organization, and work. *The party leaderships must direct this process. The unity of the entire German working class can only come about through agreed on resolutions passed at two national party congresses held in an undivided Germany.*[47] (Italics added.)

In thus stressing the problem of the two parties' nationwide unification, Brill anticipated the major SPD tactic of the coming winter months and stated it more vigorously, on the whole, than the ZA was to do later.

An important factor in the thinking of the Soviet Zone's SPD leadership in the summer of 1945 was the conviction that the most fruitful policy for both the SPD as a party and for Germany as a nation involved an "Eastern orientation" (*Ostorientierung*) toward the Soviet Union.[48] The Soviet interests were thought to include a desire to foster Socialism as well as seeking guarantees for Soviet security; it would therefore have to rely on the SPD as the only German party that was "Socialist" *and* had a mass base. Thus the SPD could divert Soviet backing from the KPD to itself; this in turn would make possible a measure of reasonably free political activity for the SPD in the Soviet Zone.

A further impetus for a pro-Soviet policy was seen in Germany's prospective economic situation.[49] According to the SPD's analysis, the combination of Western economic hostility and German industrial weakness would direct the flow of German exports to the Soviet Union, where long-standing deficiencies and war-born shortages would combine to provide a ready market for German goods.

This policy could outflank both the traditional Communist and the conservative German attitudes toward the Soviet Union. The SPD would replace the KPD as the major pro-Soviet force in the German working class. At the same time, by advocating trade and security policies associated with the German right wing—in the tradition of Tauroggen, Rapallo, and the National Committee "Free Germany"—it would allow the Soviet Union to benefit from these policies without having to qualify its support of socialism. Socialist Germany would cooperate with the USSR in European and world politics, and the SPD would be the logical leader of such a Germany.

This plausible analysis rested on certain assumptions made by the ZA concerning Soviet policy. It believed that the Soviet Union favored a democratic, independent Germany and the early legalization of political parties in the Soviet Zone was taken as a sign of this. Soviet policy and KPD pronouncements were both interpreted as welcoming an indigenous German socialist development. Above all, the SPD assumed that the Soviet authorities wished to deal with an autonomous Germany that would follow policies satisfactory to the Soviet Union. The SPD was prepared to adopt social, political, and economic policies designed to satisfy those interests. In late July 1945 Dahrendorf, for example, wrote to a friend in Rostock that

> Germany must strike out on an entirely new path politically. In our view, the destiny of our country is bound especially closely to the Soviet Union. The direction of our policies will be set by our willing it, as well as just knowing it. It is self-evident in this connection that the unusual circumstances of our territory with respect to economic and social factors will have to to be kept in mind.

In expressing "our views" in this fashion, Dahrendorf went on to a familiar if dubious conclusion: that from this "Eastern" policy there would flow a "mediating" role for the SPD between the Soviet Union and the "European West."[50] Indeed, for Grotewohl even a "mediating position was undesirable."[51] He argued that Germany's economic and political development "pointed to the East." In a revealing passage, Grotewohl explained that, "The only difficulty is finding a tactically acceptable formula for this under current circumstances." Plainly put: commitment to the East and polite compromise with the West.

The fullest statement of Grotewohl's views on this matter is the speech he gave to party functionaries on August 26, 1945, in connection with the Leipzig *Bezirksparteitag*.[52] Speaking with neither SMA nor KPD representatives present, Grotewohl cited a meeting of June 1945 between Zhukov and the ZA.[53] Responding to SPD frankness concerning life in the Soviet Zone, Zhukov supposedly replied:

> Gentlemen, I have been sent to Berlin and to the occupied territory with Moscow's instructions to build up a democratic political order. I am perfectly aware that in this effort I cannot rely in the first instance on the Communist Party, but that I am rather in need of your support, for I know that you have the masses behind you.

To Grotewohl this exchange was a model for SMA-SPD relations: such plain speaking was incumbent on the SPD, for only it could do so, and the result would be further to solidify the SPD's claim to leadership. He contrasted the SPD's resoluteness in this regard with the performance of the Communists and bourgeois leaders, for whose behavior he had respectively only scorn and contempt:

> I have observed repeatedly that it is just those . . . who should have the closest connections with those circles [i.e., the SMA] who are often the least courageous when the time comes to speak up. Nor can we expect anything from the representatives of the bourgeoisie. They have never yet demonstrated any special political courage. Thus it remains for us to speak out. . . . *For this reason if for no other we deserve political leadership.*[54]
> (Italics added)

Grotewohl was equally outspoken regarding the Oder-Neisse line, the expulsion of German populations from Eastern Europe, limitations on German industry, and the impossibility of maintaining the Potsdam-approved "central European standard of living" in the shrunken Germany.[55]

The speech in Leipzig foreshadowed in detail Grotewohl's later controversial public statements, suggesting that these ideas were not new in September and November. (If, as seems likely, Grotewohl was not the sole author of those speeches, he certainly accepted their content over a significant span of time.)[56] Did he speak out in public because he thought his ideas would meet Soviet consideration, or even acquiescense? Or was it that the course of German poltics in the fall of 1945 made Grotewohl fearful that the SPD's claim to leadership could not be sustained?

In the summer and fall of 1945 the SPD maintained its interest in unity with the KPD; it acknowledged obstacles but felt that, as Gniffke wrote of past disagreements, "Although there may be wounds which ache when it rains, we will deaden the pain."[57] The KPD, by its advocacy of a democratic, parliamentary republic, and its rejection of the idea of forcing the Soviet system on Germany, had brought about a "historic turning point" in German party history, and had produced the ideological preconditions for ending the conflict with the SPD.[58] The general tenor of Social Democratic comments suggests that there was a widespread belief in a genuine Communist transformation.

In an interview with the correspondent of *Krasnaia Zvezda* in July, the SPD leaders declared that cooperation with the KPD was a freely chosen course for the SPD. It was true that "in those first days many Social Democratic workers asked that we form one united party together with the Communists, a party which the workers would then join." But what had the ZA done in those May days? In a clear misstatement of facts, they now declared that "after mature reflection we came to the conclusion (together with our Communist friends) that the time for an organizational merger had not yet come." The functionaries of both parties would require a lengthy process of ideological reeducation, something that was better handled by each party acting alone.[59]

The Communist response to such Social Democratic overtures was a cautious one. Typical was Pieck's comment that the Communists were convinced that through collaboration with the SPD in building a democratic republic the way would be cleared for the amalgamation of both parties into a united party of the toiling people, which would be the leading force in a great alliance of workers, peasants, scientists, and artists. Conversely, the united front of the four parties (KPD, SPD, CDU, and LDP) would aid the formation of a united party of the working class. But the time for this had not yet come, for the working class must first undergo a great spiritual transformation to create a firm foundation for a united party.[60]

The SPD supported the four-party Bloc, arguing that what Germany needed was a form of democracy in which the parties would speak to the public with one voice. Germans were used to regarding democracy as an arena for "wild party quarrels"; they must be shown that the middle class and working class parties were united in the face of the gigantic tasks confronting Germany.[61] This attitude may have been due in part to suspicion of the great mass of the SPD's Nazi-tainted fellow Germans; moreover, it represented the widespread conviction among German political leaders in all zones that important decisions about Germany's political future would have to be made without effective reference to the politically immature German people. This relieved unrepresentative party leaderships of the need to account for their "democratic" activities, but it therefore made more difficult any appeal to rank-and-file sentiment by such party leaders.

This interpretation of democracy suited the KPD quite well, for it had concluded from the German experiences of 1525, 1848, and 1918 that Germany needed a "concentration" of political forces. This might not seem democratic to "some countries" with long-established democratic systems, but the first rule of democracy was not to force one's ideas on others![62]

This degree of ideological convergence only serves to emphasize the degree to which interparty strife, as reflected at the provincial SPD congresses, resulted from weeks of practical "unity of action" of SPD and KPD. Complaints about parity in the filling of offices could be found throughout 1945.[63] For although the two parties continued to hold different theoretical positions, the important obstacles to heartfelt cooperation, as far as most Social Democrats were concerned, lay in the area of everyday relations. This was partly due to the fact that the SPD had been greatly impressed by the changes already announced in the KPD's theoretical position; there was also a general expectation that ideological quarrels would be solved in due time, albeit slowly, under the pressure of an overwhelming commitment in both parties to working class unity.

The occasions for friction, and the consequent revival of old suspicions, came therefore in the area of practical activity. This was especially so in the filling of administrative positions,[64] or what Siegfried Thomas refers to as the "so-called parity question."[65] Although the Communists, as we have shown, were keen to occupy certain important posts, the numerical ratio of positions was not as important to them as to the Social Democrats.

"Parity" not only reflected a traditional Social Democratic inclination towards "sober, practical work," but also a justified fear that the KPD was using its Soviet connections to dominate administration in the Soviet Zone.[66] A mid-September report from Magdeburg, for example, complained about the number of Communists in the local administration, where the KPD had eleven of fourteen *Landräte*.[67]

As early as June 1945 Berlin Social Democrats complained to Gniffke that "whenever there are positions to be filled, Social Democrats [are] shunted aside and Communists unfairly favored."[68] An SPD meeting in the Berlin borough of Wilmersdorf heard complaints that the Communists had been "surrounding" every Social Democrat in the administration with Communists.[69] In the Baltic coast city of Stralsund, the SPD organization claimed that of ten *Landräte* in the area of Mecklenburg-Vorpommern, only one was a Social Democrat.[70]

The ZA attempted to secure redress for these grievances. From June on there was ample opportunity to consult with the KPD Central Committee, but SPD representations concerning points of friction were met with meaningless reassurances.[71] When Gniffke returned in early October from his tour of the Zone, he bluntly told Dahlem that Communist tactics were hurting unity prospects in the Soviet Zone. At a meeting of Gniffke with Pieck, Ulbricht, and Dahlem on October 8, 1945,[72] Pieck complained about unsatisfactory cooperation within the Bloc. Gniffke retorted that relations with the KPD were perforce one-sided, since KPD tactics consisted of presenting prepared positions and insisting on their immediate (and favorable) consideration. The result was that "Even highly placed SPD functionaries grow skeptical and begin to ask whether the KPD wished to have meaningful joint activity or wished simply to take the SPD in tow." Ulbricht coldly ascribed such concern to "hostile class elements," who wished to "sabotage" working class unity on behalf of "finance capital." Dahlem interjected soothingly that "unity of action" had yet to be adequately developed.

The lack of significant political content in the "unity of action" agreements was demonstrated by the rather late promulgation of an SPD-KPD agreement in this matter for the Berlin organizations of the parties. The five points of this October 8 agreement show plainly that cooperation was just beginning, and that as yet there could be no talk of preparations for unity in Berlin.[73]

Such reluctance to engage fully in joint activities was also present in some provincial organizations.[74] In the Saxon SPD, party officials who were cool to close cooperation occupied important positions in Dresden and Leipzig. They made their views known both in internal party sessions and at the Saxon SPD party congress.[75]

Moreover, ZA-SMA relations continued troubled. For one thing, there were the Soviet suspicions regarding the influence of Western European and West German Social Democrats on the ZA, related to the revival of the SPD in the Western zones. The SPD leaders, in their July interview with *Krasnaia Zvezda*,[76] presented a claim to Social Democratic leadership that must have been pleasing to the Soviet authorities: "Today only we have the right to speak in the name of the [SPD]. We led the fight against Nazism [sic], and thousands of our comrades fell in this struggle. It is our holy duty to realize their aim—the unification of all the forces of the German working class." Subsequently, however, the renewal of interzonal contacts (discussed in the following chapter), meant that eventually the ZA would either be forced to abandon this claim, or to enforce it against intraparty opposition, thus increasing its dependence on the Soviet authorities.

While touring the SPD organizations of the Soviet Zone in August–September 1945, Gniffke found that the local and provincial Soviet commanders repeated suspiciously similar complaints against the SPD, leading Gniffke to conclude dolefully in his report to the ZA that "there is a system to these denunciations," whose secret origin was the influence of the KPD on the Soviet Command. SPD complaints to the SMA brought only countercomplaints of "rightist" influences in the SPD.[77]

All this was in a period that, compared to what came later, represented a honeymoon of Soviet-SPD relations. Looking back to the fall of 1945 from the summer of 1946, Soviet commentators saw in that period the warning signs of undesirable SPD attitudes. The authors of the *Bol'shevik* article marking the founding of the SED noted that

> Already in the first period of joint work by the two parties, the political heterogeneity of the Social Democratic Party showed itself. While the greater part of the Social Democratic membership, the workers, actively cooperated with the Communist Party and strove to strengthen this cooperation, many Social Democratic functionaries of the middle rank, and

many of those who came from the pre-1933 leadership, came out against cooperation with the Communist Party or wavered on this question.[78]

Siegfried Thomas criticizes the ZA leadership for having been irresolute in the fall of 1945 in pushing for cooperation with the KPD and leaving it to the initiative of the party membership to foster this cooperation. He attacks the ZA for failing to suppress the tendencies of certain functionaries to slow down cooperation with the Communists.[79]

By the fall of 1945 the prospects for a speedy merger of SPD and KPD based on wholehearted cooperation between the parties had faded amid mutual suspicion and recriminations. As Brill was to put it, in looking back on this period, "We must reconcile ourselves . . . to the fact that in this period there passed unused changes which may never recur; politics developed along other lines."[80] As the separate party organizations were consolidated during the summer and fall of 1945, the frictions and rivalries arising from daily party work contributed to a diminution of the pro-unity sentiment that had been more widely spread immediately at the end of the war.

Moreover, the growth of the SPD despite the difficulties described above, coupled with the Social Democratic leaders' conviction that Soviet interests in German affairs could best be served by reliance on the SPD as a political partner, combined to infuse the SPD of the Soviet Zone with increasing confidence in the future of the party. Such feelings augured poorly for any plan to amalgamate the SPD and KPD.

The organizational consolidation and growing self-confidence of the SPD also called into question the future validity of slogans about "unity of action." Underneath the common rhetoric, divergent concepts as to the future of party affairs were fostered by the autonomous development of the parties.

These factors helped to shape the first crisis (in the fall of 1945) in the three-sided relations of the SPD, the KPD, and the Soviet occupation regime. In this crisis there were three main elements: public display of the SPD's growing autonomy; the revival of political activity, especially by the Social Democrats, in the Western zones of Germany; and changes in Soviet policy on party politics. These changes led to an intensification of Soviet pressure on the SPD and culminated at the year's end in the SPD-KPD conference on party unity, the "December Conference."

CHAPTER 6

The Turn to Unity

September to December 1945

In the fall of 1945 the Soviet position on the question of unifying the KPD and SPD underwent a marked change. Since the spring of the year Soviet and German Communist policy had stressed the establishment and consolidation of a number of separate parties. Indeed, then Soviet policy had stressed the importance of the Communist parties in a number of countries. Unification of Communist and Socialist parties, while accepted as a long-range goal, was postponed until a later time. In Germany in the last quarter of the year, however, unification of the parties within a short time became the overriding aim of Soviet policy.

It is difficult to determine precisely the reasons for this shift in policy, but the weight of evidence points to events in Germany, and specifically political developments in the SPD, as the proximate cause. Allied arrangements for Germany, as determined at Potsdam, had offered the possibility of political gain in all of Germany if central administrations were to be established. Although subsequent developments, including the failure of the London conference of the Council of Foreign Ministers, cast some doubt on the viability of Great Power collaboration in Germany, nothing had yet happened to occasion a major change in policy.[1]

Moreover, cooperation between Socialists and Communists, which continued with political success in a number of countries such as France, had also scored some notable gains in Germany. Despite the frictions of the "unity of action" period, joint SPD-KPD action had helped to realize a number of major political and social goals. The Soviet Zone, in the fall of 1945, saw the implementation of land reform, educational reform, a reorganization of cultural life and changes in economic administration. These changes in German life not only were supported by the SPD, but were espoused by the Social Democrats in joint activity with the KPD and within the four-party antifascist bloc.[2]

From the Soviet perspective, the SPD's growing strength in this period presented an unwelcome contrast to KPD weakness. This contrast was underlined by SPD success in factory council elections in the Soviet Zone in late 1945, an ominous fact in view of known American plans for early elections in the US zone and the expectation that elections would take place within the year in the Soviet Zone.[3]

Nevertheless, the part played in hastening the pace of "unity" by a fear of KPD reverses in forthcoming German local elections is problematical. It is significant that in this period the Communist leaders began to stress the need for joint electoral lists.[4] Subsequently the ZA secured the abandonment of this demand at the December Conference, which may indicate that it had relatively low priority for the SMA and KPD. Furthermore, the Communist attitude on the eve of crucial elections later on, such as that of October 1946 in Berlin, was unquestionably (albeit unjustifiably) optimistic concerning their chances.[5] (The Austrian Communist Party held similar preelection views in November 1945.)[6] While the KPD's concern for joint candidacies may have been due to expected reversals, the overt reason given is consistent with SMA-KPD goals: a competitive election campaign was not the most useful step to take toward unity. The results of the Austrian and Hungarian elections, which were adverse to the Communist cause, are often stressed in this connection, although the special circumstances in those countries did not necessarily apply to German conditions. Actually, the relative performance of the Communists and Social Democrats was about the same in the Hungarian voting, where it was rather the Smallholders (Peasants) Party which was victorious.[7] The Austrian voting came so late in November that the outcome cannot account for earlier shifts in policy in Germany. Nevertheless, Leonhard states that after the Austrian returns became known, "the great unity campaign began. Now there was but one theme: Unity."[8] In an interview with Albrecht Kaden, Leonhard declared that "we first really 'turned it on' [for unity] after we had seen Grotewohl's speech and the Budapest and Austrian election returns."[9] (The reference here is to Grotewohl's speech of November 11, which is discussed below.)

The Communist interpretation of this turn to unity in Soviet policy, which emphasizes dangers inherent in the developing political line of the German Social Democrats, is closer to an adequate explanation.

It would have been a mistake, it is argued, to unify the parties precipitously, especially without a prior period of ideological clarification. Without explicitly addressing themsevles to the question of whether this process had reached a satisfactory level by the fall of 1945, SED historians have asserted that there was a greater political need for a unity party after some undesignated point in time during the fall of 1945. Thus, typically, Siegfried Thomas writes that

> The resurgence of reactionary forces in the Western zones and the difference in the level of development of the *Aktionseinheit* in East and West moved the Central Committee of the KPD, *in October/November 1945*, to consider unification for the very near future in the provinces of the Soviet Zone of Occupation and in Berlin, where the best chances for unification existed.[10] (Italics added.)

Such an interpretation correctly distinguishes between the strategic goal of Communist control of "progressive" political forces throughout Europe (even where, as in France, the Communists were the stronger party), and the tactical question of the timing of the unity campaign.

If unification of the Communist and Social Democratic parties was a constant Soviet objective—but one that was to take place in the context of a broad "antifascist-democratic" coalition and with a well-organized KPD, responsive to Soviet desires, as one of the merging parties—it would scarcely have been possible to have begun the unity campaign in earnest much earlier than the fall of 1945. The start of the unity drive antedated any serious threat (from the SPD or the Western occupiers) to the Communist position in Germany and the Soviet Zone; rather, it was a response to developments that brought into question the unification of the parties on a basis acceptable to Soviet policy.

Thus one must search for the origins of Communist urgency on the unity issue by examining the activities of the SPD leadership in the two months after mid-September 1945 and the responses of the KPD and

SMA to those activities. This suggests that the turn of Soviet policy toward unification in the near future was the outcome of a process of political development, rather than a single event and that this process began earlier in the fall of 1945 than the late November or December date often cited.[11]

Moreover, this series of more independent positions taken by the SPD leadership in Berlin was given greater significance by the resumption of political activity in the Western zones, which relates in an important but ironically ambiguous way to these events. On the one hand, the larger all-German purposes, both of SPD-KPD unity and of the antifascist policy generally, could not be served in the absence of party politics in the Western occupation zones. On the other hand, these Soviet policies proved difficult to put across in the other zones. The revival of the SPD in the Western zones forced a reconsideration of the ZA's utility as instrument of Soviet policy by diminishing the ZA's prospects for all-German SPD leadership.[12]

On September 14, 1945, the SPD convened an enthusiastic well-attended meeting of party functionaries in Berlin, at which Otto Grotewohl presented a full-scale review of the ZA's policies.[13] Declaring that "unity of socialist action is not only necessary, it is also possible," [sic] for neither the KPD nor the SPD was the same party it had been before Hitler, he admitted that "Whosoever conscientiously examines these preconditions for an organizational unification will agree with me that they have not yet been fulfilled. (Applause.)"[14]

The chief difficulty, he went on, lay in the doubts of rank-and-file Social Democrats about the KPD; the Communists, he declared, must cease regarding Social Democrats as traitors.[15]

It is noteworthy that Grotewohl took care to absolve the SMA and the KPD leadership of even the suspicion of uncooperative behavior. Indeed, he showed understanding for the Communist leaders' problems in "persuading every last man and woman [in the KPD], that the policy of supporting democracy has become a historical necessity."

Grotewohl's remarks on party relations were overshadowed by his projection of the SPD's future role in German affairs. Instead of picturing the party as an integral part of a pro-Soviet, antifascist bloc gathered around the KPD, he spoke of it as the logical focal point of the politics of occupied Germany. He asked his audience two questions:

1. Might Germany's current bourgeois parties possibly be considered by the Soviet Union as the chosen representatives of the German people?
2. Might the [KPD] possibly be considered by the Western powers to be the sole representative of the German working class?

The answer was clear: the role of the SPD was to act as a "focal point for the formation and expression of political purpose," a mediating force for the views of other political parties. Therefore, he concluded, if a German state was to be built, it would be done by the German working class and *by the SPD within that class* (i.e., implicitly to the subordination of the Communists).[16]

Scarcely one month later, a new force, contending for leadership among Social Democrats, made itself felt—to the discomfiture of the KPD and SMA. This was the revived West German SPD that had been organized during the summer months by Kurt Schumacher with aid from the London SPD exile group.[17] The initial effects of the Schumacher organization on the SPD of the Soviet Zone were dual: first, it provided a center of attraction for all those Social Democrats who preferred a policy less friendly to the KPD (and according to Grotewohl's speech on September 14 there were more than a few). Second, Schumacher secured an agreement with the ZA's representatives (Grotewohl, Fechner, and Dahrendorf) by which, despite occasional subsequent divergences of interpretation, the ZA's field of activity was limited to the Soviet Zone. Seen from the perspective of the SMA, the conference of October 5–7, 1945, at the Hanover suburb of Wennigsen revealed that the SPD of the non-Soviet zones was explicitly opposed to the ZA's line of cooperation with the KPD, that it was influenced by exile leaders from the Weimar period (e.g., Erich Ollenhauer), and that, despite Schumacher's rhetorical assurances to the contrary, the SPD of the Western Zones planned to use the fact of the division of Germany to prevent the adoption of the ZA's line in West Germany.[18] Although this did not become clear to the Soviet Zone Social Democrats until January–February 1946, it may be presumed that from early October on, the SMA had to calculate its policy on the basis of these assumptions. If the SPD were to continue an independent existence in the Soviet Zone, it would either come under

Schumacher's influence, or it would be isolated from the other zones. The political evolution of the Soviet Zone had been a stage ahead of that of Western Germany, when party activity had been permitted in the Soviet Zone in June 1945. The existing pro-unity sentiment in Western Germany might conceivably result in the coalescence of the party around its Soviet Zone vanguard in unity with the KPD, if the Soviet Zone could once more be a stage ahead of the West through the unification of the SPD and KPD.[19]

The Berlin delegation had arrived in Hanover prepared to negotiate all-German arrangements with Schumacher, feeling that the party should not allow the occupation arrangements to endanger its histroric nationwide unity, along with a certain smugness about the more advanced state of political life in the Soviet Zone. Accordingly, the ZA delegates proposed that "the Berlin *Zentralausschuss* be reconstituted as the provisional central leadership of the party through the inclusion of representatives of the Western Zones and the old London *Parteivorstand*." But Schumacher's supporters insisted that this project was premature, and that questions of the location of the party's headquarters, its leadership, and its program would all have to await a party congress to be called "as soon as circumstances permitted"; in the meantime, "*as long as a German central government and administration do not exist,* the *Zentralausschuss* in Berlin under the leadership of Comrade Grotewohl represents the party in the Russian Zone of Occupation, while Comrade Dr. Schumacher in Hannover is acknowledged as being the party's agent in the Western Zones."[20] (Italics added.) Despite ritual assurances of cooperation written into the Hanover agreement, the effect of the Conference was to demonstate that the SPD leaders from outside the Soviet Zone were far more hostile to the KPD than the Berlin leaders, and that the SPD was dividing into two rival organizations.

Although there is some evidence that the ZA did not accept this arrangement too literally,[21] the Berlin leadership's minor and tentative organizational feelers toward the other zones (given the difficulties of interzonal action) were less important than the lack of political and ideological contacts. Grotewohl and his colleagues tried to establish these, but the Schumacher forces made no effort to participate in the life of the Soviet Zone SPD. For them, the agreement of Hanover had erected an absolute wall between the ZA and the rest of the German

Social Democracy.[22] It is clear that Schumacher's motives in this were mixed at best. Although there is no reason to doubt his genuine conviction that real cooperation with the SMA and KPD was impossible, it remains true that he regarded the Hanover rearrangements as a vital prop to his own leadership within the party.[23] Schumacher's response to the increasing pressures on the *Zentralausschuss* was one of total withdrawal from contact with it. Whatever assistance continued interzonal activity might have been to the *Zentralausschuss*, it faced its crisis largely in isolation from the Social Democrats of the Western zones. The hopes of the ZA and the SMA that the Soviet Zone SPD leadership might speak for the all-German party (as the Berlin KPD leadership continued to do) could no longer be realized. This increased the urgency, from a Soviet standpoint, of SPD-KPD unification, since such a united party might still cancel the influence of the "Hanover" SPD on all Germany.[24]

Communist and Soviet reaction to these developments was quickly apparent. The stronger national emphasis in the SPD's attitude produced a KPD counterclaim that it had a key national role. In his speech to a KPD meeting on October 12, Walter Ulbricht proclaimed that the KPD was the "Party of Struggle for National Unity," and that its program of the previous June was serving as a rallying point for antifascist forces in all four zones of Germany. It must have been clear to Ulbricht that Communist leadership in the new Germany would be incompatible with two Social Democratic aims: to mediate between East and West—that is, between the USSR and bourgeois German political forces and between the Western allies and the KPD—and to define the KPD-SPD relationship in accordance with the relative size and popular appeal of the two parties. Ulbricht therefore declared:

> There are some Social Democratic comrades who believe that they must assume a certain middle position. We believe that this is a skewed position. There is only one correct position, namely that of the common antifascist struggle. The *Aktionseinheit* of the KPD and SPD does not allow for a "middle position." Any attempt to occupy such a middle position would damage the unity of the working class.[25]

What was meant was plain enough. The two parties should not seek to ascertain their relative strength but rather to strengthen their collaboration. Future elections "must be used to strengthen and protect the unity of the workers . . . through joint Communist-Social Democratic leadership of the election campaign."[26]

When it came to the question of intensified collaboration between the parties, however, Ulbricht was still quite cautious. His prescription for further action was still firmly in the framework of the collaboration of the summer of 1945, and not yet that of organizational unity. He listed three chief measures for party cooperation: preparations for the winter, implementation of land reform, and joint efforts toward reform of the school system. Fulfillment of these objectives, he continued, would depend on the closest possible cooperation of the functionaries of both parties, on joint consultations, and on "comradely discussions" to handle minor points of friction. In short, both the tasks ahead and the means for grappling with them were those of the preceding period of close collaboration rather than those of the forthcoming organizational unity.[27]

Ulbricht's caution reflected the unhappy state of interparty relations. Communist concern about the possibly rising influence of anti-KPD and anti-Soviet elements in the SPD had led to public criticism of some Social Democrats by Communist speakers. Thus Pieck publicly attacked the SPD supposedly having come under the influence of such pre-Hitler leaders as Noske, Severing, and Stampfer. (Severing was unofficially active in the British Zone.)[28] This attack, launched on September 19 in Berlin and repeated in Erfurt on October 14,[29] aroused considerable Social Democratic resentment, first, because these particular individuals played no role in the Soviet Zone SPD, and secondly, because to many Social Democrats it seemed that the Communists were reverting to the "united front from below" tactics of attacking SPD leaders while appealing to the SPD membership.[30] Franz Dahlem explained that the KPD would not cooperate with enemies of unity or of the Soviet Union (whom he saw as identical), including "certain forces in the *Reich* [which] seek to establish an SPD *Parteivorstand* which would *follow a policy opposed to that of the 'Berlin line'* . . . *a clear policy of opposition to the Communists.*"[31] (Italics added.)

This concern with Social Democrats who might follow a different line from that of the ZA was shared by the SMA. Thus, in an interview with Gniffke on September 27, General Botov reeled off a list of complaints about "reformist" Social Democrats,[32] while in November General Kotikov worried about Grotewohl's "movement to the Right,"[33] and

Tiul'panov inquired whether Grotewohl was not "looking to the West more than to the East"?[34]

In fact, Grotewohl soon gave the SMA public cause for concern in a major address on November 11, 1945.[35] Although it was obvious that in giving such a major address Grotewohl would be speaking for the SPD, the actual writing of the speech seems to have been left to him by his colleagues.[36]

In this speech Grotewohl said publicly what he had said privately as early as August 1945. While he must have anticipated a virgorous Soviet reaction, he presumably felt that, as long as he observed certain pieties such as calling for eventual unity,[37] he could establish himself as the spokesman for a German party that was democratic and socialist, would cooperate with the Allies, and was committed to a reconstruction of German society, but was still a candid spokesman for legitimate German interests.[38]

In both tone and content Grotewohl's speech vertured into new ground.[39] For example, along with the standard acknowledgment of the SPD's errors during the Weimar period, Grotewohl gave a notable public defense of the SPD record in that era:"What the German Social Democracy accomplished after 1918, and especially between 1924 and 1932, will some day receive recognition in the pages of political history."[40] Moreover, in the terrible circumstances in which the German people now found itself, the Social Democrats, unlike "some" (unnamed) parties, did not claim to have a prepared, completely valid solution for the nation's problems:

> We do not belong to those who believe that they bring political and social salvation in a sack whose contents they must without delay pour out over the poor German people. He who is honest and wishes to be just can not promise anything to anyone. To make promises is *criminal*! (Italics in original.)

Nevertheless, the Social Democrats did offer a diagnosis and a prescription for the German condition. Some of it was unimpeachable from the Soviet or Communist standpoint; on the other hand, the SPD's disturbing (to the SMA) call for "socialism" was never more strongly put.

According to Grotewohl, Germany had no more capitalists because all accumulated capital had been wiped out. A class of would-be capitalists could and should be prevented from reacquiring capital by proletarian political action. Grotewohl stated this at just that time when the KPD was pointing to a supposed rising tide of reactionary machinations by (among others) capitalists to justify its policies. From the KPD reaction to this assertion of Grotewohl's, it is clear how sharply stung the Communist leadership was.[41] Grotewohl's explanation as to why this socioeconomic condition was not perceived more widely was hardly flattering to either the SMA or KPD, for what was lacking was not an objective basis for Socialism, but the vision to "dare to believe what should be as clear as day," even if "in the books which we have read, our current circumstances were not foreseen."[42] To carry out its mission of democratic and socialist reconstruction, the German working class will "one day" have to unite despite "petty organizational inhibitions and frictions." How would this be done? Grotewohl's answer to this question amounted to a detailed criticism of the mounting pressure for unification from the SMA and KPD. His indictment shattered the facade of party cooperation, revealing a fundamental divergence in SPD and KPD views as to the method, timing, and scope of unity. Having heard Pieck, at the KPD rally two days before, call for the "full unification" of the two parties "as soon as possible,"[43] Grotewohl listed four points to be heeded in the unification process. Taken together, they amounted to a clear call for indefinite delay of SPD-KPD unification.

The four points were as follows:[44] first, that "the unity of the workers' movement cannot be the work of resolutions of formal bodies, but must rather reflect the unambiguous and sincere will of all German class comrades." Although this seemed to transfer the decision on unity from the party leaderships to the mass of party (and non-party?) workers, it is clear that Grotewohl was not thinking of haphazard or spontaneous local amalgamations; the decision on unity was to be centrally taken, but only after an overwhelming rank-and-file demand had been registered. Second:

> the unity of the workers' movement can not be, even in the least degree, the result of external pressure or indirect force. It can only result from the conviction arrived at through fully free self-determination by the last and least class comrade. It is incompatible with this free decision of even the most ordinary class comrade for any party to claim priority in the question of unification.

Inasmuch as Grotewohl cannot have meant literally that an overwhelming majority desire for unification should be balked by the objections of scattered party members, this demand must be understood as a veiled legitimization of the still quite substantial opposition (or at least doubt) among Social Democrats concerning the unification of the parties. It was also a rejoinder to the view, expressed most prominently by Ulbricht, that those who were not (yet) for unity were "enemies" of the working class, to be possibly excluded from that class's political and economic organizations.

Grotewohl's third point was that "unity must be brought to full fruition through common striving for socialist and democratic reconstruction before it can be achieved organizationally through resolutions." Here Grotewohl seemed to be slipping into the plausible but dubious contention that had formed a major element of both parties' rhetoric in 1945: that joint effort would dissolve the differences between them. Of course this point may have been a tactful way of expressing Social Democratic disillusionment with the results of the cooperative work thus far.

Grotewohl's fourth point was the most direct disavowal of any plans for speedy unification of the parties, for in it he set up conditions extremely unlikely of rapid fulfillment. He said that

> The creation of unified nationwide parties of the German working class in the very near future is an imperious necessity. A zonal unification would only hamper the cause of national unification rather than advancing it, and might perhaps break apart the nation. To defend and preserve the unity and cohesion of the entire state and economic area of Germany is, however, the highest task of the German working class. [For this purpose] the creation of united nationwide parties of the German workers' movement is undoubtedly a decisive prerequisite.

Grotewohl's position is clearly indicated here. The German working class is the strongest force safeguarding Germany's unity: its principal means to this end is the formation of united nationwide political parties. A fundamental step such as unification of SPD and KPD, if undertaken on a zonal basis, would endanger the unity of the nation by breaking the unity of *each* of the parties. Thus a three-step progression is advocated: united nationwide parties, national unity, and finally a decision on unity between the parties.

Naturally, this question took on a different aspect from the Communist perspective. The KPD was already a centralized national organization; it could plausibly create precedents in whichever zone offered the best possibilities for practical action, in the expectation that its branches in the rest of the country would follow suit as circumstances indicated. The *Zentralausschuss* had no such assurance and, after the confrontation with Schumacher, had little hope of obtaining the necessary nationwide authority.

What cannot be decided with any degree of certainty is to what extent the SMA and the KPD were aware of this. Did they anticipate that the fact of unity in the Soviet Zone would arouse so powerful a rank-and-file response in the Western Zones that organizational and leadership obstacles there would be swept away? Were they prepared to chance the creation of a rump SPD in the Western Zones for the sake of establishing a unity party with its base in the Soviet Zone? As far as can be judged, the Soviet and German Communist advocates of unity in the Soviet Zone were not planning to forego influence in all of a united Germany. Yet if German unity required united national proletarian party organizations, only a misplaced trust in their own strategy can explain such a statement as that of Ulbricht in a speech in Erfurt on December 12, 1945. Ulbricht declared on that occasion that the

> Unification of the working class is a fundamental precondition for the unity of the nation. Much is being said in this connection about the unity of Germany. Those who do so [Social Democrats] refer to the opening up of the zonal borders. It seems to us that this is not the issue. The unity of Germany can be assured only through a united, antifascist, democratic policy in all parts of the *Reich*.[45]

Ulbricht did not explain how such a unified policy was to be reconciled with a program that might well split the SPD.

It must also be asked, however, whether this fourth point of Grotewohl's was intended as a serious political program or as a tactical device to ward off Communist importuning. In Kaden's view, Grotewohl knew as he spoke that there was "no real chance" for his essential precondition for unification: nationwide parties.[46]

After his experience at Hanover, and in view of the difficulties of interzonal activity, Grotewohl could not have been very hopeful of national unification in the near future. There is a bit of evidence for this in his pessimistic remark in Weimar the previous August: "A national party congress or party conference can be considered feasible only when the problems of the zonal borders have been resolved."[47] Nevertheless, while for Schumacher the line between the Soviet and the other zones was the axis of his political calculations, Grotewohl and the other ZA members seem to have believed (as their efforts to establish West German contacts demonstrate) that the zonal borders were a temporary arrangement. They cited the Potsdam commitment to Germany as an economic unity; they remembered the centralizing traditions of their party; they hardly cared to be isolated from the other sections of their party.

Whatever the ZA's hopes, however, German national unity was evidently not at hand, and the effect of Grotewohl's stance was to postpone indefinitely the unification of the two parties. In this context one can readily understand the bitter comment of Wilhelm Pieck after leaving the meeting of November 11; Leonhard, who had accompanied him, reports him as saying, "With today's speech, Grotewohl has openly and clearly revealed himself to be an enemy of unity."[48]

The effect of this portion of Grotewohl's speech was to make the issue of the scope of unity—zonal or national—the central point of conflict over unity between the parties. From mid-November 1945 to early February 1946, the *Zentralausschuss* clung to the rejection of zonal unity as the basis for maintaining the cohesion of the SPD structure in the Soviet Zone and for fending off the KPD. Its increasing isolation in this position was accentuated when both the KPD and the Schumacher leadership demonstrated their willingness to act on the basis of the zonal divisions.

If Grotewohl's statements on unification of the parties were an unwelcome departure from the public stance of cooperation with the KPD, his utterances of November 11 on national questions were even more provocative of SMA concern. The spirit of this speech was not one of humble support for occupation policies but rather a fervent (albeit "democratic") espousal of German interests. For example, Grotewohl spoke of a German working class that, despite its joy over its liberation from Hitler, had by that "liberation" become an unfree class in an unfree Germany. The cry "Workers of the world, unite!" no longer reached German ears, he declared; the once-proud German working class had, without even being aware of it, become the world's charity case.[49]

In his closing passages, Grotewohl directed his remarks to the world outside Germany. After stressing that the world rightly demanded guarantees against renewed German aggression, and pledging working class action within Germany as the best barrier against such as danger, he went on to say:

> But this request we do make of the world: Leave us enough land to feed ourselves, sufficient raw materials for the production of basic requirements, and leave us that portion of large-scale industry which does not serve war purposes (as the only rational form of industry for the utilization of our labor force), so that we eventually secure for ourselves a meager livelihood through the import and export of goods.

Thus in the space of a few sentences, Grotewohl managed to criticize the loss of territory east of the Oder-Neisse line, the dismantling program, and the Allied plans for German industrial production levels. In November 1945 each of these counts could figure in an indictment of all the occupation powers; nevertheless, Kaden's view that this was a criticism directed at the USSR but veiled as a general thesis may well have been the reaction of the SMA.[50]

A comparison of these remarks with Grotewohl's private talk to the Leipzig SPD the previous August, as well as his speech of September 14, reveals the consistency of his views on the related problems of Germany's borders, industry, and trade, and the need for socialism in its economic reconstruction. Never before, however, had he said these things so openly, so forcefully, and all as parts of a single statement. Although he was careful to disclaim any attempt to establish a distinctive partisan Social Democratic position, this is precisely what his speech did, in relation to both the KPD and the SMA.[51] As we have already seen, this conformed to Grotewohl's view of the proper stance for a German political leader, destined by his place in the political arena to be the spokesman of his people. That Grotewohl felt his speech to be such a statement is indicated by his deliberate citation of Luther's words: "Here I stand, I can do no other."[52]

Grotewohl's speeches of September 14 and (especially) of November 11 provided an indication of the ideas held in the Soviet Zone SPD leadership; more importantly, the public pronouncement of these ideas by Grotewohl amounted to a concrete political challenge to the views of the KPD and (although Grotewohl himself did not seem to think so) of the SMA as well. The turn of Soviet and KPD policy in the fall of 1945 toward party unification was bound up with the growing perception that the Soviet Zone SPD might turn out to be an unsuitable instrument for extending Soviet political influence throughout Germany.

Soviet and Communist response was prompt, agitated, and extensive. The day after the speech (November 12) Pieck called Gniffke to ask for a meeting of party leaders. Despite some critical remarks among Grotewohl's SPD colleagues concerning his failure to consult with them on the speech's contents, they resolved to support him against the KPD. Thus, when Pieck burst forth upon entering the room, "Well, Otto, you surely don't think that a single Social Democrat still supports you today?" Gniffke's rejoinder was, "There are only five of us here, but these five stand behind Grotewohl."[53] A considerable part of the Communist irritation with Grotewohl's remarks may have resulted from their consistent stand in support of the Oder-Neisse border, a stand calculated to please the Soviet Union but not an attractive one among the German people. Immediately after the Potsdam Conference, Ulbricht had declared:

> If one asks us, well, just where do you Communists stand on the matter of the cession of former German territories and their annexation by the Polish democratic republic, we answer as follows:
> "Hitler and German imperialism have gambled these territories away. If we must cede this territory, you can thank Hitlerism and all those imperialist and militarist forces which led Germany into this war."[54]

Wilhelm Pieck, writing on the question of the "Eastern territories" (*Ostgebiete*), declared that, "We Communists find these losses to be painful also," but the blame for their occurrence rests on Hitler and on those who preached hatred of the Slavs.[55] The KPD had had the bloc recorded in support of this position, but now the SPD's once-private contrary opinions had been publicly voiced.[56]

The Soviet response took the forms of a direct ban on making the contents of the November 11 speech known and attempting to split the common front of the *Zentralausschuss*. There was a flurry of snide remarks by SMA and KPD figures about Grotewohl's political proclivities.[57] Efforts were made to drive wedges between members of the ZA with overtures to Gniffke and Fechner to become more active and more prominent as speakers for the SPD, rather than leaving the spokesman's role to Grotewohl. Some ZA members had their various wishes (often of a material nature) suddenly answered by the SMA.[58] These efforts, however, were not effective.

More effective were steps taken by the SMA to prevent distribution of the Grotewohl speech in the Soviet Zone. The ZA's own newspaper did not report the speech at all, although it had carried excerpts from Pieck's address of November 9. The SMA's *Tägliche Rundschau* carried a version edited so as to make it appear that Grotewohl had delivered a standard pro-unity speech.[59] Especially striking were the tactics used to keep the speech off the Berlin radio.[60] The station had planned to carry Grotewohl's remarks on its series "Democratic Forum" and for that purpose had tape-recorded the talk, but the broadcast never took place. A ZA representative was told that the "official" (i.e., Soviet) reason was that the manuscript of the broadcast had not yet been returned by the Soviet censor at the station. Although Gustav Klingelhöfer apparently organized the private distribution of the November 11 speech to the SPD provincial headquarters via the ZA's courier service, and although he pledged to try to have the speech published in *Das Volk*, the SMA successfully prevented Grotewohl's speech from having its desired impact on the SPD membership and the population of the Soviet Zone. Kaden correctly calls this a serious defeat for the ZA that should have made clear to them the precarious nature of their political existence under Soviet control.[61]

The *Zentralausschuss* did not seem overly disturbed. The chief response it made to this Soviet displeasure was to stand firm behind Grotewohl, so that the SMA gave up, for the moment, its attempts to undermine Grotewohl's position within the top SPD leadership.[62] A sign of this is the fact that the SMA allowed him to make a trip (with Dahrendorf) to the American Zone late November. It is indicative of Grotewohl's conception of his relations with the SMA that he did not try to publicize his November 11 views in speech or press articles while out of the Soviet Zone. There is at least one bit of evidence that he subsequently made speeches within the Soviet Zone whose contents were similar to that of his November 11 speech. He was reported to have spoken critically at Halle in Late November about German refugees from beyond the Oder-Neisse border and about KPD tactics on the unity question.[63]

There is no sign that Grotewohl changed his position in any important particular in November–December 1945, although one may speculate that his indecisive stance subsequently had its origin in the hostile Soviet reaction to his initiative on November 11. Judging by the tone of his November 26 report to Grotewohl, Klingelhöfer feared that the effect of these varied reactions on Grotewohl would be to make him doubt the utility and significance of his having spoken out. Klingelhöfer assured him that the speech had been a "historic deed."[64] Since by this time Klingelhöfer was well aware of how little actual effect the November 11 speech had had in altering the situation of the SPD in the Soviet Zone, his enthusiasm was presumably directed toward insuring that the November 11 speech would become the first in a series of initiatives through which the *Zentralausschuss* (on behalf of the SPD in the Soviet Zone) would establish the party's role as spokesman for the German masses to the SMA and in place of the KPD. Such an aim would certainly have suited Grotewohl; one wonders whether Klingelhöfer should have expected the SMA to accept such ambitions.

A further response to the evidence of Soviet displeasure was the decision, taken in early December by Grotewohl, Fechner, and Gniffke, to send Tiul'panov a statement embodying the ZA's position of the previous summer advocating an "Eastern Orientation" for the party and the nation. This gesture may be understood as a belated addition to Grotewohl's remarks on Germany's territorial extent and industrial capacity in his November 11 speech; Soviet suspicions were to be allayed by this evidence of the ZA's fundamental orientation toward a pro-Soviet policy. Judging from Gniffke's account of the incident, it was a gesture made without excessive expectations of success, and as far as can be discovered, no overt Soviet reaction was ever forthcoming.[65]

This development confronted the SMA with a difficult decision as to further implementation of the Soviet policy of utilizing German political parties to further Soviet aims. The Soviet response was to increase the pressure on German party leaders to secure leaders and policies in keeping with Soviet objectives. In the case of a major "bourgeois" party, the Christian Democratic Union (CDU) of the Soviet Zone, the Soviet authorities removed the party chairmen, Andreas Hermes and Walther

Schreiber, in November 1945. Toward the SPD, Soviet policy was more circumspect. The SMA granted the SPD the tactical concession of an easing of pressure in early December 1945 while preparing a major strategic move to undermine Social Democratic resistance to Soviet policies. This move was the sponsorship of a major Soviet Zone interparty conference for the end of December 1945.

CHAPTER 7

The December Conference

The SMA's approach to the problem of dealing with the SPD of the Soviet Zone—relaxation of immediate pressure on the ZA while preparing the December Conference—can best be appreciated against the background of SPD-KPD relations on the local and provincial levels in the Soviet Zone. By the end of November it must have been clear to Soviet authorities that the ZA's striving for political autonomy reflected similar sentiments among Social Democrats throughout the Soviet Zone. If anything, these sentiments may well have been more widely spread and deeply felt at these lower party levels than in the ZA. Therefore, before considering the events leading up to the December Conference and then the Conference itself, it would be well to examine this situation at the lower levels of the SPD.

The SPD in Berlin: November 1945

Illustrative of this situation was the first district party congress of the Berlin SPD on November 25, 1945.[1] Located in the four-power city and former capital, the Berlin SPD was the most prominent of the party's subordinate organizations; in the spring of 1946 this circumstance was to make of the Berlin SPD the central arena for the final struggle over unification of the SPD and KPD. In November the Berlin SPD met to organize itself as a local body separate from the ZA.[2] The speeches made at that meeting reflected substantial agreement with the ZA's positions on the party's present and future role.

Thus the district party secretary, Erich Lübbe,[3] reported that the consequences of years of mutual hostility between SPD and KPD were still very much in evidence, especially on the lower levels of the party structure; "lengthy cooperation" would be needed to allay this mistrust.[4] Max Fechner warned against squabbling over administrative positions, against personal intrigues and meanness, for "we wish to be comrades and friends."[5] Such exhortations show clearly how little had been accomplished in the period since the war's end toward the creation of genuine comradely relationships between Social Democrats and Communists. Moreover, speaking two weeks after Grotewohl's November 11 speech, Lübbe also touched on the tender subjects of the land reform in the Soviet Zone[6] and the need to retain (under control) large industrial plants to produce for export.[7]

Otto Meier, the editor of *Das Volk*, was even more direct. After establishing the SPD's unquestioned priority in advocating a single working class party, Meier stressed that, in the intervening months, party developments had taken quite different forms in the various occupation zones. The danger thus arose that "a zonally-limited unification would under these circumstances not remove but rather perpetuate the division of the German working class. He who would prevent that must create conditions for the unification of the [party] organizations over the whole *Reich*." Meier urged the speediest creation of an all-German party organization; he specifically rejected postponement of a national party until after the establishment of a united nation with a national government.[8]

What remained unanswered were the questions of timing and feasibility. What if the lack of national unity hampered effective nationwide organizational work (as it did)? What would happen to unity with the KPD if no all-German intraparty consensus, let alone organization, could be achieved? Like the rest of the SPD leadership, Meier did not answer these questions. In part, no doubt, this was because the appeal to all-German decisions served as an unimpeachable excuse for delay. However, as has been pointed out, the SPD leadership did not anticipate insurmountable obstacles to all-German political work.

A clearer notion of the triangular relationship between SPD and the SMA and KPD at the local and provincial levels during the period of

October to December 1945 may be had by examining the record of events in Thuringia.[9] What emerges from such an examination is a picture of spasmodic and uncoordinated, but intense, pressure on the SPD below the zonal level from both the Communists and the Soviet authorities. The general tendency of this pressure was not (yet) to bring about a decision in favor of unity, but rather to hamper the work of the SPD and especially to inhibit the development of Social Democratic political initiatives.

Some local Communist organizations seem to have exceeded the limits for action set by the party leaders. Policy at the zonal level called for the establishment of a Social Democratic party, but local KPD pressure threatened to disrupt SPD activity altogether. Thus aggressive local KPD organizers tried to force Social Democrats on local police forces to switch their party membership to the KPD in one locality, intimidated would-be SPD members in another, and tried to hinder the formation of any SPD organizational at all in yet a third.[19] In some cases, political pressure was accompanied by the threat of physical reprisal—a threat that seemed plausible when it came from policemen who were also KPD officials.[11]

A KPD report on a speech of November 4, 1945, by the LV's political secretary, Hans Freiburg, fell into the hands of the local SPD group before which the talk had been given and was sent on to Weimar.[12] It described Freiburg's talk as lacking in any historical or developmental structure; Freiburg had failed to trace the causes for Hitler's rise and for the split in the working class back to their true roots—monopoly capital and the financial oligarchy in the one case, the reformism of the SPD since before 1914 in the other. Worse yet were Freiburg's prescriptions for the future: the SPD's prospects were outlined in terms that directly quoted the passages of Grotewohl's September 14 speech relating to the SPD as the focal point of German politics, while the timing of party unification was made dependent on centralized national-party resolutions. These passages, which repeated the ZA's and, indeed, the SPD's position, were characterized as "nothing less than an attempt to galvanize the political corpse of Social-Democratism." According to the KPD report, the SPD had lost its historical justification, lacked any clear program, and was unfit to provide leadership for the German working class. The KPD would have to make this clear to the Social Democratic rank and file so as to lead them into a truly Marxist and revolutionary party.[13]

In these circumstances it is hardly surprising that, as one SPD report put it, "the state of collaboration of the parties may be described, to put it as mildly as possible, as unsatisfactory."[14] The incidents of pressure, harassment, intimidation mounted up with every report reaching the *Landesvorstand*. Brill put it rather gloomily in mid-December:

> Were we now to report all that has taken place in the local party organizations, our report would run to at least 100 typed pages. It is simply impossible to give a complete picture of conditions. One may generally say, however, that there are only a few cases of . . . satisfactory cooperation. These rare instances are based on good personal relationships. Even they are put to the test from time to time. The relations of the party organizations to one another is sometimes simply shocking.[15]

Pressure against individual Social Democrats, harassment of SPD organizational activity, disparagement of the SPD's stand on issues, efforts to simply "swallow" local SPD groups whole, ideological bickering, disregard of interparty arrangements reached at provincial (or even zonal) levels—these were some aspects of SPD-KPD relations in Thuringia in November–December 1945.

Of course, there were examples of fruitful collaboration, or improvement of previously unsatisfactory conditions.[16] Both parties had their difficulties with recalcitrants in their ranks. It is significant, however, that the relationship between the parties should have been so strained in the period just preceding the December Conference, that is, the period capping six months of cooperation, because the supposed "successes" of this phase of interparty relations were to justify the Conference's decision to move on to the next and "higher" phase.

SPD-SMA relations also grew worse on the local level after the beginning of November, with the initiative for actions by local commanders sometimes coming from the KPD—perhaps to the eventual discomfiture of the SMA. Considerable friction was also generated directly by actions of the Soviet commanders. Here the chief cause for complaint was the continued hampering of local SPD activity by detailed, complicated, and often unclear requirements for the needed permission to engage in political activity. The possibilities for harassment were endless.[17]

Soviet-SPD relations in Thuringia were further complicated by the extremely poor relations that persisted between the *Landesvorstand* under Brill's leadership and the provincial SMA. One striking example of this is provided by the fact that when, after the Thuringian party congress in October, Grotewohl wrote to the Thuringia SMA on October 28, suggesting that he might "present" the newly elected Thuringian SPD leaders to the SMA, he received no response; nor was there an answer to an identical request by Brill himself on the following date.

In such a setting, SPD suspicions of Soviet intentions flourished. Publication of lectures delivered in late September at an SPD school was held up for nearly two months awaiting Soviet approval. When the censor's decision came, it was unfavorable; the reason given by the SMA's Major Babenko to Hans Freiburg was that Brill's talk had insulted the KPD, which was equivalent to insulting the SMA (!). To drive his point home, Babenko told Freiburg that the future "looked black" for the SPD in Thuringia unless it replaced the incumbent *Landesvorstand* (which had been freely and democratically elected at the party congress less than a month before). Various measures of control over SPD activity, which on the whole reflected normal occupation practices in all zones in 1945, were seen by Social Democrats as "calling into question the honor and reputation of the party."

Clearly the SMA regarded Brill as the source of policies hostile to its aims, as well as the chief basis for effective SPD leadership of an independent sort. Later, more harmonious, SMA relations with Brill's more pliant successor, Heinrich Hoffmann, bear out this judgment. Consequently, every effort was made to split the rest of the LV away from Brill. Beginning on December 14, Babenko interviewed separately each LV member except Brill, requiring them to state their position on the LV's *Circular Letter No. 18* and a September speech by Brill at Probstzella.[18]

In the course of these interrogations, Babenko made the SMA's stand quite plain. It was, as quoted by Brill, that

there no longer existed an SPD in Thuringia, but only a party of Dr. Brill's. . . . [Dr. Brill] had insulted the occupation regime, was opposed to unification, wished to reestablish employers' associations, had not publicized joint SPD-KPD resolutions, and was responsible for the fact that the SPD had become a fascist organization by the inclusion of former members of the . . . [Nazi party].[19]

This particular effort to divide the SPD leadership had no immediate consequences, but it was the prelude to the final anti-Brill drive in the last days of December, and it may also have helped to induce the *Landesvorstand* to take an accommodating position on the question of its *Circular Letter No. 18*.

The genesis of this document was a meeting of the LV of November 5, 1945, at which formal notice was taken of the complaints coming in from the local SPD organizations.[20] On Brill's proposal, the LV decided unanimously both to bring these matters to the KPD's attention at a joint provincial party meeting, and to send a circular letter to all local organizations which would clarify the LV's position, reaffirm the decisions of the Thuringian SPD congress, and inform the lower echelons of the party of the KPD's tactics in seeking a "mass basis" for its policies by cannibalizing the local bodies of the SPD. Two points were to be stressed especially: maintenance of party discipline (i.e., resistance to KPD demands on the local level), and the need to obtain LV approval for any joint activities with local organizations of the KPD.[21]

The LV's *Circular Letter No. 18*, dated at Weimar November 6, 1945, and addressed to the chairmen of all district and local party organizations, was devoted to the subject of "The Relationship of the SPD and the KPD."[22] The text was bluntly critical of the KPD. The Communists were charged with "pursuing their old so-called United Front tactics," tactics designed to make the KPD the one dominant party of the working class, by disintegrating the Social Democratic movement, isolating its leaders, and absorbing the SPD rank and file.

This charge was more than a matter of sharp polemics; in making it, the LV was challenging one of the fundamental tenets of the KPD's current policy. Both the Communist approach to the SPD, as well as their more general claim to political leadership, rested in part on the assertion that the KPD had abandoned its policies of the 1920s. To the SPD, it now offered collaboration and reconciliation; Brill branded this "new line" as fraudulent.

The *Circular Letter* then went on to detail the complaints of the SPD against Communist practices in political affairs, including, most seriously, Communist efforts to pressure local SPD groups into actions and commitments that violated *Land*-level interparty agreements. The complaint on this point deserves quotation, for it describes concisely the

Communist tactic in regard to local joint meetings and their pro-unity resolutions, tactics soon to be used more extensively throughout the Soviet Zone. The *Circular Letter* described it as follows:

> In a whole series of cases [the KPD] approached our local organizations with requests for joint functionaries' and membership meetings. At these sessions the KPD representatives offer meaningless resolutions, whose only purpose is to disrupt the organizational cohesion of our party.[23]

Such party meetings on local initiative were in violation of interparty agreements, as well as of the pertinent resolutions of the *Landesparteitag* in October, which the *Circular Letter* quoted for the local groups' benefit. Whether the resolutions adopted at such meetings were as "meaningless" as stated above may be questioned; even if the KPD or SMA leaderships were not fooled as to the source of such protestations, many Social Democrats may well have been influenced by the steady drumfire of such resolutions, especially as the press response could not be critical. Brill seems to have recognized this, for in the *Circular Letter* he assured local SPD leaders that all "official" agreements on joint actions would be publicized in good time by the LV.

As the logical consequence of this admonition, the LV enjoined all local party chairmen to maintain strictest party discipline in rejecting KPD overtures for meetings not authorized by the *Land* party leadership. All such Communist requests were to be promptly reported by telephone to the LV in Weimar, there to be checked against a list of centrally agreed upon meetings. Violators of these instructions were threatened with party disciplinary action.

The LV's vehement insistence on centralized provincial authorization of interparty contacts was intended as a relief for local party bodies.[24] As to the complaints of local organizations mounted, it became clear to Brill and his associates that they could defend the party's structure against the disintegrating pressures applied by the SMA and KPD only be locating decision-making authority in party bodies (hopefully) too important to intimidate.

The November 6 *Circular Letter* was the LV's major effort in this direction. The outcome was to show that there was insufficient power at Weimar to protect the local party units. As these local units had appealed to the Thuringian leadership in Weimar, so did the *Landesvorstand* now appeal to the SPD's zonal leadership in Berlin.[25]

One may speculate that this show of Social Democratic organizational cohesion (of which Thuringia is a well-documented example) actually served to increase Soviet determination to secure a speedy SPD acceptance of the Soviet line on unification of the parties. It had taken the SPD, with its familiar traditions of organizational solidarity only a few months to erect effective political structures in several parts of Germany. Further delay in the unity drive might mean even greater powers of resistance on the part of the Social Democratic cohorts.

A few days before the December Conference convened in Berlin, Brill sent Grotewohl two long letters (with supporting materials) describing SPD relations with the SMA and the KPD.[26] Unfortunately, these letters already included an account of the consequences of having issued the *Circular Letter No. 18,* indicating that the Thuringian provincial organization would probably be unable to withstand the pressure brought to bear upon it.[27]

The KPD's "sharp protest" in response to the policies of the SPD's Thuringian leadership resulted in a joint SPD-KPD meeting on November 23.[28] The resolution adopted at the meeting amounted to a drastic defeat for the SPD. In direct contradiction of the charges made and evidence cited in the *Circular Letter* of November 6, the later resolution took the "public" KPD position that the cooperation of the two parties was a growing success. All difficulties were simply ignored. The resolution read:

> The representatives of the *Bezirksleitung* Thuringia of the KPD and the Thuringia *Landesvorstand* of the SPD, in a session of November 23, 1945, have taken a position on problems and questions affecting the introduction of joint party activities. Inasmuch as the joint activity held pursuant to the agreement of August 8, 1945 has been carried out in a notably comradely way, [the leaderships] express their firm decision to continue advancing the cause of a united German workers' party through the closest cooperation at all levels of the party organization.[29]

Not only did the SPD representatives subscribe to a statement that was plainly contrary to the facts about and the interests of the life of their organization, but they also endorsed a viewpoint on party unification that ignored their own rejection of any unity scheme limited on one zone.

At the meeting of November 23 the Communist delegates insisted on publication of the resolution equivalent to the offending *Circular Letter* of November 6. Consequently it was sent out by the LV on December 10, 1945, as its *Circular Letter No. 27*. The dismay and confusion in the local party organizations upon receipt of this letter may well be imagined.[30]

Even before Brill's detailed reports reached Berlin, the members of the *Zentralausschuss* had become aware that party life throughout the Soviet Zone was becoming increasingly difficult. Gniffke returned from a speaking tour through the zone in late November with the impression that interparty relations had worsened sharply; unity of the working class had become "a covering slogan for Communist ambition."[31] Increasingly aware of Communist and Soviet pressure on their organization, and determined to avoid a commitment to an immediate unification of the parties, especially if limited to the Soviet Zone, the Social Democratic leaders welcomed the opportunity to settle outstanding issues in direct confrontation with the KPD. They wanted to discover to what extent the rise in pressure for unity on the local level, the "unification fever" as Gniffke termed it, was being promoted by the KPD leadership.

The response of the KPD leadership was designed to disarm SPD suspicions and prevent the ZA from responding to complaints from within the party structure by breaking with the policy of cooperation with the KPD. At a meeting on December 5, called to discuss upcoming trade union elections, the Communist representatives (Pieck, Ulbricht, Anton Ackermann, Franz Dahlem) were all in a friendly good humor, and Pieck assured the Social Democrats that relations between the parties would soon improve. Indeed, there was ample time for such a development; according to Pieck, organizational unity of the parties was "in any case not to be thought of before at least another year had passed."[32] At another early December meeting Pieck denied that the ZK was responsible for lower-level KPD unity pressure or that, indeed, the KPD even had a target date for unification of the parties. First, he declared, relations between the parties must be improved, and he thought that this might take until the fall of 1946.[33]

This combination of pressure and reassurance, applied selectively to different levels of the SPD party structure, had a dual purpose. It was evidently intended to preclude coherent organizational resistance by the SPD to external pressures; in addition, it was to prepare the ground for a major interparty conference where the SPD leadership, aware of its inability to protect subordinate party units, could be induced to make major concessions on the unity question.

At this juncture, as in October, the KPD received unintended assistance in its efforts to isolate the ZA from the West German SPD leadership under Schumacher. The occasion for this was an unhappy meeting between Gniffke, Schumacher's aide Herbert Kriedemann, and possibly also Kurt Schumacher in the latter's Hanover offices in December 1945.[34] The accounts of this meeting that Kriedemann and Gniffke have given us are in disagreement on whether Schumacher was present.[35] However confused the accounts of this meeting may be, its consequences are plain. Any possibility that the ZA would go into the December Conference with strengthened ties to the West German branches of the party, or that its stand in favor of an all-German basis for unity might be made more credible, disappeared in the fog of mutual misunderstanding.

Schumacher's and Kriedemann's suspicions may well have been enhanced by the trip through the United States Zone taken by Dahrendorf and Grotewohl in late November, and by the resulting ZA arrangement to maintain a liaison office in Regensburg.[36] The intentions of the ZA in this connection remain unclear. As was indicated in the previous chapter, the Berlin leaders tended to regard the Wennigsen agreements of October as a convenient division of labor between provisional party bodies.[37] In this the ZA not only overlooked the practical impossibility of Schumacher's "agents" working in the Soviet Zone; in effect, the ZA sought to rally political support for a program that challenged the Schumacher position. The Hanover leaders, for their part, looked to the agreements of October to insulate the three Western zones from intrusions from the Soviet Zone.[38]

Preparations for the December Conference

Although the genesis of the December Conference is somewhat obscure, it is clear that the SMA and the KPD had every reason to seek a commitment to their own schedule and scope of unity from the *Zentralauss-*

chuss. Pressure on the SPD had prepared the occasion, but the SPD's growing reluctance to follow the Soviet and Communist lead heightened, from the Communist point of view, the need for a program that would bind the SPD more firmly to Soviet plans. On the other hand, the ZA increasingly felt the need for a clarifying confrontation with the KPD to relieve the lower ranks of the party of the intensifying pressure to which they were subjected. In any case, it was clear to both sides that the ideological formulas and patterns of practice adopted in June 1945 could no longer serve as an adequate basis for interparty relations and future activities.[39]

According to Gustav Dahrendorf, the KPD had called as early as October for a meeting of the "central leadership and district representatives" of both parties to discuss intensified cooperation.[40] Most sources suggest that the decision to hold such a conference was taken sometime early in December 1945.[41]

Still earlier, at an extraordinary session of the Thuringian LV on November 16, ZA Treasurer August Karsten reported that the SPD had received a Communist proposal for a meeting of thirty representatives of each party in order to discuss joint electoral lists for forthcoming communal elections. Like the Thuringia LV, Karsten went on, the ZA rejected the notion of joint lists, but it felt that it would be unable to avoid holding the proposed conference. However, the ZA did not intend that the party go to the Conference unprepared. It was therefore convening a special meeting of delegates from all Soviet Zone party subdivisions to be held in Berlin; at this meeting the questions of *"Reich"* unity and relations to the KPD" were to be considered. Only afterwards would the confrontation with the KPD take place.[42]

The SPD meeting referred to by Karsten took place on December 4 and 5. The major items discussed were a plan for regular consultations between the ZA and representatives of the West German SPD, with the first scheduled to take place in January 1946. Furthermore, a special five-man commission was to formulate, in "clear and concise" theses, the position of the SPD regarding working class unity and cooperation with the KPD.[43] The discussion held one ominous note that foreshadowed intraparty tensions both at the December Conference and at the decisive party meeting of February 11, 1946. According to the report of one participant, several provincial representatives warned the *Zentralausschuss* not to be surprised if their organizations adopted a pro-unity stand more advanced than that of the ZA, for they felt themselves to be under intense and increasing pressure from the Soviet authorities and from the KPD.[44] The outcome of this session is not known, but it is definite that each party, shortly thereafter, prepared a statement of its views on the future course of interparty relations. The SPD proposals, dated December 15, were submitted to the ZK no later than December 17.[45] The KPD's draft did not reach the ZA until the evening of December 19, and the Conference was scheduled to start the following morning. A hasty meeting of the Social Democratic delegates was called for the evening of the 19th,[46] and a postponement of the Conference's start until the afternoon of the 20th was arranged.[47]

Meeting on the eve of the Conference, the Social Democratic delegates could produce neither a unified response to the KPD proposals nor an effective presentation of their own viewpoint. The impulses of the delegates were irresolute and contradictory; the ZA did not exercise effective leadership over the SPD caucus. A proposal to respond to the KPD draft by withdrawing from the Conference was defeated.[48] In a different vein entirely, the delegates, acting apparently under diffuse but powerful pressure from provincial representatives, accepted the KPD draft as the basis for the Conference's deliberations.[49] At the same meetings, however, Grotewohl was instructed by the delegates to reject the heart of the KPD draft in a "clear and unmistakable" fashion.[50]

Moreover, the delegates further instructed Grotewohl to present to the Conference a statement of SPD grievances drawn up in ten points by Gustav Dahrendorf.[51] These ten points contained the sharpest criticism of KPD and SMA that was still consistent with a renewed pledge of mutual cooperation in the construction of a democratic Germany. Had they been presented as a formal SPD statement, it would have been tantamount to an SPD ultimatum most likely presaging the end of any meaningful policy of close cooperation. As will be shown below, this step was not taken by Grotewohl, who utilized the latitude given him as SPD spokesman to soften the impact of the Dahrendorf statement. Nonetheless, the ten points did summarize the SPD's objections to months of pressure on its organizations and members and to favoritism shown the KPD by the SMA in material and political matters. It drew from this the conclusion that even continued, let alone expanded, cooperation between the parties would depend on relief of these abuses. Joint electoral activity in *any* zone of Germany was rejected pending a decision by an all-German party congress.

Although Dahrendorf's statement in effect indicted the course hitherto pursued by the *Zentralausschuss* in its relations to the SMA and KPD, he continued to believe that a united working class party was a goal that, far from having been adopted under "some exceptional pressure," reflected the class struggle and European power politics. He concluded from this that "the unity of the socialist movement in Germany must come without fail," although certain objective preconditions would have to be met, such as a guarantee of the autonomy and independence of a new German workers' party, and internal party democracy.[52]

Dahrendorf's ambivalent attitude was shared by his colleagues in the Social Democratic leadership. Their commitment to the SPD and their anger over Communist actions emboldened them in their complaints; a misrepresentation of their position relative to the SMA and KPD, together with a lack of viable alternatives, kept them committed to the long-range goal of a united socialist party. This attitude helps to explain why, in the end, Dahrendorf and others signed the Conference statement, why Grotewohl did not press the SPD's case over its mistreatment more vigorously, and why, finally, the Conference avoided the real and central issues between the parties—the six months of "unity of action," and their divergent views of future policy.

Certainly the confrontation between the parties was as clear as anyone could wish when it came to the programs they respectively submitted to the Conference. Both parties' drafts for the December Conference began with general declarations involving a call for unity.[53] But while the SPD's began with the situation of the German people after a lost war, deduced the necessity of a "united German socialist workers' party," and then promptly pledged the maintenance of each party's organizational autonomy (following this up with a list of conditions for unity that included most of the Social Democratic complaints of Communist behavior), the Communists opened their statement with praise for the fact that the restoration of German political activity under SMA aegis had not been accompanied by renewed divisions among the toiling masses. Pointing to the accomplishments of the four-party bloc as well as of the KPD-SPD cooperation the KPD draft attributed these successes to six months of antifascist-democratic cooperation: "these differences of opinion which have appeared within the framework of the unity front have always proven capable of resolution."

The Social Democratic draft proposal, in obvious divergence from Soviet and KPD views, called on the parties to abjure unification in one portion of Germany alone,[54] to desist from putting up a single candidate list, and to insure fair and equal treatment of both parties on the part of the Soviet occupation authorities.[55]

The SPD's motives in insisting on separate electoral activity were indicated by its further statement that, "Equal rights and true parity must be based on the relative strength of the two parties." This view was anathema to the KPD—publicly since Ulbricht's speech of October 12— and the KPD's draft was steadfastly opposed to apportioning political influence in relation to electron returns.

The KPD recommended common programs and joint lists of candidates in future elections, arguing that

> "Furloughing" unity between KPD and SPD for the duration of an election campaign (even if the parties desist from mutual attacks) would only have [a harmful] result, because only working class power that is anchored in unity can impress the broad mass of the population and attract it to the side of the working class.[56]
>
> As the experience of other countries shows,[57] separate lists of candidates can never bring about an increased vote total for the two workers' parties, but only for the others. If the *Aktionseinheit* is taken seriously as regards its coherent [*konsequent*], antifascist and democratic goals, then it follows that the workers' parties must contest elections jointly, with closed ranks.

A draft resolution of Franz Dahlem's concerning forthcoming U.S. Zone communal elections declared that the working class parties should conduct a joint campaign with common programs and candidates. These candidates should be selected in each locality by means of joint membership and functionaries' meetings, and no candidates were to be nominated who did not support unconditionally the goal of uniting the workers' parties.[58]

This program, if applied literally, would have meant the *de facto* unification of local branches of the two parties—precisely the sort of piecemeal unification for which Soviet and KPD pressure was most effective, and to prevent which was a major aim of the ZA. Maintaining the separate identity of the SPD in forthcoming elections was thus not only a means to establish the SPD as the party of greater public support, but also to avert the logical culmination of a common electoral effort based on a common program—a common organizational structure that might well outlive the campaign.[59]

While acknowledging the desirability of all-German unity, the KPD draft statement declared that "in view of the situation in the whole of Germany," a program that involved national unity as a prerequisite for party unification would delay unity "by many months," and this would be "unjustifiable." There was therefore a clear duty for the "more progressive districts" of Germany to set the rest an example,[60] and this could be done through unity on a provincial basis, if the following procedures were observed:

1) The local or county [*Kreis*] or district [*Bezirk*] organizations of both parties must have approved organizational unification by a free and unpressured majority vote;

2) A merger can be finally consummated only by provincial party congresses chosen for each party by free election;

3) Such unification of KPD and SPD at the provincial level requires the approval of the joint working committee [*Arbeitsausschuss*] of the Central Committee of the KPD and the *Zentralausschuss* of the SPD.

Where such a unification takes place, the new leaderships, [and all other positions] from top to bottom, must be filled on the basis of parity by members of the SPD and KPD.

These provisions for piecemeal unification must be interpreted against the background of the disciplined organization of the KPD in contrast to the looser SPD structure, and the KPD's recurrent exhortation to drive foes of unity or close cooperation out of their positions in the SPD. Consequently, the process described above would amount to a homogeneous KPD adsorbing such SPD units as had been equipped with suitably pro-unity leaderships. It was because this plan could not be adopted officially at the December Conference over SPD opposition that the position of the *Zentralausschuss* became a crucial question in the weeks that followed.

Both the call for joint lists of candidates and the effort to arrange for unification *seriatim* also served the KPD's purposes of further isolating the ZA from the SPD leaders of the other zones. Had these policies been adopted by the ZA, it would have committed itself to seeking simultaneously the expansion of its influence outside the Soviet Zone by searching out and supporting candidates for office who followed its version of SPD policy—a version that would have stood in the sharpest possible contrast to the policies of Schumacher and other West German SPD leaders. While it may not have been a major factor in their calculations, the KPD and SMA planners must have been pleased by the expectation that the ZA could be maneuvered into competing for all-German Social Democratic leadership on the basis of the KPD's policies; an attempt in 1945–1946 to rally all pro-unity elements in the West Zones SPD against Schumacher's line would have had some chance of success. At the least, a major internal struggle in the SPD would have ensued.

The Conference itself opened at 3 P.M. on Thursday, December 20, 1945, with Wilhelm Pieck and Max Fechner as co-chairmen. There were three items on the agenda: Pieck and Otto Grotewohl were to report on "the unity of the working class," Franz Dahlem and Helmut Lehmann were to report on the question of the US Zone communal elections, and Ulbricht and Fechner were to speak on trade union questions. The sixty participants included all the members of the SPD's *Zentralausschuss* and the KPD's *Zentralkomitee*, as well as representatives of both parties' organizations in each of the *Länder* of the Soviet Zone plus Greater Berlin. No effort was made to exclude SPD delegates who might be presumed to hold views on questions of interparty relations opposed to those of the KPD or SMA. The provincial delegates were the incumbent party leaders from their respective districts, and so the SPD's sixty delegates included persons cool toward the KPD's unity drive.[61] Their presence at the Conference and their signatures under the Conference's resolution has given subsequent SED historians ample opportunity to charge hypocrisy and double-dealing.[62]

As Grotewohl rose to speak at the Conference his position as SPD spokesman was stronger than ever. The Social Democratic position over the preceding three months had been in large measure defined in his speeches. Within the ZA there was no noteworthy opposition to his role as spokesman for the party in the Soviet Zone. Support was forthcoming also from the provincial organizations. For example, on December 7, the Thuringia LV, on Brill's initiative, unanimously passed a vote of confidence in Grotewohl's leadership.[63]

Nor was Grotewohl unaware of the moods and opinions, the fears and hopes of the party. He had Gniffke's reports and his own travel experiences to go on, and he had received Brill's two letters (with their supporting material) on affairs in Thuringia. Dahrendorf's ten points and the discussion of the KPD draft on December 19–20 were but further evidence of what his party wished him to say. Grotewohl himself was aware of the problems confronting the SPD. According to Rudolf Rothe,[64] Grotewohl told the SPD caucus on December 19 that the pressure on the party was greater than ever and could be resisted only if they remained firm. And indeed Grotewohl set out to speak as though he would make adequate consideration of the SPD's views a precondition of further political collaboration with the KPD.

It must have startled his listeners, who had just heard Pieck, in his opening remarks, give a standard account of the ills of Germany's working class movement in the Weimar era, to hear Grotewohl in effect blame the split on the presumption of the Comintern and the Communist parties to be a "centrally directed vanguard" with a calling to impose Russian solutions for the problems of a world in revolutionary turmoil.

Grotewohl noted that powerful Communist parties, like that of France, had become nationalistic and not overly revolutionary. Moreover, he continued, the French CP has indignantly rejected de Gaulle's charge that it is the agent of a foreign power; turning to the KPD, Grotewohl remarked slyly, "We would be pleased to hear from our German fraternal party what its answer would be, were we to ask it the same question." The KPD remains a party with a "centralized, undemocratic" party structure; but even a proletarian dictatorship, he felt, could be combined with internal party democracy and free discussion. The SPD membership considered that progress on this point was an indication of how far the KPD would respect the SPD's right to its own decisions. Were the Communists truly committed to a parliamentary democracy? Was the KPD a truly *German* party? One heard the KPD's public avowals, Grotewohl continued, but many people would be reassured by a specific public affirmation of these positions.[65]

Grotewohl thereupon embarked on a most dubious tactic. Hoping, as he said, to prevent the KPD from presenting its disagreements with the SPD as though they were a matter of the latter's opposition to the principle of unity, he described in detail the SPD's efforts to form a single "workers' party" in April, May, and June of 1945. It would seem that Grotewohl felt it important to respond to KPD initiatives and justify the SPD's responses. Here was one more example of the basic contrast in party styles: the KPD pressed for action, the SPD avoided commitment. For all of Grotewohl's complaints, his chief practical recommendation was a request to the KPD to desist from objectionable tactics.[66]

The six months since these offers were made, Grotewohl went on, had been a period of deep disillusionment for the SPD:

> It is in just these six months that we have had the unfortunate experience of seeing the Communist Party act otherwise than as we were prepared to act, and to be treated otherwise than we were treated. This has not exactly improved the conditions for cooperation and merger. A profound resentment against the Communist fraternal party has arisen among our members . . . [as well as] bitterness . . . over the wholly uncomradely attitude of especially the middle and lower rank personnel of the KPD, as well as over the preferential treatment accorded the KPD by middle and lower level agencies of the [SMA].[67]

These developments were a pointed commentary on SMA and KPD policies from June to December, but Grotewohl promptly weakened the effect of his statement. He dissociated the ZA from these complaints, and furthermore carefully absolved both the SMA and the ZK of the KPD from responsibility for such actions, although he himself pointed out that neither the ZK nor the Soviet command was unaware of this situation, thanks to repeated ZA representations. According to Grotewohl, the SMA was "deeply impressed" by the SPD's account and promised to discipline its subordiantes; he was equally sure that the ZK would lead all KPD units back to the "correct path."

In saying this he overlooked the weighty fact of the *pattern* of discrimination and harassment, a pattern that hardly spoke of isolated initiatives. Moreover, it made little sense to criticize the KPD for its excessive organizational centralization and then absolve the party leadership of the sins of the subordinate units.

The problem for the SPD was to stop the erosion of the party's position through criticism of its leaders and policies, impairment of its activities, and harassment of its members and officials. The December Conference presented an opportunity to secure redress of grievances in advance of SPD agreement to further cooperation; this required an insistent and aggressive concentration on the SPD's complaints and its views on the timing of unity. Grotewohl himself pointed out that (as the ZA had understood it) the agreement to hold the Conference had not implied that it would produce detailed plans for unification, but rather deal with the accumulated problems of interparty relations.[68] In the course of the December Conference, however, the initiative in directing the discussion was held by the Communist delegation, and the Conference (despite the attempts of some SPD delegates) centered on the KPD's proposals for the future rather than the SPD's complaints about the past. The fact that the KPD draft said "not a word about those great concerns" that afflicted the SPD was neither surprising nor accidental.

Responding to Grotewohl's speech, Pieck gave a pained rebuttal of the former's argument. According to Pieck,[69] all these complaints against the KPD were really disguised attacks on unity and democracy; the KPD was for speedy unification because the need for it had grown great; separate lists of candidates would produce "reactionary victories," as was shown by "a very drastic example of such faulty calculation," namely Austria.

Pieck stressed that Grotewohl's claim of SPD priority in advocating unity made it hard to understand why, after five months, so many difficulties suddenly appeared, as in Dahrendorf's Ten Points. The KPD believed in ignoring rumors and quashing troublemakers and if it were up to Pieck the Ten Points would not have been read at all!

Turning to the question of Soviet favoritism, and the SPD's request that the KPD help in asking for a balanced approach, Pieck conveniently misunderstood the matter and righteously declared that, "The Soviet military authorities let no one, least of all us, tell them how to carry out . . . their political work." As for the opposition to KPD zonal unity plans within the SPD, Pieck called on the ZA to show a more robust leadership and, in getting the local organizations to act on unity, show that there was no "pressure" to unite, while at the same time setting a good example for the whole of Germany.

The debates that followed, during the two days of the Conference, did little but amplify and illustrate these arguments. One revealing aspect of the first day's proceedings was the efforts by Dahrendorf and Klingelhöfer to focus the discussion on the SPD's complaints. The Communists had been polite to Grotewohl but, in responding to Dahrendorf and Klingelhöfer, various Communist delegates interrupted, heckled, scorned, and misrepresented the Social Democratic speakers. Thus when Dahrendorf brought up the discrepancy between SPD and KPD newspaper allotments, Ulbricht interrupted to suggest that, if the parties were to unite, they would both benefit from the KPD's advantage.[70] When Dahrendorf protested later that a recital of useful joint initiatives in the work of reconstruction evaded the points raised by the SPD, an unidentified Communist speaker asked whether he was then opposed to such efforts.[71]

Klingelhöfer began with a rather remarkable cry from the heart, "Friends from the KPD, you can talk, you have nothing to fear. You can say everywhere what you wish; no one calls you to account." At this point the Conference protocol records: "Laughter." When, upon citing the KPD's greater material support for its political activity, Klingelhöfer asked whether this was just, a heckler answered: "So let's unite!"[72] Klingelhöfer's statement, that he was speaking up for those afraid to do so for themselves, was attacked as an "affront to the Conference," and the notion that speaking freely in the Soviet Zone might lead to reprisals was deemed a "dangerous" and "unfounded" idea.[73]

The arrogant lack of comprehension for the traditions and opinions of the Social Democrats displayed by the Communist delegates in these and similar exchanges at the Conference is an indication of the scanty progress that had been made toward replacing attitudes of mutual hostility between Communists and Social Democrats.

At the end of the first day of the Conference, the positions of the two parties seemed further apart than ever on the issues; the.SPD attempt to obtain satisfaction for the abuses of Soviet Zone politics had been evaded; personal relations had worsened; and neither side showed great appreciation of the nature of the other. The KPD delegates seemed deliberately to misunderstand the inability of the SPD leadership to impose its views on the party; the Social Democrats continued to search for hopeful signs that the KPD had become a German, internally democratic, and parliamentary party.[74] Notwithstanding the gloomy prospects, on the following morning the Conference was presented with a joint ZA-ZK draft resolution (discussed below) that was adopted after only desultory debate. What had happened?

The caucus of the two leaderships had come to an agreement whereby the basic KPD draft was accepted in return for three major concessions to the SPD: the demand for joint candidacies was dropped, the proposed joint meetings were limited to ideological discussion, and the KPD schedule for piecemeal unification was abandoned.[75]

Although the SPD thus secured the omission of the most objectionable Communist clauses, the SPD's own views on such crucial issues as the timing and scope of unification or the future nature of interparty relations were nowhere evident. The consequence of this failure was that the Conference resolution awakened the impression that the SPD had acceded to the KPD schedule and conception of the future party. The weakening of the SPD position was implicit in the ZA's fundamental commitment to collaboration with the KPD, its unwillingness to consider that its own visions of a purified, national, and democratic socialist movement might not be shared by those who in effect held power over the SPD.

Grotewohl had begun his speech on the first day of the Conference with the declaration, "Concerning the unity of the working class there can be no discussion. It is necessary."[76] If this unity was further defined in terms of closing the gulf that divided the SPD from the KPD, a break with the KPD became inconceivable. The tremendous tactical advantage that this gave to the more resolute leadership is apparent at every stage of the two parties' relationship, not least at the December Conference.

In fact, the SPD's stand for nationwide unity was weakened by Grotewohl's remark that while the SPD would make every effort to have a national party congress vote on working class unity: "We will draw the conclusion that new decisions may be required of us, if the political development in the West, should it not proceed along the lines we all believe to be necessary, places us in a new situation."[77]

Here is the first mention of the eventual rationalization for the ZA's abandonment of its opposition to zonal unity; this line was to become prominent especially after the Grotewohl-Schumacher confrontation of February 8, 1946.

It might be objected that posing the question of unity in institutional terms of KPD and SPD overlooks the problem of the content of that unity. Here the presumed process of "ideological clarification" is important, for the holding of the Conference made sense only if progress toward ideological clarification had indeed taken place.

In 1966 Ulbricht described the process of ideological clarification as "one of the most important prerequisites for the unification" of the two parties. In this process "[the December Conference] was of exceptional significance."[78] In support of this he cited passages (quoted below) from the final resolution of the Conference on the arrival of the "historic moment" for the achievement of unity.

In 1945, however, Ulbricht was less sanguine. On November 9 he criticized ideological clarification as "having just begun," and warned against underestimating how deeply "false notions" had penetrated into proletarian thinking.[79] Siegfried Thomas admits that "Despite a good start, this joint ideological work had shown only scanty results by the year's end. The most important reason for this was undoubtedly, that, with few exceptions, the Social Democratic leaderships gave this subject too little attention."[80] Moreover, unity foes in the Berlin organization worked to hinder ideological activities—a view borne out for Thomas by the record of the Berlin *Bezirksparteitag* of November 1945.

This situation provides the background for the ideological decisions of the December Conference. The one form of intensified joint activity agreed to by the SPD, and specified in the Conference's final resolution, was the holding of joint sessions for ideological clarification.[81] The Conference also resolved to establish a joint publishing house and publish a joint theoretical journal.[82] In addition, the final Conference resolution incorporated passages implying that a clarification of ideological questions had taken place during the Conference.

During the preceding months the lack of such clarification had been cited by the KPD leadership as a primary obstacle to unification. It might therefore have been expected that the Conference would deal in detail with this matter; actually, the question of ideological clarification was not on the agenda, was not raised by central or provincial representatives of either party, and was ignored in the general dis-cussion. The Conference's recommendations on this subject amounted to making a fresh start in pursuit of ideological consensus. Meanwhile, the major ideological questions that divided the parties from one another—democracy in party and state, the timing of socialist demands, the responsibility for Hitler—remained during and after the Conference in the same state of controversy.

This omission becomes explicable if one keeps in mind the varied purposes of the SPD, KPD and SMA in holding the Conference. The Social Democrats were certainly aware of the need for ideological clarification; the party's theoretical position, as expressed in the speeches of Otto Grotewohl, had been shown to be quite divergent from that of the KPD. In their view, however, this clarification process was just beginning— indeed, some tentative areas of agreement had been called into question by Communist practices.

For the KPD the situation was clearer and simpler. The Communist position needed no reexamination beyond that already undertaken by the Pieck-Ulbricht leadership in the decade of 1935-1945. The KPD's self-criticism of its Weimar role rarely went beyond abjuring a sectarian underestimation of the "united front" approach; Communist hostility to Weimar was excused on the grounds of that regime's flaws. For either party, a critical evaluation of the Soviet Union or of the Stalin leadership was inconceivable. Not only was the USSR an occupying power that could limit any criticism of itself, and not only was the KPD of this period a Stalinist party, but the SPD had its own reasons for not candidly examining the Soviet background of the KPD, or that party's role in German affairs. The SPD wished to convince the Soviet authorities that it eschewed its Weimar anti-Soviet hostility, and that it thus deserved Soviet confidence as a leading political force in Germany.

Thus any effort to base a unity party on an explicit ideological foundation—"on the basis of consistent Marxism," as Ackermann put it— was hampered by tactical considerations.[83] To be sure, the need for some revision of attitudes was generally recognized; hence the Communist effort to stress their commitment to parliamentary, national, and generally accepted social goals.

Ideological clarification, in addition, presented few internal problems to the KPD leadership. As indicated previously, sectarian waverings in the KPD were straightened out without undue public fuss.[84] The opposite deviation was an "opportunism" that took the accommodation with the SPD seriously and welcomed the admixture of Social Democratic ideas and organizational style. These potential deviators were content to apply a party line with which they agreed, which they had helped to formulate and whose practical consequences they welcomed.[85]

It is hard to escape the conclusion that the KPD leaders, however seriously they may have taken ideological questions in the summer of 1945, had by the December Conference largely abandoned "clarification" as a prerequisite for unification. What had happened between June and December 1945? The KPD and SMA felt greater urgency about recruiting the SPD for their organizational plans, but the presumptive ideological basis for such an accord was not within reach. Some of the hottest disputes had come over programmatic passages in Grotewohl's speeches or in the Buchenwald Manifesto. On the other hand, although practical cooperation between the parties had brought with it many instances of friction, an impressive number of joint actions in social and administrative areas were undertaken (especially if one keeps in mind the pre-1933 relations of SPD to KPD).

In the Germany of the "Year Zero," practical cooperation on reconstruction and denazification is perhaps not too surprising. What is surprising is that such collaboration should have been considered equivalent to a process of ideological clarification. The KPD speakers made no claims at the Conference that any significant ideological consensus had been reached in the previous six months, nor that any particular crisis of ideological contention had occasioned the meeting. The growing urgency of the unity campaign was ascribed to aspects of Germany's political development.[86] Nevertheless, the continued attention paid by the pro-unity forces to ideological questions in the first four months of 1946 indicated that this issue was far from settled in the minds of the rank-and-file members of the two parties.

The final Conference resolution recapitulated the familiar KPD line as to the relationship between working class disunity and the rise of Hitler, the post-war acknowledgment of the need for unity, the accomplishments of the "unity of action" in expediting reconstruction, and the need for a unified working class party in the building of a new, democratic, peace-loving Germany.[87] It declared that the "deepening and broadening" of the interparty cooperation would be the "prelude to the realization of the political and organizational fusion" of KPD and SPD.

Although no timetable for unification was specifically indicated, the wording of the resolution (reflecting its origins in the KPD draft) suggested that important steps would be taken in the near future: "Currently . . . the historic moment has arrived to learn the lesson taught by the whole history of the workers' movement and prepare the workers' unity party." The resolution contained no suggestion of past difficulties in interparty relations; nor, even more significantly, was there any mention of the SPD's stand against unity on less than a nationwide basis.

The Conference called for the establishment of study group of four members from each party, whose task it would be to work out in detail the structure and program of the new party. The suggested program was divided into a "minimum" section (antifascist, parliamentary republic with enlarged scope for workers' political action) and a "maximum" section (socialism via the political rule of the working class in the spirit of consistent Marxism); this content was unobjectionable from the SPD standpoint, although its formulation implied a greater degree of progress toward unity than the Conference warranted. The suggested structure of the new party was deined in terms of orthodox Leninist democratic centralism, which could hardly have allayed the SPD's doubts concerning the internal organization of the KPD.

In an anticipation of Ackermann's soon-to-be-published theses on a "German road to socialism," the resolution called for a party whose task it woud be

> to develop its policies and tactics in accordance with the interests of the German toilers and the special conditions existing in Germany. It should strike out on its own way [both in the immediate future and in the transition to socialism], basing itself on the peculiarities in the development of our people. The ruthless smashing of the old power structure of the state and the resulting further development of the democratic renewal of Germany *can create new and special forms of the transition to the political leadership of the working class and to socialism.* (Italics added.)

This striking formulation, which received no discussion during the Conference itself, may be seen as an answer to Grotewohl's semirhetorical question as to whether the KPD was a "German party."

The outcome of the December Conference must have been a disappointment to both Communist and Social Democratic participants. Indeed, the latter signed the final resolution with some reluctance.[88] Since it incorporated much of their draft, the Communists were presumably happier with the resolution, but scarely satisfied with the Conference itself. They had succeeded in committing the SPD to an affirmation of the pro-unity generalities of the preceding months, but not to a plan of action that would in fact inaugurate what the KPD proclaimed as "the second phase" of the unity movement. For their part, the Social Democrats had secured no improvement in their situation or in their relations with the KPD; while they had avoided the more aggressive KPD formulas, their own position was not apparent from the announced results of the Conference, unless one already knew their original stand.[89]

This mutual dissatisfaction with the December Conference was illustrated after the Conference by the divergent interpretations each of the parties sought to give it. The SPD felt it had made some cautious arrangements for further cooperation toward the yet-distant goal of unity; for the KPD, the Conference marked the start of an intensive campaign for unification of the two parties—in the near future and in the Soviet Zone alone. Which interpretation would determine the actual course of events depended on factors that heavily favored the KPD: SMA opinion, access to information channels, disciplined party organization, allies within the SPD. Despite these advantages, however, it required six eventful weeks to bring about *Zentralausschuss* adherence to the KPD's position, and another ten weeks after that to consummate the unification of the parties.

CHAPTER 8

The Unity Campaign in the Aftermath of the December Conference

January and February 1946

On December 27, 1945, Wilhelm Pieck sent Otto Grotewohl a copy of the protocol of the December Conference (the SPD not having kept its own record). In an accompanying letter he wrote

> Please take personal care of this stenographic record, lest it fall into the hands of those outside your own immediate circle. There is nothing in the contents that could not be made public, but there were a few remarks made here and there concerning the relations of our parties to the occupation authorities, remarks which do not let it seem opportune to allow the protocol to circulate.[1]

Pieck's expression of caution, while understandable, is incomplete; the Conference protocol contained not only critical remarks concerning the SMA, but also a clear record of interparty disagreement and, more importantly, of KPD initiatives rejected by the Conference at Social Democratic insistence. By concealing the details of the Conference, the KPD influenced its outcome. The Communist origins of the text of the final resolution, the KPD initiatives going beyond the Conferences decisions, and the ZA's failure to publicize its own version of the Conference all helped the KPD to utilize the Conference in its own interests.

In Communist eyes, the Conference inaugurated "the second phase of unity,"[2] a phase marked, in Pieck's words, by the commitment of both parties to further "develop practical cooperation into organizational fusion," for which there were no more "insurmountable organizational or ideological obstacles."[3] In March 1946, when the possible political impact of his revelations were much lessened, Pieck gave a more truthful picture of the parties' respective responses to the December Conference. According to Pieck's later version:

> At first there were elements of confusion and differences of opinion between the party leaderships over implementation of the December Conference decisions, as well as over the territorial scope of unity. There arose the question of whether unity was possible only in all of the occupation zones, that is, in all of Germany, or just in the Soviet occupation zone . . . whether after a nationwide party congress . . . or at a party congress . . . [for] the Soviet Zone.[4]

In short, the Conference had not changed the divergent party positions.

The official announcement of the Conference resolutions helped to produce reactions of alarm and hostility in the Western zones among both the occupying powers and the Social Democrats. Waldemar von Knorringen,[5] came to Berlin as an official British representative and told Klingelhöfer that in British circles the December Conference was seen as the start of a "German crisis" in which the SPD would be forced to "surrender" to Soviet and KPD unity demands.[6]

The American authorities were likewise alerted. In the military government reports for October and November 1945, the SPD's resistance to Communist importuning on the unity issue had been featured,[7] but the report for December clearly considered the results of the December Conference a major reversal of SPD policy in the Soviet Zone, as well as an implementation of Communist ideas on the timing and scope of unity.[8]

Although the Americans (if not the British) still tended to regard the unity issue as a Soviet affair and concerned themselves mainly with defeating efforts to influence US Zone politics from Berlin, the Western powers' reaction to the December Conference presaged their later involvement in the struggle within the SPD in Berlin.

While the official Soviet reaction to the December Conference was rather perfunctory, one may speculate that SPD behavior at that meeting may well have been perceived as unjustifiably provocative. Given the pre-Hitler record of Social Democratic hostility to the Soviet Union, and adding the fact that the SPD leaders were, after all, spokesmen for a very recently defeated and occupied people, it cannot have been a light matter for Soviet political personnel in Germany to accept SPD strictures on their activity. In public, however, the Soviet response was brief and correct. The Soviet press reported no statements from officials in Moscow or Berlin; in an article published in a Soviet journal just after the conference, the conference resolutions were said to have found a wide response among members of both parties. A retrospective survey of the unification process in July 1946 gave a standard KPD account of the meeting. The SMA daily discussed the conference in the context of general "democratic" cooperation needed to solve Germany's problems.[9]

The SPD of the Western zones reacted promptly, incisively, and with great effect to the resolutions of the December Conference. On the initiative of Schumacher and his allies among the SPD leaders, conferences were called in early January for the British Zone at Hanover, and for Hesse and (in February) for the whole American Zone at Frankfurt/Main. The conferees declared the December Conference resolutions to be inapplicable outside of the Soviet Zone and denounced the intensified drive for unification of the SPD and KPD.[10] In this fashion the conflicting pressures on the ZA heightened ominously.

Kaden has criticized the widely held view that the December Conference marked a turning point in the unity campaign.[11] In his judgment the Conference only "brought to light" the steady downward slide of the *Zentralausschuss* after its failure to secure publication of Grotewohl's November 11 speech. This view fails to take into account the fateful omissions of SPD policy discussed in the preceding chapter (failure to secure redress of grievances, etc.); it also overlooks the use that the KPD made of the very fact of the Conference and, even more important, the style and content of the Conference resolutions.

The Schumacher reaction is a case in point here. The actual ZA position at the Conference on the need all-German decisions had been such as to strengthen the position of Social Democrats outside the Soviet Zone. Thanks to the total lack of contact between Schumacher and the Berlin leaders (for which Schumacher, as we have seen, bears much of the responsibility) and to the omissions of the Conference declaration, the ZA's stand on this issue was not known in the West. This helped account for the virulence of the reaction to any move toward zonal unity. The blasts from Hanover and Frankfurt, however, helped further to isolate the ZA, to discourage those who genuinely wished unification but only on a nationwide basis, and to weaken the argument of those who hoped to postpone a decision on unity by raising the question of nationwide decisions.

Both the SPD and the KPD leaderships realized the implications of this news from the West. Gniffke complained that it complicated the ZA's tactical maneuvers. Dahrendorf, in a letter of January 9, complained that the Frankfurt meeting's resolutions showed an "especially blameworthy insensitivity." Klingelhöfer feared that Schumacher's stand, by foreclosing the prospects for an all-German SPD, would leave the ZA no alternative but to agree to unification with the KPD in the Soviet Zone alone.[12]

Walter Ulbricht saw in the decisions of Hanover and Frankfurt a threat to the prospects for a democratic Germany, an attempt to lead the working class down the Weimar path of a bourgeois coalition. In his view, both parties should take advantage of the advanced stage of party organization and "democratic" political development in the Soviet Zone to foster joint action. He reminded his listeners that the KPD was already the most unified and widely spread, as well as the most democratic party in Germany.[13]

Possibly unaware of the emerging KPD strategy, the SPD leaders were mystified that their intramural successes at the December Conference should be so misunderstood and little appreciated. Gustav Klingelhöfer encouraged Grotewohl to think ahead of "victory" in the partisan competition of 1946,[14] and Dahrendorf declared that the Conference resolutions, albeit "historic," were nevertheless "no sensation." There was no organizational unity "because then [June 1945] *as now* essential objective preconditions" had not been fulfilled. (Italics added.) The conference had recognized, Dahrendorf went on,

> that the national organization cohesion of the workers' parties must be established before any organizational merger is possible. Such a merger can only result from a decision of a representative body of the whole party. Logically, therefore, the presentation of joint lists of candidates at future elections must be subject to similar preconditions.[15]

Grotewohl tried to account for the hostile reaction from the West by insisting that the ZA's stand and the Conference resolutions had been misunderstood or insufficiently known; of course the SPD would have to be established as a united nationwide party before there could be unity.

The Social Democrats of the Soviet Zone continued to insist that unity with the KPD, despite immediate obstacles, would represent a deep-felt and spontaneous recognition of the dictates of history. This line was held to all the more tightly as Soviet and KPD pressure increasingly sought to isolate "enemies of unity" and "saboteurs" from the ranks of honest Marxists and democrats. Thus by April Ulbricht could declare that, "Only he is a consistent democrat who is for the unification of the working class."[16] The ZA's chief means of escaping this contradictory pressure was delay, pending party formation on the all-German level. In early January the ZA suggested, briefly, another alternative, in an article by Max Fechner, suggesting a decision either through an all-German party congress, or "if need be, through a referendum of the membership."[17] Gniffke reports that this suggestion was discussed at a meeting of the two parties' leaderships with Tiul'panov. Pieck and Ulbricht opposed the referendum idea, Tiul'panov was noncommital, Ackermann was surprisingly in favor. At Soviet suggestion the idea was referred to the Study Commission called for by the December Conference.[18]

The idea of a referendum had already been raised in the aftermath of the December Conference by the Berlin SPD organization.[19] In March, party functionaries in Berlin would revive this idea to good effect; the *Zentralausschuss* did not advocate this step at either time. Scanty evidence available indicates that this idea could have found a response outside of Berlin—in Saxony, for instance, had Soviet policy permitted it.

The problems faced by the ZA in maintaining an independent and critical attitude toward the KPD's unity plans, while remaining fully committed to the goal of party unification, are well illustrated by the incident of Pieck's birthday celebration. The SMA and KPD decided, on the occasion of Pieck's 70th birthday (January 3, 1946), to organize a public demonstration for unity and at the same time advance Pieck's claim to be the leader of a united working class movement with broad, nationally acceptable goals.[20]

The SPD leadership sensed in this affair a Communist attempt to "steal" the seniority and thus leadership of a future unity party, and tested this supposition by proposing that the 70th birthday of Paul Löbe (a long-time SPD leader and former Reichstag president), which had recently occurred, be celebrated together with Pieck's. Neither the KPD nor the SMA would allow this; indeed, the Soviets had arranged for the Berlin city government to extend to Pieck a symbol of the KPD's new position as a party of state power—the honorary citizenship of Berlin.[21] The exaggerated tributes to Pieck in the KPD newspaper were perhaps to be expected;[22] Grotewohl's effusive remarks, however, form a startling contrast, not only to Pieck's own, but to the advice and sentiments of his fellow Social Democrats.

According to Grotewohl, Pieck was the "Trustee of the people," who had spent over fifty years defending the common cause of the workers' movement.[23] The delegates at the December Conference had recognized this common cause, and those Social Democrats in the Western zones who declared ZA resolutions to be not binding on them would have to realize that, "Only those resolutions which give expression in Germany to the vital necessities of the people and their ties of kinship can be considered as binding." Grotewohl then turned to Pieck and, in what became a famous political gesture, clasped his hand, declaring, "We have no testimonial to give you, and yet we do have this: a handclasp that is not meant just for today, but until a time when these hands can no longer separated." Grotewohl's political handshake has been attributed to everything from rhetorical improvisation to devious calculation; whatever the motive may have been, the result gave seeming substance to fears that the ZA had embraced the notion of rapid unification.

The startling contrast between Grotewohl's position on this occasion and his remarks at the December Conference a fortnight earlier is but one illustration of Grotewohl's puzzling role throughout this period. Various explanations for Grotewohl's behavior have been offered. Some explanations were flattering to him, centering on his desire to rescue the substance of the SPD position in the Soviet Zone, especially in anticipation of a greater future role for the SPD on the basis of the "Eastern orientation" analysis. On the other hand, Grotewohl was perceived as a vain, ambitious, weak person whose brief moments of willingness to defend the SPD soon gave way, in the face of Soviet pressure, to behavior likely to please the SMA and KPD and also, not incidentally, secure a prominent place in German politics for himself. Both before and after unification, Grotewohl apparently felt that he stood an excellent change of becoming the natural leader of German socialism and, as such, the German leader most acceptable to the Soviet Union.[24] "I have the trust of the Russians, and they know that I know Germany better than Ulbricht does," he is supposed to have said in March 1946.[25] In this mixture of analysis and illusion, of ambition for himself and calculation about his party lay the puzzling personality of Grotewohl, whose ambiguity aroused a great many unmet expectations and proved a shifting anchor for the SPD.

In fact, doubts about the ZA's apparent course were expressed not only by Schumacher or by Western observers, but by substantial bodies of Social Democrats in the Soviet Zone. As the party leaders assembled for Pieck's birthday celebration, they presumably knew that only five days previously the leadership and functionaries of the Berlin SPD had met to express serious doubts about the ZA's policies and to pass resolutions that ran counter to those policies.[26]

This meeting of December 29, 1945,[27] which must be seen as the beginning of the movement leading to the establishment of a separate Berlin SPD in March and April 1946, took place in a tense and emotional atmosphere. Kaden judges the relationship of the Berlin leadership (after its formation in November) to the ZA to have been exceptionally close; this increased resentment against the ZA following the announcement of the December Conference decisions.[28] Klingelhöfer described the meeting as one in which "There was an extraordinarily strong feeling of depression, but even stronger were the suspicions of the ZA and feelings of indignation at not having been consulted . . . twice, motions expressing lack of confidence in the ZA were almost brought to a vote."[29]

It required strenuous efforts by Klingelhöfer and Fechner to calm the delegates; even so, the two resolutions passed on December 29 should have been a warning signal to the ZA that, as perceived by important groups within the party, the resolutions of the December Conference were unacceptable.[30]

This meeting may have derived its impetus from the shock of the December Conference resolutions, but the sentiments expressed reflected a prior trend within the Berlin SPD. Joint action with the Berlin KPD had been unpopular with a segment of the SPD apparatus since the fall of 1945,[31] and the Berlin KPD leader, Waldemar Schmidt, had complained at the December Conference of the poor relations between the parties in Berlin.[32] It must be stressed here that there was no majority in the Berlin SPD for a break with the ZA and with its policy of cooperation with the Communists. Further divisions within the party were the last thing the Berlin Social Democrats desired. In all parts of the organization, however, up to and probably including the vice-chairman, Werner Rüdiger, there was rising and substantial disquiet over the course of the SPD in the Soviet Zone.[33] The resentments of the moment were stilled by ZA reassurances, but clearly the ZA's stand would have to be made explicit to the party organizations in the Soviet Zone. Moreover, a way would have to be found to implement this stand as the party's actual policy in the face of increasing Soviet pressure. To this pressure, and to the ZA's response in mid- and late January we must now turn.

An examination of the situation in Thuringia will demonstrate the ZA's problems, Soviet tactics, and the nature of the struggle at the lower levels of the party structure. The predicament of the *Zentralausschuss,* a predicament from which it failed to extricate itself between January 15 and February 11, was fashioned largely by events outside Berlin that were the result of effective Soviet actions. Ironically, Thuringia had been a major area of resistance to Soviet policy; now, its provincial SPD and KPD were to become the pace setters of that policy.

Despite Brill's difficulties in Weimar, he had attended the December Conference as the sole representative from the Thuringian SPD.[34] His presence in Berlin seems to have been the occasion for arranging his departure from Thuringia and his resettlement in Berlin as an employee of the American authorities.[35]

The problem of Brill's personal position in Thuringia was only a part of the larger issue between the SMA and the regional units of the SPD. His removal, however, was the prerequisite for implementation of the SMA's program: installation of a more amenable leadership, loosening of the ties between the ZA and its Thuringian affiliate, and recruitment of the Thuringian SPD for the SMA-KPD unity drive.[36]

In a feverish atmosphere of Soviet pressure on local SPD organizations to renounce Brill and the former stands of the provincial party,

Brill, after reporting on the December Conference to the Thuringian leadership, resigned and was replaced by a veteran SPD leader, August Frölich. But the Brill issue was not disposed of quite so easily.

During the LV's early-morning session on December 31, the SMA summoned Hoffmann to its offices.[37] In successive interviews with successively higher ranking Soviet officers, he had to explain his opinion of Frölich (favorable), how Frölich had come to fill Brill's post, and how he (Hoffmann) felt about the December Conference. It was solemnly explained to him that it was undemocratic to have Frölich, as head of the Control Commission, also act as head of the LV—a successor to Brill should have been selected from among the LV members. The Soviet officers hoped the LV would replace Frölich with "a young person with a modern outlook." Furthermore, the SMA demanded that Hoffmann arrange for a resolution of the LV endorsing the December Conference decisions, revoking the *Circular Letter No. 18,* and condemning Brill's activities, because, in the words of the SMA's Col. Kirsanov, "Dr. Brill . . . is not a political tactician; he is a deceiver, a saboteur of the workers' will [to unity]. That is what you must tell your members and write in your newspaper." Hoffmann was to produce a *Tribüne* editorial in which he "would attack especially sharply the duplicity of Dr. Brill and unmask him as a saboteur of unity efforts by contrasting *Circular Letter No. 18* and the December Conference resolutions, both of which [Brill] signed . . . [and] justify the necessity for speedy organizational unification of KPD and SPD because of the fight against fascism."

Finally, agreement was reached whereby Brill's name would not be mentioned in newspaper article or resolution, but both would contain attacks on "saboteurs" of unity; Frölich would be replaced by a "younger, more modern" member of the LV. After further SMA interviews with the SPD leaders, at an LV session of January 2, 1946, Hoffmann replaced Frölich as acting SPD chairman for Thuringia.[38]

Thus the SMA had taken the first steps to dictate the Thuringian SPD's response to the December Conference and to select the personnel to carry out their wishes. Hoffmann was already known as an SMA "candidate" for the party leadership. In a bitter exchange at a meeting on November 26, 1945, Hoffmann had responded to Brill's speech by presenting his own dissenting views on relations of the SPD to the KPD and SMA. This had prompted Brill to declare openly, "That since

August of this year Comrade Hoffmann has been the candidate of the [SMA] for the leadership of the Social Democratic Party in Thuringia. (Hoffmann: That's news to me!)" Brill insisted (sincerely?) that is was *not* a matter of what *Hoffmann* had done, but rather a "self-evident, unsurprising" piece of Bolshevik tactics to find (if necessary, to create) opposing factions whose mutual tensions they could then exploit.[39]

Hoffmann's behavior at the end of December was decent toward Brill personally; presumably, however, Hoffmann knew that the SMA favored him, as it might well have, for his views were no secret. Inasmuch as Hoffmann was aware of the complaints of local SPD organizations, his attitude toward the unity issue is significant and representative of that wing of the SPD receptive to Soviet and Communist plans. Calling on the Social Democrats to see the Communists as partners rather than enemies, he pointedly asked: "Comrades, let's be clear about one thing: were we to unleash a struggle against the KPD, it would mean carrying on a fight against the occupation forces. Can we let ourselves in for that?"[40] The Potsdam accords, he went on, had made clear that the political life of each zone would be determined by the respective occupying power; Soviet Zone politics must be exercised in harmony with Soviet views.

In these circumstances, the Thuringian SPD leadership received a letter from Grotewohl and Gniffke on behalf of the ZA that clearly expressed the SPD conviction that the agreements of the December Conference did not involve immediate steps to unity.[41] The letter stressed that, in direct contradiction to KPD proposals, there was to be no fusion "from below" or on a local, provincial, or zonal basis. Hopefully, the Berlin leaders noted, "It is thereby made clear that we have reached an understanding with the Communists not to have a regional unification." This passage seems to express a "tactical" naivete on the ZA's part, for neither the SMA nor the KPD interpreted the December Conference decisions in this way. That the ZA was in fact concerned about possible Communist and Soviet interpretations is made clear by a passage in the letter stating that, "We hereby authorize you *to make these [SPD] principles expressly clear to the SMA, should that be necessary.* Any Communist efforts to act contrary to these principles are a breach of the Berlin agreements." (Italics added.)

But the Thuringian leaders were no longer willing (or able?) to shore up the ZA's position in this fashion. A resolution presented to the LV's January 5 session, which would have fully backed the Berlin stand, was not adopted. Instead the LV published and circulated statements calling for formation of an "independent, consistently Marxist unity party."[42]

Hoffmann and the LV proclaimed in articles and circular letters that while difficulties and differences still persisted in interparty relations, the leaderships of both parties were working together to remove the occasions of friction.[43] Hoffmann dismissed those who could not place the need for unity above concrete disagreements as "self-seekers, party egotists, party fanatics," who were infected with "political arrogance," and "egotistical pride."[44] At the same time, it was very important for Hoffmann and his party that assurances were given by Kolesnichenko for the SMA, promising equality for treatment for both parties, and even offering relief from local Commandants who pressured lower party organizations into joint meetings.[45]

At a meeting of sixty leaders from each party in Weimar on January 6, the two parties agreed on intensified cooperation in agricultural, welfare, and educational matters, and intensified interparty contacts and activities.[46]

However, the discussions of the conference showed that interparty differences were still substantial; the SPD committed itself wholeheartedly to unity, but expressed concern over the timing of the projected fusion. Commenting on the conference, the *Tribüne* warned that unity at "lightning speed" would be inimical to the necessary "maturation process." The same article, however, admitted that "One can understand the position of the Communist Party and agree with it that in this matter speed is of the essence."[47]

The conferees of January 6 also decided on a mass meeting of both parties to be held in Jena on January 19 and 20, with Pieck and Grotewohl as the speakers. This conference was another step in the Thuringian parties' approach to unity, it moved them beyond the stage of January 6 or of the December Conference, but did not yet quite fulfill the SMA's plans.

The "Conference of 1200" that met at Jena on January 19 and 20, 1946, may serve as a good example of such conferences, a series of which were held in the Soviet Zone in mid-January. By mobilizing visible public support for a rapid unification of the parties, the organizers of these conferences hoped to demonstrate that such support existed. These great mass occasions were irregular bodies in terms of party organization, but were evaluated (by the KPD) as genuine expressions of proletarian will. That they were not regularly constituted bodies made it easier to arrange the attendance of pro-unity crowds; where official party bodies balked at cooperating in the arrangements, other "representatives" of the working class could be mobilized.

Moreover, these meetings formed a capstone to the ever-larger number of rallies throughout the Soviet Zone devoted to encouragement of unity.[48] Their composition was as varied as circumstances and opportunity could make them: factory assemblies, party meetings (some called jointly and others, ostensibly "joint," called by the KPD), rallies of public employees, and general public rallies of various sorts. What these meetings had in common was fervid advocacy (much of it quite genuine) of unification of the parties in the Soviet Zone in the near future, little or no mention of the SPD objections on these issues, and mounting attacks on opponents (largely Social Democratic) of the unity drive.

For the Thuringia SPD, the gathering in Jena was seen as an opportunity for a "decisive step forward on the admittedly steep and weary way to the democratic unification of the still divided German working class." Careful and clear-headed examination of the remaining obstacles would enable the delegates to· build a lasting unity.[49] In the Communist view, the "little diagreements . . . about side issues" could not halt the advance, through cooperative work, to a "strong, Marxist, united" party; let Thuringia be the first to create such a party.[50] Indeed, the Jena meeting was to be exploited by the SMA and KPD (in a manner reminiscent of their use of the December Conference) as a mandate for a breakthrough on the unity issue in Thuringia.

The proclamation adopted by the Conference was vague on specific actions to be taken, but loud in its enthusiasm for unity and attacks on those who "opposed" this process:

> We pledge our every effort to fulfill the tasks set for us by these resolutions [of the December Conference and the Weimar meeting of January 6] and, by this heightened activity, *to bring about in the near future the orga-*

nizational unification of the two parties. We wish to overcome all obstacles and difficulties through joint effort. Whosoever hinders the unity of the working class, helps the reactionaries. The workers' movement, in the strength of its millions, will roll on over him.[51] (Italics added).

In the speeches of the participants, however, especially in those of Pieck and Grotewohl, the differences in outlook between the parties was more apparent.[52] Each expressed his party's outlook in familiar and, in Pieck's case, aggressive terms.

In this connection, Pieck delivered one of the first public KPD attacks on Schumacher. Sarcastically denying Schumacher's legitimacy as a party leader, and referring to the ZA as the "leadership of the German Social Democracy," Pieck caled Schumacher's activities the concern of all "Social Democratic friends of unity." This open intervention by a KPD leader in the internal struggles of the SPD was justified by Pieck as long as the Social Democrats did not themselves—in factories, trade unions, everywhere they met antiunity sentiment—resolutely oppose all foes of unity. Here was the tactic Brill had warned against: making the KPD the arbiter of intra-SPD conflicts.

The effectiveness of this approach was determined by the rise of a corresponding attitude among Social Democrats, that they had more in common with pro-unity Communists than with antiunity members of their own party. If it was necessary, as Hoffmann, for example, had stated, to "feel" as a member of the future unity party, then were those who stood aside comrades any longer? For those who were concerned about the SPD as an historical community, such disruption of the SPD was a serious matter. One aspect of the Social Democrats' insistence on avoiding merely zonal unity was concern for their comrades in the other zones.

At the Jena meeting, Pieck directly confronted the matter of unification of the parties in one zone, declaring that

Although we strive with all our might for a unity party in all of Germany [we know] that a situation might arise in which unification should not be made to depend on its simultaneous realization in all zones. That would mean allowing ourselves to become dependent on the policies of foreign powers in the realization of this great historical deed. . . . *so very likely we shall have to content ourselves with first accomplishing the unification of the two parties only in that zone in which the most favorable conditions for it exist.* (Italics added.)

Pieck blandly added that he saw "no dangers" in this proposed course for the unity either of the German working class or nation.[53] The SPD's Thuringia newspaper dissented cautiously. Amid generally approving comments on the Conference, the writer remarked that Pieck had advocated zonal unity if necessary, and that

> Activists among the Thuringian delegates generally agreed with Wilhelm Pieck: push ahead as far as possible, set an example in Thuringia. . . . On the other hand, the discussions showed that many Thuringian workers are sufficiently farsighted not to view the question of unity only with respect to the exceptionally favorable circumstances of this *Land* alone, but to show their political sense of responsibility by thinking of the unity of the whole German working force.[54]

If some Thuringian Social Democrats thought they could treat the Jena meeting as a noncommittal exchange of differing views, they were soon disabused by the urgency of the Soviet occupation authorities in the province. The intentions of the Jena rally's sponsors can best be appreciated by considering the interview of Werner Eggerath (KPD) and August Frölich (SPD) with the SMA's General Kolesnichenko, on January 23, 1946.[55]

The General wished to know how the Jena conference had gone, and why unity was not forthcoming. As Frölich paraphrased him, "Why not unite in the Zone or Thuringia? The working class demands unity!" Frölich objected that the December Conference resolutions, as well as the Jena statements of Pieck and Grotewohl, had called for a national party congress. With calculating innocence, Kolesnichenko replied, "There's nothing in the resolution about that." In any case, as Eggerath put it, "in Jena the decision was made, in principle," for the rapid consummation of the unity drive in Thuringia.

The method to be employed was made clear by the Soviet general. Told that unity had been "practically established" in two Thuringian districts, Kolesnichenko was reported as saying,

> Utilize sentiment for unity ideologically and execute organizationally. Carry it out from below, where ripe, i.e., where the fewest obstacles. Begin! Joint meetings, united leaderships in the factories . . . register members. It is known to him that not all members of both parties wish to join a unity party. That is of no interest . . . the line has been set.

Kolesnichenko firmly assured his listeners that the working class would be "happy" and "thankful" for a pro-unity initiative of the leaderships. Enemies of unity must be shunted aside through such means as exposure in the press: "In a struggle, someone must be defeated."

Repeatedly, Kolesnichenko stressed that the Thuringian organizations must act for unity without heeding possible opposition from the West or even from the *Zentralausschuss*. Thuringia was to set the pace:

> Thuringia must set an example, then the other parts [of the Soviet Zone] and the other zones would follow. . . . Don't listen to what the West says. . . . Make a start in Thuringia, the others will follow, that is the dialectic of life. . . . *It is not necessary to wait for the Zentralausschuss,* lest workers say, "But you are not little children." (Italics added.)

Above all, there was the continuous drumfire of prompting to speedy action, lest the propitious moment pass, lest "bourgeoisie and fascism" return.

How Kolesnichenko's pressure was translated into local action may be glimpsed from the February 4, 1946, report of the Schmalkalden SPD to the LV.[56] The spokesmen for the local SPD was confronted by four KPD representatives and the local command's political officer. The Social Democrat's stress on the importance of party discipline as a reason for not agreeing to local unity measures was branded as "fearful," and he was assured that "the *Zentralausschuss* awaits such prompting, and that such measures would inspire the top leadership to speed up matters." He was told that he had no courage and was not yet himself permeated with the thought of unity. Finally, the SPD functionary referred further actions to the decisions of the joint expanded Thuringian party leaderships scheduled to meet in Weimar on February 5.

If any Thuringian Social Democrats looked to the joint leadership meeting of February 5 to provide an opportunity for further delay, they were sorely disappointed. Already on January 24, the KPD *Bezirksleitung* had proposed to the LV that a joint session of the two leaderships be held to decide on immediate Thuringian unity. Hoffmann had agreed to a session of the "enlarged" leaderships (35 delegates each) for February 5.[57] When they met after a surge of pro-unity declarations in press and radio,[58] the party leaderships announced that the SPD and KPD in Thuringia would unite within sixty days.[59] Declaring that the Jena rally had produced an "unmistakable will to the speediest organizational unity," they resolved to hold provincial party congresses

(*Landesparteitäge*) for each party on April 6 in the tradition-rich town of Gotha, followed by a joint founding congress of the new unity party on April 7.

Provisions were made for the election of delegates; a special joint committee was established to work out such requirements as a party statute, a party program (in conjuction with the December Conference's work) an agenda for the unity congress, and the election of the new party's leadership.[60] In the interim there was to be an intensification of joint activity at every party level, and especially in ideological matters, and in all those localities where joint efforts had hitherto lagged. Finally, the "sharpest struggle" was pledged against "opponents of a united workers' party."

The impact of this sudden decision may be gauged by the careful words of the *Tribüne's* pro-unity editor, Karl Doerr.[61] Commenting on the "bold and historically memorable" decision of February 5, he wrote that in retrospect it will seem "unimaginable . . . how fast the development" from the December Conference to this date had been. Of course, the former meeting had rejected unity in a single zone, and Doerr was concerned to explain that

> Of course it was not a *Land* party matter, *but rather a great, decisive national question.* Sooner or later, all provinces and zones will have to follow the Thuringian example, because the dynamic, elemental unity movement will sweep over all zonal and provincial borders and create the conditions for unity also there where today favorable circumstances do not yet exist. (Italics in original.)

For those in the party who were not merely uneasy but actually opposed the rush to merge, Doerr had harsher words. In an editorial first published in the *Tribüne,* but considered so valuable that it was reprinted in both central party organs, Doerr warned: "We declare most resolute war, against all saboteurs and disrupters of the proletarian unity front, *regardless of who they are and where they come from,* for we cannot allow that the work of unity be disrupted by irresponsible elements."[62] (Italics added.) Those who were merely confused or in honest error were loftily dismissed from the ranks of the "volunteers" of unity.[63]

The scanty evidence available does not permit detailed account of opposition within the SPD to this sudden decision—for no matter how prefigured it may have been in the developments since the start of the year, nothing had happened on the zonal or provincial level to lessen the force of the SPD arguments that pointed to delay. At the LV meeting of February 4 (that preceded the joint decisive session of the 5th), there was "long, passionate, and thorough" argument centering on the need for all-German unity;[64] on the following day, while the party leaderships were in session in Weimar, speakers at an SPD rally in Erfurt "energetically" opposed unity on a zonal basis, and this position was also taken at rallies on January 30 by the SPD Secretary for Erfurt.[65]

Those Social Democrats who favored this Thuringian initiative were aware that it contradicted the announced policies of the *Zentralausschuss.* To the extent that this resulted from a divergence of opinion, it reflected the extent to which the SPD in the Soviet Zone has lost both ideological and organizational coherence. If the decision of February 5 is seen as resulting from a conviction in Weimar that no relief from Soviet pressure would be forthcoming from Berlin, then the decay of the party's structure in the Soviet Zone is all the more starkly demonstrated.

It was clear to the protagonists in Thuringia—Social Democrats, Soviet, and Communists—that the unity to be voted in Gotha, although it might not influence party affairs outside the Soviet Zone, was not, in any case, intended as a final act. Rather, it was to be a prelude to unity throughout the Soviet Zone. The significance of the decision in Weimar lay primarily in the situation it created for the central leadership of the SPD in the Soviet Zone.

There can be little doubt that the SMA could have applied the techniques that worked so well in Thuringia in each major portion of the Soviet Zone. Other provincial leaderships were as amenable, if not more so, to Soviet pressure and persuasion; local organizations in other areas could as readily be pressed into agreements going beyond the wishes of the party center. Indeed, the technique of one-sided interpretation of interparty agreements, pressure on local units, isolation of antiunity elements as "enemies of the working class," and pressure for a unity agreement on a partial basis—all these were applied in the provinces of the Soviet Zone other than Thuringia.

However, the political purpose of the Soviet effort was not to secure unification of the parties in any one locale, but rather to absorb the political forces represented by Social Democracy into an organized movement available, under Communist influence, for Soviet purposes.

The Soviet authorities desired this outcome in all of Germany if possible, in the Soviet Zone alone if need be. To achieve this aim, the cooperation of the central party leadership was important, for the unification process would have lost much of its political impact if scattered Social Democratic organizations had been incorporated piecemeal into the KPD. The crucial question was thus whether the existing central Social Democratic leadership in the Soviet Zone under Grotewohl could be brought to accept, formally and publicly, a merger with the KPD.

The contention has been advanced that resistance by the ZA would have resulted in the replacement of some or all of its members by Soviet intervention, or that the ZA might have been bypassed entirely by a coalition of pro-unity provincial organizations. These alternatives represented distinctly second-best arrangements for the SMA in contrast to a unification of the parties under the aegis of the officially functioning SPD leadership in the Soviet Zone. This was the objective of Soviet policy, and it was, of course, attained. To understand this development, and its relation to those events on the provincial level that have been considered above, the ZA's activities during the month from early January to mid-February 1946, must now be examined.

As the *Zentralausschuss* became aware that its interpretation of the December Conference was not shared by the public at large or, more important, by Social Democratic organizations in the Soviet Zone, it took several steps to preserve the cohesion of the party structure by informing the local party units of the "true" state of affairs.

The method chiefly employed in this effort is in itself revealing as to the state of the SPD in January 1946: the material involved was dispatched by mail or courier to local and provincial party offices, to be distributed by them to the party memberships and to be used in political discussions, including those with the KPD and SMA. The quickest and most obvious method, that of publication in the central party press, was only rarely available because Soviet censorship interfered.[66]

In a letter addressed to the provincial leaderships of the SPD, Berlin leadership asserted that inasmuch as piecemeal unification would be undesirable—"and the KPD fully agrees with this"—unification of the two parties should be decided only at national party congresses.[67] Declaring that a unity party limited to the Soviet Zone would make no sense, the ZA, quoting from an article of Max Fechner's, told the lower SPD units that "It is therefore a mistake for subordinate [party] organizations, acting out of an understandable desire for unity, to seek to unite on their own, without awaiting a resolution by the overall national leadership of the party."[68]

As it was important for the party rank and file to be aware of the official party stand, the ZA requested the provincial units to disseminate this material as rapidly as possible "in the most suitable way and with the means available to you." Inasmuch as the recipients of this advice were hoping that the ZA would be able to express these views so as to help *them,* their reaction to this advice may be imagined.

On January 15, concerned about the erosion of its position of the pace and scope of unity since the December Conference, the ZA met to consider its position further. Rejecting a strongly worded resolution offered by a minority of members,[69] it adopted one milder but no less firm in its insistent opposition to unity in the Soviet Zone alone. The ZA declared that, in reviewing its position in the light of the hostile reaction to the December Conference expressed by the SPD meetings at Hanover and Frankfurt/Main, it still stood by its position that unity should not be consummated on any basis other than an all-German one, and that separate electoral lists were a logical consequence of this. The ZA further asked all provincial organizations to desist from entering into agreements contrary to this view and, again, to propagate this ZA position among the party membership.[70]

In anticipation of the possible consequences of this action, it asked that "it be informed immediately concerning all events in . . . the Soviet Zone of Occupation which are relevant to the question of unity." In its letter of January 17 the ZA requested provincial recipients to use the January 15 resolutions in "negotiations of a local or provincial nature" presumably with the KPD "or with the Commandants."[71] Finally, and somewhat perfunctorily, the ZA pledged further cooperation at the "central" level with the KPD to intensify joint efforts at a nationwide unification of the parties.

It cannot be determined whether these wishes of the ZA were carried out. The Thuringia LV published the text of the resolution as its *Circular Letter No. 7* for 1946 (dated January 26), with instructions to act in exact accordance with the ZA position contained there,[72] but Curt Böhme has subsequently claimed that a ZA Circular Letter containing an unwelcome resolution on unity, which judging from his description of its contents could well be this one, was never sent on to local party organizations by himself and Hoffmann, because "we knew that this document would be clearly rejected by the members of our *Land* party organization."[73]

According to the ZA's statement, its declaration was not intended for the press; if so, the ZA was fortunate, because the SMA censorship forbade its publication. The Dresden SPD paper, having printed the January 15 resolution, was recalled from distribution points and destroyed on Soviet orders.[74] An incident reflecting the difficulties met by the SPD in honestly reporting party views in the party press occurred in Rostock in January 1946. The local unit of the SPD met on January 6 and resolved, in reference to the decisions of the December Conference, that unity, while remaining its goal, would have to be realized throughout all of Germany, and the decision to merge parties could flow only from the will of the membership as expressed in a referendum.

According to Dahrendorf, this resolution was reprinted in the central party organ through an oversight of the censor, but its publication in the provincial party newspaper in Schwerin was blocked by SMA censorship. Instead, the paper had to run a story attacking Social Democrats who held opinions similar to those of the Rostock resolution as "saboteurs of unity."[75] The appearance of this dispatch in the SPD press—something that could not be done for the ZA's own pronouncements—remained an isolated case. As for the Rostock and Schwerin branches of the SPD, they had both fallen into line by January 20.[76]

At its meeting on January 15 the ZA also decided to call a meeting of provincial representatives for January 25 to hear reports on the status of the unity campaign. What the ZA members already knew was ominous enough. They had heard Pieck's speech at Jena. Gniffke had just returned from a trip through the Soviet Zone and reported hearing sentiments that the leadership finally concede to SMA demands on unity so that the lower party organizations might have "peace and quiet."[77]

The reports of the provincial leaders were no more encouraging. Hoffmann reported that "the General" (i.e., Kolesnichenko) had insisted that Thuringia set an example of unity by May Day; Chemnitz officials reported that the local SMA branded as reactionary anyone not favoring immediate unity; Willi Jesse reported from Mecklenburg-Vorpommern that, while he welcomed the January 15 resolution and stood for national unity, the SMA pressed for provincial unification; Leipzig delegates complained about KPD trickery and Soviet favoritism to the Communists, but pledged firm adherence to the ZA position. Other reports were along similar lines.[78] As Gniffke put it in describing his impressions of his trip: "There was uniform pressure throughout the whole zone. The *Zentralausschuss* of the SPD had lost its freedom of maneuver."[79]

Toward the end of January the ZA's connection with the local organizations became still more tenuous. The Thuringian developments have already been described in detail. While no equally detailed record of similar events in the other provinces is available, some significant items may be mentioned. In Saxony the struggle against a pro-KPD policy took the form of attempts to remove the SPD leader, Otto Buchwitz. The Leipzig organization was particularly opposed to his policies; the Dresden group, in Buchwitz's absence, passed resolutions in its district, and once even at the LV level, calling for a membership referendum on unity. The Dresden party organization also made the main effort to unseat Buchwitz. Not much is known about this effort, but the contrast between Brill, who aroused SMA-KPD enmity and went, and Buchwitz, who had the latter's staunch support and stayed, is instructive.[80]

Saxony's "Jena" meeting was the "Meeting of the 3,000" in Dresden on January 15. It is interesting that the Leipzig organization actually refused to send a delegation to Dresden. But when two SPD functionaries, Rudolf Rothe and Stanislaw Trabalski, went as observers, they found a Leipzig "delegation" organized by the KPD. Their protests were unavailing; indeed, the SMA took advantage of Rothe's absence at a Soviet interrogation in this connection to have him removed as SPD secretary in Leipzig.[81]

The resolution adopted by this large-scale, albeit irregular, conference pledged both parties to a substantial intensification of cooperative effort leading to the goal of unity. The most important step taken was the creation by the existing joint action committee of a "joint bureau" to coordinate the work of the two parties and to settle disputes. Moreover, the ideological training of members and functionaries was to be considered on a unified basis with jointly prepared instructional material. However, unlike the Jena resolution, no specific date was set for unification in Saxony.[82] That the Dresden resolution represented a compromise with SPD opposition is clear from the speech at the rally by the KPD's Hermann Matern. Although "the forces who are most actively opposed to unity sit on the other side of the [zonal] demarcation line," there were also obstacles in Saxony. At one time, Matern asserted, Leipzig workers were proud of "being Left. Now I have the impression that the SPD leadership is not of the Left."[83]

As has been described, Soviet action was taken to remedy this "defect" in the Leipzig SPD. Despite the oppositional forces in various parts of Saxony, ever-closer collaboration with the KPD in pursuit of speedy zontal unity could not be averted. One reason, especially significant for the zonal scene, was that the provincial leadership of the SPD was used (or allowed itself to be used) to commit the party ever more closely to this policy.[84] In Dresden the SMA had at hand the instrument that had to be created in Weimar and whose forging in Berlin was the focus of politics in the Soviet Zone during January 1946.

At Magdeburg a similar situation had developed. Early cooperation with KPD and SMA, although not without its problems, had functioned tolerably well. In January, pressure for progress on unity mounted steadily; the familiar tactics were used, including lengthy interrogations, maneuvers to isolate particularly resistant SPD functionaries, and threats of arrest. The result was an enlarged district meeting with local representatives on January 31, 1946, which resolved that "certain signs" of political life in the Western zones had produced a new situation since the January 15 ZA resolution, which required that the SPD "carry out immediately all preparations for the organizational merger of the two workers' parties, and expects to receive immediately the necessary authorization for this from the [ZA]." Magdeburg would have its "peace and quiet" at last, and the ZA had lost its influence with yet another constituent unit of the party.[85]

The growing isolation of the *Zentralausschuss,* together with intensified pressure for a decision on unification in the near future, led to a last attempt to secure sort of arrangement between the ZA and the SPD leadership of the Western zones. To this end, a meeting was arranged in the British Zone city of Brunswick for February 8, 1946; Otto Grotewohl and Gustav Dahrendorf spoke for the Berlin organization, while Kurt Schumacher and a close aide, Herbert Kriedemann, represented the Hanover leadership.[86]

Although the ZA had arranged the meeting,[87] its spokesmen had few concrete proposals to offer. Apparently they suggested that Schumacher agree to the convocation of a national party congress in the foreseeable future, or at least agree to the establishment of a loose alliance between the parties on a national basis. Schumacher's reaction to this was negative. Indeed, aside from Schumacher's characteristic concentration on blocking the efforts of the ZA to extend its activity outside the Soviet Zone, most of the discussion in Brunswick centered on two issues: the divergent views of the two sides respecting long-range Soviet intentions in Germany, and the alternatives immediately available to the ZA.

Grotewohl upheld the notion, contained in so many of his speeches and articles of the previous months, that the aim of Soviet policy was to achieve security vis-a-vis Germany by bringing about specific transformations of Germany's political arrangements. Chief among these arrangements was the creation of a political representation of the working class that would prevent the future rise of a Germany hostile to the USSR. To this end, Soviet policy would acquiesce in the establishment of a parliamentary system in Germany, if such a system were dominated by a strong socialist political force. To Schumacher the chief aim of Soviet policy was to dominate Germany and central Europe by political means; for this purpose, the Soviet Union required "standing political armies" to be "at its disposal" at all crucial points of European politics. In Germany this was to be the unity party, which would be created by the KPD's "conquest" of the SPD. Soviet power made this unavoidable in the Soviet Zone. Given this divergence of views, it is not surprising that the two sides failed to come closer on questions of the party's future.

As far as the situation in the Soviet Zone was concerned, the ZA representatives conceded

> that the pace and content of the movement toward a unity party were no longer under their influence. . . . The tactic of playing for time was no longer feasible. Besides, the essential basis for this tactic—some prospect of the lifting of zonal borders—was no longer to be expected realistically.[88]

This amounted to a confession that the policy followed by the ZA since at least the December Conference was bankrupt. Logically, therefore, it could be asked (as Schumacher did) what the ZA intended to do now? It could reject unity and face Soviet opposition;[89] it could dissolve the party in the Soviet Zone, thus simultaneously escaping from and testifying to the intensity of pressures for unity; finally, it could go along with unity and hope to play a significant role in the united party. At this confrontation, Grotewohl and Dahrendorf rejected the first two of these alternatives; the decision of February 11, although not arrived at without further struggle, logically was consistent with the third.

The Berlin spokesmen correctly told Schumacher that "The ZA had sought to relieve [pressure] on the districts by assuming full responsibility for unification at the zonal level. But at the first sign of hesitance on the part of the ZA, pressure on the subordinate units [of the party] so increased that today it is from this source that demands for unity come."[90]

Continued ZA opposition would lead to SPD district organizations uniting with the KPD. Schumacher's retort that 90 percent of the SPD rank and file in the Soviet Zone opposed unity, even if true, was irrelevant—as Grotewohl promptly pointed out, by reminding him that (given public membership lists, etc.) individual opposition to unity could not be maintained. Individuals could not accomplish what collective-leadership bodies were unable to do. On the other hand, an attempt by the ZA to dissolve the party in the Soviet Zone, a measure that both speakers declared had been considered at length, was too late, since those Social Democrats susceptible to various pressures would then opt for unity.

The idea of a voluntary dissolution of the party, of political suicide as a demonstrative gesture, has been cited as the most meaningful political action available to the ZA.[91] There were, however, powerful obstacles to such a course; not least of them was the feeling that, in doing this, the ZA would be guilty of abandoning the rank-and-file members of the party. Gniffke recorded his feeling that the ZA members had an obligation to the party masses; Klingelhöfer rejected any such shifting of responsibility from ZA to the rank and file; Rothe called the idea "fantastic"—if only because too many members were for some form of unity or close cooperation, even if not for the particular form and time proposed by the KPD.[92]

The course of action that remained—to seek to maximize Social Democratic influence in the unity party—seemed the only consistent response open to the ZA. It would be necessary "to influence the unification . . . in time and content through their own initiative," which

would be possible because of the Social Democrats' greater "self-asser-
tiveness." In any event, a unity party in the Soviet Zone was now
"unavoidable"; what mattered was "to organize Social Democratic
thinking and bring it to bear politically."[93] Although many Social
Democrats in the Soviet Zone shared this point of view (and in fact took
it into the SED with them), it is possible to see it as a desperate rationalization of the ZA's situation. There was, of course, no lack of
skeptics. At the Brunswick meeting, Schumacher several times asked
whether such hopes were justified either by the party's experiences or
expectations; Klingelhöfer wrote to Grotewohl at this time that to hope
for a permeation of the unity party with Social Democratic content was
"too childish to even deserve being spoken of."[94]

No meaningful accomodation between the Eastern and Western
branches of the party emerged from this meeting, not even the loose
"cartel relationship" that Klingelhöfer had strongly hoped would give
the Soviet Union an alternative preferable to zonal unity.[95] When, at the
meeting, Schumacher arranged for a trip to Berlin later in February, it
was not to further plans for cooperation with the ZA but rather to begin,
in effect, his intervention in the internal struggle within the Berlin SPD.
Ironically, it had been Klingelhöfer's hope that Soviet policy toward the
SPD might be changed precisely in order to prevent such Western intervention in an area of Soviet influence.

The Brunswick meeting was the last occasion when SPD leaders from
the Soviet and Western zones of Germany met to consider common problems and policy. We have previously noted that the SPD, unlike the
KPD, did not have a generally acknowledged postwar national
leadership. The men of the *Zentralausschuss* (unlike Schumacher) were
never quite clear in their own minds whether they wished to be
"trustees" of the SPD in the Soviet Zone while awaiting the reestablishment of an all-German party, or whether they themselves wished
to attain national leadership. In the fall and winter of 1945-1946, in any
case, the ZA claimed only a share of the leadership of a still disunited
German Social Democracy.

If, however, the West German SPD did not go along with the policy
of merging the parties, then the ZA was thrust back into the Soviet
Zone—since the "national" aspect of the unity tissue was its remaining
argument for delay. Had the Schumacher leadership offered some com-

promise on this issue, the ZA might have been able to avoid an immediate decision on unification of the parties. To Schumacher, since the ZA's cause seemed hopeless in any case, no compromise was worthwhile.

A meeting of the SPD leadership in the Soviet Zone that would make fundamental decisions concerning the party's future course was now no longer avoidable. This was the consequence of the ZA attitudes discussed above, taken together with the outcome of the meeting with Schumacher and Kriedemann, and set against the background of ever-mounting Soviet and KPD pressure. Although there still may have been advocates of further delay, it was entirely reasonable for Grotewohl to call a meeting of the ZA together with provincial chairmen of the SPD for February 10.[96]

The SPD meeting of February 10–11, 1946, heard Grotewohl deliver the main speech. After describing to the session how the discussions in Brunswick had not brought the prospect of a national party congress nearer, but had rather produced from Schumacher the suggestion that the SPD dissolve itself in the Soviet Zone, he asked:

> I ask you, Comrades, is that what you want? In May and June 1945, were we not ready to enter a united workers' party, even if our only choice had been the party that now exists alongside ours? Just what is supposed to have changed in this fundamental position? Nothing has changed; We have just lost time. Had we carried out the unification three-quarters of a year ago, or had the Occupation regime only permitted one workers' party, not only would we not have lost any time, but we would have saved ourselves many a headache. Today the Central Committee of the KPD and the Occupation power also realize this. . . . What shall we do, now that the proposal of the KPD to merge the two parties by Easter or May 1 is before us? In my opinion we must approve this proposal and carry out the unification on one of these two dates.[97]

This statement is notable for its omissions and evasions; it was not clear that the mass of Social Democrats were prepared to join the KPD at war's end, for the "one workers' party" that many advocated was to be neither of the old parties; furthermore, as Grotewohl well knew, much had changed in the months since then: the record of the relationship between the KPD and SPD and the KPD's preferential treatment by the SMA. It was possible to overlook or minimize this history, but to ignore it was a deliberate political act. It clearly was such an act for Grotewohl; on the morning of the 11th he told Gniffke, "We cannot withdraw and allow the membership to slide into an inevitable unification."[98]

Similarly, Dahrendorf's rebuttal in the debate on February 10 reflected his decision that the ZA must reject the unity proposal and, if need be, dissolve the party in the Soviet Zone.[99] This was the substance of the resolution he presented to the meeting and, consistently, it pointed precisely to the events of past three-quarters of the year as justification for his proposals. In the course of further discussion, various ZA members expressed opposition to or reservations about the unity proposal; the views of the provincial representatives were more favorable, but even here approval of the KPD offer was justified with resigned acceptance of the inevitable.[100]

The vote that followed the discussion took place in an atmosphere of confusion. The only actual count given anywhere has the ZA voting 6 to 5 with one abstention and two absences *against unity as proposed.*[101] It seems clear in any case that the ZA at first decided to reject the project for unity before May Day. This produced what Gniffke calls an "indescribable tumult." He writes:

> Moltmann (Schwerin), Buchwitz (Dresden), and Hoffmann. (Weimar) sprang up, shouted, and gesticulated. ZA members shouted back. The session seemed about to dissolve in chaos. . . . Out of the shouting could be understood only: "We're through with the *Zentralausschuss,*" and "the [party] districts will be united."[102]

Fechner (the chairman) finally made himself heard and, explaining that two participants had mistakenly voted the wrong way, recessed the meeting until the following morning.

Further discussion on the 11th revealed no new positions and when another vote was taken the unity offer was accepted. The official resolution read:

> The *Zentralausschuss* of the Social Democratic Party of Germany, after consultation with representatives of the districts, has resolved to present the question of the unity of the two workers' parties to the membership for decision as soon as possible.
> Negotiations with representatives of the Western zones having shown that the convocation of a national party congress is not possible in the foreseeable future, the *Zentralausschuss* will therefore convoke a party congress for the Soviet Zone of Occupation, inclusive of Berlin, as soon as

possible. This party congress, which is to be preceded by district and provincial party congresses, shall decide the question of the unification of the two parties.[103]

The resolution set no dates for these meetings (this was done at a party meeting of February 19),[104] although the Thuringian decisions for meetings April 6/7, together with the goal of unity by May Day, did not leave much time for the announced party congresses.

The most interesting aspects of the resolution are one item mentioned and one omitted. With a careful reference to Western obstacles to a *Reichsparteitag*, the ZA tried to justify its retreat from all of its previously announced positions opposing unity in only a single zone. The logic of the resolution reduced the need for a nationwide, all SPD decision on unity to a desirable but hardly essential condition, whereas for many Social Democrats it had been almost self-evident that a party that traditionally and intensively advocated a centralized national state should not pursue differing policies in the various zones (the very practice that they attributed to "reactionary," "federalist" intriguers).

Moreover, the seemingly democratic, open-ended reliance on the judgment of district, provincial, and zonal congresses belied the plain and well-known situation in which the party bodies subordinate to the ZA had already succumbed to Soviet pressure on the unity issue. Only the ZA could have attempted to resist this pressure. In "asking" the lower levels of the party for guidance, the ZA was sure in advance of getting the answer that it had sought to avoid since early January— immediate unity in the Soviet Zone.

This decision of February 11 also marked the breakup of the *Zentralausschuss*. Of those who had voted against the proposal, one (Dahrendorf) would soon leave Berlin altogether; two (Germer and Neubecker) would aid dissident Berlin Social Democrats to break away from the ZA. For the record, however, the acknowledged leadership of the party in the Soviet Zone had agreed to unity with the KPD on terms that hardly corresponded to its own views. In the Soviet Zone, at least, the SMA had thus secured that image of the voluntary creation of the political instrument it desired.

After the ZA vote on February 11, Grotewohl appeared at a zonal trade union meeting to read the ZA resolution cited above.[105] As Ulbricht and Tiul'panov had done,[106] he allowed himself to be impressed by the apparent desire of provincial delegates for *political* unity of the working class. In a massive understatement, Grotewohl commented on the events of the past two days as follows: "I am . . . of the opinion that if, as now seems clear in the various districts to the Soviet Zone, the membership of both parties is more convinced than ever of the need for unification, it will soon give a positive answer to the question of an early date for unification."[107]

Or as Franz Dahlem put it, party unity was "within reach."[108] In the Soviet Zone the struggle to maintain an autonomous Social Democratic policy on the future of the party, its role in Germany politics, and its relationship to the KPD had ended. What remained to be done was to consummate the victory.

CHAPTER 9

The Establishment of
the Unity Party

February to May 1946

Following the ZA's decision of February 11, 1946, in favor of unification with the KPD, the political life of Berlin and the Soviet Zone was transformed. A new party, claiming to be the product of Communist-Social Democratic merger (the Socialist Unity Party of Germany [*Sozialistische Einheitspartei Deutschlands*], SED), was established. In the provinces of the Soviet Zone, separate SPD and KPD party congresses, followed by a unification congress, were held on April 6 and 7, 1946 (in Berlin on April 13 and 14); for the Soviet Zone as a whole, the separate party congresses took place on April 19 and 20, the unification congress on April 21 and 22, 1946. At almost the same time, an autonomous SPD, dissenting from the policies of the ZA, emerged in the Western sectors of Berlin and succeeded in establishing itself throughout the city. Its founding congress was held on April 7, 1946.[1]

From the Soviet perspective, this was an ambiguous outcome. On the one hand, an important goal of Soviet policy had been achieved after some months of strenuous effort and maneuver. There was now a party based in Berlin and formed by the official leaderships of the SPD and KPD in the Soviet Zone, which might reasonably aspire to political leadership of the working class in all of Germany. Yet in the very process of consolidating this triumph, its limitations were revealed, for although provincial resistance to SPD-KPD unification after February 11 was sporadic and ineffective, the residence of elements within the Berlin SPD organization culminated in a successful challenge to the ZA line.

In practice, Berlin politics since the end of the war had been a part of the politics of the Soviet Zone; each major political development had produced similar effects in Berlin and in the zone. This situation had not thus far been affected by the presence of the other occupation powers. It was thus quite reasonable to expect that the SPD decision of February 11 would also commit the Berlin party. This would have meant that the politics of the old capital—an area only partially under Soviet occupation—would have been fitted into the new pattern designed for all of Germany.

Despite the existence and activity of the Allied Kommandatura, by the spring of 1946 each of the four sectors of Berlin was in practice an extension of each power's zone of occupation. This difference between Berlin and the Soviet Zone points up the extent to which political developments in the Soviet Zone were dependent on the will of the occupying power, and therefore showed the limitations of the Soviet achievement. It was a first clear indication that the all-German potential of Soviet policy might not be realized; it raised the question of the political cost of the Soviet victory in the Soviet Zone in terms of Soviet aims throughout Germany; finally, it was a prophetic indication that conflicting political systems might arise from within the battered society of postwar Germany.

One limiting factor affecting the Soviet victory became apparent in the problems faced by the *Zentralausschuss* as it strove to implement its decision of February 11. To begin with, the acceptance of unity within the limits of the Soviet Zone occasioned internal conflict in the ZA. At least two of its members who had opposed that decision, Karl J. Germer, Jr. and Fritz Neubecker, became active supporters of the dissident faction within the Berlin party organization. Their increasingly open opposition to the official ZA line eventually led to their expulsion in March and April from both the ZA and the party by the Grotewohl leadership. They were joined in their oppositional activity and in its consequences by Grotewohl's once intimate staff collaborator, Gustav Klingelhöfer.[2]

More striking was the defection of the man who in June 1945 had been an enthusiastic advocate of immediate and close cooperation with the KPD—Gustav Dahrendorf. In a deeply felt letter addressed to Gniffke and Grotewohl,[3] he informed them of his intention to leave Berlin for Hamburg. While striving to assure his colleagues that his actions were not motivated by personal hostility toward them, he declared that it was important to resolve "a political problem by a political decision." The "problem" was clearly the unification of the parties in the Soviet Zone: "This is how I see things; here I must subordinate myself, there I still see a task to be done! Given the way I see Germany's problems, I cannot decide otherwise. . . . For me the place to fight is over there!"[4]

Although these incidents must have been embarrassing for the ZA leadership around Grotewohl,[5] it is significant most ZA members swallowed their disagreements with the schedule of unification to which their party was now committed and maintained an outward solidarity on this issue. Such behavior corresponded to that of the party membership as a whole. Further opposition to the projected merger from SPD organizations at the provincial level was, under the circumstances, not to be expected, and with few exceptions it was not forthcoming.[6]

Despite complaints registered by provincial delegates, the party leadership meeting of February 19 voted approval of the ZA's action of February 11, including the announced schedule of zonal party congresses for mid-April;[7] it also specifically expressed its confidence in Grotewohl and approved circulation of the drafts for the unity party's statute and programmatic declaration.[8]

The obliging Thuringia LV was used by the SMA to exert pressure on the recalcitrant Berlin organization. In an "Open Letter" from the LV to the Berlin comrades,[9] the Thuringians expressed their long-standing admiration for the Berliners, but also their concern that in the March 1 meeting (discussed below) ". . . factually unfounded complaints . . . were raised . . . against Comrade Otto Grotewohl, whom we hold in esteem. . . . It would, in any case, be tawdry and very shameful if the Berlin Social Democrats, far from assuming the leadership in the creation of the [SED], as befits the citizens of the nation's capital, were to allow themselves to be driven by adventurers into total isolation and thence into the dangerous waters of sectarianism and separation." Not revealed at the time was that this letter, (by Hoffmann's admission) had been written at the express direction of the SMA.[10]

Although overt SPD opposition to the unification of the parties in the Soviet Zone vanished outside of Berlin, the forces formerly opposed to the merger continued to press for the infusion of Social Democratic content into the new party. The chief vehicle for this attempt was the insistance that the residential party cell (*Wohnbezirksgruppe*) be made the primary unit of the new organization. The SPD had been traditionally organized in this fashion, whereas the KPD had reorganized itself in the 1920s so as to emphasize the "factory cell" (*Betriebsgruppe*).[11] Efforts had been made in the winter of 1945–1946 to increase the number of such *Betriebsgruppen* in the SPD, largely to compete with the KPD for the workers' allegiance, now that the trade unions were ostensibly nonpartisan.[12] Behind the screen provided by this issue it is easy to see the lost fight for SPD autonomy being carried on in a new guise—often by the same individuals and with the same attitudes.[13]

This issue produced the only real argument at the SPD zonal congress.[14] The joint SPD-KPD study commission set up at the December conference had agreed on a compromise whereby the two types of basic organizational units would have coordinate status.[15] Helmuth Lehmann reported to the SPD congress of April 19–20 on this point, declaring that the SPD had formerly been a vote-getting organization but should now concentrate more on the *Betriebsgruppe*. He was met with a hail of lively objections from the floor.[16]

Lehmann now had to defend the commission's formulation on its true basis, that it was a necessary compromise to secure KPD agreement. This Communist view had been put succinctly by the party newspaper when it commented that "Any workers' party is based, in the last analysis, on these very factory workers."[17] Lehmann declared:

> Comrades, let us not forget that we wish to bring about a closer and more fraternal relationship with the comrades of the [KPD]. (Objections.) That is the sense and purpose of our unification. The [KPD] has for years and with great success organized factory cells. (Disturbance.) . . . and it is perfectly clear that the KPD will not abandon this organizational principle without further ado. (Lively disturbance.) Comrades, the unification of the two parties cannot very well proceed without mutual agreements. If we wish to reach an agreement (Interjection: We want to vote!), then both parties must be ready to make concessions. (Unrest.)[18]

But, as a Leipzig delegate put it, "we must have the courage to go our own way . . . what was of value in our organization must be preserved."[19] Arno Wend denied that the advocates of the *Wohnbezirks-gruppe* were hidden foes of unity.[20] Despite conciliatory remarks by Gniffke,[21] a Dresden resolution was adopted expressing the old SPD views on this question.[22]

At the SPD-KPD unity congress that followed, the compromise providing for both kinds of primary units was restored although not without "exceptionally lively discussion."[23] In the SED Statute as adopted by the unity congress, the following formulation is used:

> The party is organized into a) residential groups [*Wohnbezirksgruppen*] and factory [i.e., place of work] groups [*Betriebsgruppen*]. . . . Party members who are active in a place of work belong to the group at work and are obligated to *participate actively in it. They are obligated in addition to participate in the activity of that residential or locality group to which they belong.* . . . Party members who do not belong to a [*Betriebsgruppe*] shall belong to a [*Wohnbezirksgruppe*].[24] (Italics added.)

Thus the primacy of the *Betriebsgruppe* was achieved in the final version of the party statute.

Although the question of the unity party's primary organizational unit was obviously of some significance for the future character of that party, it seems clear from the vehemence of the debate and from the identity of the participants in it that this issue owed its prominence to residual discontent with the unification. Under these circumstances, it is significant that this fight was lost so readily. The need to abandon the wishes of the delegates to the SPD's own congress in order to preserve the projected compromise arrangement with the KPD was but one example of the logical consequences of the primary commitment to "unity" on the scale and at the pace proposed by the KPD. The harsh reality of the situation was illustrated by the fact that many former provincial opponents of a zonal unification participated in the final unification process.

Many Social Democrats in the Soviet Zone more or less grudgingly accepted their new situation. They were still pledged to "unity" as an ultimate ideal; they hoped that the new unity party might be sufficiently influenced by an influx of Social Democrats (who would bring with them their own ideas and style of work) to be something better than a thinly disguised Communist Party; they felt ties of loyalty to comrades and subordinates in the party who were going along with the merger (for whatever reason). The only realistic alternative—if they remained in the

Soviet Zone—was retirement from political activity. This was a painful prospect for the many Social Democrats who had waited and hoped for the opportunity to resume political work during the twelve years of Nazi domination. In any case, most of the known provincial opponents of unity went along into the new party. Indeed, some of these functionaries occupied notable, albeit not leading, positions at both the SPD's zonal congress and the subsequent unity congress in April 1946.[25]

Developments in the Berlin SPD did not proceed so smoothly.[26] As noted, the Berlin SPD organization had reacted with suspicion to the announced results of the December Conference. Its members welcomed any sign that the ZA would continue to defer any zonal merger of the parties. Thus, after the ZA's ill-fated January 15 resolution, the Berlin functionaries met on the 20th and pledged their support for the ZA to the extent that this policy would be maintained.[27]

These dissident views of the Berlin membership and middle level functionaries were reflected in the wavering attitude of Berlin's SPD leadership. As the struggle over unity sharpened, it found itself increasingly attempting to mediate between the ZA and the lower levels of its organization. Unlike the other provincial leaderships of the SPD, the Berlin leadership did not press the ZA toward unity. Compared with the rest of the Soviet Zone proper, party life in Berlin continued to lag in matters of joint activities; nor were the Berliners energetic in arranging cooperation with the KPD, let alone in advocating speedy unification.[28]

Rank-and-file sentiment in the Berlin SPD did not divide along sector lines. As early as January 1946, however, overt opposition to the ZA on the part of local leaders tended to be concentrated in the Berlin boroughs located in the Western sectors. These oppositional leaders in the Berlin SPD were quite varied in age, occupation, and pre-Hitler activity; they were united by the important circumstance that they occupied lower-level positions within the party (borough chairman or secretary, for example) which they could use to mobilize sentiment and action against the ZA.[29]

Anticipating the future trend of ZA policies, they began to plan their activities as early as February 9.[30] Their first attack on the ZA came at the meeting of borough and section leaders on February 17. The events of February 11 having become known, the opposition forces introduced a resolution withdrawing "confidence" in both the ZA and the party leadership of Berlin. The ZA was characterized as a "non-elected body," and, through its February 11 decision, to have relinquished the right to reach decisions "binding on the Social Democracy of the whole of Germany." A new Berlin party congress was demanded to replace the city's leadership; the ZA, apparently, was simply to be disavowed.[31]

The possibility that this resolution might be adopted by the meeting caused the ZA to add an unscheduled speaker to the program—Otto Grotewohl.[32] His eloquence, his reputation with the Berlin Social Democrats, and, especially, one promise he made, enabled him to turn the sentiment of the meeting away from the opposition. Grotewohl's crucial promise was his statement that the forthcoming zonal SPD congress would in fact be transformed into an all-German party congress through the inclusion of the West German delegates.[33]

The conference of February 17 adopted a resolution presented by the Berlin leadership regretting that the ZA "had been unable" to insert into the December Conference resolutions an explicit statement that unity required a national party congress. This background gives added significance to the operative paragraph:

> The Conference welcomes the declaration of Comrade Grotewohl to the effect that an effort is being made to replace the zonal party congress with one at which, given the approval of the three Western [occupation] powers, delegates from the French, English, and American Zones shall participate.

The meeting was thus soothed with all-German pledges, but it also voted that, "in the event of substantive changes" in the political situation, a conference of identical composition was to be called.[34] Such changes were soon forthcoming. As has been noted, the party leadership met on February 19 to approve the February 11 decision and set up a schedule of provincial and zonal congresses to translate that decision into fact. On February 26 the "Second Conference of the Sixty"—a conference intended as the sequel to the December Conference—was held in Berlin; it received the report of the Study Commission that the earlier meeting had set up.[35] At this meeting the dates were set for the final separate zonal congresses of the SPD and KPD (the SPD's "40th" and the KPD's "15th") and for the unification congress. The draft declaration on "Fundamentals and Goals" of the unity party was approved, and the Study Commission, transformed into an organizational committee, was charged with elaborating a draft statute, preparing for the amalgamation of the party central bodies and press organs, and arranging for the publication of a joint theoretical monthly to be called *Unity* (*Einheit*). Similar bodies were to be set up on the lower levels of both parties and, as the unification progressed, each party was to elect half of the new party's leadership at each level. These steps were promptly endorsed by the provincial organizations of the SPD outside of Berlin.[36]

The Berlin Opposition came to the functionaries' conference of March 1 armed with more than resentment of the party leadership. Heartened by assurances of support from Schumacher,[37] its spokesmen were prepared to offer a positive alternative to the official unification schedule. On February 23 the SPD of the French Sector borough of Reinickendorf, under the leadership of Franz Neumann, had adopted a resolution advocating a referendum on unity within the SPD; this resolution was adopted on March 1 by over 2,000 Berlin SPD functionaries.[38] Equally important, the March 1 meeting was marked by the openly hostile reception given to the main speaker—Otto Grotewohl.[39] Grotewohl warned eloquently that only a united socialist party could guard German democracy. Moreover he sought (unsuccessfully) to dispel the chief grounds for the opposition to the ZA policy by insisting that that policy had been unchanging and consistent from June 1945 to March 1946. According to Grotewohl the only issues that had arisen were minor points of tactics; he defended the ZA decision of February 11 on the dual ground of Schumacher's intransigence and pressure from the provincial SPD. There were, he insisted, no "opponents of unity"; this was possibly true but irrelevant if the abstract idea of unity was what Grotewohl meant, inasmuch as the grounds for opposition to the ZA lay precisely in the immediate experiences of political activity since the formation of the parties. Actually Grotewohl seems to have recognized the sources of disaffection, for a major portion of his speech dealt with the record of the KPD. Arguing in great detail, he defended the KPD on its past record and its commitment to democracy and to a genuinely national German policy.[40]

The meeting on March 1 signified that a psychological rift had opened between the ZA and the Berlin functionaries over the legitimacy of the ZA's leadership in the party. The adoption of a call for a referendum signified disapproval of the ZA's stewardship of the party and especially

of its decisions on unity during February 1946. To the contestants for
SPD leadership in Hanover, Berlin, and London there had now been
added a dissident Berlin group. This group, by threatening to withdraw
from ZA control a part of the party that had been operating under SMA
influence since the war's end, embodied a potential limitation to the
reach of Soviet policy. It thus drew upon itself the political wrath of the
SMA and KPD. Soviet opposition to the proposed referendum, however
dubious on tactical grounds, was a consistent application of this fundamental hostility.

The ZA's and KPD's first reactions to the tumultuous scenes of the
first of March were ones of cautious and evasive disapproval. *Das Volk*
was jolly but vague as to what had occurred:

> It was a very lively meeting! Well, there have always been stormy
> disagreements in the socialist movement, and they didn't always do us
> harm! The Berlin Social Democracy, in particular, can pride itself on
> having always had lively discussions which were filled with a spirit of
> honest conviction and deep commitment to socialism, and which were useful
> for the party as a whole.[41]

Speaking on March 2 to a national KPD conference, Grotewohl
served notice that ZA policy would continue as before; the views of the
Berlin opposition were to be disregarded: "I am certain that yesterday's
meeting of functionaries in Berlin did not represent the clear position of
Berlin's Social Democrats. *I am especially certain that there cannot be
the slightest doubt concerning our decision on unification*"[42] (Italics
added.)

This assertion, which doubtless pleased his KPD audience, meant that
Grotewohl viewed the March 1 vote not as an injunction to be implemented but rather as a challenge to be defeated. Moreover, in identifying
the causes for this split, he declared that the Berlin developments were
"by no means in the first instance" a dispute among Social Democrats,
but rather a consequence of the fact that "Berlin is a city divided into
four zones. The whole situation in Berlin would be different, if Berlin
were not thus divided." The alternatives posed here were by no means
exclusive: there *was* genuine disagreement among Social Democrats, and
Berlin's four-power status *did* make a difference. What is difficult to see
is how this view of Grotewohl's can be reconciled with his oft-repeated
assertion that Social Democrats of the Soviet Zone had never "inwardly"

recognized the zonal divisions. Why the Social Democrats of Berlin, who had been sharing the same political world as those of the Soviet Zone, should now react differently was not explained.

The KPD stand on a referendum, as expressed on March 2 by Wilhelm Pieck, was rather conciliatory. Calling the demand for a referendum understandable, he warned that the "SPD comrades" must remember that a great mass of new members had joined the SPD within the last few months. These members are poorly instructed concerning the "history of Social Democracy, about the old struggles, and especially about the Communist Party and about the necessity which demands unification." A thorough campaign of "education" was needed so that the projected referendum would produce a pro-unity result.[43]

In these circumstances the SPD leadership responded by arranging for a referendum in the Berlin party but not elsewhere in the Soviet Zone. First the Berlin party leadership met on March 4 and 7 and announced that a referendum open to those who were party members as of March 1 would be held in Berlin on March 31. This announcement, although accompanied by pro-unity arguments, was a concession to the Berlin Opposition qualified only by the assertion that the "final position of the Berlin party" would be decided at the Berlin party congress on April 7.[44]

On that same day, the ZA and provincial leadership, meeting together, rejected the recommendation of the March 1 resolution that a referendum be held throughout the Soviet Zone. A referendum was rejected "fundamentally and on technical grounds. . . . Votes of this sort cannot encroach upon the resolution of the party congresses."[45] The notion of a referendum in the Soviet Zone outside of Berlin was, under the circumstances, a forlorn and perhaps naive hope.[46] Although the idea of a referendum had come up at various times in some provincial organizations, there was not organized support for it. This relieved the SMA of the onus of prohibiting it; in Berlin, however, the local SPD leadership had arranged for the referendum and, as March 31 approached, the SMA faced the tactical decision of whether to allow it to be held in the Soviet sector of the city.

Meanwhile the SPD in Berlin slowly disintegrated under the pressure of the struggle between the ZA and the opposition. The ZA gradually backed away from its conditional approval of the referendum. An editorial in *Das Volk* attacked the whole idea as unprecedented, in conflict with the system of party congresses, and too open to influence by recent members.[47] In a public appeal to Berlin's Social Democrats, the ZA reviewed and defended its policies on unity, attacked the opposition for its actions (especially the conduct of the March 1 meeting), and called upon the party's factory group officials "who must undertake the major share of the task of opinion-formation in a working class party," to demonstrate the requisite sense of unity and discipline.[48] Finally, on March 27, while again inviting all SPD organizations in Germany to send delegates to its party congress in Berlin, and disparaging the standing of a referendum, the ZA formally called on the Berlin Social Democrats not to participate in the planned referendum.[49]

The referendum of March 31, 1946, concerned the scope and nature of SPD-KPD relations. There were two questions. The first asked: "Are you for the immediate merger of both workers' parties?" The second question asked: "Are you for an alliance of both parties that would guarantee cooperative effort and exclude fratricidal conflict?"[50] Although electoral arrangements were somewhat harried and informal, there is no significant evidence of fraud or administrative distortion of the results. (Perhaps in consequence of the informality of the arrangements, the precise vote totals are hard to determine, but the returns do not vary significantly.) The crucial figure is that of the total potential electorate; the most reasonable figure for SPD membership in the three Western sectors of Berlin (where the referendum was permitted) is 33,247. The total vote cast was 23,755. On the first question, 2,940 voted for immediate fusion, 19,529 against; on the second question, 14,763 approved cooperation with the KPD, 5,559 did not.[51] Most Communist and pro-merger comment has been based on the membership figures for all of Berlin, so as to demonstrate that only a minority of Social Democrats opposed immediate unity. A more sophisticated version of this view is based on a western-sector membership figure of 39,000-plus and thus (by ignoring the matter of the *actual vote cast*) can claim that less than half of the SPD opposed immediate unity.[52]

The immediate postreferendum reaction of the KPD and SPD (i.e., pro-ZA) press was to denigrate the results. Thus the KPD's newspaper headlined, "For Workers Unity," and "Defeat of the Foes of Unity in Berlin," claiming that "only" 5,559 were "against workers' unity."[53] *Das Volk* proclaimed the "Defeat of the Splitters," and stressed supposed irregularities and an allegedly small turnout.[54] As for the prohibition of the vote in the Soviet Sector, *DVZ* claimed that those eight boroughs had "already decided for unity"; *Das Volk* commented that "preparations" had not been completed in time for a vote there.[55]

By any reasonable interpretation of the results, however, the referendum was a defeat for the SMA's policy on the unity question. The advocates of that policy held the positions of authority in their party organizations, and had available far superior material means to disseminate their views and organize support for them. The vote in Berlin was a vote against "unity of action" as it had been practiced for nine months, against the unity program being offered by the ZA. It provided eloquent testimony to both the potential for cooperation among SPD members and the extent to which this potential had been dissipated in actual practice.

Both the referendum questions and results pretty accurately reflected the outlook of the SPD in Berlin. Most Social Democrats saw unity as a desirable step. Their objections centered on the particular tactics of the KPD since the war's end. An outright rejection of the KPD, no matter how "logical," simply did not correspond to the political ideals of most Social Democrats; on the other hand, their idea of "cooperation" was not simple acceptance of KPD proposals. To hold that an SPD vote for cooperation indicates a misguided but genuine urge to "really" support unity as proposed by the KPD, is to assume that either cooperation or unity is possible only on the KPD's terms.

The very fact of holding the referendum reflects the lack of legitimate party leadership. For a provisional leadership in a turbulent and unprecedented situation, the ZA was hardly the least legitimate party leadership imaginable; the dispute that produced a referendum concerned whether the ZA had enough authority to take so important a step—especially one that, no matter how limited in intent or effect to the Soviet Zone, could not help but deeply influence the SPD in the remainder of Germany.

The ZA was firmly committed to as great an extent of party cohesion as possible. Its overtures to the Western zones, if futile, were nonetheless sincere; its ready response to provincial pressures in early February demonstrated similar motives. Quite aside from responding to Social Democratic tradition, and without necessarily seeking a solid front against the KPD, the ZA had an interest in leading a cohesive party; indeed, the closer the collaboration with the KPD, the greater the incentive to match the latter leadership's solid party base. Thus the ZA was extremely reluctant to break with any substantial group within the SPD. Not until mid-March did it accept the logic of the KPD's view that those who resisted the unity schedule, regardless of their party membership, were to be considered enemies and fought as such.[56]

In the end, of course, the ZA's efforts to maintain a united SPD in the Soviet Zone—and to lead that united party into a merger with the KPD—collapsed. By April 1946 the ZA was presiding over a party that, in the provinces of the Soviet Zone, had been used against it by the SMA and that, in Berlin, had successfully challenged its leadership.

It is ironic that in these circumstances the ZA undertook deliberately to proclaim itself to be an all-German SPD leadership and claimed to be planning an all-German party congress in Berlin April. This was, in fact, a fairly obvious tactic, practically forced on it by the circumstances of its position. That these claims would be challenged and lead to a further exacerbation of relations between Schumacher and the ZA was assured by Schumacher's declaration, during his visit to Berlin, that no official delegates from the Western zones would appear at the ZA's party congress.[57] When a ZA invitation was officially extended anyway, the Hanover leadership responded with a threat to expel from the SPD anyone attending the zonal congress in Berlin.[58]

The ZA responded to this with an "Open letter" to Schumacher, repeating the claims to legitimacy of the "Fechner-Weimann group," pointing out truthfully enough that between October 1945 and February 1946 all the initiatives for Social Democratic cooperation had come from the ZA side.[59] Now the ZA appealed to the party in the Western zones, and to its leadership, to aid in the cause of unity by sending delegates to the forthcoming SPD congress in Berlin.

In this connection the events of June 17, 1945, were embellished to suggest that among the functionaries assembled on that date were 300 acting as "representatives" of the party in the Western zones. This claim was repeated and expanded in the following weeks and has become a staple of SED accounts.[60] This mythical "all-German endorsement" indicates how strongly the ZA felt the need to counter the argument that in agreeing to zonal unity it was splitting the SPD, the workers' movement, and Germany itself. Fechner declared that the ZA had always regarded the zonal borders as "temporary technical arrangements of the Occupation forces" and had always tried to act on a national basis "as the KPD has done."(!)[61]

Speaking to the Berlin functionaries' meeting of March 1, Grotewohl complained that

> The Berlin *Zentralausschuss* and the Social Democrats of the eastern zone have never, as Socialists, inwardly acknowledged the validity of the zonal borders. Whereas we wished to create conditions favorable for German unity through our influence on the party rank and file throughout Germany regardless of zonal borders, Hanover has always insisted on the zonal borders and demanded decision-making powers [*Bestimmungsrecht*] for itself.[62]

Thus in Grotewohl's view, the lack of a unified SPD was attributable to various Social Democrats' incorrect subjective attitudes toward the zonal borders. Questions of reconstructing a party leadership were ignored, and differences in policy, most especially on the unity issue, were treated as nonexistent. Hence the deplorable condition, for which Grotewohl offered no deeper explanation, that "despite all zonal borders, the views of the KPD formed the basis of a political line *for all of Germany*, whereas in the Social Democratic Party each zone developed its own political viewpoint."[63] (Italics in original.)

The ZA's good intentions in this regard are beyond question, but disregarding the zonal lines was hardly realistic, and comparing the KPD's centralized party structure, with an intact emigré leadership, to the fragmented postwar condition of the SPD, was typical of the ZA's willful misperception of the KPD.

By inviting delegates from the Western zones to a party congress called by the ZA, the Berlin leadership hoped to establish the claim that this congress was not a zonal congress but was, in fact, the widely desired all-German congress. According to Gniffke, "the *Zentralausschuss* [has] not convoked a zonal party congress, but rather a [national] party congress."[64] Having in its view done all it could to secure the convocation of such a party congress, and having been blocked by Schumacher, the ZA felt justified in claiming an all-German basis for the forthcoming zonal congress. Some Western-zones Social Democrats did come to Berlin—and in sufficient numbers to give substance to the "fiction" of an all-German congress.[65] SPD leaders maintained at the congress that the ZA had "always" acted on an all-German basis, had always regarded itself as an all-German, if provisional, leadership.[66]

In fact, these claims, and the whole ZA line about the ostensibly all-German nature of its activities, were predicated on a future vindication through the establishment of the unity party in all the occupation zones. This stand on the part of the ZA could not but please the Soviet authorities, for it presumed the extension into other parts of Germany of the authority of an organization by now thoroughly amenable to Soviet wishes. Moreover, given the still-fluid structure of the SPD and the absence of concerted opposition by the other occupation powers, the outcome of a contest for SPD leadership was by no means clear. There was a Berlin center espousing the ancient Social Democratic principle of "unity" able to appeal to like-minded comrades in the West, and having the material support of an all-German KPD apparatus and of the SMA. Opposed to it was an unofficial party bureau in Hanover, unable to be certain of the support of the Western occupiers, unable to mobilize potential allies within the Soviet Zone, and lacking equal material backing.

As the SPD's internal conflict over unity worsened, the KPD saw its own function chiefly as that of supporting and spurring on the ZA leadership. For the most part, Communist attacks were concentrated on overt opponents of their unity policy. The *DVZ* editorialized that Schumacher's visit to Berlin was an attempt by the "renegade" to stem the tide of "events sweeping over" him.[67] The Berlin dissidents were alternately scorned as inconsequential or denounced as shameful. Thus Ulbricht on March 26 predicted that "In a few months no one will be able to recall the name of these people who today here in Berlin do so much screaming against unification."[68]

While attacking certain hostile elements within the SPD, the Communist leadership remained careful to identify the bulk of the Social Democrats with their policy. Pieck again provides a typical example. Speaking in early March, he expressed his conviction that

> The will to unity of Berlin's Social Democratic workers, as expressed in a multitude of unity resolutions by the factory groups of both parties, is the best guarantee that unity will soon be realized here in Berlin, despite lingering doubts and misunderstandings. Moreover, all the hesitant Social

Democrats in the residential party units will also come to see that unification is a pressing necessity, and that their often real mistrust of the Communist Party rests on illusions concerning the nature of the KPD.[69]

There is even some indication that informal contacts were made between members of the Berlin Opposition and ZK representatives—albeit without results.[70]

The major statement of KPD attitudes in this question, and the most severe criticism of the ZA were to be found in a policy speech by Wilhelm Pieck at the KPD's *Reichskonferenz* of March 2–3, 1946. (This conference, which was attended by 400 delegates from all four zones, formally ratified the proposals of the joint conference of party leaderships of February 26—the draft program and statute of the unity party, as well as the time schedule of party and unification congresses.)[71] Pieck was in part quite conciliatory, seeking to show the Social Democrats that the KPD understood their "emotional" obstacles to acceptance of immediate unity: their attachment to their party and even to those leaders who had erred; the memories of the old mutual antagonism between SPD and KPD; the harmful effects in Berlin of the four-power occupation; the relative weakness of the proletarian elements within the SPD. Furthermore, the Communists had not always bothered to inquire whether their own behavior might not be the cause of the SPD's suspicions.

Having presented the KPD's self-criticism, Pieck turned to the "political errors" of the SPD leadership, in which he saw the *chief* cause of the Berlin problems. These errors related primarily to two questions: the timing and the territorial extent of unity. Mercilessly, Pieck exposed the hesitations and evasions with which the ZA had sought to maintain its good relations with the KPD and agreement with it on principles, while yet rejecting its program for unity.

> Instead of starting a large-scale campaign for unity, once the necessity of unification was acknowledged . . . the comrades [of the ZA] made certain concessions to the emotional objections of the Social Democratic rank and file members in Berlin and in that connection introduced arguments *which are now being used against them by membership*.[72] (Italics added.)

Such concessions were made particularly concerning the "sincerity" of the Communists, their "supposed dependence on Moscow," and the "supposed pressure from outside" (i.e., the SMA), among other things. Once the SPD members were exposed to such arguments, Pieck continued, it was difficult to change their minds, and so in Berlin the unity process has run into "very serious difficulties."

Pieck's statement on this issue provides a curious confirmation of the Berlin dissidents' contention that not they, but the ZA, had strayed from the commonly accepted SPD course of the previous winter. They would readily have agreed with Pieck that the dissidents were throwing up the ZA its own former positions on the issues!

In his concluding address to the gathering, Pieck, having ascribed the difficulties within the Berlin SPD to the fact of four-power occupation (by this time a standard point), paid one of the most open tributes to the activities of the SMA to be publicly uttered in this period. Although Pieck pledged that the KPD would make every effort to cooperate with all the occupying powers, the Soviet occupiers clearly occupied a special place:

> Here in the Soviet Zone of Occupation we have the great good fortune to have an occupation regime which stems from a socialist land; a regime which tackles the different problems connected with the occupation of a foreign country with full understanding for the interests of the toiling masses. The Soviet occupation authorities attempt in every respect to help the toiling masses in this part of Germany.[73]

Such emphasis on the contributions of the SMA gains added meaning in the context of KPD statements to the effect that, while forcing Germany to adopt a Soviet social system would be wrong, it would be equally wrong to adopt mechanically any other foreign social or political system.[74] One of the major Communist arguments in favor of unity turned on the KPD's "German" commitment. At every step in the continuing relationship between the parties, the question of the KPD's ties to Soviet policy had been raised in one form or another.

The Communists were certainly aware of this circumstance. In the ideological effort that accompanied the organizational consummation of the unity decision, the crucial question was that of "a German road to socialism," a concept that included a commitment to democracy in party and state, a peaceful transition to socialism, and defense of German interests.

Insofar as the Social Democratic perception of the KPD as an undemocratic, antinational party was a major hindrance to gaining support for unity, the Communists were concerned to show that, whatever the errors of the KPD in the Weimar period may have been, the KPD was now firmly committed to democratic politics and to action on the basis of German conditions.

The „repeated Communist emphasis, beginning in June 1945, on a "parliamentary democratic republic with all rights and freedom for the toiling masses" was designed to provide reassurance on the former point. As the prospect of unification limited to the Soviet Zone came nearer in the spring of 1946, there was a rising stress on the KPD's national stance. Thus Dahlem in February:

> Our SPD friends have often asked us, "Just what is your course of action in politics? What is your orientation in respect to the national questions facing Germany?"
> Our clear and candid answer is, "*We orient ourselves exclusively on Germany!* The policies of the German working class and of the toiling people of Germany can only be derived from the specific circumstances of our nation. It can and will be nothing other than a German Policy."[75]
> (Italics in original.)

The question remained, however, as to what a "German policy" might mean to a party that had been notorious for seeking solutions for German problems by appeal to "Bolshevik" models. To give a satisfactory answer to this question, both to Social Democrats and to members of the KPD itself, a major restatement of KPD theory was needed.

This was the function of the widely noted article by Anton Ackermann, "Is there a Special German Road to Socialism?"[76] The contentions advanced in this work were implicit in the KPD's postwar line; their explication served the political purpose of lending credibility to that line. Apparently written in the winter of 1945, the article's publication in February 1946 coincided with the climax of the campaign to win over Social Democratic support for immediate unity.[77]

Ackermann began by stressing that there was not any specifically *German* set of Marxist principles; the chief relevant principle, that of the working class attaining the "whole of the state power" was generally valid. From this follow tactical questions—How is this power to be attained? Must the working class use revolutionary force? May it achieve its goals through parliamentary-democratic means?—and here national differences were possible. Which path might Germany follow? Ackermann was careful to stress that the revolutionary method had much to recommend it: the Soviet success and everyone else's failure. There could be no question of utilizing the existing bourgeois state, be it ever so democratic, in order to pass gradually to socialism.

But not all "state machines" are alike. Might there not be a nonbureaucratic, nonmilitary state? Such a state would not need to be smashed. How might such a situation arise? In the crucial passage of his essay, Ackermann wrote:

> it [would be] incorrect . . . to deny the possibility, for all times, for all lands, and under all circumstances, of an exceptional transition to a state that incorporated the whole power of the working class. Such a transition is possible on relatively peaceful lines, if the bourgeois class, due to extraordinary circumstances, cannot dispose of the military and bureaucratic apparatus of force of the state.[78]

Just such a unique situation existed in Germany in 1945–1946, thanks to the fact that the old state machine had been smashed by war and occupation. Ackerman had written previously that the new administrative organs of the Soviet Zone were not yet a workers' government, but that they might become one.[79] Expounding Ackermann's thesis in late March, Wolfgang Leonhard wrote that "The new democratic state organs . . . are already something other than organs of repression. . . . To parrot the thesis of the "smashing of the bourgeois state" today is to look to the dead letter and not the living spirit of Marxist teaching."[80] Ackermann's own conclusion, in the February article, was that the future nature of the Soviet Zone administration was uncertain, but that a prime factor insuring the indicated peaceful development would be the unification of the SPD and KPD into a united proletarian force.[81]

What would be the consequences for Germany of such a road to socialism? To begin with, a great deal of violence might be avoided; as for the KPD, "No one wishes it more fervently than we, that new open struggles, a new blood bath might be avoided." The fact that the German population had a proletarian majority, and that a unity party would have "no Mensheviks" (unlike Russia in 1917!) would create better chances for speedy realization of socialist democracy. Moreover, Germany's more developed economic and cultural life would make socialist economic construction and the development of socialist culture easier. Not to take advantage of such "national" opportunities would be a tragic error.[82]

In the context of the unity struggle, the vision of these benefits to be derived from a "German road" was crucial to the argument. By suggesting a non-Soviet development toward socialism for Germany, it supplied credibility to the postwar change in the KPD line and for many Social Democrats made cooperation with the Communists palatable. The Communists seemed to have oriented themselves toward German desires and requirements. An essential part of their postwar line was to declare their nationalism, to proclaim that the KPD was the truest exponent of distinctively German interests.[83] In the same month that saw the publication of his article on the "German Road," Ackermann asserted in a speech that all culture is essentially national in character. In an interesting counterpart to the political stress on German conditions, he stated that, "In our age, culture generally appears in national forms, and can develop only in its national forms."[84]

At the same time, those Social Democrats following the ZA lead, by stressing a "rediscovered" Marxist orthodoxy, felt themselves to be approaching the Communist position. A typical example of this is Max Fechner's speech of March 12, in which he denied that "democracy" was a fundamental aim of the German working class, although it was, of course, an important tactical goal: "The German working class is uninterested in democracy as a merely formal type of state. . . . That does not alter the fact that the working class can go along for part of the way with the antifascist-democratic forces in those elements of the bourgeoisie committed to reconstruction."[85]

The primary political emphasis of the SPD, he went on, must lie in a coalition with the Communists, which is the only alternative to a Weimar-style coalition with the bourgeoisie. This attitude on the part of some Social Democrats helped the KPD to ward off the criticism that its espousal of democracy was merely a tactical decision. For example, the statement of the new party's program spoke of the unity party "resorting to revolutionary means if the capitalist class abandons democratic procedures."[86] Many critics of the unity campaign had seized upon this to claim that the KPD had only a temporary commitment to democracy. In his speech on March 1, Grotewohl had insisted that the Social Democrats were not bourgeois democrats; for them, a democratic state was important but not essential.[87] At the founding meeting of the SED in Berlin on April 14, he returned to this theme with the assertion that the SPD had never regarded democracy as an "end in itself," but rather as a form of government subject to the effects of social transformation. If the SPD was democratic now, it was because Germany could be reconstructed only on a democratic basis.[88]

Kaden has argued that the Ackermann thesis of a "German road to socialism" was convincing only to those Social Democrats who already accepted the ZA's views on relations with the KPD.[89] While this may be true, it is largely irrelevant. The function of the Ackermann thesis was to provide the ideological justification for a policy whose adoption troubled many of its protagonists. Ackermann's thesis "saved" Grotewohl and the ZA from the fear that, in agreeing to unity, they were lending themselves to unacceptable purposes.

If the Ackermann program helped to reinforce a tendency toward Communist-Social Democratic convergence on the questions of democracy in state and party, it also possessed, when shorn of its nationalist trappings, a remarkable resemblance to the policy actually followed by the KPD-SED leadership in the Soviet Zone. This policy was one of gaining power through the use of the instruments of state power, rather than by opposing them with the weapon of insurrection. In this perspective, the "peaceful transition" is feasible because special circumstances (in this case, Soviet military occupation) permit the party to seize and utilize the state machinery. For the party itself, this situation was characterized by the shift from a "party of opposition" to a "party of state responsibility."[90]

On the whole, the Ackermann thesis made a strong case for the KPD (and thus necessarily also the unity party) as an indigenous, autonomous, democratic, and socialist party. In his address to the March 2–3 KPD conference, Pieck repeated Ackermann's arguments almost literally, recommended that all party members study them intensively and suggested that they advance it in discussions with their Social Democratic comrades. Similar advice came from the KPD party press.[91]

On the eve of the party congresses of April 1946, the KPD stood in sharp contrast to the SPD. Both parties had Berlin headquarters, but the leadership of the KPD's Central Committee was unchallenged in the Soviet Zone, in Berlin, and (insofar as it was not hampered by Western occupation restrictions) in the Western zones as well. The KPD's national conference on March 2 and 3, 1946; was the first postwar German party meeting that might reasonably be called nationwide.[92] The Ackermann theses were accepted equally in all four zones and in Berlin as well. The KPD was ready for unification with an SPD in disarray.

The emergence of organized opposition to the merger of the SPD and KPD was made possible by the presence in Berlin of non-Soviet occupation forces. The chief manifestations of this presence, insofar as the political struggle was concerned, were physical security, material aid, and specific actions by the occupation authorities.

It is difficult to assess the precise effect of physical intimidation of German political figures by the SMA. Individual experiences and local patterns differed quite widely in this regard. To some extent fear of possible Soviet action seems to have been as important as any actual deed. It must also be kept in mind that, armed with the unchecked power of occupation status, the SMA could undertake arbitrary actions as a "normal" procedure. Many Social Democrats had undergone painful imprisonment and worse under the preceding regime and, in many cases, were reluctant to endanger their regained personal freedom. These considerations tended to weigh more heavily on Social Democrats at the lower levels of the party, who were not protected by the prominence of the ZA. For such persons, even Soviet procedures that may not have had menacing intentions (e.g., late night interrogations) took on a menacing aspect. Thus the relative physical safety of Berlin may have made a considerable difference for the individuals, largely lower-level party figures, who sparked the opposition within the SPD.[93]

A potential oppositionist in the Soviet Zone had always to reckon with the probability that, even if he were to succeed in committing a party organization to a course of action of which the SMA disapproved, the organization itself might be dissolved by the occupation authorities. It was therefore important for the antiunity SPD functionaries in Berlin to have some assurance that, in the event of a split in the party organization leading to preservation of an SPD alongside a new unity party, such an SPD would have a reasonable prospect of existing and functioning. Just such assurance seems to have been given semiofficially to Berlin oppositionists by spokesmen for the British military authorities on the eve of the meeting of February 17 where the first revolt against the ZA's leadership was attempted.[94] Whereas leaders of organizations functioning under SMA control had to fear that they would be replaced if they deviated from Soviet policy (as was feared by the ZA leaders in the crucial days of February 8–11), the Berlin oppositionists had a reasonable expectation that their struggle would lead to an opportunity to continue political activity.

Furthermore, it had been shown that political views diverging from those of the SMA could not be effectively publicized in the Soviet Zone. Opposition remained isolated and its spokesmen were unable to present their case. In Berlin, however, the opposition's lack of access to any portion of their party's press was offset by the availability of newspapers in the Western sectors. Foremost among these was the American-licensed but privately published *Tagesspiegel* which, from March 15 on, formally and explicitly made space available to the expression of opposition views.[95] From March 22 on, when the militantly anti-KPD and anti-ZA *Telegraf* was licensed in the British sector, it promptly paid great attention to the unity issue.

Publicity and psychological relief from isolation were also the chief contributions of Kurt Schumacher during his visit to Berlin in late February, a visit made possible by the four-power status of the city and by travel facilities provided by the British occupation authorities. During this period the chief foreign resonance of the internal struggle within the Berlin SPD was provided by the interest in Social Democratic affairs shown by British Labour officials and MPs.[96] In a House of Commons debate on the government's German policy on March 18, 1946, several MPs (including Maurice Edelman and Michael Foot) criticized the Soviet policy in forcing the fusion of the two parties.[97]

In competition between the ZA and the Berlin opposition forces prior to the March 31 referendum, the ZA had a great initial advantage in the supplies of paper and other materials made available to it by the SMA. The intervention of Western occupation authorities helped to offset this advantage. Although the higher-level British and American personnel remained aloof from the SPD struggle, regarding it officially as a matter for the Germans to settle "democratically" among themselves, some personnel at lower levels did intervene against the ZA; their support made political competition feasible within the Berlin SPD.[98]

Moreover, the very idea of a referendum, seen as a "democratic" device, suited the grass roots approach to the democratization of Germany favored by American planners. Already in February, General Clay had declared that OMGUS did not oppose unity were it brought about through the "free, democratic choice" of the membership.[99] On March 23 he defended the notion of a referendum as a suitable device to discover whether unity was backed by the membership as well as by some party leaders.[100] Almost on the eve of the referendum, on March 29, the U.S. Commandant in Berlin, Major General Barker, issued a statement of the United States position on the upcoming referendum that made it clear that the conduct of the referendum would have American assistance.[101] On the day of the referendum such support, extending to police protection for polling places, was made available.[102]

The March 31 referendum and the various party congresses following thereupon produced conflicting claims to recognition by the newly merged organization of the SED and by the SPD organization that arose from the ranks of the Berlin Opposition. Recognition, which involved the right to function politically, was a matter for the occupation authorities; here, once more, the policies of the Western occupation powers were an important factor in producing a situation differing from that of the Soviet Zone.

Immediately after their April 7 congress, the Opposition leaders petitioned the Allied Kommandatura for official sanction as the new leadership of an already existing, continuing body.[103] In the Kommandatura debates on this request, the Western spokesmen accepted the position that the referendum and subsequent events demonstrated that the SPD had indeed maintained organizational continuity; its new leadership could simply be recognized, while the merged party might apply as a new party.[104] When the AKB discussed the matter again on April 26, SED operations in the Soviet Zone and Soviet sector of Berlin were already proceeding without having required any special SMA authorization.[105] Moreover, a request for recognition from the Berlin SED now lay before the AKB. Now the Soviet representative suggested that both parties be allowed to operate throughout all of Berlin—although he intimated that it was the SED that represented organizational continuity and the SPD that would have to "explain" itself.[106]

No agreement could be reached, however, as the three other powers insisted on their earlier formulations. The entire problem was therefore referred to the Allied Control Council. In the interim, SED activities were banned in the Western sectors, SPD activities in the Soviet sector.[107] Finally, on May 31, acting under instructions from a Control

Council Coordinating Committee session on May 28, the Kommandatura ignored the matters of priority and continuity and permitted both
parties to operate on an equal basis throuhout Berlin.[108]

While official Western support for the antimerger forces was in no
way comparable to the consistent and purposeful activity of the SMA on
behalf of "unity," the activities of the Western occupation powers were
of sufficient effect to arouse ill-concealed hostility on the part of the KPD
and SPD leaderships. An examination of the speeches at the April party
congresses, for example, reveals the extent of this bitterness, which was
directed especially at the British.[109]

The Western Commandants had indicated that they would facilitate
holding the referendum in their sectors of Berlin; KPD hostility made
Soviet approval seem unlikely. Although the question of the referendum
had been the chief topic of Berlin politics for a month, it seems that the
harried Berlin leadership did not apply to the Soviet Commandant for
permission to hold the referendum until March 29. It was thus simple
for Gen. Kotikov, citing "apparent divergences of outlook within the
Social Democratic party organization of Berlin," between, for example,
the ZA and the BV, to delay his approval pending submission of detailed
information concerning the technical arrangements for the voting—information that could not be supplied until after the appointed time. In
two Soviet sector boroughs, voting was nevertheless begun, but the polls
were quickly closed by Soviet authorities. The referendum was thus held
only in the three Western sectors of the city.

It may be argued that, from the standpoint of Soviet interests, the decision to ban the referendum in the Soviet sector was a mistaken one. Although presumably a citywide referendum would have produced a
citywide defeat for Soviet policy (much like the Berlin city elections of
October 20, 1946), in March 1946 the division for and against Soviet
policy was not a division along sector lines. This did apply to the organizational possibilities, but not to opinion and sentiment. By banning the
referendum in its part of Berlin, the SMA was stressing the dependence
of certain political tendencies on its material support. While the
referendum results were a rebuke to the manner in which the Social
Democrats had been approached, they were also an indication that a
long-range policy of political concentration around a pro-Soviet center
might still receive substantial support. The Soviet action in this case

helped to set the limits of effective returns for Soviet policy; a limit defined roughly by the imposition of Communist control over an ostensibly multipartisan movement.

The zonal party congresses on April 19–20 and the unity congress on April 21–22 were ceremonially impressive but politically anticlimatic consummations of the developments of the past months. By April the crucial battles had already been fought and the victory had been achieved, albeit on a more restricted basis than its authors must have hoped.[110] It now remains to examine what the unification of the parties in the Soviet Zone meant for the participants and, above all, for the Soviet sponsors of this development.

CHAPTER 10

Conclusions

With the establishment of the Socialist Unity Party in April and May of 1946, Soviet policy in Germany secured an ambiguous triumph that helped to shape Soviet policy in Europe in the early postwar years and that was a major factor in determining the political profile of the East German ruling party for many years to come.

Soviet policy in Germany in 1945–1946 looked to the extension of Soviet influence throughout the country and therefore favored the consolidation of all-German institutions. Thus the Soviet Union had taken the initiative in fostering German political activity, in establishing German governmental administrations in the Soviet Zone, and it maintained its commitment to the creation of viable four-power control machinery in Germany.[1] Finally, and most relevant to this study, Soviet policy was responsible for the creation of an instrument of potential political leadership throughout Germany—the Socialist Unity Party of Germany.

This Soviet policy was a politically activist one: it pointed to the creation of instruments for the realization of Soviet aims in Europe. This is not to say that Soviet policy was therefore in some abstract way aggressive or expansionist. Indeed, to raise the question in this way is to mislead by raising false alternatives of Soviet policy. The familiar distinction is often made between two opposed modes of Soviet foreign policy. One, to quote Marshall Shulman, is "essentially militant and direct . . . [involving] a detachment of the Communist movement abroad from association with other elements of the national or international community"; the other is "manipulative, flexible . . . [involving] exploitation of contadictions abroad, and collaboration with other groups, classes, or nations." As Shulman reminds us, either policy may have offensive or defensive implications, depending on "how the Soviet leadership assesses the historical character of the current period."[2] Soviet policy in Germany clearly fell into the latter mode. It is beyond the bounds of this study to elucidate in detail the often contradictory elements of Soviet policy in Germany, the conflicts between various Soviet administrative hierarchies, or the diplomatic fencing that accompanied four-power negotiations over such topics as reparations.[3] Stalin's policy was designed to secure maximum Soviet advantage while maintaining the structure of the Grand Alliance.[4] Despite increasing inter-Allied friction in the winter of 1945, the prospects for useful four-power collaboration had hardly been exhausted.[5]

This view of Soviet policy suggests that, rather than asking whether opportunities for four-power cooperation were not missed by a failure of communication or by American malevolence, it would be more to the point to ask whether such collababoration as did take place did not contain the elements of future discord. As Paul Seabury has pointed out, given the circumstances of Europe in 1945 and the nature of Soviet power, it was not to be expected that a barrier could exist "between ideology and order-building statecraft. . . . Where a moral vacuum appeared, it was filled with outside formulas for order."[6] But from the Soviet perspective, such a "formula for order" would most probably be based on strategies for manipulating European political forces—and using Communist parties as the key to such manipulation. Such a policy, while intended to be fully consonant with maintenance of the wartime alliance, was likely, in fact, to lead to suspicion and hostility on the part of the Soviet Union's intended allies. We have seen that in the particular case of Soviet policy regarding the SPD and KPD, such was the case. Despite this contradictory outcome, however, it is clear that the policy of Communist-Social Democratic unification was a general European-wide tactic of the Soviet Union, and that this tactic was related to postwar Soviet concepts of the attainment and utilization of state power.[7]

In fact, the methods used in the Soviet Zone to create the SED had the unintended consequence of arousing the hostility of both the Western occupation powers and the West German Social Democrats. This indicates the extent to which an ideological commitment to a particular political strategy caused the Soviet authorities to underestimate (disregard?) the response they might evoke. In Eastern Europe, Soviet power could effectively cancel out such hostile responses (although not without providing some of the more vivid incidents of the early Cold War); in Germany, the presence of competing power meant that the Soviet strategy would have to succeed on political merit alone. A line of action that was based on German politics coalescing around a Soviet-sponsored political instrument has the virtues of boldness and analytical depth, but in terms of available power it had at best a marginal chance of success.

If, indeed, the Soviet leadership was divided on the issue of how to advance Soviet prospects (i.e., gain political influence in various European states), and if this division turned on an estimate of the political prospects in those states,[8] then the policy under study here had the great virtue of fitting into either the "moderate" or "radical" long-range outlook. The "moderate" notion of "seizing power [so as to] pick up as much local support as possible and [conciliating] Western opinion where feasible"[9] is not a policy of withdrawal, but one of advance, albeit advance of a cautious sort.

The unresolved character of this Soviet policy in Germany suggests that the Soviet leadership had not decided on the optimal strategy to pursue in postwar European politics. Richard Lowenthal has suggested that Stalin allowed both approaches to be used.[10] Certainly Stalin's most notable pronouncement of this period, his election speech of February 1946, did not reflect the uniformly aggressive "Left" attitude often attributed to it. In a crucial passage Stalin described World War II as having *"from the outset* assumed the character of an antifascist war, a war of liberation, one aim of which was also the restoration of democratic liberties. The entrance of the Soviet Union into the war against the Axis states could only enhance, and indeed did enhance the antifascist and liberation character of the Second World War."[11] (Italics added.)

Continued cooperation with the Soviet Union's wartime allies was thus not incompatible with Soviet aims. Seen from this perspective, Soviet policy toward the SPD and KPD helped to shape the evolution of East-West relations from the wartime alliance to the Cold War.

In both the Soviet-occupied or Soviet-influenced countries of Eastern Europe and in the liberated nations of Western Europe, postwar Communist-Socialist relations followed a pattern similar to that of the Soviet Zone in Germany. Among the observable regularities one may note the following: Communist advocacy of "unity of action" agreements with Socialists, together with postponement of organizational unity;[12] stress on the common working class basis of both parties; emphasis on "antifascism" as a unifying bond, coupled with frequent references to the threat of a reactionary restoration; Communist support for "democratic" economic and social reforms (e.g., land reform) but not (yet) for "Socialism"; Communist support for "parliamentary" and "peaceful" ways to socialism; and a pattern of Communist and Soviet interference in the internal affairs of the Socialist parties, resulting in a series of purges and internal splits preceding the organizational mergers with the Communist parties.[13]

To be sure, there were distinctive features in the experiences of each country. Thus, for example, in countries with strong peasant parties (such as Hungary and Poland), the Socialist-Communist unification campaign was delayed until after the weakening or elimination of the peasant parties as rivals of the Communist parties for political power.[14] Indeed, in a country such as Rumania, thanks to its social and political history, the socialists may have been a less important target than the peasant groups. Yet it remains a striking fact that the unification of the Socialist and Communist parties was an important goal in such countries as well.

The various Socialist parties, having divergent histories, leaderships, and outlooks, reacted in different ways to this common pressure. The Czechoslovak party was at first under the pro-Communist Fierlinger leadership; not until after its November 1947 congress did the Czechoslovak Communists meet a serious obstacle there. The Rumanian party formally split in 1946 on the issue of cooperation with the Communists; the Polish party had begun as a Soviet-inspired "new party" divorced from the prewar Polish socialist organization, but it too developed autonomous ambitions in 1945–1947.[15]

Moreover, important differences arose from the fact that the possibilities for exerting Soviet pressure differed from country to country.

Nowhere in Western Europe, where Soviet power could not intervene in this struggle, was a unity party formed. A good example in this regard is Austria, where there was a Soviet occupation in a four-power setting, but where, unlike the German situation, the occupied country was formally "liberated," and a single nationwide government existed. Here the preponderance of Socialist leaders opposed to unity made itself felt in the party and helped to delay and ultimately defeat Communist efforts.[16]

Despite such differences of detail, the existence of a standard Soviet policy on the question of Socialist-Communist unification seems indisputable. In some countries, Communist policy may have concentrated on peasant parties as a more serious rival than the socialists;[17] if so, this only delayed the pressure on the Socialists. Nor is Communist restraint on organizational unity immediately upon the war's end a convincing argument against unity as the political goal of Soviet and Communist policy vis-a-vis the Socialists.[18] The evidence cited here from a variety of East European countries precludes regarding the process leading to the formation of the SED as exceptional.

Indeed, even in the countries outside the range of Soviet power where Socialist-Communist unification was sought, many of the appeals and tactics used were similar to those in Eastern Europe and the Soviet Zone of Germany. Thus, in France, the pattern included initial Communist rejection of unity proposals made by the Socialists during the war; a subsequent reversal on this point by both parties;[19] Communist appeals to the joint experience of the Resistance as a basis of future cooperation (with "Resistance" here the equivalent of "antifascist reconstruction" in Germany); an independent nationalist stance by the Communists; a new name proposed for the future unity party; immediate electoral alliances as an intermediate step toward unity; contrasting Communist appraisals of "progressive" Socialists favoring unity and old reformist leaders like Leon Blum who opposed it; and "the conquest of power by the working class" as an ultimate goal.

The Scandinavian countries were likewise the scene of attempts at Socialist-Communist mergers. In Sweden, a Communist offer of an electoral alliance with the Social Democrats in the 1944 elections was rejected by the Socialists.[20] In Denmark, efforts at some measure of cooperation failed in the summer of 1945 as a result of Socialist complaints that the Communists were attacking Socialist officials in the trade unions.[21]

The most serious effort at unity came in Norway, which had long possessed the most radical Socialist party in the area, the Norwegian Labor Party (NLP). Contacts with the Communists had begun during the war in Swedish exile and in the Grini concentration camp near Oslo. A program worked out in the Grini camp served as the basis for tripartite negotiations between the NLP, the Communists, and the trade union organization. These negotiations began in June 1945 and dealt with such areas as joint economic policy, ideological training among the industrial workers, and a joint newspaper. The unification of the parties was projected to precede the first postwar elections of the fall of 1945.[22]

At some point in August 1945 all plans for unification of the "Marxist" parties collapsed. A Communist account blames lack of understanding on the part of the NLP leadership for this failure. Other sources point to Communist attacks on the political and military wartime record of certain NLP leaders. The motives for such attacks remain obscure, as do the possible Soviet connections with Norwegian CP actions. What is clear is the result: all chances of Communist-NLP unification vanished.[23]

The significance of the Soviet success in sponsoring close Socialist-Communist cooperation in Eastern Europe was made explicit in Soviet comment on postwar European politics. Writing in mid-1946, Eugene Varga noted that "An intensified struggle rages around the Social Democracy in the countries of Europe between progressive and reactionary forces. This forms the main content of the internal politics of the capitalist countries. Of course, this struggle means, simultaneously, a struggle within each Social Democratic party. . . . This struggle may best be observed in Germany." The crux of this struggle, Varga went on, was whether the social and political forces represented by Social Democracy would become, once more, a supporting pillar of the old order (the aim of the old "reformist" leaderships) or join with the Communists in building the new.[24]

A Soviet survey of the European scene revealed two groups of Socialists.[25] One, headed by the British Labourites and including the West German SPD under Schumacher, played the part of "servants of militant reaction," fearful of mass popular initiatives, abandoning their national interests for "European blocs," and, characteristically, opposing cooperation or unification with Communists. The other group, including the Socialist movements of Eastern Europe and the Soviet Zone of Germany, followed a diametrically opposed line. These more progressive Social Democrats responded to the great upsurge of democratic mass movements by cooperating with the Communists, who, for their part, had "won the confidence of the masses" by their leadership in the struggle against fascism and for a "democratic" renewal of society.[26]

This generalized policy toward the Socialist parties of Europe was one aspect of the postwar Soviet approach to the conquest of political power.[27] Characteristic of this approach was an emphasis on Communist domination and manipulation of broad political coalitions, adaptation of Communist tactics to the special conditions of individual nations, and a notable stress on the use of the existing machinery of the state for Communist aims. We may briefly describe such an approach as *inclusive*, nationalist, and statist. The opposite approach may be summed up as strongly (working-) class oriented and politically *exclusive*, internationalist, and revolutionary. If we describe the former road to power as "nonrevolutionary," this is to be taken in a relative sense as implying a reliance on methods that are quasilegal but not necessarily "peaceful."[28]

In keeping with this strategy, the KPD focused its attention on acquisition of power and influence over the machinery of governmental administration, albeit within the limitations of Germany's status as an occupied country. The KPD would henceforth be a "statist" party, securing crucial administrative positions for party members, using such positions to influence the course of politics, and basing its mass appeal in part on its administrative achievements. Like other Communist parties, the KPD supported a reformed, "democratized" state; in Germany this took the form of advocating a parliamentary republic "which would avoid the weaknesses of the Weimar Republic." This allowed the KPD to explain away its Weimar-era opposition to democratic state institutions; given widespread postwar dissatisfaction with the Weimar state (especially within the SPD) this was an attractive position for the Communists to take.

Communist willingness to assume the burdens of office, along with the policy of unification with the Socialists, were designed to facilitate the

"peaceful" acquisition of power.[29] Insofar as a nonrevolutionary conquest of power depended, in the Communist thinking of this period, on a
redefinition of the role of the state machinery in politics, the presence of
Communists in administrative positions was an important condition of
such a transformation of the state. It was in this sense that Ackermann's
thesis of a "German way" was far more than a tactical appeal to na-
tionally-minded Communists and Socialists, but rather a statement of the
possibilities that penetration of the state machinery opened up to the
Communists.[30] This theoretical stance was implemented by Communist
actions in all parts of Europe after 1945; in those countries where local
politics or Soviet power made it feasible to do so, Communists occupied
important, if not crucial governmental posts.

As George Lichtheim has remarked,

> Hitler, no less than Stalin, had something to teach the Communists.
> What he taught them (and what they subsequently applied when their turn
> came in 1945) was the technique of the quasilegal *coup d'etat* and the sub-
> sequent reign of terror. The real answer to Hitler's seizure of power in
> Berlin in 1933 was the Communist seizure of power in Prague fifteen years
> later: using very similar methods. . . .[31]

But Prague in 1948 was not the first application of this technique; nor
was dramatic violence a necessary feature of it. It might be enough to
dominate the state; had Leninists not always believed so much in the ef-
ficacy of the state machinery that they advocated "smashing" it? Richard
Lowenthal has remarked that "Stalin learned how successful the new
technique of 'legal' seizure of the state machine might be, if combined
with dependence on the Soviet Union."[32] Or, as Tiul'panov put it, "By
all means let the bourgeoisie fight against the state."[33]

At the same time, the Communists not only adopted an affirmative attitude toward the state, but also became the champions of *national* states.
This constitutes another element of uniformity in Communist policies in
various parts of Europe. Communist parties aggressively advocated
traditional nationalist goals. Both Hungarian and Rumanian Communists supported their respective national claims to Transylvania;
French and German Communists differed on the future of the Ruhr and
the Rhineland.[34] This development, incidentally, demonstrated the
flexibility imparted to European Communism by the abandonment of
formal "internationalist" obligations. In the competition for power, the

Communists would no longer be outbid for nationalistic support. Whereas the "reformists" and the bourgeoisie were denounced as cosmopolitan, nationally disintegrative forces, which were accused of supranational "bloc-building," the Communists attempted to present themselves as the true representatives of the interests of the nation.[35]

Within Germany this led to a remarkable situation in which the three Western powers, after 1945, rather discouraged German nationalism, while the Soviet Union, the KPD, and the portion of the SPD under Schumacher all sought nationalist support. For the KPD, the switch was dramatic; Pieck declared at the Jena Conference in January 1946 that the Communists would not be outbid in devotion to German interests. In practice, of course, the KPD's nationalism had to give way to overriding Soviet interests in the case of the Oder-Neisse border. Nonetheless, in numerous ways, such as deliberately harking back to the traditions of the 1848 revolution, insisting on German retention of the Ruhr, and stressing their commitment to a centralized German state, the Communists sought to insure themselves against rejection for nationalist reasons. After all, the lesson of August 1914 had been reinforced by that of 1933; the Hitler years had further demonstrated the power of nationalism; the war years had underlined this lesson again.[36]

Given the Communists' new identification with the nation and the state, at least as a tactic in the political struggle, what was the significance of the effort to secure unification with the Socialist parties? It must be remembered that the Communists, while appealing to nationalist and statist elements, did so on the basis of a democratic a d reformist program. The 1944–1946 period was one in which the political forces of the "right" were on the defensive throughout Europe; "antifascism" served as a platform for and justification of Communist leadership. Serious competition could come only from political forces capable of making a parallel claim; and Socialist parties could provide such competition wherever they had some political strength.

In what became the Soviet Zone of Germany, the Social Democrats had been the leading "democratic" force prior to 1933. Now that there was a new KPD line, the SPD was the chief obstacle to Communist leadership of a "democratic, antifascist" government and political movement.

The goal of the KPD was manifestly to absorb the SPD and to enroll under Communist leadership the political forces incorporated in the Social Democratic movement. In the Soviet Zone of Germany, as in other countries, the Socialists were to be neither merely suppressed nor allowed to function in competition with the Communist party. Rather, through a combination of pressure (applied in part through the machinery of the Soviet occupation and of the state) and ideological persuasion, the Socialists were to be brought to contribute to the consolidation of political forces under Communist leadership. The labor movement, the democratic-antifascist movement, the national movement—all were to be led by Communists, and the chief potential alternative, Social Democracy, was to be neutralized through absorption.

Thus the unification of the SPD and KPD is to be understood not merely as a device for ridding the KPD of an inconvenient rival, but also as an important step in the attainment of power by the Communists by a process of inclusion rather than exclusion, by utilization of the state rather than insurrection, and by monopolization of "permissible" political movements rather than ideological purity.[37]

The KPD's absorption of the Social Democracy of the Soviet Zone was in large measure the result of the manipulation of German political activity by the Soviet occupation authorities. The techniques used by the SMA in this connection have been described in the body of this study, and need only be briefly summarized at this point.

The foundation of Soviet control was the minute supervision of party activity: appointments to office, meetings, speakers and speeches, and publications, as well as of the physical instruments of political work—cars, fuel, offices, money, and food. This made the German parties, at every level, dependent on Soviet good will; it also insured the SMA that it would never be confronted with actions born and nurtured out of Soviet sight within a given party's organizational structure. While it may be noted that these techniques, far from being uniquely Soviet, or Russian, or Communist, were to some extent applied by the other occupation powers, the very close ideological and organizational supervision of German party affairs described in this study also owes something to a characteristic Bolshevik suspicion of autonomous political impulses.

Second, the Soviet authorities contrived to play off groups, individuals, and organizational levels within a given party against one another. This has been noted especially in the relationship of the ZA to provincial party organizations. The SMA had available against provincial or local leaders all the sanctions brought to bear on the zonal leadership, including outright removal from party office; the relatively greater obscurity of the local leaders made a action against them even easier. Although the determined opposition of several major components of the Soviet Zone SPD might have given the SMA pause, it must be remembered that Soviet policy was only tactically but not strategically responsive to German (specifically, SPD) opinions.

Finally, the SMA offered the SPD attractive advantages in order to gain its cooperation. It clothed its policy in acceptable ideology and it offered a respected and active place in public affairs to men whose involvement with such activity ran deep. Such attractions only increased the effectiveness of pressure brought against men often tired from years of persecution and political exclusion.

The goal of these Soviet actions was to establish a political leadership responsive to Soviet purposes and to place it in positions of power in Germany, or, to be more precise, in positions from which such a leadership could assume power when German institutions of government were re-created.[38] Thus Soviet policy proceeded on two levels: while working to shape a reliable political instrument through the unification of the SPD and KPD, the Soviet authorities strove for the establishment of an all-German political framework within which the united party could operate.

The frustration of the latter objective lies outside the scope of this study, but even on the level of party affairs, the Soviet occupation authorities forfeited political advantages in all of Germany by the manner in which they exercised their unlimited authority within the Soviet Zone. The KPD was, of course, intended to be a unified nationwide party, although its effectiveness nationally was blocked by the circumstances of four-power control. The SPD might have become a national political force, but the chances of extending the ZA's authority or of influencing an enlarged all-German SPD leadership were lost in part by the way the unification campaign was carried out in the Soviet Zone. By the same token, the all-German prospects of the SED were limited from the start by the circumstances of its creation.

A year of political activity under Soviet occupation had very different consequences for the KPD and for the SPD. For the German Communists, the first postwar year saw the validation of an exiled leadership's claim to priority in the reconstruction of German political life (at least within the Soviet Zone). This claim was successfully asserted against other political parties generally, against the SPD in particular, and not least against possible opponents within the KPD itself.[39]

The Communist leaders who returned to Germany from Soviet exile easily repressed attempts to base the KPD on the rejected attitudes and policies of the Weimar period, i.e., "sectarianism." These "sectarians" were mainly older party members who had survived the Hitler period in Germany; no important party leader rallied to their side. Another group advocated a "German road to socialism," genuine accommodation with the SPD, and long-range commitment to democratization of party and state. In 1945–1946 its members felt their position to be largely identical with that of the party as a whole. In striking contrast to other East European countries such as Poland or Rumania, in the Soviet Zone no group of leaders from within Germany (from the jails or concentration camps) or from Western exile strongly challenged the KPD's "Muscovites." Later disputes resulting in purges of the party leadership did not reflect the postwar situation.[40] The most important figure of the 1945 KPD, Walter Ulbricht, dominated the SED for a quarter century.

The successful Communist absorption of the greater part of the Soviet Zone Social Democracy formed a striking climax to thirty years of competition for the mantle of Marxist proletarian leadership in Germany.

The SPD had a more indigenous leadership, greater popular appeal, and a more democratic party structure than the KPD. Nonetheless, and despite an impressive achievement in building up the party structure in the face of severe material handicaps, the SPD leadership failed in its bid to achieve political leadership of the Soviet Zone and, perhaps, of all Germany. The ZA could not attain the Soviet backing it wanted for its claim to leadership, although it offered the SMA its broad popular support, close cooperation with the Soviet authorities, and policies designed explicitly to meet legitimate (in the eyes of the SPD) Soviet requirements. This policy (should one rather say "hope"?) of the ZA had clearly failed by the end of 1945, by which time there could no longer be any doubt of Soviet desires for immediate unification. A weak SPD would probably not have been spared this Soviet pressure in the long run, but, ironically, the SPD's very strength, which the ZA hoped would qualify it as a repository of Soviet trust and support, evidently prompted the Soviet authorities to intensify their own pressure for a merger with the KPD. Such merger was needed if the overall Soviet strategy of coalescing political forces under Communist leadership was to succeed in the Soviet Zone.

Until the late winter of 1945–1946, Grotewohl appears to have believed that the SPD would be accepted by the Soviet authorities as the true representative of the German working class.[41] Even after this expectation waned, Grotewohl continued to hope that, in the newly united party, the numerical, intellectual, and personal superiority of the Social Democrats would make itself felt. This gave added intensity to Grotewohl's desire to spread the unity across all of Germany. From the west could come Social Democratic reinforcements, in both numbers and leadership personnel, in greater amounts than were available to the KPD. Seen under this aspect, every Social Democrat in Berlin or the Western zones who balked at unity weakened those who, whether willingly or not, were politically active within the SED.[42]

Soviet policy toward the SPD was not based entirely on the overwhelming power of the occupation regime. Instead, it combined pressure with ideological inducements to secure support of Social Democrats for the program of uniting the parties. Nor was the SPD completely unresponsive to these overtures. The difficult predicament of the Social Democrats arose partly from the fact that so many of them shared the premises of the KPD while drawing different conclusions from them.

The basis of the ZA's position regarding the Soviet Union was a conception of the USSR as a "socialist state." This identification formed the basis for the "Eastern orientation," which inclined the ZA to believe not only that Germany's future could be assured by none but the Soviet Union, but also that German Social Democratic leadership could appeal to the Soviet authorities on this basis. The Soviet Union would offer markets and "Socialist aid" for the German economy; German socialists would offer a guarantee of Soviet security by creating a socialist, democratic Germany.

Indeed, it was basic to the ZA's stance that no critical examination of either recent Soviet or KPD history was feasible. Thus the commitment of the USSR to democracy and socialism was not tested against the record of Stalinist rule, and the KPD's postwar pronouncements were held to outweigh that party's record and internal structure. Consequently, Social Democratic arguments against unification with the KPD were restricted to points of friction in the two parties' postwar collaboration.

The ZA's inclination toward common action with the KPD was further buttressed by an analysis of German history that saw in the disunity of the German working class, which was due to faults on both sides, the factor that had reduced the 1918 revolution to a nearly empty shift in the political facade and had then made possible Hitler's rise to power. Thus the first task of postwar German politics was seen as insuring that these mistakes were not repeated. In all the many speeches and articles on this theme, there was little analysis of this phenomenon of working class disunity. To put it unkindly, this was a policy of guilt and nostalgia for lost opportunities.

The capstone of this ideological edifice was the concept of a "German road to socialism." Ackermann's thesis was introduced to resolve Social Democratic doubts about the Communist commitment to a parliamentary system, and to policies based on German perspectives. The notion of a "German road" was designed to show that the KPD had not only changed its tactics, but its strategy as well, and that commitment to a "parliamentary, German road" had a foundation in doctrine.

Acceptance of this Communist position was in part an expedient for the ZA. Like the entire set of beliefs described here, it not only allowed Grotewohl and his colleagues to "draw lessons" from the past, but also to bow gracefully to Soviet pressure. Any distintion between serious analysis and wishful thinking in this Social Democratic position can no longer be made—if indeed it ever could be. However, the idea of a "German" or, more broadly, a parliamentary road to socialism was not merely a convenient ideological evasion by the Social Democrats; it also represented a conscious effort by the Soviet authorities and the KPD to provide *themselves* with an ideological justification for their policy and for their approach to the SPD.[43]

In holding these views, the ZA members may have mistaken their own half-wishful slogans for reality; if so, they were in good company. Many of their illusions concerning the USSR and local Communist parties were widely shared in 1945–1946, and if they concentrated too much on repairing supposed "errors" for the future of Germany, few German leaders in this period showed superior analytical powers.[44]

Although these doctrinal considerations helped shape the behavior of the participants in Soviet Zone politics, the ultimately decisive factor was "the presence and employment of Soviet power."[45] It was the painful destiny of the Social Democrats in the Soviet Zone to be confronted with this overwhelming power; it was this power that determined that the traditional German Social Democracy would cease to exist in the Soviet Zone of Germany.

Notes

Introduction

1. This lack is taken into serious account by a recent study of American policy in this era. John Lewis Gaddis, *The United States and the Origins of the Cold War 1941–1947* (New York: Columbia University Press, 1972), p. xvii.

2. Adam Ulam, in *The Rivals: America and Russia Since World War II* (New York: Viking Press, 1971), p. 25, has recently written that "On such crucial issues as Germany, Stalin's mind was obviously not quite made up. The Soviet position depended to some extent on what the Americans wanted and how strenuously they would stick to their demands."

3. John Gimbel, "Cold War: German Front," *The Maryland Historian*, II (Spring 1971) 41. The reference to Germany as the "chief prize" is from William H. McNeill, *America, Britain and Russia, Their Cooperation and Conflict 1941–1946*. Survey of International Affairs, 1939–1946, III (London: Oxford University Press, 1953), 724.

4. This is true of such a major Soviet monograph on this subject as P. A. Nikolaev, *Politika sovetskogo soiuza v germanskom voprose 1945–1964* (Moscow: Izdatel'stvo Nauka, 1966).

5. James L. Richardson has pointed out that postwar European politics cannot be understood without reference to prewar organizational and ideological cleavages, and the various postwar responses to them. See his "Cold War Revisionism: A Critique," *World Politics*, 24, no. 4 (July 1972), 606.

6. Studies of occupation regimes as political phenomena are rare. Noteworthy ones of American occupations include: John Gimbel, *A German Community under American Occupation: Marburg, 1945–1952* (Stanford University Press, 1961), and the same author's *The American Occupation of Germany* (Stanford: Stanford University Press, 1968); John D. Montgomery, *Forced to be Free: The Artificial Revolution in Germany and Japan* (Chicago: University of Chicago Press, 1957). See also Carl J. Friedrich, "Military Government and Dictatorship," in *Military Government*, Sidney Connor and Carl J. Friedrich, eds., 267, *Annals of the American Academy of Political and Social Science* (January 1950), 1–18.

1. The German Communist and Social Democratic Parties

1. See, among others, Carl E. Schorske, *German Social Democracy, 1905-1917* (Cambridge, Mass.: Harvard University Press, 1955); A. Joseph Berlau, *The German Social Democratic Party, 1914-1921* (New York: Columbia University Press, 1950); Peter Gay, *The Dilemma of Democratic Socialism* (New York: Columbia University Press, 1952).

2. Wolfgang Leonhard, *Die Revolution entlässt ihre Kinder* (Cologne-Berlin: Kiepenheuer & Witsch, 1955), p. 437. For a perceptive discussion of the myth of "Bebel-ite" party unity, see Vernon L. Lidtke, *The Outlawed Party: Social Democracy in Germany 1878-1890* (Princeton, N.J.: Princeton University Press, 1966), ch. 13.

3. Thus, for example, Bebel's portrait hung above the stage at the April 1946 unity congress; see the illustration following p. 640 in Fanny Rosner, Ilse Schiel, Heinz Vosske, eds., *Vereint sind wir alles: Erinnerungen an die Gründung der SED* (Berlin: Dietz, 1966), cited hereinafter as *Vereint*. Even after the establishment of the SED, Leonhard was told at the highest party school that Bebel was to be handled in lectures "with kid gloves" (Leonhard, *Die Revolution*, p. 490). See also Anton Ackermann, "August Bebel und die sozialistische Einheitspartei," *Deutsche Volkszeitung*, cited hereinafter as *DVZ*, February 22, 1946.

4. As early as the unity party congress of the SPD and KPD in April 1946, however, this issue was being won by the Communists, as is clear from the wording of the Manifesto approved there. See Institut für Marxismus-Leninismus beim Zentralkomitee der [SED], ed., *Dokumente und Materialien zur Geschichte der deutschen Arbeiterbewegung* (Berlin: Dietz, 1959), Series III, I, 628.

5. Ossip K. Flechtheim, *Die Kommunistische Partei in der Weimarer Republik* (Offenbach A. M.: Bollwark Verlag-Karl Drott, 1948); Sigmund Neumann, *Die Parteien der Weimarer Republik*, 2d ed. (Stuttgart: W. Kohlhammer, 1965); Herman Weber, ed., *Der deutsche Kommunismus: Dokumente* (Cologne: Kiepenheuer und Witsch, 1963); Herman Weber, *Von Rosa Luxemburg zu Walter Ulbricht: Wandlungen des Kommunismus in Deutschland*, 4th ed. (Hannover: Verlag für Literatur und Zeitgeschehen, 1961); Horst Duhnke, "German Communism in the Nazi Era," Diss. University of California, 1964, pp. 1-54, cited hereinafter as Duhnke dissertation; Richard Lowenthal, "The Bolshevization of the Spartacus League," in *International Communism*, David Footman, ed., St. Anthony's Papers No. 9 (London: Chatto and Windhus, 1960), pp. 23-71.

6. See especially Siegfried Bahne, "Die Kommunistische Partei Deutschlands"; Erich Matthias, "Die Sozialdemokratische Partei Deutschlands"; and Alfred Milatz, "Das Ende der Parteien im Spiegel der Wahlen 1930 bis 1933," in *Das Ende der Parteien 1933*, Erich Matthias and Rudolf Morsey, eds. (Düsseldorf: Droste, 1960); Horst Duhnke, *Die KPD von 1933 bis 1945* (Cologne: Kiepenheuer und Witsch, 1972), pp. 63-78.

7. The relevant chapter is aptly entitled "The Leap into the Abyss," in Franz Borkenau, *World Communism* (Ann Arbor, Mich.: University of Michigan Press, 1962).

8. This particular doctrine, although not characteristic of Soviet and Communist thought until after 1928, was originated by Stalin in his 1924 statement calling Fascism and Social Democracy "not antipodes" but "twins"; J. V. Stalin, *Works* (13 vols.; Moscow: FLPH, 1953), VI, 294. For a Thälmann quotation of this in 1932, see Weber, *deutsche Kommunismus*, p. 185. These points are well made by Siegfried Bahne, " 'Sozialfaschismus' in

Deutschland," *International Review of Social History*, 10, Part 2 (1965), 211–45. Bahne provides an excellent summary of the genesis and utilization of this slogan, as well as its significance within the KPD and the Comintern.

9. Such as the ZK's call for a general strike on January 30, 1933. See Bahne, *Ende der Parteien*, pp. 684–86; Duhnke, *Die KPD 1933–1945*, pp. 78–88.

10. For Friedrich Stampfer's efforts to contact the Soviet embassy to secure a change in the KPD stance, see Matthias, *Ende der Parteien*, pp. 156–57.

11. *Ibid.*, p. 158; Ex-Insider, (pseud.) "Moscow-Berlin 1933," *Survey*, no. 44–45, (October 1962), 156; generally, Lewis J. Edinger, *German Exile Politics* (Berkeley and Los Angeles: University of California Press, 1956).

12. The validity of this argument will not be considered here.

13. Ex-Insider, pp. 157–59; Margarete Buber-Neumann, *Von Potsdam nach Moskau* (Stuttgart: W. Kohlhammer, 1957), p. 284.

14. Quoted in David J. Dallin, *Russia and Postwar Europe*, trans. by F. K. Lawrence (New Haven: Yale University Press, 1943), p. 62.

15. From a May 1933 ZK resolution quoted disapprovingly by Pieck in 1935. See Wilhelm Pieck, *Der neue Weg zum Gemeinsamen Kampf für den Sturz der Hitlerdiktatur Referat und Schlusswort auf der Brüsseler Konferenz der Kommunistischen Partei Deutschlands, Oktober 1935* (Strasbourg: Editions Promethee, n.d.), pp. 22–23, cited hereinafter as Pieck, *Brussels speech.*

16. Borkenau, p. 377.

17. B. M. Leibzon and K. K. Shirinia, *Povorot v politike Kominterna (K 30-letiiu VII Kongressa)* (Moscow: Mysl', 1965), p. 170. The ECCI worker is identified as "B. Vasil'ev, a responsible worker in the party affairs department of the IKKI." For the resolution of the 13th Plenum, see Jane Degras, ed., *The Communist International 1919–1943: Documents* (London: Oxford University Press, 1965), III, 296–306.

18. Carola Stern, *Ulbricht: Eine politische Biographie* (Cologne: Kiepenheuer and Witsch, 1964), p. 83; Duhnke, *Die KPD 1933–1945*, pp. 148–49.

19. See Siegfried Vietzke, *Die KPD auf dem Wege zur Brüsseler Konferenz* (Berlin: Dietz, 1966), pp. 137–44. Vietzke offers a useful survey of both Communist and other literature in the field. *ibid.*, pp. 19–35; Stern, *Ulbricht*, pp. 82–86; see also Edinger, *Exile Politics*, pp. 151–52.

20. "Ein interessanter Brief Georgi Dimitroffs zur Vorbereitung des VII. Weltkongresses der Kommunistischen Internationale," *Beitrage zur Geschichte der deutschen Arbeiterbewegung*, cited hereinafter as *BzG*, 5, no. 2 (1963), 282–84.

21. Georgi Dimitroff, "The Fascist Offensive and the Tasks of the Communist International," *The United Front* (New York: International Publishers, 1938), pp. 9–93.

22. Edinger, *Exile Politics*, p. 153; Vietzke, *Die KPD*, p. 144; Stern, *Ulbricht*, p. 83.

23. "Walter," "Der Weg zum Sturz des Hitlerfaschismus," *Die Kommunistische Internationale*, XVI, no. [?] (August 20, 1935), 1318–40.

24. In 1946 the conference was inserted into the series of KPD party congresses as the 13th.

25. Vietzke, *Die KPD*, p. 215.

26. *Ibid.*, p. 218.

27. As shown by the composition of the new party leadership, for which see Weber, *deutsche Kommunismus*, p. 649; Duhnke, *Die KPD 1933–1945*, pp. 183–89.

28. Pieck, *Brussels speech*, p. 4.

29. *Ibid.*, p. 14.

30. *Ibid.*, p. 79.

31. *Ibid.*, p. 79.

32. Thus Wilhelm Florin's speech at the Brussels meeting is noticeably cooler toward the Social Democrats than those of Pieck and Ulbricht. See Wilhelm Florin, "Unser Verhältnis zur Sozialdemokratie und zu den sozialdemokratischen Massen," *Die Kommunistische Internationale*, 16, no. 20 (November 30, 1935), 1769–76.

33. "Ercoli," "Die antifaschistische Einheitsfront und die nächsten Aufgaben der KPD," *Die Kommunistische Internationale*, 16, no. 20, (November 30, 1935), 1741–55.

34. Texts of the resolution are in Pieck, *Brussels speech*, pp. 87–103, and in *Rundschau*, 4, no. 73 (December 12, 1935), 2817–22.

35. Edinger, *Exile Politics*, p. 156; for this period generally, see Erich Matthias, *Sozialdemokratie und Nation* (Stuttgart: Deutsche Verlags-Anstalt, 1952), especially pp. 35–43; Duhnke dissertation, pp. 262–82.

36. For the Prague meeting, see Stern, *Ulbricht*, pp. 87–90; Edinger, *Exile Politics*, p. 157; Otto Findeisen, "Zu den Einheitsfrontverhandlungen am 23. November 1935 in Prag," *BzG*, 8, no. 3 (1966), 676–94. For a detailed documentary account of the SPD-KPD negotiations, see Werner Link, ed., *Mit dem Gesicht nach Deutschland* (Düsseldorf: Droste, 1968), pp. 241–50, cited hereinafter as *Mit dem Gesicht*.

37. Edinger, *Exile Politics*, p. 157.

38. Walter Ulbricht, "Die Einheitsfrontvorschläge der KPD," *BzG*, 5, no. 1 (1963), 75–81.

39. Edinger, *Exile Politics*, p. 235 (the phrase is Edinger's).

40. *Ibid.*, p. 236.

41. Edinger, *Exile Politics*, pp. 161–68.

42. Erich Matthias, *Die deutsche Sozialdemokratie und der Osten 1914–1945* (Tübingen: Arbeitsgemeinschaft für Osteuropaforschung, 1954), p. 98.

43. Max Braun had been SPD leader in the Saar, where a proto-United Front had come into being during the Saar plebiscite campaign in January 1935. See Vietzke, *Die KPD*, p. 129.

44. Willi Bredl, "Volksfrontbesprechungen in Lutetia," in *Walter Ulbricht: Schriftsteller, Küntler, Wissenschaftler und Pädagogen zu seinem siebzigsten Geburtstag*, Alexander Abusch *et al.*, eds. (Berlin: Dietz, 1963), pp. 40–42, cited hereinafter as *Ulbricht 70th birthday*; Stern, *Ulbricht*, pp. 87–90; Duhnke dissertation, pp. 262–82; Babette L. Gross, "Die Volksfrontpolitik in den dreissiger Jahren. Ein Beitrag zum Verständnis der kom-

munistischen Taktik," *Aus Politik und Zeitgeschichte* (Beilage zur Wochenzeitung "Das Parlament"), October 24, 1962, pp. 521–48. See also Carola Stern, "Ulbricht und die Volksfront," *SBZ-Archiv*, 14, no. 10 (May 1963, 2d half), 148–55 (including two letters from non-Communist participants to the ZK/KPD); "Zwei Richtungsweisende Beiträge Walter Ulbrichts zur Entwicklung der Strategie und Taktik der KPD in den Jahren 1935-1937," *BzG*, 5, no. 1 (1963), 75–84—included are a letter to the PV in Prague of November 1935, and one to Heinrich Mann, May 25, 1937; Heinrich Mann's comments on Ulbricht, both oral and written, are in Alfred Kantorowicz, *Deutsches Tagebuch* (Munich: Kindler, 1959), I, 48, 63. For Breitscheid's attitude, see his letter of October 13, 1937, to Friedrich Stampfer, cited in *Mit dem Gesicht*, pp. 295–96.

45. From Pieck's speech at the Berne Conference cited in Gerhard Nitzsche, "Zum 25. Jahrestag der Berner Konferenz der [KPD]," *BzG*, 3, no. 1, (1964), 95.

46. Edinger, *Exile Politics*, pp. 210–25.

47. Klaus Mammach, "Die Berner Konferenz der KPD," [II] *BzG*, 8, no. 2 (1966), 228–29.

48. For details of the "Berne" proceedings, see Klaus Mammach, "Die Berner Konferenz der KPD," *BzG*, 7, no. 6 (1965), 971–89; Weber, *deutsche Kommunismus*, pp. 640, 649.

49. Nitzsche, p. 89.

50. *Ibid.*, p. 90 (these last two citations refer to ZK material provided to the Conference); Mammach, *Berner Konferenz*, pp. 984–85.

51. Resolution adopted at Berne Conference, in Weber, *deutsche Kommunismus*, 337.

52. Nitzsche, p. 95.

53. Duhnke dissertation, p. 630.

54. Weber, *deutsche Kommunismus*, pp. 336–37.

55. Nitzsche, pp. 95–96; Mammach, *Berner Konferenz,* pp. 988–89.

56. *Ibid.*, p. 989, n. 86.

57. See *inter alia*, Benedikt Kautsky, *Teufel und Verdammte*, 2d ed., (Vienna: Verlag der Wiener Volksbuchhandlung, 1961); H. G. Adler, "Selbstverwaltung und Widerstand in den Konzentrationslagern der SS," *Vierteljahreshefte für Zeitgeschichte*, 8, no. 3 (July 1960), 221–35; Eugon Kogon, *Der SS Staat*, 2d ed. (Frankfurt: Verlag Frankfurter Hefte, 1947); Duhnke, *Die KPD 1933-1945*, pp. 518–20; Margarete Buber-Neumann, *Als Gefangene bei Hitler und Stalin* (Stuttgart: Deutsche Verlags-Anstalt, 1958); Walter A. Schmidt, *Damit Deutschland lebe* (Berlin: Kongress, 1959); Günther Weisenborn, ed., *Der lautlose Aufstand* (Hamburg: Rowohlt, 1953), esp. pp. 145–237. For an account of Communist attitudes in the Sachsenhausen concentration camp in 1941–1942, see Heinz Brandt, *Ein Traum, der nicht entführbar ist* (Munich: Paul List, 1967), 153–56.

58. Kautsky, p. 135; a variety of interviewees expressed this opinion. In a Soviet Zone obituary notice for Grotewohl, it is claimed that he had "heard with satisfaction" of "permanent and heartfelt" community of effort between Social Democrats and Communists in Buchenwald. See Walter Bartel, "Zum Tode Otto Grotewohls," *Zeitschrift für Geschichtswissenschaft*, 12, no. 8 (1964), 1330, cited hereinafter as *Zfg*.

59. For incarceration of Schlimme and Lehmann, see Schmidt, pp. 407–8. For further biographical material on the experiences of many ZA members during the Hitler period, see Klaus-Peter Schultz, *Auftakt zum Kalten Krieg, Der Freiheitskampf der SPD in Berlin 1945/46* (Berlin: Colloquium, 1965), pp. 361–81.

For political reasons, every effort was made to present Grotewohl as active in the resistance to Hitler. Thus in August of 1945, a biographical sketch writer in *Das Volk* implied that Grotewohl's commercial traveling was a cover for underground work. See "O. M." [Otto Meier?], "Wir stellen vor—Otto Grotewohl," *Das Volk,* August 26, 1945.

60. *Grundriss der Geschichte der deutschen Arbeiterbewegung* (Berlin: Dietz, 1965), pp. 199–200, 205; Leibzon and Shirinia, pp. 326–27.

61. Duhnke dissertation, p. 185; Duhnke, *Die KPD 1933–1945*, pp. 282–84.

62. Kermit E. McKenzie, "The Soviet Union, the Comintern and World Revolution: 1935," *Political Science Quarterly,* 65 (June 1950), 236.

63. Thomas P. Thornton, "The Foundations of Communist Revolutionary Doctrine," in *Communism and Revolution: the Strategic Uses of Political Violence,* Cyril E, Black and Thomas P. Thornton, eds. (Princeton: Princeton University Press, 1964), p. 60.

64. Lowenthal, p. 31.

2. *The Occupation Regime*

1. The best source for the EAC negotiations is the 1950 essay of Philip E. Mosely, deputy American representative in 1944–1945. Philip E. Mosely, "The Occupation of Germany: New Light on how the Zones were Drawn," *Foreign Affairs,* 28, no. 4 (July 1950), 580–604.

The date of early April 1945 and the contents of the resumed EAC negotiations are based on Professor Mosely's letter to the writer, August 12, 1964.

2. "Declaration regarding the defeat of Germany and the assumption of supreme authority with respect to Germany by the Governments of the United Kingdom, the United States of America and the Union of Soviet Socialist Republics and the Provisional Government of the French Republic (June 5, 1945)," Beate Ruhm von Oppen, ed., *Documents on Germany under Occupation 1945–1954* (London: Oxford University Press, 1955), pp. 29–35, cited hereinafter as *Documents on Germany.*

The passage relevant here is in Article 13 (b): "The Allied Representatives will impose on Germany additional political, administrative, economic, financial, military and other requirements arising from the complete defeat of Germany."

3. "Order No. 2," Berlin, June 10, 1945, *Documents on Germany,* pp. 37–39.

4. Letter from Wolfgang Friedmann, May 20, 1964; Professor Friedmann was with the British military government in 1945; letter from Philip E. Mosely, June 30, 1965.

5. U.S. Department of State, *Foreign Relations of the United States, The Conference of Berlin (The Potsdam Conference) 1945* (2 vols.; Washington: Government Printing Office, 1955), "Document no. 855, Memorandum by Central Secretariat (Archibald Macleish), Washington, July 18, 1945," II, 783, hereinafter cited as *Potsdam I* and *Potsdam II*: "We must assume, although we have no explicit knowledge, that the Russians are clear as to their intentions. . . . Presumably they propose to substitute for a Nazi Germany a Germany at least sympathetic to Communism."

6. "Document no. 345, Deputy Military Governor, USZIG (Clay) to War Department, July 5, 1945," *Potsdam I*, pp. 489–90.

7. "Document no. 226, Acting Secretary of State (Grew) to the President, June 27, 1945 (including Murphy memorandum of June 2, 1945)," *ibid.*, p. 276.

8. OMGUS, *Monthly Report of the Military Governor*, no. 1 (August 20, 1945), p. 17. In an *Annex* on the political situation there is a comment on the four-party bloc established two months earlier in the Soviet Zone: "It is not yet clear just how much real independence these parties have within the framework of this bloc and who really determines its objectives. However, the bloc follows the pattern which has emerged in the last year in many countries . . . under Russian influence. It is also evident that the leaders of these four parties now wish to get into the (Western Zones) and organize there as well."

9. "Document No. 850, Director of Political Affairs, US Group, CCG (Heath) to Political Advisor in Germany (Murphy), July 17, 1945, with a Sub-Memo by Perry Laukhoff, July 16, 1945," *Potsdam II*, p. 761.

10. "Document No. 848, United States Delegation Working Paper, July 16, 1945," *ibid.*, p. 751. Drawn up by Philip E. Mosely and Emile Despres, it provided that "anti-Nazi political parties together with freedom of assembly and of public discussion shall be allowed and encouraged throughout Germany." The American delegation's formal proposal, submitted July 17, 1945, provided that "non-Nazi political parties with rights of assembly and public discussion shall be allowed and encouraged throughout Germany." "Document No. 852, Proposal by the United States Delegation," *ibid.*, p. 777.

11. "Document No. 1383, Protocol of the Proceedings of the Berlin Conference, August 1, 1945," *ibid.*, p. 1482.

12. Letter from Philip E. Mosely, June 30, 1965.

13. *Ibid.*

14. *Potsdam II*, p. 75.

15. Letter from Philip E. Mosely, June 30, 1965.

16. McNeill, pp. 617–18.

17. "Istoricheskiie resheniia Berlinskoi Konferentsii triokh derzhav" *Bol'shevik*, no. 15 (August 1945), 6.

18. I. Lemin, "Berlinskaia Konferentsiia triokh derzhav," *Mirovoe Khoziaistvo i mirovaia politika*, no. 9 (September 1945), 15–17.

19. Sergej Ivanovic Tjulpanow, "Die Rolle der SMAD bei der Demokratisierung Deutschlands," *ZfG*, 15, no. 2 (1967), 248, cited hereinafter as Tjulpanow, "Die Rolle."

20. V. M. Molotov, *Problems of Foreign Policy: Speeches and Statements, April 1945–November 1948* (Moscow: Foreign Languages Publishing House, 1949), p. 356.

21. "Draft Directive on Political Parties in Germany: Note by Allied Secretariat," (23 March 1946) (CORC/P(46)111). To the text of this draft, which was approved by the Control Council's Political Directorate on March 14, 1946, the Soviet delegate had proposed adding the following: "When, in the opinion of the Control Council, the conditions in Germany warrant it, and insofar as this action conforms to the democratically expressed desire of party members, Political Parties may unite throughout Germany."

The American and British delegations agreed to this change, but the French delegation, acting on "definite instructions from its Government," refused to go along.

22. Lucius D. Clay, *Decision in Germany* (Garden City, N.Y.: Doubleday, 1950), pp. 118–19, quotes the Soviet delegate as saying, "It seems to me we should not raise obstacles for German democratic parties to form on a national all-German basis."

23. F. Roy Willis, *The French in Germany 1945–1949* (Stanford: Stanford University Press, 1962), p. 27; John Gimbel, "On the Implementation of the Potsdam Agreement: An Essay on U.S. Postwar German Policy,"*Political Science Quarterly,* 87, no. 2 (June 1972), 259–63.

24. *Documents on Germany,* pp. 39–40.

25. By a process of amalgamation of historic German areas plus the absorption of remnants created by the drawing of the Oder-Neisse border, five such provinces (designated both *Land* and *Provinz*) were established. They were (roughly from North to South) Mecklenburg-Vorpommern, Brandenburg, *Provinz* Sachsen (Saxony), roughly the former Sachsen-Anhalt, *Land* Sachsen (Saxony), and Thüringen (Thuringia). The five provincial centers were at Schwerin, Potsdam, Magdeburg, Dresden, and Weimar respectively. The population of the Soviet Zone in 1946 was slightly over 17 million; in area it measured somewhat over 100,000 square kilometers.

26. J. P. Nettl, *The Eastern Zone and Soviet Policy in Germany 1945–1950* (London: Oxford University Press, 1951), ch. 3; Gregory Klimow, *Berliner Kreml* Cologne: Kiepenheuer and Witsch, 1951), pp. 204–10, has a description of the SMA organization. See also Kurt Glaser, "Governments of Soviet Germany," in *Governing Postwar Germany,* Edward H. Litchfield, ed. (Ithaca, N.Y.: Cornell University Press, 1953), cited hereinafter as *GPG;* ch. 6, is almost entirely devoted to political party affairs. The official SMA newspaper for the German population, the *Tägliche Rundschau,* rarely mentioned the Soviet military government. The SMA did not issue an official gazette; the published collection of SMA orders and directives does not go beyond 1945. *Befehle des Obersten Chefs der Sowjetischen Militärverwaltung in Deutschland: Aus dem Stab der Sowjetischen Militärverwaltung in Deutschland. Sammelheft 1, 1945* (Berlin: SWA-Verlag, 1946), cited hereinafter as *Befehle.*

27. "Order No. 1," Berlin, June 9, 1945, *Befehle,* p. 9. The SMA's provincial commands were established by "Order No. 5," Berlin, July 9, 1945, *Befehle,* p. 13 (see also *Pravda,* July 11, 1945). The provincial commanders were (names are as given in the cited Order): Colonel General I. I. Fediuninskii (Mecklenburg-Vorpommern); Marshal of Armor [?] Bogdanov (Brandenburg); Colonel General V. I. Kuznetsov (*Provinz* Saxony); Colonel General M. E. Katukov (*Land* Saxony); Colonel General V. I. Chuikov (Thuringia).

28. The other deputies were Major General M. A. Skosyrev (Mecklenburg-Vorpommern), Major General V. M. Sharov (Brandenburg), Major General D. G. Dubrovskii (*Land* Saxony). The Soviet commandants of Leipzig and Dresden were, respectively, Colonels Morozov and Gorokhov. See Hermann Matern, "In Mai 1945 begannen wir mit dem Aufbau eines neuen Deutschlands," *Vereint,* p. 308, and "Manuscript by Erich W. Gniffke dealing with party developments in 1945–1946," p. 78, cited hereinafter as Gniffke Manuscript.

For the changes in Personnel see "Berliner Chronik," in *Berlin: Kampf um Freiheit und Selbstverwaltung 1945–1946,* Albrecht Lampe, ed. 2d ed. (Berlin: Heinz Spitzing,

1961), pp. 87, 408. Berzarin is described by Alexander Werth in his *Russia at War 1941–1945* (New York: Dutton, 1964), pp. 990–91; for Berzarin's death see the story in the *DVZ*, June 17, 1945. Kotikov's political sharpness is mentioned by Erich W. Gniffke in his *Jahre mit Ulbricht* (Cologne: Verlag Wissenschaft und Politik, 1966), p. 161; see also Gladwyn Hill, "Political Officer Governs in Saxony," *The New York Times*, December 28, 1945. The published memoirs of General Gorbatov stop short at the war's end and thus do not deal with his tenure as Berlin Commandant; the abridged English version is A. V. Gorbatov, *Years Off My Life*, trans. by Gordon Clough and Anthony Cash (New York: Norton, 1965).

29. Until 1949 each Soviet Commander was at the same time chief of the occupation regime and commander of Soviet forces in his area. Nettl, p. 60.

When Harry Hopkins spoke with Stalin on May 28, 1945, Stalin commented on Harriman's suggestion that the military representative on the Control Council work "with little practical interference" by declaring that "military men were so practical they could often be fooled politically; therefore it was necessary to give them a political directive to work by." *Potsdam I*, p. 51.

30. Interviews with Joseph Baritz (March 21, 1960) and Sergei Gol'bov (March 28, 1960). Both of these former SMA officers treated the political officers' role as a well-known fact within the SMA. An East German reference is Horst Schützler, "Die Unterstützung der Sowjetunion für die demokratischen Kräfte Berlins in den ersten Nachkriegsmonaten," *ZfG*, 13, no. 3 (1965), 400. A hostile SPD account of their activities is *Die Ausschaltung der SPD in der Sowjetzone durch die sowjetische Besatzungsmacht* (Bonn: SPD Parteivorstand (1951?), pp. 7–8.

According to Klimov, one must differentiate between the Political Advisor to the Supreme Commander, who handled political coordination between the SMA and Moscow, and the Political Administration of the SMA, whose field was the political life of the Soviet Zone. Klimow, pp. 205–7.

31. For Tiul'panov's background see Nicholas Nabokov, *Old Friends and New Music* (Boston: Little, Brown, 1951), pp. 273–82 (but Nabokov is wrong in dating Tiul'panov's arrival in Berlin in the fall of 1945); Boris Meissner, *Russland, die Westmächte und Deutschland: Die sowjetische Deutschlandpolitik 1943–1953* (Hamburg: H. H. Nölke, 1953), pp. 81–82; Heinrich Graf von Einsiedel, *Tagebuch der Versuchung* (Berlin: Pontes, 1950), pp. 24–26, 86; interview with S. I. Tiul'panov, April 16, 1960. For story of Tiul'panov's 1969 lecture at a West Berlin university, see "Former Soviet Aide Visits West Berlin," *The New York Times*, December 7, 1969.

32. Von Einsiedel, p. 86.

33. Tiul'panov's role was rarely mentioned in earlier DDR writings on this period. One exception is Elly Winter, "An der Seite Wilhelm Piecks in den ersten Monaten des Neubeginns." *Vereint*, p. 127. Tiul'panov himself has begun to comment publicly on this period in recent years. For example, in April 1966 Tiul'panov participated in a joint DDR-USSR historians' meeting in Moscow in connection with the 20th anniversary of the SED. His was one of the three main talks given. For an account of this meeting, see N. M. Lebedev, "20 Let sotsialisticheskoi edinoi partii Germanii (ob'edinennaia nauchnaia sessiia)," *Novaia i Noveishaia Istoriia*, no. 4 (1966), 191–92.

34. Von Einsiedel, pp. 24–26; Leonhard, pp. 494–97. Tiul'panov's interest in German

literature was also remarked on by Alfred Kantorowicz. Interview with Alfred Kantorowicz, March 15, 1960.

35. Gniffke Manuscript, pp. 42–45.

36. *Ibid.*, p. 41.

37. *Ibid.*, pp. 42–45.

38. That there was nothing mysterious about the role of the hierarchy of political officers is shown by Nettl's statement (Nettl, p. 67) that ". . . it was responsible for liaison with, or control of, the German political parties in the Russian Zone. The amalgamation of Socialists and Communists in April 1946 took place under its auspices." There are numerous accounts of detailed Soviet interference in party activities. For an instance connected with trade union elections in the winter of 1945, see Interview with Rudolf Dux, February 19, 1960.

39. Sergei Ivanovic Tjulpanov, "Gedanken über den Vereinigungsparteitag der SED 1946," *ZfG*, no. 5 (1970), 620.

40. Wolfgang Friedmann writes that "On the whole, military government has been in the hands of regional and local commanders. This has meant a much greater reliance on indirect control through sponsored German instruments." Why this last conclusion follows is not quite clear. W. Friedmann, *The Allied Military Government of Germany* (London: Stevens, 1947), pp. 35–36. Nettl stresses local variation in Soviet military government quite strongly. Nettl, pp. 57–59.

41. Leonhard, pp. 369–73.

42. Horst Schützler, p. 399, quoting Order of the Day No. 5 (April 23, 1945) of the First Belorussian Front (i.e., Zhukov's command).

43. The story of Walter Frank is taken from *Berlin nach der Kapitulation,* Tonband no. 684 (Tonbandarchiv, Landesbildstelle Berlin). Orlopp's story is in Gniffke Manuscript, pp. 101–11, and V. N. Vysotskii, *Zapadnyi Berlin i ego mesto v sisteme sovremennykh mezhdunarodnykh otnoshenii* (Moscow: Mysl', 1971), pp. 65–66. See also Leonhard, pp. 365–68.

44. *Ibid.*, pp. 443–44; Gniffke Manuscript, pp. 129–31; Brandt, p. 171, declared that some Soviet commandants behaved like "little kings." Brandt has also stated that Soviet commanders who were charged with arbitrary behavior replied that this was the treatment they were used to at home. Interview with Heinz Brandt, March 8, 1960.

45. See, for example, Heinrich Hoffmann's remarks to a session of the Thuringia SPD *Landesvorstand* (Protocol of January 19, 1946).

46. Friedmann, p. 35.

47. Nettl, p. 63.

48. Interview with S. I. Tiul'panov, April 15, 1960. Tiul'panov has written that the Soviet Union had no previously worked out "theory of occupation administration." Tjulpanow, "Die Rolle,"p. 243.

49. This emerged from numerous interviews; e.g., interview with Fritz Sarow, July 25, 1960.

50. A full treatment of the background of German-Russian relations is Walter Laqueur, *Russia and Germany: A Century of Conflict* (London: Weidenfeld and Nicolson, 1965), ch. 1. A detailed description of German goals and methods in the Soviet Union is Alexander Dallin, *German Rule in Russia 1941–1945* (London: Macmillan, 1957).

51. Quoted by Deutscher as having been made to Mikolajcyzk in August 1944, in Isaac Deutscher, *Stalin: A Political Biography* (London: Oxford University Press, 1949), p. 537.

52. Milovan Djilas, *Conversations with Stalin* (New York: Harcourt, Brace and World, 1962), p. 79.

53. Franz Neumann wrote that "Stalin had a deep contempt for Germany's working class and more particularly for her Communist Party." Franz L. Neumann, "Soviet Policy in Germany," in *The Soviet Union since World War II*, Philip E. Mosely, ed., *The Annals of the American Academy of Political and Social Science*, 263 (May, 1949), 166. See also McNeill, p. 354. According to McNeill, Stalin at Teheran showed "admiration for the discipline and efficiency of the German people, but was bitter in his remarks about the attitude of the German working class toward the Soviet Union."

An American memorandum circulated at the Teheran Conference described Stalin's views as follows: "He appeared to have no faith in the possibility of the reform of the German people and spoke bitterly of the attitude of the German workers in the war against the Soviet Union." Robert E. Sherwood, *Roosevelt and Hopkins: An Intimate History* (New York: Harper, 1948), p. 782.

54. Djilas, p. 114. More than a little honest feeling may have underlain Stalin's statement of November 6, 1944, that "Everyone knows the rulers of Germany are already preparing for a new war. History shows that a short period of 20 or 30 years is enough for Germany to revive her power." *Soviet Foreign Policy during the Patriotic War. Documents and Materials*, tr. by Andrew Rothstein (London: Hutchinson, n.d.), II, 31–32, cited hereinafter as *SFP*.

55. *Vneshniaia Politika Sovetskogo Soiuza v Period Otechestevennoi Voiny. Dokumenty i Materialy* (Moscow: Gosizpollit, 1944), I, 30.

56. *Ibid.*, pp. 50–51.

57. "Obrashchenie tov. I. V. Stalina k narodu" *Bol'shevik*, no. 9 (May 1945), 4. The statement also appeared in the daily press; see *Pravda* and *Trud*, both May 10, 1945.

58. Molotov, p. 63.

59. Booklet in files of the *Landesarchiv Berlin—Abteilung Zeitgeschichte*.

60. Of course Ehrenburg was not alone in writing in this vein. Stalin, for example, said the German army wished to turn the Soviet people "into slaves of German princes and barons," *SFP*, p. 21, which was no less frightening for being true. See also Werth, pp. 416–17.

61. *Krasnaia Zvezda*, April 11, 1945.

62. Ilya Ehrenburg, *The War, 1941–1945*, tr. by Tatiana Shebunina and Yvonne Kapp (London: Macgibbon and Kee, 1964), V (*Men, Years, Life*), 175–77.

63. *Pravda*, April 14, 1945. Alexandrov was head of the Agitation and Propaganda Department of the Central Committee of the Soviet Communist Party. The article was re-

printed on May 16, 1945, in the *Tägliche Rundschau* with the following explanation: "In his article "Enough," published in the Moscow newspaper "Red Star," the well-known Soviet author Ehrenburg deals with the question of the German people's responsibility for the crimes of the Hitler gang in an overly simplified and false manner. This was the reason for the publication of Alexandrov's article in "Pravda" . . . [an article] which correctly reflected Soviet public opinion on this question."
According to Ehrenburg, p. 178, the article against him was inspired directly by Stalin.

64. Interview with Joseph Baritz (March 21, 1960) and Sergei Gol'bov (March 28, 1960).

65. Even Tito and his comrades had cause to complain. See Djilas, pp. 87–89. For Stalin's casual responses, see *ibid.*, pp. 95, 110–11.

66. See Leonhard, p. 372, and Sokolovskii's comment to Alexander Werth in Werth, p. 986. Zhukov declared to an SPD delegation in June 1945 that, in his efforts to halt excesses by "demoralized" individual Red Army men, he would not hesitate to order shootings. Gniffke Manuscript, pp. 43–45.

67. In response to a question from Alexander Werth at a press conference held in early June 1945 jointly with Vyshinsky, Zhukov, having previously announced a "strict occupation regime," declared that this necessarily excluded "fraternization" (*Pravda*, June 10, 1945). Werth does not mention his question in the account of the press conference in his book. Werth, pp. 995–99.

68. Leonhard, pp. 382–83. Leonhard comments, "This ticklish question was never referred to again at any meeting."

69. Franz Dahlem, "Die antifaschistische Einheit in den Konzentrationslagern," *Einheitsfront der antifaschistischdemokratischen Parteien* (Berlin: Neuer Weg, n.d.), p. 41.

70. Walter Ulbricht, "Das Aktionsprogramm der KPD in Durchführung," *DVZ*, October 14, 1945.

71. Gunther Benser, "Über den friedlichen Charakter der revolutionären Umwälzung in Ostdeutschland," *BzG*, 7, no. 2 (1965), 189–90.

72. Heinz Brandt lists rape, dismantling, and the Oder-Neisse border as three major Soviet handicaps in any attempt to win mass support. Interview with Heinz Brandt, March 8, 1960.

73. For Mikoyan's trip to Dresden and Berlin and his impressions as to the food supply situation and general material conditions, see the interview with him upon his return, *Pravda*, May 19, 1945, and Vysotskii, p. 78.

74. For Western testimony to the extent and effectiveness of these activities, see Friedmann, p. 23, n.1; Nettl, p. 57; OMGUS, *Monthly Report of the Military Governor*, No. 1 (August 20, 1945), *Annex: Civil Administration*, p. 11. Communist accounts are understandably favorable toward the SMA's efforts in this field. See, for example, Siegfried Thomas, "Der Wiederbeginn des politischen Lebens in Berlin und die Aktionseinheit der Arbeiterparteien," *ZfG*, 8, no. 5 (1960), 1312, and Vysotskii, pp. 70–79.

75. As reported in the Halle *Volks-Zeitung* August 18, 1945, Wilhelm Pieck tried to explain that the "Measures taken to dismantle large war industry plants . . . are often misunderstood, because they appear to limit the employment opportunities of workers native to a given locale. . . . We know that these measures make for difficulties, but we also know that help is being given us to cope with these difficulties."

According to a Soviet journalist, however, German workers did not really want heavy industry; in any event, there were jobs available in light industry. See V. Avarian, "In Postwar Germany," *New Times*, no. 3 (February 1, 1946), 30–31. See also Gniffke, *Jahre*, pp. 193–96; Leonhard, pp. 421–22.

76. Gniffke Manuscript, pp. 43–45, 124–25.

77. Gniffke has recorded his impression that most Soviet officers tried to establish frank and friendly relations with the German Social Democrats. *Ibid.*, p. 39. He was less happy with the tendency of Soviet commanders to present lengthy speeches along with frequent toasts. *Ibid.*, p. 78.

78. *Ibid.*, p. 39.

79. *Ibid.*, pp. 36–38.

80. S. I. Tulpanow, "Der Kampf der SED für den proletarischen Internationalismus," *BzG*, 8, no. 5 (1966), 792.

81. For a postunification example, see Leonhard, p. 472.

82. *Ibid.*, p. 353. Franz Dahlem, "Mit Wilhelm Pieck im Flugzeug zurück nach Deutschland," *Vereint*, p. 24; Dahlem writes that upon Pieck's and his arrival in Berlin, Ulbricht took them to "one of the daily joint consultations with the Soviet Military Administration at Comrade Semenov's."

83. Interview with Karl J. Germer, Jr., July 12, 1960. This same theme is sounded in reports from local SPD organizations to the provincial leadership (LV) of Thuringia; see, for example, Letter from the SPD, Erfurt district (*Kreis*) to the LV in Weimar, November 23, 1945.

84. Richard M. Scammon, "Political Parties," *GPG*, ch. 19.

85. Tjulpanow, "Die Rolle," p. 243.

86. For instance, in September 1945 Otto Grotewohl declared: "In approaching the Soviet occupation authorities we have found them receptive to our requests and willing to help." Although Grotewohl knew, as he spoke, that he was improving upon reality, it must be remembered that for an anti-Nazi German, any cooperation on the part of the victorious powers must have appeared as a voluntary gesture of support. Otto Grotewohl, *Wo stehen wir, wohin gehen wir? Weg und Ziel der deutschen Sozialdemokratie* (Berlin: "Das Volk," 1945), p. 30, cited hereinafter as Grotewohl, *Wo stehen wir?*

87. In 1956 Hermann Matern wrote: "In Eastern Germany, the socialist occupation power gave the working class . . . ample opportunity for development. . . . The Soviet Army acted as a class brother of the German working class. . . . Thanks to its presence, the foreign and West German imperialists were not in the position to undertake armed intervention; nor did the reactionary forces in East Germany dare to resist the people with armed force." Hermann Matern, "Zehn Jahre Sozialistische Einheitspartei Deutschlands: aus einem Vortrag vor dem Parteiaktiv der WISMUT, April 1956," *Aus dem Leben und Kraft der Deutschen Arbeiterbewegung* (Berlin: Dietz, 1958), p. 253.

88. Siegfried Thomas, *Entscheidung in Berlin*, 2d ed. (Berlin: Akademie-Verlag, 1966), p. 242.

89. Walter Ulbricht, "Referat zum Entwurf 'Grundriss der Geschichte der deutschen Arbeiterbewegung,'" *BzG*, 4, no. 3 (1962), 601–2.

90. Walter Ulbricht, "Die geeinte Arbeiterklasse führte das Volk aus der Katastrophe: Rede des Genossen Walter Ulbricht auf dem Empfang der Aktivisten der ersten Stunde im Berliner Rathaus am 12. Mai 1960," *Neues Deutschland*, April 17, 1965, cited hereinafter as Ulbricht, 1960 speech. An editorial note identified this as the first publication of these remarks.

91. Heinz Vosske, "Über die politisch-ideologische Hilfe der KPdSU, der Sowjetregierung und der SMAD für die deutsche Arbeiterklasse in den ersten Nachkriegsjahren 1945 bis 1949," *BzG*, 14, no. 5 (1972), 725–39.

92. Tjulpanow, "Die Rolle," p. 249.

93. Leonhard, p. 498.

3. Communist and Social Democratic Postwar Plans

1. For the ideas that activated the refounding of the SPD in the Western Zones, see Albrecht Kaden, *Einheit oder Freiheit: Die Wiedergründung der SPD 1945/46* (Hannover: J. W. H. Dietz Nachf., 1964), chs. 1 and 4; for those of the SPD organizations in British exile, ch. 5. For the latter, see further *Mit dem Gesicht*, pp. 706–10. For the ideas of the influential SPD leader in the Western Zones, Kurt Schumacher, see Lewis J. Edinger, *Kurt Schumacher: A Study in Personality and Political Behavior* (Stanford: Stanford University Press, 1965), pp. 77–93.

2. In his speech of May 12, 1960, Ulbricht declared that "At the moment when Soviet troops were crossing the Vistula [i.e., about January 12, 1945] our [KPD] party leadership had formed a commission to determine the first steps to be taken in the struggle to liquidate the remnants of Hitlerite Fascism. I was the chairman of this commission. We settled all the details inclusive of the organization of the public administration and even of cultural life." See Ulbricht, 1960 speech. Between March and August 1944, a KPD "working group" of twenty members is said to have held eighteen sessions on ideological questions. Horst Laschitza, *Kämpferische Demokratie gegen Faschismus* (Berlin: Deutscher Militärverlag, 1969). pp. 90–91, cited hereinafter as Laschitza, *Kämpferische Demokratie*. Some work had apparently been done as early as 1943. See Duhnke, *Die KPD 1933–1945*, p. 395.

3. "Aktionsprogramm des Blockes der kämpferischen Demokratie," *BzG*, 7, no. 2 (1965), 261–63, cited hereinafter as "Aktionsprogramm." The document is marked "3rd draft," but this is not further explained. See Horst Laschitza, "Zwei Dokumente aus den Jahren 1944 und 1945 für das neue, demokratische Deutschland," *BzG*, 7, no. 2 (1965), 258–60. Laschitza, *Kämpferische Demokratie*, pp. 88–90, ascribes the first draft to Pieck and dates it October 1944.

4. Ackermann claims authorship as of October 1944 (Ackermann, *Vereint*, p. 77); Laschitza, giving the same date, attributes it to Pieck, Ulbricht, and Ackermann. Since the first two names may be there for piety's sake. Ackermann's claim seems strong. See Horst Laschitza, "Über Inhalt und Programm eines Blockes der kämpferischen Demokratie," *BzG*, 6, no. 6 (1964), 1037.

5. "Aktionsprogramm," p. 262.

6. *Ibid.*, p. 261.

7. *Ibid.,* p. 262.

8. Leonhard, pp. 331–35; Lothar Berthold, "Der Kampf gegen das Hitlerregime—der Kampf für ein neues demokratisches Deutschland," *BzG,* 6, no. 6 (1964), 1017–18.

9. Leonhard, p. 334. Describing KPD discussion in the period between the Yalta Conference and V-E Day, Ackermann mentions that "At this time, we already had available to us the experiences of Poland, Bulgaria, and Rumania, which we studied thoroughly and which we discussed with Comrade Dimitrov." Ackermann, *Vereint,* p. 78. The idea of a "national bloc of militant democracy" for postwar Germany is traced back to a talk given to the KPD working group in Moscow by Wilhelm Florin on March 6, 1944, by Laschitza in *Kämpferische Demokratie,* p. 92.

10. "Richtlinien für die Arbeit der deutschen Antifaschisten in dem von der Roten Armee besetzten deutschen Gebiet," *BzG,* 7, no. 2 (1965), 263–68, cited hereinafter as "Richtlinien."

11. The name for the proposed "antifascist" newspaper to be published by the local administrative authorities was *Deutsche Volkszeitung,* which in time became the name used for the KPD newspaper in Berlin. The newspaper which fits this description was the second one to publish in postwar Berlin, the *Berliner Zeitung.* Ostensibly a nonpartisan organ of the Berlin city government, it was edited by the KPD's Rudolf Herrnstadt.

12. "Richtlinien," p. 264. See "An unsere Leser!" *DVZ,* June 13, 1945.

13. Sensibly enough, history, civics, and geography were to be stressed; Weimar-era texts were to be discarded. "Richtlinien," p. 267.

14. *Ibid.,* pp. 265–66.

15. "Aufruf der Kommunistischen Partei Deutschlands. Schaffendes Volk in Stadt und Land! Männer und Frauen! Deutsche Jugend!" *DVZ,* June 13, 1945.

16. It was also accepted as binding by the party's organizations in the Western Zones. See Hans Kluth, *Die KPD in der Bundesrepublik* (Cologne and Opladen: Westdeutscher Verlag, 1959), pp. 29–30.

17. A Soviet author has recently reiterated the claim that the KPD had realized that Germany was not "objectively" ready for a socialist transformation in 1945. See V. P. Ierusalimskii, *Gody stanovleniia i bor'by* (Moscow: Nauka, 1970), p. 30.

18. At this point in time, the KPD already knew of organizational stirrings among former Social Democrats and former members of the *Zentrum.*

19. For similar Polish views expounded early in the war years, see Andrzej Korbonski, "The Polish Communist Party 1938–1942," *Slavic Review,* 26, no. 3 (September 1967), 436. Korbonski writes that "Only the Bulletin Group managed to go beyond . . . narrow doctrinaire ideas. . . . [it] anticipated the outbreak of the Soviet-German war—which brought with it an entirely new line to be followed by Communists throughout the world— by calling above all for the regaining of Polish independence and for the establishment of a "true democracy," to be followed later by a social revolution. To achieve this objective the group envisaged the formation of a wide liberation front resembling the original concept of the popular front."

Speaking on April 8, 1945, Klement Gottwald told the Czech Communists that "the nation is looking for another leader, and this can only be the working class and ourselves, as the party of the working class." Quoted in Zdenek Elias and Jaromir Netik, "Czechoslovakia," in *Communism in Europe: Continuity, Change, and the Sino-Soviet Dispute*, William E. Griffith, ed. (Cambridge: MIT Press, 1966), II, 193.

20. *DVZ*, June 27, 1945; Walter Ulbricht, *Die Entwicklung des deutschen volksdemokratischen Staates 1945-1948* (Berlin: Dietz Verlag, 1959), pp. 16–33, cited hereinafter as Ulbricht, *Staat*. According to Leonhard, pp. 408–10, more than one-third of the delegates represented the KPD of Provinz Brandenburg rather than of Berlin.

21. Ulbricht, *Staat*, pp. 26–27.

22. *Ibid.*, p. 29. In a letter to Wilhelm Pieck dated May 17, 1945, Ulbricht complained that a "majority of our comrades have sectarian leanings." Walter Ulbricht, *Zur Geschichte der deutschen Arbeiterbewegung: Aus Reden und Aufsätzen* (Berlin: Dietz,1966), II, Supplement 1, 205.

23. Ulbricht, *Staat*, p. 30.

24. *Ibid.*, pp. 31–32. Such groups included "millions" who were antiwar, concentration camp victims from different social classes, those Germans disgusted by the bankruptcy of the leadership of the Weimar parties (not including the KPD), deracinated bourgeoisie, and others.

25. According to Leonhard, p. 410; the definition given by Ulbricht had been worked out by Fred Oelssner.

26. Fred Oelssner, "Die Anfänge unserer Parteischulung," *Vereint*, pp. 156–57; Leonhard, p. 426.

27. "Der Sieg des Faschismus in Deutschland und seine Lehren für unseren gegenwärtigen Kampf," *Vortragsdisposition* No. 1 (Zentralkomitee der Kommunistischen Partei Deutschlands, Abteilung Kultur und Volksbildung), July 9, 1945. Oelssner does not list this title in the essay cited in note 26, above.

28. The KPD position on this issue in 1945 is summarized in "Der Klassencharakter des Faschismus und die Probleme der Einheits-und Volksfront. Die Politik der KPD von 1933 bis August 1939," *Vortragsdisposition* No. 2 (Zentralkomitee der Kommunistischen Partei Deutschlands, Abteilung Kultur und Volksbildung). While discussing very frankly the resistance of the new line within the KPD in 1934–1935 (*ibid.*, pp. 6–7), the lecture comes to the conclusion that "The fault for the continuation of the split in the working class after 1933 rests solely and alone on the old SPD leadership (*ibid.*, p. 8).

29. Kautsky, p. 135, n.1, and p. 287.

30. "Buchenwalder Plattform vom 1. Mai 1944," cited in Herman L. Brill, *Gegen den Strom* (Offenbach A. M.: Bollwerk-Verlag, 1946), p. 94.

31. *Ibid.*, p. 88. According to Brill, a wave of arrests in November-December 1944 resulted in the loss of the original manuscript. The platform was the subject of lively discussions that were incorporated in an expanded version prepared by Brill in August 1944 (and circulated in the camp in April 1945).

32. *Bericht über die Tätigkeit des Volksfront-Komitees des ehem. Konzentrationslagers Buchenwald*. Besides Brill, the committee included Werner Hilpert (Christian Democrats), Ernest Thape (SPD; after 1945, chairman of the SPD in Provinz Saxony), and Walter Wolf (KPD). Duhnke, *Die KPD 1933-1945*, pp. 519–20.

33. *Manifest der demokratischen Sozialisten des ehem. Konzentrationslagers Buchenwald.* The Manifesto is dated April 13, 1945. My copy is headed "League of democratic Socialists *(Bund demokratischer Sozialisten)*/For Peace/Freedom/Socialism!"

34. Brill, *Gegen den Strom,* p. 96.

35. Duhnke, *Die KPD 1933-1945,* p. 519.

36. "Vom Chaos zur Ordnung. Aufruf der Sozialdemokratischen Partei Deutschlands. Männer und Frauen! Deutsche Jugend!" *Das Volk,* July 7, 1945.

37. The Soviet Union was nowhere referred to.

38. At the KPD-SPD meeting of June 19, 1945, Gniffke declared that "we are, after all, a socialist party and cannot, as you [the KPD] can, put forward a capitalist program. No one would believe us if we did." Gniffke Manuscript, p. 32. For an interesting discussion of this question, and a comparison of the two parties' appeals in this matter, see Ulla Plener, "Zum ideologisch-politischen Klärungsprozess in der SPD der Sowjetischen Begatzungszone 1945," *BzG,* 14, no. 1 (1972), 37–39, cited hereinafter as Plener, *Klärungsprozess.*

39. Subsequently, the SPD's failure to accept the border raised a storm in its relations with the SMA. During the election campaign of fall 1946, the SED drew back from acceptance of the border but subsequently it returned to the original Ulbricht position. Leonhard, pp. 459–60.

40. *Ibid.,* p. 333.

4. *The Formation of the KPD and SPD in the Soviet Zone*

1. Alfred J. Rieber, *Stalin and the French Communist Party 1941–1947* (New York: Columbia University Press, 1962), pp. 212–15.

2. For the pronouncements, orders, and proclamations attendant upon the formation of parties, the four-party bloc, cultural and social groups, and provincial administrations during June and July 1945, see *Um ein antifaschistisch-demokratisches Deutschland: Dokumente aus den Jahren 1945–1949* (Berlin: Staatsverlag der Deutschen Demokratischen Republik, 1968), pp. 54–96.

3. The best general account of the National Committee "Free Germany" is Bodo Scheurig, *Freies Deutschland: Das National Komitee und der Bund deutscher Offiziere in der Sowjetunion 1943–1945* (Munich: Nymphenburger, 1960). Scheurig has also edited a collection of relevant documents, *Verrat hinter Stacheldraht?* (Munich: Deutscher Taschenbuch Verlag, 1965). Heinrich Graf von Einsiedel, *Tagebuch der Versuchung* (Berlin: Pontes, 1950) and Jesco von Puttkamer, *Irrtum und Schuld: Geschichte des National-Komitees "Freies Deutschland"* (Berlin: Michael, 1948) are memoirs by officer participants. The Communist cochairman of the Committee has written his account: Erich Weinert, *Das Nationalkomitee "Freies Deutschland" 1943–1945* (Berlin: Rütten and Loening, 1957). Leonhard's participation is described in Leonhard, pp. 287–317, 325–31. A Soviet history is A. S. Blank, *Natsional'nyi Komitet "Svobodnaia Germaniia": Tsentr antifashistskoi bor'by nemetskikh patriotov (1943–1945 gg.)* (Vologda: Vologodskoe Knizhnoe Izdatel'stvo, 1963).

4. Although GDR historians and political leaders have in recent years increasingly stressed the NK"FD" as a forerunner of their subsequent efforts, the areas in which the

Committee's work is praised are other than with enemy forces. See Ulbricht, 1960 speech. Ulbricht's own activities in speaking over loudspeakers at the front lines, etc., have been favorably noted in SED literature. See, for example, Willi Bredl, "Zwischen Don und Volga," *Ulbricht's 70th Birthday*, pp. 43–46, and Stern, *Ulbricht*, p. 113.

5. Leonhard, pp. 330–31; Meissner, pp. 20–36.

6. Matern has stated flatly that the "KPD was the initiator" of the Committee; Herman Matern, "Die führende Rolle der Kommunistischen Partei Deutschlands in der antifaschistischen Bewegung 'Freies Deutschland,' " *Einheit*, 18, no. 5 (May 1963), 18. The same point is made more cautiously by Weinert, pp. 14–17, although he cites the fact that the actual implementation of plans for the Committee's establishment needed Soviet approval. A. S. Blank, pp. 3, 16, gives German Communists only limited credit for the formation of the Committee.

Western analysts do not accept this attribution of sponsorship; see Scheurig, p. 38; von Einsiedel, p. 48; Leonhard, pp. 285–86, gives the credit for selecting the Imperial German colors of black-red-white as the Committee's colors, rather than the Republican black-red-gold or the proletarian red, to Manuilsky. See also von Puttkamer, pp. 36, 41.

7. Peter Kleist, *Zwischen Hitler und Stalin 1939–1945* (Bonn: Athenäum, 1950), pp. 230–84; Alexander Dallin, "Vlasov and Separate Peace: A Note," *Journal of Central European Affairs*, no. 4 (January 1957), 394–96.

8. Leonhard, pp. 332–34, 398. Leonhard has maintained his position on this issue; See Wolfgang Leonhard: " 'Es muss demokratisch aussehen . . . ': Vor 20 Jahren begann die 'Gruppe Ulbricht' ihre Arbeit—Legende und Wirklichkeit," *Die Zeit*, May 14, 1965.

9. In what may be an effort toward retroactive justification, an East German historian has declared the Bloc of Militant Democracy to have presupposed the prior existence of political parties. See Horst Laschitza, "Über Inhalt und Programm eines Blocks der kämpferischen Demokratie," *BzG*, 6, no. 6 (1964), 1038. For Communist historians this problem does not exist. Siegfried Thomas, pp. 43–45, passes from a description of the spontaneous revival of KPD organizations among survivors of the Hitler era to a description of the work of the Ulbricht Group.

10. This was true at the zonal level. Once four "democratic," anti-Fascist" parties had been authorized, local Soviet commanders sometimes did hasten the desired process. Leonhard, pp. 413–14.

11. *Ibid.*, p. 412.

12. Kluth, p. 19.

13. A list of the membership of the Central Committees elected at the "Brussels" (1935) and "Berne" (1939) party conferences (later designated as the 13th and 14th KPD Congresses) is to be found in Weber, *deutsche Kommunismus*, p. 649. A different listing is given in Klaus Mammach, "Die Berner Konferenz der KPD." *BzG*, 7, no. 6 (1965), 977. He omits Alexander Abusch, Philip Dengel, and Gerhart Eisler from Weber's list, while adding Walter Hähnel, Emil Svoboda, and Ernst Thälmann (in absentia). Mammach lists, as members of the new Politburo, Thälmann, Pieck, Ulbricht, Florin, Dahlem, and Merker. Both sources list the five latter persons as ZK members. The continuing leadership of the KPD might well have included the influential Wilhelm Florin, had he not died of natural causes in Moscow in 1944.

14. Dahlem, *Vereint*, p. 23: Anton Ackermann, "Der Neue Weg zur Einheit," *Vereint*, p. 81; Leonhard, p. 405.

15. For the SED's *Zentralsekretariat*, see Carola Stern, *Porträt einer bolschewistischen Partei: Entwicklung, Funktion und Situation der SED* (Cologne: Verlag für Politik und Wirtschaft, 1957), after p. 327. These seven also headed the list of KPD members of the SED's *Parteivorstand*. See *Protokoll des Vereinigungsparteitages der Sozialdemokratischen Partei Deutschlands (SPD) und der Kommunistischen Partei Deutschlands (KPD) am 21. und 22. April 1946 in der Staatsoper "Admiralspalast" in Berlin* (Berlin: J. H W. Dietz Nachf., 1946), pp. 154–55, cited hereinafter as *Unity Congress.*

16. Leonhard, p. 406.

17. Walter Ulbricht, Anton Ackermann, Hermann Matern, Gustav Sobottka, Otto Winzer, and Hans Mahle.

18. This term, which has become standard SED terminology, is a convenient label for the three groups of Communists dispatched to recently liberated territory at the end of April 1945: the Ulbricht Group in Berlin; the Ackermann-Matern Group in Dresden, and the less important Sobottka Group in Mecklenburg-Vorpommern.

19. Dahlem, *Vereint*, p. 23; Ackermann, *Vereint*, p. 81. The convenient symmetry of this occasion—the leaders of the three *Initiativsgruppen* returning to Moscow for consultation—is slightly suspicious in view of the political reality of Sobottka's lesser importance in 1945. Interestingly, one of the editors of this volume, Heinz Vosske, is the source of the assertion that Sobottka was only informed about the Order # 2 in early June near Berlin at a meeting with Ulbricht. Of course, the one meeting does not necessarily exclude the other. Heinz Vosske," Über die Initiativgruppe der ZK der KPD in Mecklenburg-Vorpommern (Mai bis Juli 1945)," *BzG*, 6, no. 3 (1964), 424–37.

20. According to Richard Gyptner, "Die Vorbereitung der Vereinigung durch das Zentralkomitee der KPD," *Vereint*, p. 104, the KPD in June 1945 had a "Büro des Zentralkomitee," of which Gyptner was the Secretary and whose members were Pieck, Ulbricht, Dahlem, and Ackermann. This is the only reference in print to this Bureau.

21. Leonhard, pp. 358–60.

22. Kaden, p. 163, n.357, writes: "It has almost been forgotten today how significant was the role played in all occupation zones in the first postwar year by former concentration camp inmates. Many a political argument was settled in their favor without further discussion thanks to the moral weight of their demonstrated resistance to National Socialism." This did not apply to the KPD.

23. Leonhard has described the activities of the Ulbricht Group in great detail, pp. 341–401. His previously cited article in *Die Ziet* (May 14, 1965) includes a critical review of some recent East German literature on the Group. Two other participants have written memoirs of the Ulbricht Group: Richard Gyptner, "Die ersten Tage in der Heimat: Das Wirken der Gruppe Ulbricht im Mai 1945," *Neues Deutschland* May 5, 1964, cited hereinafter as *Gyptner ND*; Karl Maron, "Unerschütterlicher Optimismus," *Ulbricht 70th birthday*, pp. 150–58.

Thomas, p. 30, incorrectly names Arthur Pieck as a member of the Group while omitting Leonhard, Gustav Gundelach, and Hans Mahle. Aside from ignoring Leonhard, Gyptner (*Gyptner ND*) gives the correct list: Walter Ulbricht, Richard Gyptner, Karl

Maron, Otto Winzer, Gustav Gundelach, Hans Mahle, Fritz Erpenbeck, and Walter Koppe. Leonhard, pp. 342–47, describes the members of the Group and also mentions the anonymous German "technical secretary." See also Vysotskii, p. 62, n.4.

24. Leonhard, p. 355, has the Group leaving Moscow and arriving at Bruchmühle on the same day, April 30. Gyptner agrees as to the departure date but has the arrival on May 1. Maron dates the departure April 29 and the arrival at Bruchmühle April 30; Maron, *Vereint*, p. 150. But Leonhard, Gyptner, and Maron all place Ulbricht in Berlin, to the exclusion of the remaining members, on May 1. Ulbricht himself has stated that he arrived in Germany on April 30 and visited Berlin on May 1. See Ulbricht, 1960 speech.

25. Little has ever been written on the Dresden Group, perhaps because Ackermann fell from party grace just as the Ulbricht Group first appeared in print in the DDR (1953), while Matern has always remained in Ulbricht's shadow. The Ackermann-Matern chapters in *Vereint* are largely silent on this matter.

26. Vosske, pp. 424–37. It is clear from Vosske's account that this group was not really the peer of the Ulbricht and Ackermann Groups. It had a strong admixture of non-KPD personnel; only Sobottka signed the *Aufruf* and none of the members were among the forty Communists elected to the SED's *Parteivorstand* in April 1946. The area in which they arrived had been notoriously poor Marxist territory prior to 1933; part of it became Polish, and it probably did not help that, as Vosske puts it: "Most of the members of this Group hardly knew the area and its population from former times."*Ibid.*, p. 426. Ulbricht, by contrast, had been the KPD's Berlin-Brandenburg district secretary in 1929-1933.

27. Thus the Sobottka Group went to the Berlin suburb of Rüdersdorf in early June to hear the announcement of the Order No. 2. *Ibid.*, p. 433.

28. Leonhard, pp. 363ff.

29. *Ibid.*, pp. 358–60.

30. This concentration on key governmental posts, rather than on the more prominent "representative" positions was part of a general Communist pattern in Eastern Europe after 1945. For an overall account, see Hugh Seton-Watson. *The East European Revolution*, 2d ed. (London: Methuen, 1950), p. 170; ch. 8 gives specific country-by-country examples, e.g., Czechoslovakia, p. 179ff. Appearing on East German television, Ulbricht was shown inspecting an exhibit on the Ulbricht Group. At one point he remarked: "The Personnel Office should have been placed in the hands of a Communist, i.e., the Friedrichsheiner [party members in a Berlin borough] had been careless." Quoted in Stern, *Ulbricht*, p. 274.

31. Leonhard, pp. 387–88; *Tägliche Rundschau*, May 17, 1945. The three were respectively: Karl Maron, Arthur Pieck and Otto Winzer, who on this date was still referred to by his party name from Soviet days, "Lorenz." Maron was described by the Soviet paper as a "locksmith, social welfare expert," and Pieck (who had come to Berlin as a Red Army Major) as an "active functionary in the trade union movement." Gyptner (*Gyptner ND*) and Leonhard make vivid how reluctant Maron was to take on the burdens of high administrative position.

32. In the Central Administrations established in 1945, Communist representation was concentrated at the vice-presidential level; Nettl comments that since this position of second-in-command "carried with it control over internal administration and staff ques-

tions, the Communists from the very beginning occupied the majority of vice-presidencies." Nettl, p. 117.

When the provincial ministries who organized after the *Land* elections of October 1946, SED men who were formerly KPD members occupied four of the five Interior Ministries (or their equivalents). *Ibid.,* p. 93.

33. Thomas, p. 39, writes, quoting from the minutes of the Berlin district KPD party congress in April 1946, that "It was by no means the case that the Communists scrambled for administrative positions. On the contrary, a party command was frequently necessary to induce these comrades to assume such positions."

Gyptner states that during the Ulbricht Group's flight to Germany many of its members thought to themselves "We have always fought in the opposition, but now we are to take things in hand and provide leadership. Thus one of us declared during the flight, "We are now the party of the new democratic [state] order." *Gyptner ND.*

34. For the borough of Wedding, Leonhard, p. 382; for the boroughs of Steglitz and Schöneberg, Franz Wohlgemuth, "Vor dem Einzug der Westmächte in Juli 1945 bestand in ganz Berlin eine antifaschistisch-demokratische Ordnung," *BDI,* 1, no. 1 (January 1964), 10; for Neukölln, Thomas, p. 151; for Friedrichshein, Stern, *Ulbricht,* p. 274.

35. Thomas, p. 145.

36. Leonhard, p. 396; Ulbricht, *Zur Geschichte,* II, Supplement 1, 223–34. Gyptner has written (*Gyptner ND*) that "Furthermore,the [Ulbricht] Group took up connections with . . . above all . . . Brandenburg; the district leadership of the KPD for Brandenburg was set up on its [the Group's] initiative." Vosske, pp. 435–36, indicates similar problems in the Sobottka Group's operations.

37. Ulbricht, *Zur Geschichte,* II, Supplement 1, 205.

38. Leonhard, pp. 425–28; Johannes R. Becher, *Walter Ulbricht, ein deutscher Arbeitersohn,* 8th ed. (Berlin: Dietz, 1964), p. 191; Gyptner, *Vereint,* pp. 108–19; *Gyptner ND.*

39. The voluntary activism of former SPD and KPD members extended to all parts of Germany. An American military government report noted that "Immediately after the occupation, "anti-fascist" organizations developed in many communities. . . . Such organizations have been almost wholly of leftist orientation [and] led principally by former Social Democrats and Communists." OMGUS, *Monthly Report of the Military Governor,* no. 1 [August 20, 1945], p. 17.

40. Interview with Wolfgang Leonhard, January 7, 1960. For deviant local groups see Leonhard, pp. 396–97. The leader of the "Party of Working People" in Thuringia, Werner Eggerath, later became provincial KPD chief.

41. Thomas, p. 35, attacks Leonhard's position on this issue. According to him, the "real reason" for shutting down the Antifa committees was that "After the cessation of hostilities, the situation in Berlin demanded the mobilization and utilization of all forces available for dealing with the chaotic circumstances on an area-wide basis. The mutually isolated [committees] . . . contributed to a further disintegration of a municipal organism which was in any case already overly divided. [They also] diverted too many useful cadres."

Ulbricht makes a similar point in a letter to Georgii Dimitrov in May, 1945. See Ulbricht, *Zur Geschichte*, II, 417. A later Soviet commentator has conveniently telescoped the activities of the Ulbricht Group and the Antifa Committees: "The Ulbricht Group carried out the immense task of mobilizing the population in the struggle for the quickest normalization of life in Berlin. Immediately after the Liberation antifascist people's committees were set up in many sections of the city. . . . The task of the Ulbricht Group consisted of unifying the work of the people's committees." B. M. Tupolev, "Vosstanovlenie politicheskoi zhizni v Berline posle krakha fashizma" *Voprosy Istorii*, no. 5 (May 1961), 190–91.

42. Thomas, pp. 45–46.

43. Vosske, pp. 435–36.

44. Schulz, *Auftakt*, pp. 15–18.

45. That is, at a time when no parties had yet been registered, although the Communists had already made all their preparations.

46. Letter from "Der Magistrat der Stadt Berlin/Der Oberburgermeister," June 18, 1945.

47. Schützler, p. 405.

48. Leonhard, p. 379, for concentration on Western sectors; Siegfried Thomas, "Der Wiederbeginn des politischen Lebens in Berlin und die Aktionseinheit der Arbeiterparteien (Mai–Juni 1945)," *ZfG*, 8, no. 6 (1960), 1322–23; *Gyptner ND.*

49. Ulbricht, 1960 speech.

50. *Referat von Walter Ulbricht am Sonntag den 10. Juni 1945 aus Anlass der legalen Wiederkehr der KPD*, p. 8, cited hereinafter as Ulbricht, *June 10 Referat*. To my best knowledge, this speech has not been published. See also, Thomas, pp. 46–47, and Leonhard, pp. 399–403. According to Leonhard, when Ulbricht, at the June 10 meeting, had finished reading the proposed KPD proclamation, he was asked how a party that had such a program differed from any other democratic party. Ulbricht winked and grinned and replied, "That you'll soon see, Comrade. Just wait a bit."

51. Ulbricht, *June 10 Referat*, p. 1.

52. When Ulbricht made a similar comment at the first public meeting of the Berlin KPD, "cries of astonishment" were heard in the audience. Leonhard, p. 410.

53. Ulbricht, *June 10 Referat*, p. 6. How many Germans, he asked a heckler, had had an opportunity to study Marxism under Hitler?

54. Ulbricht took this opportunity to announce that the KPD would not establish a new atheists' organization. Ulbricht, *June 10, Referat*, p. 81. .

55. *Ibid.*, pp. 3–5. This new image was reflected in the party's agitational material. One Berlin branch stressed "Elimination of the Housing Shortage"; *Aufruf*, KPD, Bezirk, Berlin-Schöneberg, May 15, 1945. This same organization informed its branches that, "We must see to it that by our willingness to work and through our initiatives we let the KPD appear before the public as the leader of the antifascist struggle for the rebirth of a democratic Germany"; *An alle Unterbezirke.* KPD Bezirk Berlin-Schöneberg, June 14, 1945

56. In the progression of synonyms "Arbeiter," "Werktätigen," and "Schaffenden," the last has the broadest social connotation; almost anyone who receives a wage, salary, or commission could be included. These three terms were used alternatively but not interchangeably in 1945–1946 depending on the occasion and audience, for support in the name of general social goals. Discussions of KPD-SPD unity almost always involved "Arbeiter," and sometimes "Werktätigen," but almost never "Schaffenden."

57. For the text, see also Ossip K. Flechtheim, ed., *Dokumente zur parteipolitschen Entwicklung in Deutschland seit 1945* (Berlin: Dokumenten Verlag, 1962), I, 313ff.

58. "An unsere Leser," *DVZ*, June 13, 1945. It would represent the just demands of the broadest strata of working people and act as "guardian of traditional German cultural values and as sponsor of a progressive and truly national culture." It would throw open its columns to everyone willing to lead the German people out of the current catastrophic situation; cooperation was asked of workers, salaried employees (*Arbeiter und Angestellte*), the middle classes, peasantry, intellectuals, scientists, artists, writers, and educators.

59. "Eine bedeutungsvolle Beratung," *DVZ*, June 13, 1945; "Kommunisten, Sozialdemokraten, Demokraten und Zentrum in einheitlicher Front!" *DVZ*, June 14, 1945. In these stories the *DVZ* still referred coyly to Ulbricht as a "former Reichstag Deputy."

60. *Ibid.;* see also Ulbricht, *Zur Geschichte*, II, 418–21.

61. Leonhard, pp. 407–8.

62. "Stimmen zum Aufruf der KPD," *DVZ*, June 16, 1945.

63. Thomas, pp. 49–50. Thomas assumes that this was obviously a good thing.

64. Later claims by SPD organizations both in the Soviet Zone and in the Western Zones to represent organizational continuity with the pre-1933 party is not based on fact. For the problems of the London emigrés' return, see Edinger, *Exile Politics*, p. 238, and *Mit dem Gesicht*, pp. 710–23.

65. The reestablishment of the SPD in all parts of Germany has received a thorough treatment in the previously cited book of Albrecht Kaden, whose analysis is marred chiefly by his identification with Schumacher's policies.

The best accounts of events in the Soviet Zone are Gustav Dahrendorf, "Zwangsvereinigung der Kommunistischen und Sozialdemokratischen Partei in der Russischen Zone," in *Der Mensch das Mass aller Dinge: Reden und Schriften zur deutschen Politik 1945–1954*, Ralf Dahrendorf, ed. (Hamburg: Verlagsgesellschaft deutscher Konsumgenossenschaften, 1955), cited hereinafter as *Zwangsvereinigung*, as well as a number of shorter pieces collected in that volume; and the two works of Gniffke (Manuscript and *Jahre*). A ZA member's account, notable for its errors, is Max Fechner, "Zentralausschuss der SPD und Zentralkomitee der KPD gingen zusammen," *Vereint*, pp. 42–64.

66. The term *Zentralausschuss* translates literally to "Central Committee," but the latter is preempted in German and Communist terminology by the KPD. The pre-1933 SPD was led by a *Parteivorstand* (literally "Party Directorate"). The term "Zentralausschuss" was clearly chosen as a provisional expedient to apply to a particular institution in special circumstances, and it seems best to acknowledge this by using the term without translation or by reference to its abbreviation, ZA.

The first recorded use of the term is by Gniffke in relation to Social Democratic overtures to the KPD on May 24, 1945, its official use in the application to the SMA after June 10, 1945; was apparently suggested by Fechner in the style of "Zentralausschuss der Sozialdemokratischen Partei Deutschlands mit den Sitz in der Reichshauptstadt Berlin" [Zentralausschuss of the (SPD) with its seat in the Reich capital Berlin]. Gniffke Manuscript, pp. 12, 28.

67. Among them were the Fechner claim of a "mandate" (discussed below), the meeting on June 17, 1945, their daily work, approval by provincial and local SPD organizations, and their "caretaker" function.

68. *Mit dem Gesicht*, pp. 703–4.

69. Gniffke Manuscript, pp. 1–9.

70. Orlopp was *Stadtrat für Handel und Handwerk*; Pieck was *Stadtrat für Personal und Verwaltung. Tägliche Rundschau*, May 18, 1945.

71. This phrase about "organizational unity" has been omitted from the account in the published memoirs. See Gniffke, *Jahre*, p. 24.

72. Gniffke Manuscript, p. 12.

73. *Ibid.*, pp. 13–14.

74. Gustav Dahrendorf, "1946-Berlin-Deutschland-Europa," *Der Mensch das Mass aller Dinge*, pp. 159–60.

75. A shadow side of the liberation was the Red Army command's insistence that the prisoners take part in a "liberation march" through the streets of Potsdam. Interview with Ralf Dahrendorf, January 18, 1960.

76. Dahrendorf (note 74), pp. 159–60; Ulbricht's 1960 account mentions meeting only Otto Buchwitz. See Ulbricht, 1960 speech.

77. Maron seems to have lost his eagerness for Social Democrats rapidly, for he apparently said nothing on this topic to Gniffke, Grotewohl, and Graf when they visited him two days later.

78. Letter from Gustav Dahrendorf to [name unclear], Hamburg, July 15, 1945.

79. Dahrendorf had been strongly anti-Communist before 1933, but had been very strongly affected by his prison experiences, especially his connection with Wilhelm Leuschner (a trade unionist and Social Democrat executed in connection with the July 20 plot). From this Dahrendorf derived a conviction that socialist unity was a German necessity. At this early date the presumptive content of that unity had not yet become a problem. Interview with Ralf Dahrendorf, January 18, 1960.

80. Statement by Karl J. Germer, Jr., June 5, 1956, hereinafter cited as Germer Statement. This account of the activities of the Germer circle was prepared for the *Landesarchiv Berlin-Abteilung Zeitgeschichte* chronology of postwar Berlin history. See also interviews with Karl J. Germer, Jr., July 12, 1960 and July 4, 1962.

81. The Germer Statement has May 16; the account of Fritz Neubecker has May 15. Neither remembers the exact date.

82. Interview with Karl J. Germer, Jr., July 12, 1960; Germer Statement.

83. Draft Program for the May 15 Meeting (Germer files).

84. Letter from Karl J. Germer, Jr., to Hermann Schlimme, May 18, 1945. See also Germer's Draft for a Youth Appeal.

85. Thomas, pp. 63–64.

86. Gniffke Manuscript, p. 15. Fechner was disliked, perhaps unfairly, for his pseudointellectual pretensions and for his suspected weakness for material allurement.

87. *Stenographische Niederschrift über die gemeinsame Konferenz des Zentralkomitees der KPD und des Zentralausschusses der SPD mit den Vertretern der Bezirke am 20. und 21. Dezember 1945 in Berlin, SPD-Haus, Behrenstrasse,* cited hereinafter as December Conference. Possibly, Grotewohl said, wartime confusion had made delivery difficult. Ulbricht interjected at this point, "I never received it." (December Conference, p. 8.) According to Siegfried Thomas, this letter, "which in those days never reached its addressee," is in the SED files. Thomas, p. 62, n.156.

88. From the previously cited accounts of Leonhard, Maron, and Gyptner it is clear that on April 28, 1945, Ulbricht was still in Moscow. Although the letter could well have lain over at the *Bezirksamt* until Ulbricht stopped by on his rounds in Berlin, the April date is impossible to explain except through confusion on Fechner's part. This point was not raised at the December Conference.

89. December Conference, p. 7.

90. A month after supposedly writing to Ulbricht, Fechner was still unsure as to whether any party activity would be permitted and was willing to work in a nonpartisan antifascist organization. See his letter to a "Herr Fuchs," sent through Germer, May 21, 1945.

91. According to Fechner, when the regularly elected PV went into exile in 1933 it authorized a twelve-member committee to continue the PV's work on an "illegal" basis within Germany. Of the original number only two had survived: Fechner and Richard Weimann. Now, by coopting suitable newcomers, they would reconsttitute the legitimate leadership of the SPD throughout Germany. Fechner's claim was advanced primarily on three occasions: in his report on the meeting with Schumacher in Hanover in October 1945 (Max Fechner, "Hannover—ein Beitrag zur Klarheit," *Das Volk,* October 16, 1945); in a radio address on January 10, 1946 (Max Fechner, "Was ist der Zentralausschuss?"); and in a newspaper polemic against Schumacher (Max Fechner, "Offener Brief an Dr. Schumacher," *Das Volk,* March 21, 1946), and reiterated at the Soviet Zone Congress ("40th") of the SPD: *40. Parteitag der Sozialdemokratischen Partei Deutschlands am 19. und 20. April 1946 in Berlin* (Berlin: Vorwärts-Verlag, 1946), p. 38, cited hereinafter as *SPD 40th Congress.* Fechner's story first appeared in print during the summer of 1945, but without mentioning himself or Weimann by name. See Max Fechner, "Vermächtnis," *Das Volk,* July 19, 1945.

92. Kaden, pp. 28–29, n.32.

93. For a supposedly powerful argument, it was scarcely mentioned by others and never in print by Weimann, who later denied its factual basis (*ibid.*). Also an Interview with Erich W. Gniffke, August 3, 1960.

94. Horst Duhnke accepts it without further comment. Duhnke, *Die KPD 1933–1945,* p. 521, n.256.

95. Thomas, p. 52; Gunter Benser, quoted in *Wir sind die stärkste der Parteien! Eine Bibliographie zum 15. Jahrestag der Grundung der Sozialistischen Einheitspartei Deutsch-*

lands, Günter Herting and Günter Aurich, eds. (Leipzig: VEB Verlag für Buch-und Bibliothekswesen, 1961), p. 29.

96. Thus he suggested a referendum (*Urabstimmung*) in the SPD on the unity question. Max Fechner, "Um die Einheit der Schaffenden." *Tägliche Rundschau,* January 1, 1946.

97. For example, Grotewohl and Dahrendorf had both been Reichstag deputies, and the former had been a cabinet minister in Brunswick as well. Gniffke and Fechner had been *Landtag* deputies; Schlimme and Göring had been prominent trade union officials. See Tupolev, p. 191; Thomas, p. 52.

98. Thus, in a talk in August 1945, Dahrendorf proclaimed that "The bourgeois era is over and done with. All toiling people must combine their efforts socially and economically . . . [Germany must be a] new social and democratic community." Gustav Dahrendorf, "1945—Was wird aus Deutschland?" *Der Mensch das Mass aller Dinge,* p. 158.

99. In writing about the immediate postwar period, Gniffke remarks that he and his Social Democratic colleagues had to inform themselves quickly about the Soviet Union. Gniffke Manuscript, p. 39.

On the other hand, opportunities for acquiring broader perspectives were soon available. Gniffke points out that most members of the ZA lived in the Western sectors of Berlin and had the opportunity, not least through contacts with American and British trade unionists, of informing themselves about the other occupying powers. *Ibid.,* p. 75.

100. Chairs were lacking, windows were broken, and, thanks to the confusion caused by the death one day earlier of the Soviet Commandant, it was not possible to obtain a permit for the meeting until after the announced starting time. Gniffke Manuscript, p. 29; *DVZ,* June 19, 1945; *Das Volk,* July 7, 1945.

101. Leonhard, p. 409; Gniffke Manuscript, p. 29.

102. From the text of one of the posters announcing the meeting as quoted in Kaden, p. 38, n.56. Germer remembers that the process of authenticating delegates broke down and that, in any case, the meeting admitted pre-1933 rank-and-file members as well as former functionaries. Interview with Karl J. Germer, Jr., July 12, 1960.

103. No formal vote was taken at the meeting.

104. The *Zentralausschuss* consisted of: Otto Grotewohl, Max Fechner, Erich W. Gniffke (as co-chairmen), Gustav Dahrendorf, Helmuth Lehmann, Fritz Neubecker (as added members of the "executive committee"), plus Richard Weimann, Otto Meier, Hermann Harnisch, Karl Litke, Josef Orlopp, Hermann Schlimme, Bernhard Göring, Karl J. Germer, Jr.; their places of origin ranged from East Prussia to the Ruhr, their occupations from carpenter to party worker, and their ages from 63 to 32. ZA data compiled largely from Germer Papers.

105. The Appeal was dated June 15, 1945, but apparently was not made public until the meeting of the 17th. At this time the SPD did not yet have a newspaper.

106. *SPD 40th Congress,* p. 20.

107. See the cogent technical objections of Kaden, p. 39. The Berlin meeting was the first of its kind for the SPD in postwar Germany.

108. Gniffke Manuscript, p. 29. Gniffke notes that as Grotewohl read the party's Appeal "The meeting was soon under his spell. . . . Grotewohl was the outstanding public speaker of old, addressing himself to the emotions as well as to reason. He was an artist with words and captured the hearts of the Berliners." *Ibid.*, p. 30.

109. Grotewohl's speech was published as part of a booklet together with the SPD Appeal and other documents: *An die Arbeit! Aufruf der Sozialdemokratischen Partei Deutschlands vom 15. Juni 1945 und Begründungsrede ihres Vorsitzenden Otto Grotewohl* (Berlin: "Das Volk," [1945]), pp. 3–9, hereinafter cited as *Begründungsrede*. See also Otto Grotewohl, *Im Kampf um Deutschland: Reden und Aufsätze*, 2 vols. in 1 (Berlin: Dietz, 1948), I, 7.

110. He absolved the honor of German antifascists from the charge of not having overthrown Hitler: see what effort it required of the three great Allies! *Begründungsrede*, p. 3.

111. *Ibid.*, p. 7.

112. *Ibid.;* this important decision was taken without even the dubious legitimization of the June 17 meeting having been obtained. The true source of legitimacy, the SMA, had already granted its approval.

113. *Ibid.*, pp. 5–6.

114. Kaden, pp. 23–25.

115. Kaden's book contains convincing refutation of Thomas's contention that "In 1945 Berlin became the starting point for the re-establishment of the SPD in all of Germany." Thomas, p. 50.

116. Such is the viewpoint of Georg Kotowski, "Der Kampf um die Selbstverwaltung in Berlin: Ein Beitrag zur Vorgeschichte der Spaltung der Stadt," *Das Hauptstadtproblem in der Geschichte: Festgabe zum 90. Geburtstag Friedrich Meineckes*, Jahrbuch für Geschichte des deutschen Ostens, I (Tübingen: Max Niemeyer, 1952), p. 173; see the sources for the CDU and FDP/LDP in Kaden, p. 25, n.24.

117. Thus Dahrendorf, writing in mid-July 1945, mentions SPD organizations in the *Länder* of the Soviet Zone and adds, "We hope to be able to establish connections with the district organizations [of the party] in the next few weeks." Letter from Gustav Dahrendorf to [name unclear] Hamburg, July 15, 1945. Members of the ZA did not get to the various provincial centers until late August-September 1945. SPD leaders in the West seemed equally ill-informed about ZA activities. For an account of how eagerly Social Democratic exiles in London devoured information on Berlin developments, see *Mit dem Gesicht*, pp. 705–6.

118. For the formation of the LDP in the Soviet Zone, see Leonhard, p. 142; Ekkehart Krippendorf, "Die Gründung der liberaldemokratischen Partei in der sowjetischen Besatzungszone 1945," *Vierteljahreshefte für Zeitgeschichte*, 8, 3 (July 1960), 292–95. For the formation of the SPD in the Western zones, Kaden, ch. 3.

119. The former organization secretary of the Leipzig SPD in 1945–1946 remembers that American officials seemed more interested in trade union than political party organization. Interview with Rudolf Rothe, February 6, 1960. For the American position generally, see *GPG*, chs. 3 and 19; for relevant portions of the controlling American directive, JCS 1067,

see *Documents on Germany*, pp. 14–21. For an SED view of Halle under the Americans, see Robert Siewert, "Erinnerungen an die Zusammenarbeit mit der sowjetischen Besatzungsmacht in den Jahren 1945/46," A. Anderle et al., eds., *Zwei Jahrzehnte deutsch-Sowjetische Beziehungen 1945–1965* (Berlin: Staatsverlag der DDR, 1965), pp. 75–76.

120. There is a description of early covert contacts between the KPD in Leipzig and the Dresden Group in Fritz Selbmann, "Die sowjetischen Genossen waren Freunde und Helfer," *Vereint*, pp. 354–55. Some information on the Dresden Group may be found in Hermann Matern, *Vereint*, pp. 303–4. In a generally similar account published a year earlier, Hermann Matern, "Gedanken nach 20 Jahren (Rede im Kurhaus Dresden-Bühlau am 21. April 1965)," *BzG*, 7, no. 4 (1965), 598, Matern omits Ackermann's name. See also Klaus Drosbich, "Der Kampf um die Einheitspartei der Arbeiterklasse in Leipzig 1945–1946," *BzG*, 2, *Sonderheft* (1960), 131–32.

121. In addition to the Matern accounts cited above, see Ackermann, *Vereint*, pp. 78–81, and Fred Oelssner, "Die Anfänge unserer Parteischulung," *Vereint*, pp. 154–56.

122. Matern, "Gedanken nach 20 Jahren," *BzG*, p. 599.

123. Matern, *Vereint*, p. 309.

124. Joseph Lapus, "Das Leipziger Nationalkomitee Freies Deutschland: Ein Opfer des Faschismus und des Stalinismus," *Der dritte Weg*, I, No. 7 (November 1959), n.p.; Duhnke, *Die KPD 1933–1945*, pp. 492–504.

125. In addition to its organizational autonomy, the Leipzig group apparently advocated policies that differed from those of the ZK on the subjects of dismantling and formation of central administrations in the Soviet Zone. Lapus, in *Der Dritte Weg*.

126. Selbmann's tactful account omits mention of these difficulties but is otherwise compatible with Lapus's. The men arrested, Plesse and Rosenberg, were later released and given minor administrative posts. Selbmann, *Vereint*, pp. 348–49, 359. In the fall of 1945 Matern told Gniffke that he had "intervened" in Leipzig and recalled Selbmann to Dresden—ostensibly to improve relations with SPD. Gniffke Manuscript, p. 76.

127. Otto Buchwitz, *Brüder, in eins nun die Hände* (Berlin: Dietz, 1956), pp. 22–23.

128. Interview with Rudolf Rothe, February 6, 1960; interview with Arno Hennig, March 4, 1960.

129. *Protokoll vom Parteitag des Sozialdemokratischen Partei Deutschlands-Landesgruppe Sachsen: Stenographischer Bericht über die Verhandlungen des Landes-Parteitages, abgehalten am 7., 8. und 9. Oktober 1945 in Dresden (Freital)* (Dresden: Schrift und Kunst [1945]), p. 30, cited hereinafter as *Saxony SPD Congress*.

130. Buchwitz, p. 32.

131. Gniffke Manuscript, p. 71.

132. Liselotte Thoms and Hans Vieillard, *Ein guter Deutscher: Walter Ulbricht—eine biographische Skizze aus seinem Leben* (Berlin: Staatsverlag der Deutschen Demokratischen Republik, 1963), pp. 71–75.

Basing herself on this, Carola Stern writes incorrectly (*Ulbricht*, pp. 129–30) that Ulbricht was in Thuringia *prior to* the departure of American troops. Her comment on Ulbricht's activities stresses the familiar pattern of his work (although neglecting his party activity): "There too he prepared for the new organization of the administration according to those principles which had been established in Moscow prior to the war's end and which had already been applied in Berlin to the organization of the municipal and borough administrations."

Ulbricht's trip to Thuringia is also mentioned by Becher, pp. 209–11. In 1965, documents relating to an Ulbricht visit to Jena on July 5, 1945, were published in Ulbricht, *Zur Geschichte*, II, Supplement 1, 241–45.

133. According to Ulbricht, *Zur Geschichte*, Ulbricht had to restrain "sectarian" comrades who complained that the program of the British Communists went further than that of the KPD. See also, Thoms and Vieillard, pp. 71–72.

134. *Dokumente und Materialien*, pp. 47–48 (for the "Anti-Nazi" Group), and pp. 62–65 (for the resolution of July 15, 1945).

135. Protocol of the Meeting of the Thuringia LV, November 26, 1945.

136. Ulbricht, *Zur Geschichte*, II, Supplement 1, 244. At a meeting in Jena, Ulbricht scolded the local KPD, "You're no longer in opposition! The responsibility is yours!"

137. For a brief reference to the earlier career of both Brill and August Frölich in Thuringia, see Werner T. Angress, *Stillborn Revolution: The Communist Bid for Power in Germany, 1921–1923* (Princeton: Princeton University Press, 1963), pp. 229, 380–81. See also Gross, pp. 540–42, for his underground work in the Hitler period.

138. The text of the call for the conference is dated at Weimar July 5, 1945. See Plener, *Klärungsprozess,* pp. 40–41.

139. *Bund demokratischer Sozialisten—Richtlinien* [Summer 1945]. The *Richtlinien* are undated; I presume Brill's authorship from his general position as chief ideologue of the Thuringian SPD, and from remarks in interviews with former associates.

140. *Protokoll der ersten Landeskonferenz der Sozialdemokratischen Partei Deutschlands, Bezirksverband Thuringen*, p. 2. During this early period, provincial organizations of the SPD sometimes used their pre-Hitler designation of *Bezirksverband* and sometimes their new Soviet Zone designation *Landesverband*.

141. Letter from Thuringia LV, to *Bezirksleitung* Thuringia (KPD) July 10, 1945.

142. Possibly the tone and contents of this letter were part of Brill's plan to force the SMA to take the SPD "seriously." Gniffke reports (*Jahre*, p. 54) that a member of the Thuringian LV, Cäsar Thierfelder, who was visiting Berlin in early July, told the ZA that at the first Thuringian SPD Conference (just held), Brill had declared that the Social Democrats "must not allow the Communists to press them to the wall. They must make [people] aware of their presence; in the end even the Russians will be convinced that they will have to deal with the Social Democrats as a major social factor."

Both Brill and Grotewohl hoped that the SMA would, in its own interests, eventually deal with the SPD; the conclusions as to their own actions that they drew from this premise were quite opposed. In a letter written in 1947 Brill wrote that, after the Soviet forces had occupied Thuringia, he had refused to bow to Soviet demands not to advocate immediate moves toward Socialism, and he had opposed the unification of the KPD and SPD, preferring the "realization of the unity of the working class." Bitterly he concluded that, therefore, "I was not only threatened with a court-martial, but also . . . arrested by the NKVD, harassed for months, intimidated, threatened with deportation, with being shot, and so forth." Letter from Herman L. Brill to [name withheld], April 19, 1947.

143. Letter from the *Bezirksleitung Thüringen, KPD* to *Landesvorstand Thüringen, Sozialdemokratische Partei, Bund demokratischer Sozialisten,* July 21, 1945.

The letter read in part: "How shall Socialism be achieved while the majority of the population is the captive of a hostile ideology? After all, you yourselves have declared, and rightly so, that the full attainment of Socialism requires the participation of the entire toiling people. We therefore maintain that we must first carry out a patient, more of less long-range educational effort amongst the German people, in order to win the masses for Socialism."

144. Gniffke, *Jahre*, pp. 41–43. This reference to Brill is not found in the earlier version of these events; see Gniffke Manuscript, pp. 36–39.

145. Letter from Hermann L. Brill to Otto Grotewohl, December 15, 1945; (hereinafter cited as Brill, SMA Letter); Gniffke, *Jahre*, p. 82. A former close associate characterized Hoffmann as an ambitious man of tactical skills, who tended always to "excuse" KPD actions. Despite later differences, Brill had at first supported him, helping to make him vice-chairman. Interview with Adolf Bremer, June 28, 1960.

146. Brill, SMA Letter.

147. Letter of *Zentralausschuss* to Thuringian LV, September 23, 1945, cited in Protocol of Extraordinary Session, Thuringian *Bezirksvorstand,* September 30, 1945; Gniffke Manuscript, pp. 79–81.

148. Protocol of the Meeting of Otto Grotewohl and Otto Meier with members of the Thuringian *Bezirkssekretariat,* August 25, 1945.

At this meeting Grotewohl said that the ZA was powerless against Soviet wishes and that Brill should perhaps withdraw from politics, both for his own safety and because his political relations to the SMA had become impossible. Hoffmann and Curt Böhme suggested ZA help in securing Brill an administrative job in Berlin. This was in fact done when Brill finally did flee Thuringia in January 1946. In the public story on Grotewohl's trip, Hoffman is referred to as head of the Thuringian LV. See "Aufbau der Reichsorganisation der SPD," *Das Volk,* September 6, 1945.

149. Freiburg was political secretary of the LV until he was injured in an automobile accident in October 1945.

150. BV Meeting of September 30, 1945; Gniffke Manuscript, pp. 79–81.

151. Letter from LV (signed Hoffman) to "Russian Commandant for Thuringia," July 12, 1945.

152. Gniffke, *Jahre,* p. 61.

153. Brill, SMA Letter.

154. This exchange was reported in *Circular Letter No. 6/1945* (August 16, 1945) issued by the LV.

155. "Notes on a Conference of the Undersigned with Major General of the Guards Kolesnichenko," August 24, 1945. There is no signature, but internal and surrounding evidence makes it probable that Hoffman represented the SPD on this occasion.

156. "In any case, socialization could not be carried out after a lost war by a government not able to take independent decisions."

157. Another of Kolesnichenko's homilies on how one educates a people was "In view of the fact that this enlightenment had not yet taken place, he [the general] could not countenance participation in the process of enlightment by a people that still found itself in spiritual confusion."

158. As late as July 27, 1945, Brill declared at a session with the Thuringia SMA that "Our *Parteivorstand* [finds itself] abroad. . . . The ZA is only competent for the Russian occupation zone, and we have recognized it in that area. However, this is an internal party matter, which will have to be clarified at a party congress or conference." Protocol of Meeting of LV, SPD Thuringia, July 30, 1945.

Grotewohl declared, at a meeting with functionaries of the Thuringia LV, in Weimar, that, "The *Zentralausschuss* considers itself to be only a substitute for a *Parteivorstand* to be set up at a party congress or conference." He dismissed the claims of the remnants of the exiled SOPADE leadership on the grounds that only two of its members were still alive. Protocol of Meeting of Thuringian *Bezirkssekretariat*, August 25, 1945.

159. Protocol of Meeting of Thuringia, LV, August 6, 1945. Hoffman repeated this contention in the fall in the first issue of the Thuringian SPD's newspaper. See Heinrich Hoffman, "Neuaufgaben der Partei," *Tribüne*, September 15, 1945.

160. Protocol of the meeting of the extended LV, August 11, 1945.

161. The reference is presumably to Brill's meeting with members of the ZA in Berlin during the first days of August 1945.

162. Protocol of the Meeting of Thuringia LV, August 6, 1945; Protocol of the Meeting of Thuringia LV, August 11, 1945. On this occasion Hoffman declared that "We must try to arrange a *Reich* party congress or party conference as soon as possible so as to work out a uniform program for the party."

163. Brill reported with satisfaction that "All the members of the *Zentralvorstand* [sic] were active in illegal work and served time either in a concentration camp or in prison. The *Zentralausschuss* is also of the opinion that the new SPD cannot simply pick up where the old SPD stopped in 1933."

164. Undated copy, signed Heinrich Hoffman. The six points were:
   1) Orders of the SMA;
   2) Decisions of the Potsdam Conference;
   3) ZA Appeal of June 14 [sic], 1945;
   4) further ZA resolutions, as well as those of future *Reichsparteitäge* and *Reichskonferenzen*;
   5) agreements on cooperation between the KPD and SPD in Thuringia;
   6) the four-party bloc agreements for the Soviet Zone and for Thuringia.

165. Brill, SMA Letter.

166. *Ibid.;* Protocol of Meeting of BV, SPD Thuringia, September 30, 1945.

167. "Aktionseinheit für ganz Thüringen," *Thüringer Volkszeitung*, August 16, 1945. The SPD signatories were: Curt Böhme, Gustav Brack, Adolf Bremer, Marie Canarius, Heinrich Hoffman, Cäsar Thierfelder; Ernst Busse, Richard Eyermann, Stefan Heymann, Hanna Melzer, Georg Schneider, and Walter Wolf signed for the KPD.

168. Walter Ulbricht, "Über unsere Aufgaben," *Thüringer Volkszeitung*, August 16, 1945.

169. But probably after it had applied for a license to operate; judging by Dahrendorf's remark quoted below, this was most likely done on June 11.

170. There is no trace of the action that sent Dahrendorf to the meeting as a *Zentralausschuss* spokesman, but that he would commit the ZA and the party on his sole initiative is implausible.

171. Dahrendorf's remarks are in *DVZ*, June 14, 1945, and were reprinted in a pamphlet, *Der Weg zur Einheit* (Berlin: Union-Druck, n.d.), pp. 12–14.

172. *Begründungsrede*, p. 7.

173. Germer Statement.

174. "Von der Einheit der Parteien zur Einheit des Volkes," *DVZ*, June 20, 1945.

175. They were, for the KPD: Walter Ulbricht, Anton Ackermann, Ottomar Geschke, Hans Jendretzki, Otto Winzer; for the SPD; Otto Grotewohl, Erich W. Gniffke, Gustav Dahrendorf, Helmut Lehman, Otto Meier.

176. Gniffke records Grotewohl as saying of Ulbricht after the meeting, "That fellow will do us in yet!" On the other hand, Ackermann made a favorable impression on Gniffke by saying that "we" would have a hard time putting German and socialist ideas across. Gniffke Manuscript, p. 33.

177. *Ibid.*, p. 31.

178. "Vereinbarung des Zentralkomitees der Kommunistischen und des Zentralausschusses der Sozialdemokratischen Partei Deutschlands," *DVZ*, June 20, 1945.

179. The agreement of June 19 between the ZK and the ZA was repeated between party organizations at lower levels throughout the Soviet Zone; thus: July 3 in *Land* Saxony, August 8 in Thuringia, September 1 in Brandenburg, October 5 in Mecklenburg-Vorpommern, and October 6 in Berlin.

180. The language of the agreement clearly reflects that of earlier KPD documents. Germer ruefully remarked, in connection with a different SPD-KPD conference, "They [KPD] always had the thicker drafts." Interview with Karl J. Germer, Jr., July 20, 1962.

181. Letter from Gustav Dahrendorf to Albert Schulz, Rostock, July 28, 1945.

182. Dahrendorf wrote that "[The KPD] has decisively influenced the personnel composition of the local administrations, which have been almost literally created from scratch. It did this thanks to its better relationship with the occupying power. We [the Social Democrats] recognize this fact very clearly." *Ibid.*

183. *Ibid.*

5. Party Activity

1. Anton Ackermann, "Wohin soll der Weg gehen?" *DVZ*, June 14, 1945.

2. Fred Oelssner, "Die Kommunisten sind die konsequentesten Kämpfer für die Demokratie," *DVZ*, July 15, 1945.

3. Anton Ackermann, "Aber es geht doch nicht, . . . !" *DVZ*, July 8, 1945; report of a speech by Wilhelm Pieck, *DVZ*, July 21, 1945; Wilhelm Pieck, "Antifaschistische Einheitsfront der demokratischen Parteien," *DVZ*, July 17, 1945; Franz Dahlem, "Die antifaschistische Einheit in den Konzentrationslagern," *DVZ*, July 14, 1945.

4. "[Let us] stress clearly and unmistakably that the *close cooperation of Social Democrats and Communists* is no obstacle to the attainment of cooperation of all democratic parties; on the contrary, as is being shown by experience everywhere, it is *a decisive precondition for the speedy creation of a unified bloc* of anti-fascist-democratic parties." (Italics in original.) "Das Ziel unseres gemeinsamen Kampfes," *DVZ*, July 6, 1945.

5. "Zum Neuaufbau Berlins. Offener Brief der Gross-Berliner Bezirksleitung der KPD," *DVZ*, September 23, 1945. See also, Walter Ulbricht, "Die Bewältigung der Aufgaben des Aufbaus," *Zur Geschichte*, II, 477. The 1963 edition of this work, cited here, dates this interview as of August 29, 1945. In the 1955 edition it is marked as having been *broadcast* September 15, 1945; (pp. 482–85). The text is the same in both cases.

6. "Partei des schaffenden Volkes," *DVZ*, June 27, 1945.

7. Thomas, p. 139.

8. Franz Dahlem, "Deutschland braucht eine starke Kommunistische Partei," *DVZ*, November 2, 1945.

9. *Das Volk*, July 8, 1945. Compare this with a feature article on Otto Grotewohl: "Wir stellen vor—Otto Grotewohl," *Das Volk*, August 26, 1945.

10. "Öffentliche Massenversammlung der KPD—Wilhelm Pieck spricht," *DVZ*, July 20, 1945.

11. Gniffke Manuscript, p. 52; Leonhard, p. 415.

12. Ulbricht, Zur Geschichte, II, Supplement 2, 327; Thomas, pp. 139–141; Stern, *Porträt*, p. 282; Frank Wohlgemuth, "Zum Kampf der Berliner Arbeiterklasse für die Gründung der Sozialistischen Einheitspartei Deutschlands (1945/1946)," in *Beiträge zur Geschichte der Sozialistischen Einheitspartei Deutschlands*, Stefan Doernberg et al., eds. (Berlin: Dietz, 1961), p. 139. See also the report of Franz Dahlem to the KPD XV Congress in April 1946; *Bericht über die Verhandlungen des 15. Parteitages der Kommunistischen Partei Deutschlands am 19. und 20. April 1946 in Berlin* (Berlin: Neuer Weg, 1946), p. 66; cited hereinafter as *KPD 15th Congress*.

13. Kaden, pp. 319–23.

14. Thomas, pp. 138–40.

15. This growth gives some credence to Nettl's statement that "the period May 1945 to October 1946 was really the period of ascendancy for the Social Democrats in the Eastern Zone," Nettl, p. 81. For the period ending in the winter of 1945–1946, this is fairly accurate.

16. For an uninformative account of the trip taken in late August 945 by Grotewohl and Meier through Magdeburg, Halberstadt, Gotha, Erfurt, Weimar, Leipzig, and Dresden, see "Au. ·ı der Reichsorganization der SPD," *Das Volk*, September 6, 1945. See also Gniffke Manuscript, p. 69.

17. Gniffke Manuscript, pp. 71–82.

18. *Ibid.*, p. 67.

19. *Ibid.*, pp. 90–92. Typically, after Gniffke had listed his complaints, General Bokov of the SMA agreed to look into these complaints, and then presented Gniffke with a long list of the SPD's political "sins."

20. See Protocol, Meeting of the SPD *Bezirkssekretariat* August 25, 1945, for Grotewohl's statement that only Zhukov's personal intervention had made his trip to Weimar possible.

21. Gniffke Manuscript, p. 34; interview with Fritz Schreiber, December 29, 1959.

22. Gniffke Manuscript, p. 72. Commenting on his first trip outside of Berlin (to Schwerin), he writes that "It was in Schwerin that I first experienced that organizational disproportion between KPD and the SPD which must necessarily follow from the fact that in the SPD the full-time staff is outnumbered by unpaid, part-time volunteers, whereas in the KPD it is difficult simply to find an unpaid or part-time employee." Similar conditions prevailed at the local level in Saxony. Interview with Walter Ramm, December 4, 1959.

23. Gniffke Manuscript, pp. 87–89.

24. There was obvious symbolism in the shift from "Red Flag" to the new "democratic, antifascist" title.

25. The daily *Berliner Zeitung* was published by the SMA from May 21 to June 18, 1945, when it was formally turned over to the Berlin city government. The KPD's Rudolf Herrnstadt became its editor.

26. One of the *Tribüne's* editors suspected that the sudden grant of permission to publish may have been due to a desire for an SPD voice in support of the land-reform campaign. Interview with Fritz Sarow, July 25, 1960. This period was also one of a temporary easing of relations between Brill and the Thuringia SMA.

27. Dates of publication mentioned here are from the first issues of the newspapers cited, plus: Heinrich Hoffman, Report delivered at the 2d Thuringian SPD party congress, April 6, 1946; *Dokumente und Materialien*, p. 48; Buchwitz, p. 79; Interview with Fritz Koch, February 19, 1960; Karl Urban, "Der Kampf um die Wiedervereinigung der Arbeiterbewegung in der Provinz Brandenburg (Mai 1945–April 1946)," *ZfG*, 7, no. 7 (1959), 1550.
    These contrasts extended to the matter of names and formats. As part of its general line, the KPD often chose names including the phrase *Volkeszeitung*; in addition, the SPD suspected the Soviet authorities of deliberately denying to the Social Democrats their old newspaper names. Thus in Berlin *Vorwärts* remained unavailable until the central party daily until the newly formed Berlin SED was permitted to use the name in April 1946. In Dresden the Social Democrats were convinced that the names of the respective party dailies were consciously chosen to reverse the symbols of the Weimar period—and showed detailed Soviet knowledge of German affairs. Interviews with Arno Wend, December 30, 1959, and with Rudolf Rothe, February 6, 1960.

28. Gniffke, Manuscript, p. 48. The continuing difficulties in getting paper and equipment for the *Tribüne* are described in the Protocol of the Meeting of the BV, SPD Thuringia, September 24, 1945.

29. On one occasion the *DVZ* provided partial circulation figures, according to which its circulation in Brandenburg, Mecklenburg-Vorpommern, and portions of Saxony at the end of July 1945 totaled 43,210. *DVZ*, July 28, 1945.

30. OMGUS, *Monthly Report of the Military Governor*, no. 4 (November 20, 1945), Annex: Information Control, p. 3.

31. *Tribüne*, November 1, 1945.

32. Hoffmann, Report at 2d Thuringian SPD Party Congress, p. 8.

33. Reporting to the Berlin SPD *Parteitag* in November 1945, Erich Lübbe remarked that, when it came to the content and circulation of *Das Volk*, "After all, we are not free to act in this matter [of circulation] and must keep within prescribed limits. This applies [equally] to the contents of the newspaper." Quoted in *Sozialdemokratische Partei Deutschlands, Bezirksverband Berlin. Bezirksparteitag am Sonntag, dem 25. November 1945 vorm. 9 Uhr im "Prater,"* Berlin, Kastanienallee 7/8 [*Abschrift*], cited hereinafter as *SPD Berlin—November Congress*, p. 8.

34. Sarow relates that he had to carry the copy from Weimar to Jena, where the relevant SMA office was located! Interview with Fritz Sarow, July 25, 1960. There were sometimes differences in practice from one locale to another within the Soviet Zone. For a Berlin and Halle contrast in September 1945 see, Report of October 18, 1945, from Gustav Klingelhöfer to Otto Grotewohl. Detailed Soviet press rules were published in "Vorläufige Regeln . . . ," *Das Volk*, August 8, 1945. The proclamation is dated August 2, 1945; and signed "Chief Censor of the [SMA] in Germany, I. Filippov."

35. Dahrendorf, *Zwangsvereinigung*, p. 92.

36. The stress placed herein on press statistics is accounted for by 1) the availability of this data, as opposed to other material, and 2) the intrinsic importance of the press as an instrument in building the parties, establishing central control within the parties, and setting the programmatic line for the parties.

37. The busy organizational life of the party is reflected in press accounts of meetings of all sorts. See for example, *Das Volk*, August 9, 15, and 31, 1945, and October 16, 23, and 28, 1945, as well as *Tribüne*, October 13, 1945, and November 10, 1945. Starting with the issue of October 30, 1945, the *Tribüne* ran a front-page box headed "Sozialdemokratie im Aufbau." See also the report of August Karsten, "Die Partei im Aufbau," *Das Volk*, December 2, 1945.

38. As of December 31, 1945, the SPD had 58,000 members in Greater Berlin; 45,000 in Thuringia; 85,000 in the Saxon districts (*Bezirke*) of Dresden, Leipzig, Zwickau, and Chemnitz; in the entire Soviet Zone, the SPD had 376,000 members. By March 31, 1946, this figure had almost doubled to over 700,000. See also the reports on the SPD press and party membership given by Gniffke and the party treasurer, August Karsten, at the zonal SPD party congress in April 1946. *SPD 40th Congress*, pp. 73–83.

39. I have been unable to find evidence for such party gatherings in the provinces of *Provinz* Saxony, and Mecklenburg-Vorpommern prior to the general round of congresses in anticipation of unity in April 1946. At that time the four districts mentioned here held "second" party congresses. However, the Magdeburg *Bezirk* (District) held a party congress on October 20–21, 1945. See "Die Sozialdemokratie im Vormarsch," *Das Volk*, October 28, 1945.

On October 6–7, 1945, a district party congress was held in Halle-Merseburg. *Das Volk*, October 14, 1945. *Bezirk*-organizations had been characteristic of the SPD before 1933; the SMA insisted on provincial (*Land*) organizations to correspond to their occupation organizational structure. Gniffke Manuscript, p. 71. See also Plener, *Klärungspro-zess*, pp. 53–54.

40. At the party congress for *Land* Saxony, Rudolf Rothe, speaking for Leipzig, suggested setting up only *Landesausschüsse* ("provincial committees") rather than formal *Länderorganisationen* ("provincial organizations") because the former would have lacked the formal competence to decide a question like that of unity with the KPD; Rothe felt this would help the party resist Soviet pressure. Interview with Rudolf Rothe, February 6, 1960.

41. Hennig was at that time Mayor of the congress locale, Dresden-Freital.

42. *Protokoll vom Parteitag der Sozialdemokratischen Partei Deutschlands-Landesgruppe Sachsen; Stenographischer Bericht über die Verhandlungen des Landes-Parteitages ab-gehalten am 7., 8., und 9. Oktober 1945 in Dresden (Freital)* (Dresden: Schrift und Kunst, [1945]), pp. 6–7, cited hereinafter as *SPD Saxony Congress*.

43. *Ibid.*, pp. 13–14, 34.

44. For Brill's speech in Dresden, see *ibid.*, p. 40; for the party congress of the Thuringian SPD, see *Tribüne*, November 1–5, 1945.

45. "Neu Beginnen," *Tribüne*, November 1, 1945. Brill had previously written that "new organizations make sense only if they are filled with new thought." "Verpflichtende Geschichte," *Tribüne*, October 27, 1945.

46. "Neue Humanität und Neuformung der Partei," *Tribüne*, October 9, 1945.

47. Hermann L. Brill, "Die Sozialdemokratie im heutigen Deutschland," talk given at Jena at an unspecified date and quoted in *Tribüne*, October 27, 1945. Brill's was not the only voice of dissent in the Thuringian SPD. For resolutions critical of the KPD, see "Resolutions on unity submitted to the first Thuringian *Landesparteitag*," Brill papers; see also Hans Freiburg, "Politischer Rückblick und Ausblick," and "Herstellung der sozialistischen Einheit der Arbeiterklasse," *Tribüne*, November 1, 1945.

48. For a lengthy statement of the ZA's position, see *Stellungnahme und Beschluss des Zentralausschusses der Sozialdemokratischen Partei Deutschlands vom 20. August 1945.* The copy I saw was marked "Secret."

49. The reputed author of this aspect of the report was Gustav Dahrendorf.

50. Letter from Gustav Dahrendorf to Albert Schulz, July 28, 1945.

51. Letter from Otto Grotewohl to Karl J. Germer, Jr., July 16, 1945.

52. Otto Grotewohl, speech of August 26, 1945, to party functionaries at the first party congress, SPD *Bezirk* Leipzig, cited hereinafter as Grotewohl, Leipzig speech. This speech was never published.

53. Kaden, p. 83.

54. Grotewohl, Leipzig speech.

55. Grotewohl grew abusive in this connection, remarking that "The nationalist demands of our Eastern neighbor Poland have risen sky-high. Never in its long history has Poland given evidence of any particular state-forming powers (Very true!). Poland has never yet shown that it is even capable of creating the most elementary organizational preconditions

for an organized state." Grotewohl's explanation for the failure of the Statement on Potsdam issued by the four-party Bloc (see *DVZ*, August 14, 1945) to reflect these views was that the KPD had not given "the support we would have normally expected." Grotewohl, Leipzig speech.

56. Schreiber credits Klingelhöfer with their authorship (interview with Fritz Schreiber, December 29, 1959), a contention borne out by Kaden's researches in the Klingelhöfer files. Kaden, pp. 183, 192.

57. Erich W. Gniffke, "Politisches 'Soll und Haben,' " *Das Volk*, July 12, 1945.

58. Otto Grotewohl, quoted in "Geschichtsbildende Kraft der Demokratie," *Das Volk*, August 14, 1945.

59. The interview appeared in *Das Volk* and *DVZ*, both of July 13, 1945, under the heading "Die Sozialdemokratie auf neuen Wegen."

60. *DVZ*, July 21, 1945.

61. "Aussprechen, was ist!" *Das Volk*, August 14, 1945; also, "Auf dem Wege zur Freiheit," *Das Volk*, July 15, 1945.

62. Fred Oelssner, "Über die historische Verantwortung der Kommunisten," *DVZ*, October 28, 1945. See also Walter Ulbricht, "Festigung der Einheitsfront—eine nationale Aufgabe," *DVZ*, October 28, 1945.

63. *SPD Berlin November Congress*, p. 4; *SPD Saxony Congress*, p. 36.

64. Dahrendorf, *Zwangsvereinigung*, p. 94.

65. Thomas writes that the chief causes of misunderstanding were not "the actual key ideological problems of the future unity party, the dictatorship of the proletariat and the question of internal party democracy," but rather differences arising from daily work, "above all: the so-called parity issue. . . . [which was] the sorest point in the two parties' collaboration in Berlin." Thomas, p. 148. The same writer had earlier expressed what (even in 1945) was the truer Communist view of this matter when he wrote that while "revolutionary" and "reformist" organizations might cooperate on questions of detail, a unity party needed a sound ideological basis. See Siegfried Thomas, "Der Kampf um die Vereinigung von KPD und SPD in Berlin," *ZfG*, 10, Sonderheft (1962), 127.

66. Thomas explains the preferment of Communists as follows: "It was often the case that Soviet commandants preferred to appoint Communists. Firstly, because for the Soviet occupation forces, understandably enough, the most politically reliable elements were those who had not only fought most actively against fascism, but had also been true to the Soviet Union. Furthermore, as a rule the Communists volunteered first for reconstruction work. For these reasons there were, in the borough and local administrations of Berlin after the liberation, relatively more Communists than Social Democrats." Thomas, pp. 148–50.

67. "Report of the BV (Magdeburg) . . . on Relations with the Communist Party," September 15, 1945.

68. Gniffke Manuscript, p. 49.

69. Protocol of the session of August 14, 1945, SPD Kreisleitung 10-Berlin-Wilmersdorf.

70. Letter from SPD *Kreisvorstand* Stralsund to ZA, November 9, 1945.

71. Gniffke manuscript, p. 67. Gniffke notes, "They listened to us patiently, took notes, promised to investigate, promised to report back to us. But nothing happened."

72. *Ibid.*, pp. 113–14, for this meeting and the quotations following.

73. "Arbeitsgemeinschaft KPD-SPD für Gross-Berlin," and Waldemar Schmidt, "Berlins Kommunisten und Sozialdemokraten gemeinsam beim Aufbau," both *DVZ*, October 9, 1945.

74. "Erfolge der Einheit KPD-SPD. Arbeitsgemeinschaft auch in der Provinz," *DVZ*, October 10, 1945. Writing of party affairs in Mecklenburg-Vorpommern, the paper speaks of first creating the "Preconditions for the political unity of the toiling people."

75. An East German study, quoting from a letter in the *Privat-Archiv Buchwitz*, to Buchwitz from Arno Wend (then political secretary, SPD LV Saxony) claims that Wend advocated, "The attempt to create one party, [make common cause] in local . . . organizations before a party congress has voted on unification must be opposed." Quoted in Willy Peter, "Die Gründung der Sozialistischen Einheits-partei Deutschlands in Sachsen (1945/1946)," Doernberg et al., *Beiträge*, p. 91, n.27. Buchwitz wrote that the discussion at the October party congress revealed who the opponents of unity were.

76. DVZ, July 13, 1945.

77. Gniffke Manuscript, pp. 87–89, 92.

78. G. Korotkevich and P. Pol'iakov, "Sozdanie sotsialisticheskoi edinoi partii Germanii" *Bol'shevik*, 23, no. 13–14 (July 1946), 57.

79. Thomas, p. 148.

80. Hermann L. Brill, "Ein wichtiger Schritt zur Einheit der Arbeiterklasse," [? *Tribüne*, December ?, 1945].

6. The Turn to Unity

1. Gaddis, pp. 264–81; John Gimbel, *The American Occupation of Germany: Politics and the Military, 1945–1949* (Stanford: Stanford University Press, 1968), pp. 19–23. That American policy in German affairs was undergoing a substantial and anti-Soviet change is the view of Athan Theoharis, "Roosevelt and Truman on Yalta: The Origins of the Cold War," *Political Science Quarterly*, 87, no. 2 (June 1972), 227–29. The underlying hostility sometimes present in the political maneuvering over the future of Germany is demonstrated by the interview of Louis Wiesner (labor advisor to the American occupation authorities) with Ulbricht on November 13, 1945. Wiesner describes Ulbricht as making "no attempt to conceal his hostility toward the United States." United States Department of State, *Foreign Relations of the United States, 1945*, III, 1075–77.

2. Hermann Weber, *Von der SBZ zur DDR 1945–1968* (Hannover: Verlag für Literatur und Zeitgeschehen, 1968), pp. 25–28; Nikolaev, *Politika sovetskogo soiuza*, pp. 41–42; *Dokumente und Materialien*, pp. 174–79, 210–18.

3. Stern, *Porträt*, p. 26. Interview with Rudolf Rothe, February 6, 1960. Gustav Dahrendorf felt that adverse results in factory council elections motivated the KPD shift on the timing of unification. Interview with Ralf Dahrendorf, January 18, 1960.

4. See Pieck's speech of November 9, 1945, in *DVZ*, November 10, 1945.

5. Leonhard, pp. 461–62.

6. *Ibid.*, p. 435.

7. In the Budapest municipal elections of October 7, the Smallholders received 295,197 votes and 121 seats, while a Communist-Socialist combination received 249,711 votes and 103 seats. When, on November 4, the latter two parties ran separately, the totals for the national elections of that date showed little change. The Smallholders had 57% of the votes and 245 seats, the Communists 17% and 70 seats, the Socialists 17.4% and 69 seats. Stephen D. Kertesz, *Diplomacy in a Whirlpool* (South Bend: University of Notre Dame Press, 1953), pp. 140–41. See also *The New York Times*, October 9, 18, 19, 22, 24, November 10, 1945; *DVZ*, October 11, 1945.

8. Leonhard, p. 435.

9. Quoted in Kaden, p. 191, n.421. While the Hungarian voting was barely mentioned in the SPD and KPD press, the Austrian election received some comment. The *DVZ* reported straightforwardly that the Austrian Communist Party had suffered a setback, ascribing it to Austria's lack of those new political forces, born in anti-Hitler resistance movements, that had transformed the politics of such countries as France or Yugoslavia. Whatever the flaws of this analysis, it was a great deal better than the timid SPD appraisal, which avoided the uncomfortable topic of Social Democratic gains and Communist losses by going into a long-winded historical analysis concentrating on the Hapsburg period. *DVZ*, December 5, 1945. The results of the Austrian voting were givne on the front page of *Das Volk* on November 27 and 28, 1945; the commentary, "Österreich," by "P.L.," appeared on November 30, 1945. At a session of the *Kreisvorstand* of the Berlin-Wilmersdorf SPD on November 27, 1945, the Austrian results were considered "good news," made possible by the "clear differentiation" between Socialists and Communists in Austria. Protocol of *Kreisvorstand* session, November 27, 1945.

10. Thomas, p. 170.

11. As Kaden has written: "The reasons for the change in the Communist position cannot be . . . fully ascertained. Equally we cannot determine . . . at what point in time the KPD began to press for the speedy merger of the KPD and SPD. Our investigations show, however, that this point came substantially earlier than other accounts maintain." Kaden, pp. 172–73, n.382.

12. OMGUS, *Monthly Report of the Military Governor*, no. 4, (November 20, 1945), p. 5. See also, the discussion of the Wennigsen Conference in this chapter, below.

13. Gniffke Manuscript, p. 83; "M. N.," "Neue Welt," *Das Volk*, September 18, 1945.

14. Grotewohl, *Wo stehen wir?* pp. 76–77.

15. *Ibid.*, p. 78.

16. *Ibid.*, pp. 82–83.

17. See generally Kaden, especially chs. 1, 2, 4, 6; Edinger, *Schumacher*, ch. 6.

18. For this Conference see *Die Wiedergeburt der deutschen Sozialdemokratie. Bericht über Vorgeschichte und Verlauf der sozialdemokratischen Parteikonferenz von Hannover vom 5. bis 7. Oktober 1945* (London: [Union of Social Democratic Organizations in Great Britain], 1945); cited hereinafter as *Wiedergeburt*. An edited version is in Ossip K. Flechtheim, ed., *Dokumente zur parteipolitischen Entwicklung in Deutschland seit 1945*

(Berlin: Dokumenten Verlag, 1962), I, 60–69. See also "Die SPD Tagung von Hann-over," *Das Volk*, October 11, 1945; Kaden, ch. 7.

19. Albrecht Kaden, "Entscheidung in Wennigsen: Die Wiedergründung der SPD in 1945 und die 'Einheit der Arbeiterklasse,' " *Die Neue Gesellschaft*, no. 6 (1960), 237–56. A review of this article from an SED standpoint is Gunther Benser, "Bemerkenswerte Ein-geständisse," *BzG*, 3, *Sonderheft* (1961), 139–48.

20. *Wiedergeburt*, pp. 9–10.

21. Gniffke Manuscript, p. 109; OMGUS, *Military Government Weekly Information Bulletin*, no. 19 (December 1, 1945), pp. 16–17. Reporting on ZA activities in US Zone, the report states: "It is known that representatives of the [ZA] in Berlin have traveled ex-tensively in the Zone. . . . actively engaged in organizing the Regensburg group of the SPD." See also Kaden, pp. 165–68.

22. Kaden, p. 169. This stance resulted from the exiled Social Democrats' long record of anti-Communism and their suspicions of Soviet constraints on the Berlin SPD leaders.

23. Edinger, *Schumacher*, p. 102.

24. As one author has written, the Wennigsen Conference "gave the Communists reasons to increase their pressure on the Social Democrats of the Soviet Zone." See Jürgen Fijalkowski et al., *Berlin: Hauptstadtanspruch und Westintegration* (Cologne and Oppladen: Westdeutscher Verlag, 1967), p. 24.

25. "Die KPD Funktionär-Versammlung der 4000. Walter Ulbricht vor den Berliner Funktionären," *DVZ*, October 13, 1945. See "German Reds Exhorted," *The New York Times*, October 13, 1945. The *Times* called it the "biggest and most enthusiastic political rally since the fall of Berlin." Ulbricht's speech was reprinted in the *DVZ*, October 14, 1945 and in Ulbricht, *Zur Geschichte*, II, 478–98; cited hereinafter as *Ulbricht October 12 speech*.

26. This view may be contrasted with the Social Democratic notion, as expressed most openly by Brill, that separate election campaigns (albeit with a mutually agreed upon program) "would give the people an opportunity to speak their minds clearly. That is a true step toward democracy; it would make it possible to determine the actual state of public opinion, in contrast to that political will which is now represented only through political parties." Brill, "Ein wichtiger Schritt" [Tribüne?]

27. Ulbricht's public position on these issues corresponded to the remarks he made pri-vately to Gniffke on October 8. (Gniffke, *Jahre*, p. 101). Later in October Ulbricht still spoke only of a "gradual fusion" of the workers' parties. Walter Ulbricht, "Festigung der Einheitsfront—eine nationale Aufgabe," *DVZ*, October 28, 1945.

28. Kaden, p. 93, n.189; p. 109, n.222; p. 111. Edinger remarks that Severing became "what he himself termed 'a sort of personnel manager' for the military government." Edinger, *Schumacher*, p. 96.

29. Brill, KPD Letter; Thuringia LV, *Circular Letter No. 18*, November 6, 1945.

30. Thomas, p. 154, n.293. At the December Conference, Pieck apologized for his remarks as follows: "Comrades, I must confess to having been taken aback by Comrade Gro-tewohl's speech on September 14. . . .Unfortunately, his speech was so permeated with doubts and complaints concerning Communists that I did in fact say at a closed

membership meeting in Erfurt that such utterances were grist for the mills of those who oppose the unity of the workers' parties." Pieck further insisted that the speech had been published against his will. December Conference, pp. 94–95.

31. Franz Dahlem, "Betrachtungen zu zwei Reden," *DVZ*, September 29, 1945.

32. Gniffke Manuscript, pp. 90–92.

33. His remark to Gniffke was quoted in a report to Grotewohl from Gustav Klingelhöfer, dated November 26, 1945; cited hereinafter as Klingelhöfer Report.

34. Gniffke, *Jahre*, p. 109. Judging by the subsequent testimony of a British visitor who met Grotewohl in October 1945, the SPD leader was, at that time, cool to closer ties to the KPD. Great Britain, Parliament, *Parliamentary Debates* (House of Commons), 5th ser., 420 (4–22 March 1946), 1640.

35. The very occasion on which Grotewohl spoke was itself a cause of controversy. At the end of October 1945, (Gniffke, *Jahre*, p. 102. Earlier, Gniffke had it as of the beginning of November. Gniffke Manuscript, pp. 122–23.), Pieck suddenly asked for a meeting of the KPD Central Committee Secretariat with the core of the *Zentralausschuss*. At this session Ackermann announced that he had been charged by the KPD with the organization of a celebration of the anniversary of the 1918 revolution as a joint SPD-KPD event and now wished to work out a program for the occasion. Dahrendorf replied heatedly that the Communists should abandon the practice of presenting the ZA with previously discussed proposals, and then asking for an immediate decision. The upshot of this was that the ZA decided to hold its own public meeting. The KPD celebrated on November 9, and the SPD two days later on the eleventh. Gniffke Manuscript, p. 122.

36. Gniffke, *Jahre*, p. 106; Klingelhöfer himself claimed authorship in an article in the Berlin SPD weekly; see "Zehn Jahre Kampf um die Freiheit Berlins," *Berliner Stimme*, March 13, 1956; and Kaden found a draft of this speech in Klingelhöfer's handwriting in the latter's files. Kaden, p. 192, n.425.

37. In his criticism of these passages in Grotewohl's speech Kaden misstates the time factor when he charges that Grotewohl wished to delay unity until after a "democratic and socialist Germany" had been built, whereas for Grotewohl unity would grow out of that process; moreover, Kaden overlooks the tactical importance of a pledge for unity, which was a *sine qua non* of meaningful political activity for the SPD in the Soviet Zone by this time. Kaden, p. 193.

38. In this, as in so many ways, Grotewohl's ambition paralleled that of Schumacher.

39. Otto Grotewohl, "Rede vom 9. November 1945." The occasion of the speech was the anniversary of the proclamation of the Republic on November 9, 1918. The meeting at which the speech was given was held on Sunday, November 11, 1945; the speech is therefore cited hereinafter as Grotewohl, November 11 speech.

40. For this and following quotations, see Grotewohl, November 11 speech.

41. At an SMA reception some weeks later, Ulbricht went out of his way to needle the Social Democrats present to the effect that "there were still some capitalists around." Klingelhöfer Report.

42. Grotewohl, November 11 speech.

43. Pieck's speech is reprinted in full under the heading "Grosskundgebung in Berlin," *DVZ*, November 10, 1945. The needs of Germany in the postwar era were so great, Pieck declared, that no one party could meet them. Hence the Communists advocated the antifascist unity of the four democratic parties in the Soviet Zone and "sought the closest collaboration especially with their Social Democratic comrades, in order to create not just a firm leadership for the antifascist-democratic united front, but also *to bring about as soon as possible the complete unification of the Communists and the Social Democrats into one single workers' party."* (Italics added.)

44. Grotewohl, November 11 speech.

45. Walter Ulbricht, "Einheitliche Gewerkschaften sichern Aufbau und Frieden," *Thüringer Volkszeitung*, December 15, 1945.

46. Kaden, p. 193. For a Communist critique of this view, see Ulla Plener, "Kurt Schumachers Konzeption der demokratischen Republik—die Grundlage seiner antikommunistischen Politik (1945/1946)," *BzG*, 8, no. 5 (1966), 819–20.

47. Protocol of Meeting of SPD Thuringia, *Bezirkssekretariat*, August 25, 1945.

48. Leonhard, p. 434. For a recent comment that Grotewohl's speeh lacked "full clarity" as to the relationship between socialism and democracy, see Plener, *Klärungsprozess*, p. 41.

49. Grotewohl, November 11 speech.

50. Kaden, p. 191.

51. "Our call and our stand is no disengagement or delineation from other parties, but rather an appeal for reflection and reconsideration. We do wish to be tricky or to engage in maneuvering; rather we wish to speak to the German in all his depression and insecurity with absolute honesty and total fairness." Grotewohl, November 11 speech.

52. *Ibid.;* Kaden, p. 192, n.425.

53. Gniffke Manuscript, pp. 123–24.

54. Walter Ulbricht, *Thüringer Volkszeitung*, August 16, 1945. A large portion of this article was reprinted *ibid.* on August 23, 1945, under the heading, "Zur Frage der deutschen Ostgrenze."

55. Wilhelm Pieck, "Das Dorf im demokratischen Deutschland," *DVZ*, August 18, 1945. See also Pieck's speech at the first public rally of the four-party bloc on August 12, 1945, reprinted in *Einheitsfront der antifaschistisch-demokratischen Parteien* (Berlin: Der neue Weg, [1945]), pp. 56–59.

56. "Erklärung des Blocks der antifaschistisch-demokratischen Parteien vom 12. August 1945 zu den Beschlüssen der Potsdamer Konferenz," *DVZ*, August 14, 1945.

57. Gniffke Manuscript, p. 124. One amusing consequence was that Marshal Zhukov's aide supposedly rushed to friends of Grotewohl and exclaimed, "Grotewohl spoke before 5000 people in Berlin. Speech no good, painting pictures better. [A reference to Grotewohl's hobby] . . . you must tell him, no more speeches, just paint pictures."

58. Gniffke, *Jahre*, p. 108.

59. "Bekenntnis zur Einheit der Arbeiterbewegung," *Tägliche Rundschau*, November 13, 1945.

60. The details of the following passage are based on a memorandum by Dr. Antoine to the economics section (i.e., Klingelhöfer's section) of the *Zentralausschuss*, dated November 19, 1945. It was included in the Klingelhöfer Report.

61. Kaden, p. 194; Klingelhöfer Testament.

62. Some ZA members thought of this crisis as a "Grotewohl affair" rather than an SPD stand. See Klingelhöfer Report.

63. Friz Schenk, *Im Vorzimmer der Diktatur* (Cologne: Kiepenheuer and Witsch, 1962), p. 12.

64. Klingelhöfer Report.

65. Gniffke Manuscript, p. 137; Klingelhöfer Testament.

7. *The December Conference*

1. The record of this party meeting has been previously cited as *SPD Berlin-November Congress*.

2. This meeting established a Berlin SPD organization distinct from the ZA, which had hitherto exercised supervision over Berlin party affairs. See Kaden, p. 243.

3. Lübbe spoke as provisional *Bezirk*-secretary. The meeting elected the following officers: Hermann Harnisch and Werner Rüdiger as Chairman and Vice-Chairman, Erich Lübbe, Emil Barth, Georg Wendt, and Dora Lösche as Secretaries (among other posts). *SPD Berlin-November Congress*, p. 23.

4. *Ibid.*, p. 7.

5. *Ibid.*, p. 4.

6. Lübbe criticized the Soviet-inspired program, in part as follows: "We make no secret of the fact that the current land reform corresponds neither to the party's former plans nor to its present-day expectations. But we live in extraordinary times." *Ibid.*, p. 9.

7. *Ibid.*, pp. 9–10.

8. *Ibid.*, p. 14.

9. The documents on the SPD in Thuringia used for this study fortunately contain material from three levels of the party organization: the zonal (ZA), the provincial (LV Thuringia), and the local (letters and reports sent to the provincial headquarters in Weimar by *Ort* and *Kreis* organizations).

10. Report from Küchler (Gössnitz), November 11, 1945; letter from *Ortsgruppe*, Neustadt, received November 26, 1945; letter from *Kreisstelle* Langensalza, October 22, 1945; letter from *Kreisverband* Langensalza, November 10, 1945. It was presumably as part of this pattern of general intimidation, rather than as a specific prophecy of forthcoming party unification, that Social Democrats were warned that by Christmas or New Year's, or in some cases by Eastertime, there would be no more SPD in existence. Letter from *Ortsgruppe* Neustadt, received November 26, 1945; letter from *Kreisstelle*, Langensalza, October 22, 1945.

11. Letter from *Ortsgruppe* Nordhausen, September 21, 1945; letter from *Kreisverband*

Langensalza, November 10, 1945; Report from *Ortsgruppe* Alach to *Kreisleitung* Erfurt, November 12, 1945.

12. The report is enclosed with a letter from the *Kreisverband* Langensalza, November 17, 1945.

13. The report of Freiburg's speech in the KPD *Thüringer Volkszeitung*, November 16, 1945, contains no hint of this critical view but rather quotes excerpts with approval.

14. Letter from *Kreis* Erfurt-Weissensee, November 23, 1945.

15. Brill, KPD Letter.

16. Letter from *Kreisverein* Meiningen, October 23, 1945; letter from *Kreisverein* Arnstadt, October 22, 1945.

17. Brill, SMA Letter, quoting local reports.

18. All the instances discussed in the preceding passages are cited from Brill, SMA Letter.

19. *Ibid.* A serious controversy between the SPD and KPD (and later a difficult problem for the SED) was policy toward "nominal" Nazi party members. We have refrained from going into this complex issue, but it should be noted that each party accused the other, with great vehemence and bitterness, of bidding for the ex-Nazis' support.

20. According to the Protocol of the LV meeting of November 5, 1945, Brill was authorized to write it on the basis of received complaints and past SPD and interparty decisions.

21. Brill, KPD Letter.

22. *Rundschreiben [Circular Letter] No. 18: An alle Kreisverbänds-und Ortsvereins-Vorsitzenden. Betr.: Das Verhältnis SPD und KPD*, November 6, 1945.

23. *Ibid.*

24. In keeping with this line was the LV's stand on unification of the parties, as embodied in the *Circular Letter*: "We want this unity to be arranged between central party bodies on a national level . . . so-called unifications in single . . . provinces let alone localities are out of the question for us." *Ibid.*

25. For the receipt of the Thuringian *Circular Letter* by the ZA in Berlin, see Gniffke, *Jahre*, p. 117.

26. The text of Brill's two letters indicates that they were drawn up at Grotewohl's request.

27. Werner Eggerath of the Thuringian KPD complained of the *Circular Letter's* harmful effects on KPD-SPD relations at the December Conference. See December Conference, p. 59.

28. Brill, KPD Letter.

29. Brill, KPD Letter.

30. *Ibid.* Brill wrote on this point: "My attitude toward this declaration is made plain by the fact that it was publicized on November 26 without any initiative on my part."

    On November 26, after reading the Resolution of the 23rd, Brill commented, "Nothing wrong with that." After describing a passage on "thoroughly comradely" cooperation as a "tactful evasion," he added that, "This working was chosen on purpose. I think it can be accepted." Herman L. Brill, "Wie kommen wir zur sozialistischen Einheit der deutschen Arbeiterklasse?" Protocol of Meeting of LV (*Gesamtvorstand*, including local delegates) Thuringia, November 26, 1945. When reference is only to Brill's report at this session it is cited as Brill, November 26 Report.

31. Gniffke Manuscript, pp. 131–32.

32. *Ibid.*, p. 135.

33. Gniffke, *Jahre*, p. 114. In a talk to Thuringian KPD officials on December 13, 1945, Ulbricht is said to have urged that, "We must block the unification of party organizations at the local level. We must not give the SPD an opportunity to claim that we only wish to destroy that party or strengthen ours. We must do all we can to achieve unification of both parties as wholes." Ulbricht, *Zur Geschichte*, II, Supplement 2, 378.

34. A date of Dec. 18 is derived by Kaden from an examination of Schumacher's ap-. pointment calendar (Kaden, p. 195, n.432), but the sequence of events given by Gniffke (in *Jahre*, pp. 117–19), plus Klingelhöfer's date of December 10 for when the December Conference date was fixed (Kaden, p. 196, n.436), suggests that Gniffke's visit may have taken place in the first ten days of December.

35. Kaden, p. 195, n.433; Gniffke, *Jahre*, p. 118, where he says that he was "immediately received" by Schumacher and Kriedemann upon his arrival. According to Gniffke, Schumacher, after some discussion of the ZA's position, left for lunch—which Gniffke took as a personal and political affront. According to Kriedemann, Schumacher had been at lunch when Gniffke arrived, and the latter spoke only of administrative matters connected with former SPD property.

36. Kaden, p. 165; Gustav Dahrendorf, letter to Wilhelm Busch, January 9, 1946.

37. Dahrendorf seems to have regarded the trip as a harmless exercise in information exchange and organizational assistance. See letter from Gustav Dahrendorf to Hans Venedey, January 4, 1946.

38. Kaden, p. 169, n.368.

39. Fijalkowski's remark that the SPD went into the December Conference in a state of "dangerous misperception of the intensity of the Communist unification campaign" is unjustified. Fijalkowski, p. 27.

40. Dahrendorf, *Zwangsvereinigung*, pp. 95–96.

41. Kaden, p. 196, n.436; Thomas, p. 165; Gniffke, *Jahre*, p. 119.

42. Protocol of extraordinary session of LV Thuringia, November 16, 1945. Karsten also said that any resolutions adopted at such a meeting would be valid only for the Soviet Zone even if delegates attended from the Western zones.

43. *Konferenz der Bezirksvertreter mit dem Zentralausschuss der Sozialdemokratischen Partei Deutschlands, 4. Dezember 1945 im Parteihaus Berlin.* See also "Sozialdemokratische Konferenz," *Das Volk*, December 6, 1945.

44. Interview with Karl J. Germer, Jr., July 12, 1960; Kaden mentions a draft report from this meeting, quite critical of the SMA, in the Klingelhöfer files. Kaden, p. 197.

45. Gniffke, *Jahre*, p. 120; Dahrendorf, *Zwangsvereinigung*, pp. 96–97.

46. An invitation to "an *urgent* extraordinary *Zentralausschuss* session" for December 19, 5 P.M., is in the papers of Karl J. Germer, Jr. (Italics in original.)

47. Dahrendorf, *Zwangsvereinigung*, p. 100.

48. By what margin is not known.

49. Gustav Klingelhöfer, "Zehn Jahre Kampf um die Freiheit Berlins," *Berliner Stimme*, March 13, 1956.

50. Dahrendorf, *Zwangsvereinigung*, p. 100.

51. *Ibid.*, pp. 97–99.

52. Letter to Hans Venedey, January 4, 1946. In this letter Dahrendorf was optimistic as to the SPD's future in the Soviet Zone and as to agreement with the KPD, but rejected unification of parties without prior national unity.

53. All references to and quotations from the SPD and KPD draft proposals in the following paragraphs are taken from these unpublished documents: for the SPD—*Verhandlungsvorschlag der SPD zum 20. 12. 1945;* for the KPD—*KPD Entwurf* and *Streichungen aus dem Entwurf der KPD-Vorschläge.*

54. The SPD statement proposed that "any unification of local, county [*Kreis*], district [*Bezirk*], provincial or zonal party organizations must await a resolution calling for overall organizational merger. . . . An attempt at zonal merger of the workers' parties would . . . call into question . . . the future unity of the working class [as it would endanger the creation of a truly democratic republic and the conversion of Germany into a peaceful nation. The parties] therefore seek the speedy formation of united workers' parties for the whole territory of the state, [parties] whose *first party congresses* are to discuss and begin the organizational merger of the parties." (Italics in original.)

55. It is revealing that after six months of activity under the SMA, the SPD should find it necessary to ask that "in order to remove any doubts concerning the sincerity of the will for unity and the actual equality of the parties, each of the two parties will approach the occupation powers to insure that every *advantage or disadvantage* accruing to one party cease—be it in respect to freedom of organization or means of publicity." (Italics in original.)

56. This paragraph was among those deleted from the final Conference declaration at SPD insistence.

57. During the Conference itself, Pieck specified Austria and Bavaria (by anticipation) as horrible examples. December Conference, pp. 21–24.

58. Undated draft proposal by Franz Dahlem for the Conference discussion of joint electoral plans.

59. December Conference, p. 31; *Tägliche Rundschau*, December 27, 1945.

60. Ulbricht wrote in this connection that "It is precisely to the extent that the Communist and Social Democratic parties in the territory east of the Elbe provide a good example of unity, that their activity will have a fruitful effect on developments in the other parts of Germany. In this way the true unity of Germany will be achieved on a progressive basis." Walter Ulbricht, "Wo ist der Ausweg aus der Katastrophe?" *DVZ*, December 19, 1945.

61. *Wir schaffen die Einheit. Beschlüsse der gemeinsamen Konferenz des Zentralkomitees*

der KPD und des Zentralausschusses der SPD mit den Vertretern der Bezirke Beilage für die *Deutsche Volkszeitung* (Berlin: Einheit, n.d.), pp. 14–15, cited hereinafter as *Wir schaffen die Einheit*. This supplement (which also appeared in *Das Volk*) contains the text of the resolutions adopted at the Conference and the list of signatories.

62. Thomas, pp. 167–69.

63. Protocol of meeting of Thuringia LV, December 7, 1945.

64. Interview with Rudolf Rothe, February 6, 1960.

65. December Conference, pp. 3–4, 5–6.

66. Interview with Rudolf Rothe, February 6, 1960. Rothe would have balked at further joint meetings.

67. December Conference, pp. 9, 11, for this and following passage.

68. *Ibid.,* p. 13.

69. *Ibid.,* pp. 18–31, gives Pieck's speech. See also for following passages.

70. *Ibid.,* p. 51.

71. *Ibid.,* p. 70.

72. *Ibid.,* p. 74–75.

73. *Ibid.,* p. 89.

74. Thus the reaction of Eggerath is not surprising and may well have been widespread: "But when the discussions were broken off that evening, I had little hope that the next day would bring a positive result." Quoted by Thomas, p. 168.

75. According to Dahrendorf, *Zwangsvereinigung*, p. 104, the SPD delegates accepted the revised KPD draft because it contained "no specific determination of a date for unification of the parties on a zonal basis."

76. Grotewohl's speech at the Conference exists in a number of unpublished copies, cited hereinafter as Grotewohl, December 20 speech.

77. December Conference, p. 89.

78. "Die Bedeutung der marxistisch-leninistische Theorie für die Entwicklung der Politik der SED (Interview mit Genossen Walter Ulbricht. . . .)," *Einheit*, 21, no. 2 (February 1966), 151.

79. Walter Ulbricht, "9. November 1918 in Deutschland," *DVZ*, November 9, 1945; Thomas, p. 158.

80. Thomas, pp. 163–64.

81. *Wir schaffen die Einheit*, pp. 12–14.

82. This appeared as *Einheit* in February 1946; these projects had already been broached in October 1945; see *Ulbricht October 12 speech*, p. 494.

83. In an article on the anniversary of Engels' birth in the *Tägliche Rundschau*, December 4, 1945.

84. December Conference, p. 27.

85. As, for example, Wolfgang Leonhard. Such considerations, quite apart from the role of proper ideological justification in establishing the KPD's legitimacy and self-image, make it difficult to accept Melvin Croan's contention that "ideological clarification" was merely a tactical exercise to fool the Social Democrats. See Melvin Croan, "Dependent Totalitarianism," Diss. Harvard University, 1960, p. 46.

86. Stefan Doernberg, "Die Entstehung der Sozialistischen Einheitspartei Deutschlands und ihr Kampf um die Schaffung einer antifaschistisch-demokratischen einigen deutschen Republic (1945–1949)," Doernberg et al., *Beiträge*, p. 46.

87. See *Wir Schaffen die Einheit*, pp. 4–14, for the text of the resolution adopted.

88. In the list of signers printed in the party press, the name of Karl J. Germer, Jr. appears incorrectly in *Das Volk*, December 23, 1945, but it is (correctly) omitted from the *DVZ* of the same date. After some pressure from his colleagues not to spoil the Conference's harmony and unanimity, Germer added his name, which then appeared with an explanatory note in the *DVZ*, December 24, 1945. Interview with Karl J. Germer, Jr., July 12, 1960.

89. Richard Lukas is mistaken when he asserts that the KPD *viewpoint* was put across at the Conference: "The Communists had put across their views on unification; limitation to the Soviet Zone, creation of *fait d' accompli* in individual districts, splitting the SPD, and isolation of the ZA." Richard Lukas, *Zehn Jahre sowjetische Besatzungszone* (Mainz: Deutscher Fachschriften-Verlag, 1955), p. 65.

8. The Unity Campaign in the Aftermath of the December Conference

1. Letter from Wilhelm Pieck to Otto Grotewohl, December 27, 1945.

2. *DVZ*, December 23, 1945.

3. Wilhelm Pieck, "Auf dem Wege zur vollen Einheit der Arbeiterklasse," *Wir schaffen die Einheit*, p. 19. Walter Ulbricht claimed that "representatives of both parties from the outlying districts reported on the ever-closer and more trusting cooperation of the functionaries of both workers' parties. These reports convinced all the Conference participants that the second phase of unification had already begun." Walter Ulbricht, "Die Vereinigung der Arbeiterparteien—eine nationale Aufgabe (Interview mit einem Vertreter des Berliner Rundfunks 11. Januar 1946)," Ulbricht, *Zur Geschichte*, II, 53.

4. See Pieck's speech to the KPD Conference on March 2, 1946, in Wilhelm Pieck, *Probleme der Vereinigung von KPD und SPD* (Berlin: Neuer Weg, 1946), p. 10, cited hereinafter as *Pieck March 2 speech*.

5. During the 1930s a member of the *Neu Beginnen* group and later head of the SPD in Bavaria.

6. Kaden, p. 219.

7. See for example, OMGUS, *Monthly Report of the Military Governor*, no. 5 (December 20, 1945), Annex: Political Activity, p. 5.

8. *Ibid.*, no. 6 (January 20, 1946). Annex: Political Activity, p. 3.

9. D. Mel'nikov, "Vnutripoliticheskoe polozhenie Germanii," *Mirovoe khoziaistvo i mirovaia politika*, no. 1–2 (January–February 1946), 66–67; Korotkevich and Poliakov, p. 57: "Einheit der demokratischen Kräfte—Grundlage für die Wiedergeburt Deutschlands," *Tägliche Rundschau*, December 27, 1945.

10. For the places and dates of these meetings, see Kaden, pp. 220–21, especially nn.492–93. It was in this connection that Schumacher used a phrase that vastly annoyed the KPD: that the SPD must not become a "blood donor for the weakened party body" of the KPD. See also *Mit dem Gesicht*, p. 714.

11. Kaden, p. 214, especially n.476. But Kaden himself points out that by agreeing to the text of the Conference resolution, the ZA surrendered a major weapon, because "no letter, no newspaper article, no radio interview or circular letter could change the fact of what had been surrendered in the Resolution." *Ibid.*, p. 217.

12. Gniffke Manuscript, p. 158; letter from Gustav Dahrendorf to Wilhelm Busch (Regensburg), January 9, 1946; letter from Gustav Klingelhöfer to Otto Grotewohl, January 3, 1946.

13. Walter Ulbricht, "Offene Antwort an sozialdemokratischen Genossen," Ulbricht, *Zur Geschichte*, II, 526–32.

14. Letter from Gustav Klingelhöfer to Otto Grotewohl, January 3, 1946.

15. "From a Radio Address by Comrade Dahrendorf" (early January 1946).

16. *Unity Congress*, p. 159.

17. Max Fechner, "Um die Einheit der Schaffenden," *Tägliche Rundschau*, January 1, 1946.

18. Gniffke Manuscript, pp. 156–57. According to Gniffke the idea originated with Fechner's aide, Gunther Scheele.

19. "Kundegebung der Betriebsgruppenfunktionäre," *Das Volk*, December 29, 1945.

20. Reporting on the occasion, Hoffman said, "Pieck is regarded as a future *Reich* president." Protocol of meeting of the enlarged Thuringia LV, January 5, 1946. For KPD preparations in early December, see Ulbricht, *Zur Geschichte*, II, Supplement 2, 280.

21. For the dispute over the Löbe birthday celebration, see Paul Löbe, *Der Weg war lang*, 2d ed. (Berlin-Grunewald: Arani, 1954), p. 256; Gniffke Manuscript, pp. 151–53; *Mit dem Gesicht*, p. 715, for the London SPD leaders' reaction. For the Pieck celebration itself, see Leonhard, pp. 436–38; *DVZ*, January 3, 1945.

22. "Social Democratic workers and Communist workers, even Christian workers—they all look upon you in the same way, as one of their finest." *DVZ*, January 3, 1946. Pieck's own talk was more modest, see *DVZ*, January 5, 1946.

23. Grotewohl's remarks are reported in *DVZ*, January 4, 1946.

24. See the obituary notice by Carola Stern in *SBZ-Archiv*. 15, no. 19–20 (October 1964), 305.

25. Interview with Karl J. Germer, Jr., July 12, 1960.

26. For a realistic picture of Social Democratic sentiment by a Communist observer, see

Franz Dahlem, "Ein grosser einiger des Volkes," *Wilhelm Pieck—dem Vorkämpfer für ein neues Deutschland zum 70. Geburtstag* (Berlin: Neuer Weg, 1946), p. 74.

27. A notice of the meeting, including the admonition that "Each *Kreis* must be represented without fail" appeared in *Das Volk*, December 28, 1945. No further account of this meeting appeared in the press until the *Tagesspiegel's* story of February 17, 1946.

28. Kaden, p. 243. Siegfried Thomas, citing the protocol of this meeting in the archives of the Berlin SED, states that Franz Neumann called the signers of the December Conference resolutions the "gravediggers of the majority of the Social Democracy," Thomas, p. 176, n.41.

29. Letter from Gustav Klingelhöfer to Otto Grotewohl, January 3, 1946.

30. "An die Kreisleiter!" Resolution No. 1, in Circular Letter of the Berlin SPD organization, December 30, 1945. The resolution asserted that the December Conference program was only a basis for discussion, and all new organizational commitments were to be approved by a referendum or national party congress. A second resolution banned SPD-KPD joint actions at the borough level until the zonal party leaderships had settled problems arising from the December Conference. Resolution No. 2, in Circular Letter.

31. Thomas, p. 145.

32. December Conference, p. 63.

33. Thomas claims that the resolutions of December 29 show "unequivocally" that the "overwhelming majority" of the enlarged BV "favored unity in principle and thus supported the resolutions" of the December Conference (p. 177), but in a footnote to this passage (n.43) he shows his awareness of what actually took place by his effort to discredit Rüdiger.

34. See list of signatories in *Wir schaffen die Einheit*, p. 14.

35. Gniffke, *Jahre*, p. 120; the Protocol of the Thuringian LV meeting of December 28, 1945, shows that he did return to Weimar.
    At the December Conference, Brill did not participate in the discussion, but just before the Conference's close, Pieck remarked that a local KPD paper in Thuringia had just attacked an earlier speech of Brill's. There would be no follow-up on this issue, however, because, "We request that Dr. Brill—I may speak freely here—leave Thuringia, and we have agreed to let the matter rest in anticipation of his departure." December Conference, pp. 110–11. Pieck's mild statement at the Conference, the fact that Brill was able to return to Weimar in the last days of 1945 to wind up his affairs there, and the absence of attacks on him at the zonal level, all suggest that Brill and the ZA may have profited from a tacit SMA-OMGUS arrangement.

36. Communist hostility to Brill has lasted over the years. Thus Walter Ulbricht devoted three paragraphs in a recent article to attacking Brill's activities in 1945–46. Walter Ulbricht, "Die historische Mission der Sozialistischen Einheitspartei Deutschlands (Rede auf der Festveranstaltung zum 25. Jahrestag der SED)," *Neues Deutschland*, April 22, 1971.

37. The source for the interview at Weimar SMA headquarters discussed in the following paragraphs is a memorandum of the event written by Hoffman for the LV files. It is cited hereinafter as Hoffman December 31 Memorandum.

38. Protocol of Meeting of the Thuringia LV, January 2, 1946.

39. Brill, November 26 Report.

40. *Ibid.*, pp. 45–46, 48.

41. Letter from Otto Grotewohl and Erich W. Gniffke (on behalf of the ZA) to the Thuringia LV, January 4, 1946. In the letter the basis for the agreement is said to be the ZA's "contention . . . that the question of organizational unity must be left to the decision of a nationwide party congress. Any other position would endanger the national unity of the party and perhaps even national unity altogether."

42. The text of this unsuccessful resolution has been preserved in the LV archives. For the resolution that was adopted, see "An die Arbeit," dated January 5, 1946, in *Tribüne*, January 8, 1946.

43. Heinrich Hoffman, "Das Jahr der politischen Einheit," *Tribüne*, January 5, 1946; see also the joint statement of the Thuringian SPD and KPD leaders (Hoffman and Eggerath) in the LV's *Circular Letter No. 3* (1946), January 15, 1946. But evidently, the SPD's local organizations still found cause for complaint. See Protocol of the Meeting of the Thuringia LV, December 31, 1945; report of a meeting of the Thuringia LV January 5, 1946. At this latter meeting, a local delegate (Pohle, of Hildburghausen) stated that "We must demand a change in attitude from the Communists."

44. Hoffman in *Tribüne*, January 5, 1946.

45. Protocol of the Meeting of the Thuringia LV, January 19, 1946.

46. For the resolutions adopted January 6, see the documentary collection prepared for the Jena meeting of January 20, *Wir schaffen die Einheit* (Weimar: Thüringer Volksverlag, 1946), p. 4. This item should not be confused with the resolutions of the December Conference, which had the same title. Accounts of the January 6 meeting are, "Eine historische Tagung," and "Entschliessungen zur Einheitsfrage," both *Tribüne*, January 8, 1946.

47. "Einheit," *Tribüne*, January 8, 1946. A week later, Karl Doerr, the *Tribüne's* political editor, wrote in the KPD's *Thüringer Volkszeitung* ("Durch Einheit zur Freiheit," January 15, 1946) that "There is nothing more that divides us, only what unites us; there are no theoretical, let alone practical antitheses; there is but a single will, one goal, one way, one party, one idea!"

48. Thus in Chemnitz January 12, Dresden January 15, Potsdam February 15, Potsdam January 26, and a series of trade union and plant meetings, especially in Berlin.

49. "Es lebe die Einheit—Gruss an die Delegierten," *Tribüne*, January 19, 1946.

50. "Wir schmieden die Einheit der Arbeiterklasse," *Thüringer Volkszeitung*, January 19, 1946.

51. "Es lebe die einheitliche deutsche Arbeiterpartei," *Tribüne, Thüringer Volkszeitung*, both January 22, 1946.

52. Grotewohl's speech is in *Tribüne*, January 22, 1946. On January 21, after Grotewohl had spoken of the KPD's placing "Fatherland before party" *like the SPD*, Pieck told students at Jena University: "We want no federalism. (Applause.) We place Fatherland before party, before everything that smacks of the special interests of any social stratum. (Prolonged applause.)" *Thüringer Volkszeitung*, January 22, 1946.

53. *Thüringer Volkzeitung*, January 22, 1946. For possible effects of this speech on Grotewohl, see Gniffke, *Jahre*, p. 133.

54. Fritz Sarow, "In der zweiten Phase," *Tribüne*, January 22, 1946. An SPD delegate at the conference declared that, "We belong together with our comrades across the zonal borders. . . . The zone is not our fatherland." Franz Lepinski, "Es geht um die Zukunft des deutschen Volkes," *Tribüne*, January 24, 1946.

55. "Report of [a visit] from just after 2 P.M. until 4:15 . . with General Kolesnichenko on January 23, 1946." Frölich placed this memorandum in the LV archives; it is cited hereinafter as Report of January 23. The quotations in the following passages are from this report.

56. "Content of a Meeting with the Russian political officer in the . . . [SMA] Command of Schmalkaden on February 4, 1946."

57. Protocol of the Meeting of the Thuringia LV, January 28, 1946; according to the same source, the KPD *Bezirksleitung* had made this proposal on January 24, 1946.

58. "Neunzig Percent," and "Briefe aus Ost und West," *Tribüne*, February 5, 1946.

59. "Landesparteitag der Einheitspartei im April: Gemeinsame Tagung des erweiterten Landesvorstandes der SPD und der erweiterte Bezirksleitung der KPD am 5. Februar in Weimar," *Tribüne*, February 7, 1946.

60. Heinrich Hoffman, "Thüringen schmiedet die Einheit," *Tribüne*, February 8, 1946. In this talk over the Weimar radio on February 6, Hoffman said: "The thing now, in the local organizations and district federations [of the SPD], is to elect supporters of unity to the party congresses. The democratic rights of the membership remains the highest law."

61. Karl Doerr, "Gotha als Symbol," *Tribüne*, February 7, 1946.

62. *Tribüne*, February 6, 1946; *DVZ*, February 13, 1946; *Das Volk*, February 15, 1946.

63. Karl Doerr, "Gegen Saboteure der Einheit," *Tribüne*, February 6, 1946.

64. Curt Böhme, "Wir erfüllten den Schwur von Buchenwald," *Vereint*, p. 498.

65. Fritz Gäbler, "Altes Denken musste überwunden werden," *Vereint*, pp. 484–85.

66. See Kaden, p. 228, for examples.

67. "An die Landesausschüsse und Bezirksverbände der SPD," January 12, 1946 (signed by Otto Grotewohl and Max Fechner). This letter was accompanied by an enclosure of ten items; including Grotewohl's speech at the December Conference; the SPD draft for the Conference and a list of deletions from the KPD's draft; and postconference radio interviews with Grotewohl, Dahrendorf, and Fechner.

68. See for example, *Tribüne*, January 17, 1946.

69. This resolution stated that serious differences having arisen between the parties on the unity issue, ZA members were duty-bound to adhere strictly to the letter of the December Conference decisions. Further, in order to respect fully the rights and wishes of the party membership, these decisions must be regarded only as a basis for discussion, a final decision being reached only through a referendum or a national party congress with delegates elected by the membership. Immediate talks with the SPD in the other zones were called

for. Text of the resolution in the private papers of Fritz Neubacker, who was a member of the ZA at the time.

70. "Resolution of the *Zentralausschuss* of January 15, 1946"; Dahrendorf, *Zwangsvereinigung*, p. 106. Thomas, pp. 188–89, assigns considerable effect to the January 15 ZA resolution in increasing the "wavering" of the Berlin SPD leadership on the unity issue.

71. SPD, *Zentralausschuss, Circular Letter No. 1 (1946)*, January 17, 1946.

72. Thuringia LV, *Circular Letter No. 7 (1946)*, January 26, 1946.

73. Böhme, *Vereint*, p. 498.

74. Gniffke, *Jahre*, p. 129; Gustav Klingelhöfer, "Zehn Jahre Kampf um die Freiheit Berlins," *Berliner Stimme*, March 31, 1956. For Dresden difficulties, see Interview with Walter Ramm, December 4, 1959.

75. "Stellungnahme der Sozialdemokratie Rostocks," *Das Volk*, January 13, 1946. The same story was reprinted in the *Tribüne*, "Um den Weg zur Einheit," January 19, 1946, and may have appeared elsewhere. An undated letter from Rostock supports the contents of the original resolution adopted. Dahrendorf, *Zwangsvereinigung*, p. 105; interview with Willi Jesse, February 9, 1960.

76. "Konferenzen zur Einheit," *Das Volk*, January 27, 1946.

77. Gniffke, *Jahre*, pp. 133–34. Gniffke also submitted a transcript of Frölich's January 23 interview with the Thuringia SMA.

78. This passage is based on a paraphrase of the reports made at the time by Fritz Neubecker.

79. Gniffke Manuscript, p. 165. The meeting did what it could by passing a resolution supporting the ZA, declaring that unity could not be ordered by a fixed date and would have to depend on nationwide decisions. *Ibid.*, p. 162.

80. Peter, in Doernberg et al., *Beiträge*, p. 104; interview with Arno Hennig, March 4, 1960. Hennig claims that he failed in an attempt to obtain ZA support for an anti-Buchwitz move. See also, Erich Mückenberger, "Alle kannten wir nur ein Ziel: die Einheit der Arbeiterklasse," *Vereint*, pp. 337–38.

81. Interview with Rudolf Rothe, February 6 1960.

82. "Entschliessung," *Volksstimme* (Dresden), January 17, 1946, cited in *Dokumente und Materialien*, pp. 427–30; Gniffke Manuscript, p. 165.

83. Matern's speech is in Hermann Matern, *Aus dem Leben und Kampf der deutschen Arbeiterbewegung* (Berlin: Dietz, 1958), pp. 237–46.

84. For examples, see "Beschluss der gemeinsamen Sitzung des SPD-Landesvorstandes und der KPD-Bezirksleitung Land Sachsen, vom 28. Januar 1946 über weitere Schritte zur Vereinigung der beiden Arbeiterparteien," *Dokumente und Materialien*, p. 460.

85. See Dahrendorf, *Zwangsvereinigung*, p. 110. See also, a similar resolution in Potsdam for Brandenburg, *DVZ*, January 30, 1946.

86. The major source for this meeting is the Memorandum prepared by Herbert

Kriedemann, cited hereinafter as Kriedmann Memorandum. See also Gniffke, *Jahre* pp. 138–39.

87. Gniffke, *Jahre*, pp. 138–39; see also, Kaden, p. 235, especially the interview with Kriedemann cited in footnote 525. Grotewohl seems to have hoped rather desperately that Schumacher would soften his hitherto unyielding stand.

88. Kriedmann Memorandum.

89. In these discussions Grotewohl and Dahrendorf rejected a suggestion that an anti-SMA stand could be put into effect by the ZA. In such a case the ZA was to rely on the still-united Berlin SPD organization and utilize the publicity facilities of the Western sectors. The reason given for the rejection of such a policy provides an interesting reflection on the political atmosphere of Berlin at that time. In the view of the ZA representatives, political policy in Berlin (i.e., the policy of the Allied Kommandatura) was determined by its Soviet member. Kriedmann Memorandum.

90. Kriedemann Memorandum.

91. The first suggestion of this that I have been able to find was made by Brill in reporting on the *Parteiausschuss* meeting of December 4–5. Speaking to the LV, Brill remarked, "The SPD must openly advocate its own policies even at the risk of being banned or having to dissolve itself." Protocol of the Meeting of the Thuringia LV [December] 12, 1945.

92. Interview with Rudolf Rothe, February 6, 1960; see also Klingelhöfer Letter of February 9.

93. Kriedemann Memorandum.

94. Letter from Gustav Klingehöfer to Otto Grotewohl, February 9, 1946.

95. Klingelhöfer Testament.

96. Gniffke, *Jahre* p. 139.

97. This was the first mention found of the date on which the unity congress eventually opened (April 21, 1946, Easter Sunday). See Gniffke Manuscript, p. 167. See also, Dahrendorf, *Zwangsvereinigung*, pp. 117–19; Thomas, p. 191.

98. Gnifke Manuscript, p. 171.

99. Dahrendorf, *Zwangsvereinigung*, p. 117.

100. Gniffke, *Jahre*, pp. 141–42. Gniffke objected to the enforcement of a set date in the near future but saw no practical alternatives open.

101. Gniffke's published account, *Jahre*, pp. 142–43, gives no count of the vote nor does it identify who voted how. According to Gniffke Manuscript, p. 170, Dahrendorf, Neubecker, Germer, Weimann, Harnisch, and he voted against unity, while Grotewohl, Lehmann, Litke, Meier, and Orlopp voted for, and Fechner, who was chairing, abstained. Dahrendorf speaks of an original vote of 9–5 to postpone a decision and then an 8–3 (4 abstentions) to accept the unity schedule. *Zwangsvereinigung*, p. 118.

102. The versions in Dahrendorf and the two Gniffke works differ slightly in minor detail. Gniffke Manuscript, p. 170.

103. "SPD-Parteitag. Entscheidung über die Einigung," *Das Volk*, February 12, 1946.

104. The resolution is in *Das Volk*, February 20, 1946.

105. Grotewohl's appearance is not mentioned in a Soviet account of the meeting. D. Umanskii, "Pervye shagi novykh profsoiuzov v Germanii," *Trud*, March 31, 1946.

106. *Freie Gewerkschaft*, February 10, 12, and 13, 1946.

107. Excerpts from a radio interview with Grotewohl and Ulbricht in *DVZ*, February 12, 1946.

108. Franz Dahlem, "Für die Einheit und Macht der Arbeiterklasse," *DVZ*, February 13, 1946.

9. The Establishment of the Unity Party

1. Major sources for these congresses are their published records, which are cited here again for convenience:

Protokoll des Vereinigungsparteitages der Sozialdemokratischen Partei Deutschlands (SPD) und der Kommunistischen Partei Deutschlands (KPD) am 21. und 22. April 1946 in der Staatsoper "Admiralspalast" in Berlin (Berlin: J. H. W. Dietz Nachf., 1946), cited hereinafter as *Unity Congress*.

Bericht über die Verhandlungen des 15. Parteitages der Kommunistischen Partei Deutschlands 19. und 20. April 1946 in Berlin (Berlin: Neuer Weg, 1946), cited hereinafter as *KPD 15th Congress*.

Parteitag der Sozialdemokratischen Partei Deutschlands am 19. und 20. April 1946 in Berlin (Berlin: Vorwarts, 1946), cited hereinafter as *SPD 40th Congress*.

Bezirksparteitag der SPD Gross-Berlins am 7.4.1946, nachm. 16 Uhr, (Landesarchiv Berlin-Abteilung Zeitgeschichte), cited hereinafter as *Berlin Opposition Congress*.

2. Germer and Neubecker were first expelled from the ZA (*Das Volk*, March 14, 1946) and then from the SPD (*ibid.*, April 3, 1946). The two letters of expulsion against Germer were shown the writer by Herr Germer.

3. "Lieber Erich, lieber Otto!" February 17, 1946. The letter was distributed among ZA members by Dahrendorf's authorization. See also Gniffke, *Jahre*, pp. 149–52; the letter is reproduced on p. 150.

4. Dahrendorf Letter of February 17, 1946. For the official ZA response, see "Gustav Dahrendorf wechselt in den Westen," *Das Volk*, March 31, 1946.

5. See Grotewohl's pained response to questions at a public meeting, "Grotewohls Flucht in das Gefühl," *Tagesspiegel*, March 16, 1946.

6. For opposition in Chemnitz, see Mückenberger, *Vereint*, p. 340. A Soviet account has it that "the splitters received a decisive rebuff" in "Leipzig, Halle, and other cities" of the Soviet Zone. A. Korsunskii, "Bor'ba za edinstvo rabochego klassa v Germanii," *Mirovoe khoziaistvo i mirovaia politika,* no. 12 (December 1946), 73.

7. The *Parteiausschuss* was an enlarged leadership group which included representatives of the provincial SPD organizations as well as the zonal *Zentralausschuss*.

8. Notes of Fritz Neubecker, with *Parteiausschuss* resolution of February 19, 1946.

9. "Berliner, übernimmt die Führung!" *Das Volk*, March 14, 1946. See also Thomas, p. 210, and Böhme, *Vereint*, pp. 499–500.

10. See Hoffmann's statement in Protocol of the meeting of the Thuringia LV, March 14, 1946.

11. Strictly speaking, *Betriebsgruppen* were at places of work generally; for example, at government offices, and not just at factories.

12. Kaden, p. 49.

13. Statements by Arno Wend and an unnamed Leipzig delegate in *SPD 40th Congress*, pp. 115–16; Peter in Doernberg et al., *Beiträge*, p. 106; Karl Urban, "Der Kampf um die Wiedervereinigung der Arbeiterbewegung in der Provinz Brandenburg (Mai 1945 bis April 1946)," *ZfG*, 7, no. 7 (1959), 1571–72.

14. Kaden, pp. 266–67.

15. Gniffke, *Jahre*, p. 156.

16. *SPD 40th Congress*, pp. 106–9.

17. "Das Einheitsbekenntnis der sozialdemokratischen Betriebsarbeiter," *DVZ*, March 17, 1946.

18. *SPD 40th Congress*, p. 109.

19. *Ibid.*, p. 114.

20. This was not entirely sincere. Wend himself has said that this issue was raised to "accentuate differences" between Social Democrats and Communists. Interview with Arno Wend, December 30, 1959.

21. *SPD 40th Congress*, p, 117.

22. The resolution described the "local organization" as the "basic organizational unit," and "fundamental embodiment" of the unity party. *Ibid.*, p. 121.

23. *Unity Congress*, p. 150.

24. Paragraphs 8 and 9, Sections 1–3, *Ibid.*, p. 83.

25. *SPD 40th Congress*, p. 68; *Unity Congress*, pp. 154–56.

26. For general accounts of the emergence of the dissident Berlin SPD, see Schulz, *Auftakt,* passim; Kaden, pp. 245–56; and from a Communist standpoint, Thomas, pp. 189–224.

27. *Entschliessung in der Konferenz der Berliner-SPD-Funktionäre am Montag, dem 20. Januar 1946 in der Staatsoper (Admiralspalast)*, cited hereinafter as SPD January 20 Resolution.

28. SPD January 20 Resolution; Thomas, pp. 188–89.

29. Examples are: Swolinsky (Tempelhof), Neumann, (Reinickendorf), Schulz (Charlottenburg), Lehrenz and Aussner (Spandau), Jeanetta Wolff (Neukölln).

30. Kaden, p. 246.

31. Schulz, *Auftakt,* pp. 293–94.

32. Kaden, p. 246; Thomas, p. 195.

33. Frölich's remarks in the Protocol of the Meeting of Thuringia LV, February 24, 1946, bear this out.

34. For the resolutions of the February 17 meeting, see Schulz, *Auftakt*, pp. 294–95.

35. For the discussions at the "Second Conference of the Sixty," see *Die Sozialistische Einheitspartei Deutschlands (Beschlüsse der gemeinsamen Konferenz der Parteileitungen der SPD und KPD mit Vertretern der Bezirke am 26. Februar 1946 in Berlin)* (Berlin: Verlag der Einheit, [1946]), cited hereinafter as *February 26 Meeting*; also *DVZ*, February 27, 1946. For the uneventful proceedings see Gniffke, *Jahre*, p. 156; Thomas, p. 198.

36. See the resolution of the Thuringia LV: "Es lebe die Sozialistische Einheitspartei Deutschlands. Entschliessung des erweiterten Landesvorstandes der SPD Thüringen," February 28, 1946. By way of contrast, the Berlin BV rejected a KPD proposal for a joint organizational committee; this was on February 18, 1946. Thomas, pp. 205–6, especially n.176.

37. *Ibid.*, p.197; Kaden, p. 247. Thomas's implication that Schumacher "gave orders" to the Berlin Opposition is unsupported; indeed, it is difficult to see what he did provide beyond a psychological boost.

38. The text of the resolution is in the *Tagesspiegel*, March 14, 1946; Schulz, *Auftakt*, pp. 305–6.

39. Gniffke Manuscript, pp. 181–82; Thomas, pp. 202–3, gives a partisan but fair account.

40. Grotewohl's speech included in *Das Volk*, March 2, 1946, as a booklet entitled, "Einheit der Werktätigen, Einheit Deutschlands," cited hereinafter as *Grotewohl March 1 speech*. Grotewohl was answered by Karl Germer, who criticized the KPD record in detail. See Karl J. Germer, Jr., "Vertrauen oder Mistrauen," *Tagesspiegel*, March 3, 1946.

41. *Das Volk*, March 2, 1946. The first KPD response to the proposal for a referendum was to describe it as a demand for "wider consultation" and "insufficient participation" by party functionaries in deciding the unity question. "Einheitspartei von lebenswichtiger Bedungtung," *DVZ* March 2, 1946.

42. Cited in *Das Volk*, March 2, 1946.

43. *Pieck March 2 speech*, p. 14.

44. "An die Mitglieder der SPD von Gross-Berlin," *Das Volk*, March 8, 1946. For technical arrangements set on March 12, see Thomas, p. 206.

45. *Das Volk*, March 14, 1946.

46. Kaden, p. 245.

47. Thus picking up Pieck's notion that new members were not reliable persons to be consulted on this question. The hypocrisy of this stand becomes plain if it is recalled that nonparty workers were said to be a strong and valid pro-unity force and indeed were mobilized for many of the factory meetings approving unity. For this editorial, see "Demokratisches Disziplin," *Das Volk*, March 14, 1946.

48. "An die Mitglieder der SPD von Gross-Berlin," *Das Volk*, March 15, 1946.

49. "An die Sozialdemokraten Berlins! Erklärung des Zentralausschusses zur Urabstimmung in Berlin," *Das Volk*, March 28, 1946. Two days prior to this, the Berlin SPD BV had approved arrangements for the referendum! See Thomas, p. 213.

50. Schulz, *Auftakt*, p. 306.

51. These totals have been compiled from a number of press, wire-service, and SPD sources. Minor variations in the vote total, which do not affect the outcome, are probably the result of somewhat informal voting arrangements.

52. The French-licensed *Der Kurier* asked both the BV and the Opposition's election committee for the total of qualified voters. Germer replied for the latter and listed 33,247. The BV's Erich Lübbe substantiated this, explaining that the ZA's figure of 39,716 included applicants for membership and persons in arrears on their dues. The difference between the two figures is whether an absolute majority voted "NO" on question one. See "Zwei Sieger?" *Der Kurier*, April 3, 1946.

53. *DVZ*, April 2, 1946.

54. *Das Volk*, April 2, 1946.

55. *DVZ*, April 2, 1946; "Zur Urabstimmung im sowjetischen Sektor von Berlin!" *Das Volk*, April 6, 1946.

56. For a reasoned, if partisan, attack on these "incorrect" positions of the ZA and especially of the Berlin BV, see Thomas, pp. 188–89, 205–9.

57. *Tagesspiegel*, February 26, 1946; Thomas, pp. 196–97; Gniffke, *Jahre*, pp. 152–54.

58. "Einladung zum Parteitag der SPD," *Das Volk*, March 20, 1946. It was signed for the ZA by Grotewohl, Fechner, and Gniffke. For the expulsion vote's reception by the ZA, see Erich W. Gniffke, "Unser Parteitag," *Das Volk*, March 20, 1946.

59. Max Fechner, "Offener Brief an Dr. Schumacher," *Das Volk*, March 21, 1946. Fechner incorrectly asserted that the agreement at Wennigsen had given the ZA the duty to "further party work in the West in every possible way."

60. Gniffke, "Unser Parteitag" *Das Volk*, March 20, 1946; *SPD 40th Congress*, p. 20; Walter Müller, "Die Aktionsgemeinschaftzwischen KPD und SPD in München 1945/1946," *BzG*, 3, S (1961), 133.

61. Fechner, "Offener Brief," *Das Volk*, March 21, 1946.

62. *Das Volk*, March 2, 1946.

63. Grotewohl speech, *ibid.*

64. "Die Einheit und der Westen. Rundfunkgespräch mit dem Genossen Erich Gniffke,"*Das Volk*, March 17, 1946. Such assurances found a ready echo outside Berlin. In Thuringia, for instance, August Frölich "expressed his joy" that a way had been found to turn the zonal party congress into a national one. Protocol of the Meeting of the Thuringia LV, February 28, 1946.

65. There was supposedly 127 "westerners" out of 507 KPD delegates, and 103 of 548 SPD delegates at the unity congress, *Unity Congress*, p. 146.

66. *SPD 40th Congress*, p. 44.

67. "Zu Schumachers Berliner Fraktionsbesprechungen," *DVZ*, February 24, 1946.

68. "Berlin ist für die Einheit!" *DVZ*, March 27, 1946. Pieck, referring to the Opposition's meeting place, sneered at the "Zehlendorfer invalids' club." Leonhard, p. 448.

Franz Dahlem, "Die Verantwortung der Berliner Sozialdemokraten," *DVZ*, March 17, 1946, considered that the Opposition's tactics were a "shame for the Berlin workers' movement."

69. "Nur die geeinte Arbeiterklasse wird die Reaktion endgültig vernichten," *DVZ*, March 9, 1946.

70. Thomas, p. 209, n.190.

71. *Die nächsten Aufgaben beim Neuaufbau Deutschlands. Beschlüsse der Parteikonferenz der Kommunistischen Partei Deutschlands am 2. und 3. März 1946 in Berlin* (Berlin: Neuer Weg, 1946), p. 4; cited hereinafter as *KPD March 2 Conference*.

72. *Pieck March 2 speech*, pp. 12–13.

73. *Ibid.*, p. 31. Grotewohl asserted, *Unity Congress*, p. 117, that "If the socialist state in the East shows the greater interest in and sympathy for the great work of socialist unification in Germany than do some other powers, why then as Socialists we find that quite understandable."

74. *KPD March 2 Conference*, p. 9; Franz Dahlem, "Um Leben und Zukunft unseres Volkes," *DVZ*, March 1, 1946.

75. Franz Dahlem, "Deutsche Politik: Zur Diskussion um das Ruhregebiet," *DVZ*, February 21, 1946.

76. Anton Ackermann, "Gibt es einen besonderen deutschen Weg zum Sozialismus?" *Einheit*, 1, no. 1 (February 1946), 23–32; cited hereinafter as *German Road*. This *Einheit* was published by the joint commission of the two parties for preparing unity; three issues were published until the unity congress in April. The current SED theoretical monthly *Einheit* appeared with vol. 1, no. 1 in June 1946.

77. Leonhard, p. 429, refers to "Ackermann's saving thesis." Ackermann was forced to disown his views in 1948. For a later, cautiously favorable judgment on Ackermann's ideas, see Gunter Benser, "Über den friedlichen Character der revolutionären Umwälzung in Ostdeutschland," *BzG*, 7, no. 2 (1965), 189–220. In a 25th anniversary article for the Soviet party journal *Kommunist*, Ulbricht once more disavowed the notion of a special German road. His article was reprinted in German in an anniversary collection, "Die geschichtliche Leistung der SED," *Die historische Mission der Sozialistischen Einheitspartei Deutschlands* (Berlin: Dietz, 1971), p. 47.

78. *German Road*, p. 29, Tiul'panov has written that in Germany the task of smashing the state machine was "notably more complex and had to be carried out in a more radical fashion than in other countries," because the combination of Hitlerism and state-monopoly capitalism had produced a state "unique" in its totality and social ubiquity. Tiul'panov, "Die Rolle," p. 244.

79. *DVZ*, December 4, 1945.

80. Wolfgang Leonhard, "Über den deutschen Weg zum Sozialismus," *DVZ*, March 24, 1945.

81. *German Road*, p. 30.

82. *Ibid.*, pp. 31–32.

83. It may be pointed out that Schumacher held the same idea for the SPD.

84. Anton Ackermann, "Unsere kulturpolitische Sendung," *Um die Erneuerung der deutschen Kultur. Erste zentrale Kulturtagung der KPD vom 3. bis 5. Februar in Berlin (Stenographischer Niederschrift)* (Berlin: Neuer Weg, 1946), p. 33.

85. Max Fechner, *Einheit tut not! Rede auf der Versammlung der Zentralverwaltung für Industrie in Berlin am 12. März 1946* (Berlin: Einheit, 1946), pp. 5–6.

86. *Dokumente und Materialien*, pp. 625–27.

87. *Das Volk*, March 2, 1946.

88. *Einstimmig beschlossen: SED Gross-Berlin. Die Bildung der SED in der Hauptstadt Deutschlands.* . . . (n.p., n.p., n.d.), p. 13.

89. Kaden, p. 241.

90. See, for example, Dahlem at *KPD 15th Congress*, p. 65.

91. *Pieck March 2 speech*, p. 20.

92. Commenting on the March 2–3 KPD Conference, the *DVZ* remarked (March 5, 1946), "There is only one single Communist Party for all of Germany."

93. That these were not overriding considerations in reaching a political decision regarding merger of the parties is best shown by the ZA members themselves. Doubly protected by their highly visible position and by the fact that many of them lived in the Western sectors of Berlin, the majority of ZA members nevertheless supported unification with the KPD.
For those reasons one should assign little weight to the location of the ZA's offices in the Soviet sector. Although the move to East Berlin was undertaken in June 1945 at Soviet suggestion to remove the SPD from the future American sector (with the plausible argument that parties were not yet legal in areas under American occupation), there is no evidence that the ZA's decisions were the result of its location. See in this connection Kaden, p. 205, n.452.
The statements made in the text on this matter are based on a variety of interviews and conversations with former Soviet Zone Social Democrats. See also Leonhard, p. 443; Gniffke, *Jahre*, p. 139; Kathleen McLaughlin, "Russians Imprison German Leftists," *The New York Times*, March 20, 1946.

94. Arno Scholz, *Berlin im Würgegriff* (Berlin-Grunewald: Arani, 1953), p. 16. Klingelhöfer wrote to Grotewohl that British officers had expressed interest in the Berlin political events and hinted of publicity opportunities. Letter from Gustav Klingelhöfer to Otto Grotewohl, February 9, 1946.

95. Thomas, p. 227; for example, in addition to Germer's March 1 speech, the *Tagesspiegel* on February 17 printed the Berlin resolution of December 29, the ZA resolution of January 15, a Charlottenburg resolution expressing nonconfidence in the ZA, and other items.

96. The BBC broadcasts of Patrick Gordon-Walker played a particular role here, earning him Pieck's scorn. *KPD 15th Congress*, p.202.

97. Great Britain, Parliament, *Parliamentary Debates* (House of Commons), 5th ser. 420 (4–22 March 1946), 1626–40, passim. In the course of this debate, Konni Zilliacus de-

fended the utility of Communist-Socialist cooperation in postwar reconstruction, *ibid.*, p. 1637. See also, Michael Foot, "The Reopening of Buchenwald," *Daily Herald*, March 12, 1946.

98. Brandt and Lowenthal mention the Americans George Silver and Louis Wiesner of Robert Murphy's staff, and the British officer Austin Albu. Willy Brandt and Richard Löwenthal, *Ernst Reuter—ein Leben für die Freiheit* (Munich: Kindler, 1957), p. 356.

99. Clay declared also that Social Democrats might travel to Berlin for the SPD Congress. See "U.S. eases Zone Bars for Political Rally," *The New York Times*, February 26, 1946.

100. OMGUS, *Monthly Report of the Military Governor*, no. 9, (April 20, 1946), Annex: Political Activity, p. 4.

101. *Ibid.*, p. 2.

102. Kaden, p. 255, especially n.572.

103. Allied Kommandatura Berlin (AKB) *Document* BK/R (46) 46.

104. *Ibid.*; AKB, *Document* BKC/M (46) 11.

105. Thomas, pp. 231–32.

106. The SED Letter and subsequent discussion: AKB, *Document* BK/R (46) 160.

107. Thomas, pp. 231–33; OMGUS, U.S. Berlin District, Letter of April 30, 1946, to Dr. Wittgenstein, District Mayor of Zehlendorf.

108. Fijalkowski, p. 41; AKB, *Document* BKC/M (46) 15.

109. For such statements by Pieck and Ulbricht, see *Unity Congress*, p. 19; *KPD 15th Congress*, p. 59; "German Red Hits Allies," *New York Times*, March 4, 1946.

110. At the time of the unification congresses in the provinces, in Berlin, and finally for the Soviet Zone as a whole, there was a flurry of Soviet press commentary. This commentary was of a uniform and unenterprising nature; it stressed the progressive character of the new development, the broad rank-and-file enthusiasm for the merger, and the ultimately futile opposition of right-wing Social Democrats located in the Western zones and in Berlin. As *Pravda*'s correspondent put it, ordinary party members and local organizations were "enthusiastic" for unity, while "a portion of the functionaries of the Social Democratic party" did not share this reaction. Unity, despite their "bitter opposition," was dictated "by life itself," and therefore triumphed. See I. Zolin, "Ob'edinionie rabochikh partii v Germanii," *Pravda*, April 25, 1946. See also "Ob'edinionie berlinskikh organizatsii sotsial-demokraticheskoi i kommunisticheskoi partii Germanii, "*Pravda*, April 18, 1946; "Ob'edinionie germanskikh sotsial-demokraticheskoi i kommunisticheskoi partii v sovetskoi zone okkupatsii Germannii," *Pravda*, April 15, 1946; M.M., "Na mezhdunarodnye temy," *Krasnaia Zvezda*, April 20, 1946.

10. Conclusions

1. Herbert Feis, *From Trust to Terror: The Onset of the Cold War, 1945–1950* (New York: Norton, 1970), pp. 56–62; Nikolaev, *Politika sovetskogo soiuza*, pp. 57–58.

2. Marshall D. Shulman, *Stalin's Foreign Policy Reappraised* (Cambridge: Harvard University Press, 1963), pp. 4–5. See also Alexander Dallin, "Soviet Foreign Policy and

Domestic Politics: A Framework for Analysis," in *The Conduct of Soviet Foreign Policy*, Erik P. Hoffmann and Frederic J. Fleron, Jr., eds. (Chicago: Aldine, Atherton, 1971), pp. 44-48.

3. For an illuminating incident, see Leonhard, p. 425.

4. One analyst has described Stalin's policy as "messianic in its world view, limited in its geographic and functional scope, pessimistic in its evaluation of situations, parsimonious in its acceptance of costs and risks. . . ." Charles O. Lerche, Jr., *The Cold War . . . and After* (Englewood Cliffs, N.J.: Prentice-Hall, 1965), p. 50.

5. Thus Walter Lafeber seems to rely too much on hindsight when he argues that "By the end of 1945, chances for a united, open, and self-sufficient Germany had largely disappeared." Walter LaFeber, *America, Russia, and the Cold War 1945-1966* (New York: Wiley, 1967), p. 20.

6. Paul Seabury, *The Rise and Decline of the Cold War* (New York: Basic Books, 1967), p. 20.

7. If this analysis is correct, it casts grave doubt on the common revisionist view that Stalin had few if any political ambitions in Europe. See, for example, Gardner's contention that, beyond land reform, Stalin had no need for further political moves in Germany. Lloyd C. Gardner, "America and the German 'Problem,' " in *Politics and Policies of the Truman Administration*, Barton J. Bernstein, ed. (Chicago: Quadrangle, 1970), p. 114.

8. Alexander Dallin, "The Uses of International Movements," in *Russian Foreign Policy* Ivo J. Lederer, ed. (New Haven: Yale University Press, 1962), p. 331.

9. Burks, "Eastern Europe," in *Communism and Revolution*, pp. 83-84.

10. Lowenthal, p. 33.

11. *Speech Delivered by J. V. Stalin at a Meeting of Voters of the Stalin Electoral Area, Moscow, February 9, 1946* (Washington: Embassy of the Union of Soviet Socialist Republics, 1946), p. 4.

12. In Poland, an agreement of this type on November 29, 1946, resulted from a trip of Socialist and Communist leaders to Moscow. See M. K. Dziewanowski, *The Communist Party of Poland* (Cambridge: Harvard University Press, 1959), p. 216. In Austria an agreement forming a "community of action" (*Aktionsgemeinschaft*) was approved by the Socialist and Communist leaderships (by the former in an 8-5 vote) on July 26, 1945. Kurt L. Shell, "The Austrian Socialist Party since 1945; Socialism in the 'Age of Fulfillment.' " Diss. Columbia University, 1955, p. 307.

13. See, *inter alia*, Dziewanowski, especially pp. 215-20; Henry L. Roberts, *Rumania: Political Problems of an Agrarian State* (New Haven: Yale University Press, 1951); Ghita Ionescu, *Communism in Rumania 1944-1962* (London: Oxford University Press, 1964); Valentin Thoma, "Wie es zur Liquidierung des rumänischen Sozialismus kam," *Die Zukunft*, no. 7 (July 1949), 203-7; Edward Taborsky, *Communism in Czechoslovakia 1948-1960* (Princeton: Princeton University Press, 1961); Richard T. Davies, "The Fate of Polish Socialism," in *The Soviet Union 1922-1962: A Foreign Affairs Reader*, Philip E. Mosely, ed. (New York: Praeger, 1963), pp. 257-74; William B. Bader, *Austria Between East and West 1945-1955* (Stanford: Stanford University Press, 1966).

14. Dziewanowski believes that unification in Poland was delayed until after the purge of

Gomulka, lest a Socialist-Gomulkaite bloc overturn the "Muscovite" party leadership. Dziewanowski, pp. 217–18.

15. *Ibid.*, pp. 189–90.

16. The Austrian Socialists delayed cooperation with the Communists in practice until after the elections of 1945. Bader, p. 18; Shell, p. 307.

17. Burks argues, in *Communism and Revolution*, p. 92, that "The forcible fusion of the Communist and Socialist parties was an important development only in those states in which Social Democracy had been a major force during the interwar period, i.e., in East Germany, Poland, Czechoslovakia, and Hungary."

18. Zbigniew K. Brzezinski, *The Soviet Bloc: Unity and Conflict*, rev. ed. (Cambridge: Harvard University Press, 1967), p. 16.

19. Thorez announced this just after his return from Moscow in November 1944. For France, see generally, Alfred J. Rieber, *Stalin and the French Communist Party 1941–1947* (New York: Columbia University Press, 1962), esp. pp. 212–20.

20. Ake Sparring, "Die KP Schwedens," in *Kommunisten im Norden*, Ake Sparring, ed. (Cologne: Wissenschaft und Politik, 1967), p. 25.

21. Berholt Homgard, "Die KP Dänemarks," *ibid.*, p. 53.

22. Hans F. Dahl, "Behind the Fronts: Norway," *Journal of Contemporary History*, 3 (1970), 47; Peder Furbotn, *Kampen for Norges Suverenitet* (Oslo: Norsk Forlag Ny Dag, 1948), pp. 26–27; John Otto Jahnsen, "Norway," in *Communism in Europe*, William E. Griffith, ed. (Cambridge: MIT Press, 1966), II, 328.

23. Dahl, p. 49; Willy Brandt, *Draussen: Schriften während der Emigration* (Munich: Kindler, 1966), pp. 325–26. This last selection is a partial translation of an NLP pamphlet on the subject that Brandt wrote in 1945 under the title "Facts about the Policies of the Communists."

24. E. Varga, "Osobennosti vnutrennei i vneshnei politiki kapitalisticheskikh stran v epoku obschchego krizisa kapitalizma," *Mirovoe khoziaistvo i mirovaia politika*, no. 6 (June 1946), 14.

25. S. Iwanow, *Über die Rolle der sozialistischen Parteien nach dem zweiten Weltkriege* (Berlin: SWA-Verlag, 1947), p. 10. Citations used here were checked against the Russian original: S. Ivanov, "O roli sotsialisticheskikh partii posle vtoroi mirovoi voiny," *Bol'shevik*, 13, no. 17–18 (September 1946), 50–65.

26. The Italian Socialists are handled very gingerly in this article, because of the hope that the antiunity decisions of the April 1946 Florence congress of the Socialist Party will be reversed. Iwanow, pp. 20–21.

27. Thornton, "The Foundations," and Burks, "Eastern Europe," *Communism and Revolution*; Hugh Seton-Watson, *From Lenin to Khrushchev: The History of World Communism* (New York: Praeger, 1960), ch. 13.

28. As indicated in chapter 1, above, this approach was an elaboration and extension of the Popular Front policy of the 1930s. See on this point, Horst Duhnke, *Die KPD 1933–1945*, pp. 282–84.

29. That is, "peaceful" in the sense that the overturn in Prague in 1948 was peaceful. On

this point, see Gunther Benser, "Über den friedlichen Charakter," p. 195, wherein the social conflict in the Soviet Zone is compared to the fight against collaborators in the Resistance.

30. Melvin Croan, "Soviet Uses of the Doctrine of the 'Parliamentary Road' to Socialism: East Germany, 1945–1946," *The American Slavic and East European Review*, 17, no. 3 (October 1958), 302–15.

31. George Lichtheim, "Reflections on Trotsky," *Commentary*, 40, no. 1, (January 1964), 56.

32. Lowenthal, p. 31.

33. Leonhard, p. 547. The statement was made in April 1947.

34. For further examples of such conflicting policies, and their use in Soviet foreign policy, see Philip E. Mosely, "Soviet Policy and Nationality Conflicts in East Central Europe," *The Kremlin and World Politics* (New York: Vintage, 1960), pp. 221–45.

35. Thus the KPD virulently opposed any program for a federal reform of the German state structure.

36. Carola Stern has pointed out that "When the Communist emigres returned to Germany from Moscow at the end of the Second World War, they had resolved not to repeat their grossest error of the Weimar Republic, their "underestimation of the national question." This time they would be cleverer. . . . The emigres had . . . learned from Stalin [during the war] Hitler had given them the opportunity to pose, for the first time, as the representatives of national interests." Stern, *Ulbricht,* pp. 215–16.

Joseph Starobin comments that when "Ulbricht and Rakosi, Anna Pauker and even Dimitroff were being prepared to return to the homelands where they had previously failed. . . . they did not go back as revolutionaries. For all of Moscow's hopes that they root themselves in native soil, they were intended to be the guarantors of control." Joseph Starobin, "Origins of the Cold War: The Communist Dimension," *Foreign Affairs*, 47, no. 4 (July 1969), 687. Nevertheless, despite its efforts, the KPD continued to be regarded by many Germans as "the Russian party," Leonhard, p. 463.

37. The subsequent use of such power may, of course, take many forms. Nevertheless, it seems inescapable that (at least in the short term perspective of 1945) it would be used to enhance Soviet power. Only a special unconcern with such enhancement and narrow definition of the political "left" can justify the comment of Gabriel Kolko that, "The Americans never understood that the Communist parties by virtue of Russian influence were the safest in politics, and the only group capable of aborting the left by deluding it." Gabriel Kolko, *The Politics of War* (New York: Random House, 1968), p. 346.

38. Whatever mistakes of analysis the Soviet authorities may have been guilty of, they nevertheless did undertake to identify the various social forces of postwar Germany, decide which should be backed in the interests of Soviet policy, and act accordingly. For the more abstract and less effective American procedure of reliance on formulas of "democratization" and "denazification," see the comment of John Gimbel, *A German Community*, pp. 4–5.

39. Horst Duhnke writes that "The real decision of 1945 was about who would lead German Communism in the future. To a large extent that decision had been made during the years of exile. The struggle for the leadership of the KPD had been decided during Stalin's purges." Duhnke dissertation, p. 636.

While this view is essentially correct as far as the German situation is concerned, it over-looks the potential challenges to the emigré leaders. Here a comparison with the other East European CPs is instructive.

40. For the internal history of the SED and the purges within the party, see Stern, *Porträt,* ch. 4, and *Ulbricht,* ch. 5. A presentation displaying more empathy with Ulbricht is Gerhard Zwerenz, *Walter Ulbricht* (Munich: Scherz, 1966), pp. 15–17.

41. Interview with Fritz Schreiber, December 29, 1959.

42. For a typical comment on these lines, see interview with Erich W. Gniffke, August 3, 1960.

43. Croan, "Soviet Uses," pp. 302–15. Croan underestimates the utility of this doctrine in justifying and explaining Soviet policy to *Soviet* policy-makers.

44. When criticising the ZA, one must bear in mind that the prognoses of other German political leaders were no more perceptive. How "realistic," for example, was Schumacher's insistence that only "socialism" could restore Germany's economy and society. On this point see ch. 5, "Perspectives of a post-totalitarian leader," esp. pp. 72–91 in Edinger, *Schumacher.*

45. Croan, "Soviet Uses," p. 304.

While this view is essentially correct as far as the German situation is concerned, it overlooks the potential challenges to the emigré leaders. Here a comparison with the other East European CPs is instructive.

40. For the internal history of the SED and the purges within the party, see Stern, *Porträt*, ch. 4, and *Ulbricht*, ch. 5. A presentation displaying more empathy with Ulbricht is Gerhard Zwerenz, *Walter Ulbricht* (Munich: Scherz, 1966), pp. 15–17.

41. Interview with Fritz Schreiber, December 29, 1959.

42. For a typical comment on these lines, see interview with Erich W. Gniffke, August 3, 1960.

43. Croan, "Soviet Uses," pp. 302–15. Croan underestimates the utility of this doctrine in justifying and explaining Soviet policy to *Soviet* policy-makers.

44. When criticising the ZA, one must bear in mind that the prognoses of other German political leaders were no more perceptive. How "realistic," for example, was Schumacher's insistence that only "socialism" could restore Germany's economy and society. On this point see ch. 5, "Perspectives of a post-totalitarian leader," esp. pp. 72–91 in Edinger, *Schumacher*.

45. Croan, "Soviet Uses," p. 304.

Bibliography

Because most studies dealing with the development of the Soviet Zone and Soviet politics in Germany have not focused directly on the political issues of the first postwar months, there are no detailed studies of this subject other than those produced under SED auspices. While this is due in part to the inaccessibility of source materials, it clearly reflects the greater attraction diplomatic developments and economic policy have held for many scholars.

Thus, for instance, the leading Western monograph on the early history of the Soviet Zone, that of J. P. Nettl, concentrates on economic and formal governmental developments; the only study based on Soviet defector sources (Slusser) is limited almost entirely to economic questions. (Works referred to in this and the following paragraphs are listed in the body of the bibliography.)

Soviet scholarship in this area had not been more satisfactory than Western efforts. Limited for many years to unenlightening Stalinist accounts (Mel'nikov, 1951), Soviet treatments of this period still concentrate on Great Power diplomacy, rather than on internal developments in the Soviet Zone. This is true of the otherwise useful works of Nikolaev, Galkin and Mel'nikov, and Vysotskii. Surprisingly, there is no general scholarly or documentary account of the Soviet military government comparable to studies of the American occupation regime; indeed there is no comprehensive published collection of the official enactments of the SMA.

There are extensive German accounts (both East and West) of this period. Yet here also the focus is either on the diplomatic scene (as in the important early work of Boris Meissner) or on general German developments (as in Kaden's study of the SPD; Kaden does not investigate the Soviet Zone events at local or provincial levels) or on German developments to the neglect of the Soviet involvement (as in the otherwise invaluable works of Carola Stern.)

As part of the general intensification of concern in the German Democratic Republic with the origins of the regime, there has been a substantial increase in works published on this topic; this has included publication of, or reference to, a number of documentary materials. These works have included valuable memoir accounts (especially the volume *Vereint sind wir alles*) and many journal articles, as well as some valuable monographs, of which the best by far is that of Siegfried Thomas.

Unfortunately, this literature is weakest where expectations are highest: the relations of the Soviet occupation authorities to political events,* and the internal politics of the Communist Party.† Moreover, access to the SED's party archives, which also house all GDR dissertations on the subject of party history, was in practice (although, perhaps, not in principle) unavailable to me.

The most extensive body of source material in this field is that produced by the Social Democratic Party. This reflects both the relatively open character of the SPD, as well as the fact that the party's continued existence in the Western Zones after 1946, together with the relatively fluid nature of zonal borders in the early postwar period, resulted in some Soviet Zone materials being deposited in Berlin and West Germany.

This disproportionate origin of the source materials has led to a somewhat excessive stress on the reactions of the Social Democrats to Soviet initiatives, which has thus become one of the main subjects of the work. Inasmuch as it is my contention that Soviet policy toward Social Democrats was an important aspect of general Soviet policy in this era, the stress of this work is not wholly inappropriate.

---

* See the plaintive remark of a GDR researcher that, on the subject of Soviet support for "... working class and other antifascist forces ... the archives unfortunately do not contain all too many documents." Helfried Wehner, "Dokumente internationalistischer, wegweisender Hilfe," *BzG,* 9, *Sonderheft* (1967), 139–140.

† This criticism is made of the first edition of Thomas's book by Manfred Behrend, review, *ZfG,* 13, no. 3 (1965), 510.

1. Interviews

(Conducted in 1959–1960 and 1962, with notation of subject's relevant activity in 1945–1946)

Joseph Baritz, economics officer with SMA in Dresden.

Ulrich Biel, officer in OMGUS, Berlin Detachment.

Heinz Brandt, staff worker in Berlin KPD Agitation-Propaganda department.

Adolf Bremer, organization secretary, Thuringia LV, SPD.

Ralf Dahrendorf, son of Gustav Dahrendorf.

Rudolph Dux, secretary in *Bezirk* organization, Magdeburg SPD.

Karl J. Germer, Jr., ZA member and Berlin opposition leader.

Erich W. Gniffke, member of "inner" ZA.

Sergei Gol'bov, officer in SMA, stationed near Magdeburg.

Hans Gottfurcht, visitor to German trade unions in 1945–46 on behalf of British TUC.

Arno Hennig, involved in formation of SPD, Dresden; major of Dresden-Freital.

Willi Jesse, SPD secretary for *Land* Mecklenburg-Vorpommern.

Alfred Kantorowicz, German Communist and literary figure in Berlin, 1946.

(Frau) Gustav Klingelhöfer, widow of Gus Klingelhöfer.

Fritz Koch, SPD secretary for cultural affairs, *Bezirk* Zwickau-Plauen, Saxony.

Herbert Kriedemann, close collaborator of Kurt Schumacher.

Wolfgang Leonhard, member of Ulbricht Group; active in KPD organization for Soviet Zone.

Fritz Neubecker, ZA member; active in Berlin opposition.

Walter Ramm, active in Saxon SPD, including subdistrict secretary in Dresden-Freital and Hennig secretary.

Rudolph Rothe, helped found, later served as first secretary of SPD Leipzig.

Fritz Sarow, staff member of *Tribüne*, newspaper for SPD, Thuringia.

Fritz Schreiber, ZA staff member, specialized in economic affairs.

Klaus-Peter Schulz, active in Berlin SPD opposition.

Sergei Ivanovich Tiul'panov, head of hierarchy of political officers, SMA; head of information section, SMA; head of CPSU party group, SMA.

Arno Wend, secretary of SPD Saxony LV.

2. Private Archives

The "private archives" noted below are collections of papers, organized with varying degrees of formality, in the possession of the persons indicated in the annotation. A brief description of the more important contents of each collection is provided below.

Dahrendorf Papers

Included in this collection are a number of letters to and from Gustav Dahrendorf, some documents of Gustav Klingelhöfer's circulated among the members of the ZA, and a long report on events in Magdeburg.

Germer Papers

Included in this collection is a wide variety of materials pertaining to the work of Karl J. Germer, Jr., in the ZA, materials pertaining to the organization and functioning of the ZA (agenda, resolutions, etc.), as well as drafts of speeches, resolutions, and papers circulated in the ZA.

Klingelhöfer Papers

Included in these papers is the Stenographic Protocol of the December Conference, as well as drafts of papers for that Conference; the documents cited in the footnotes as "Klingelhöfer Report" and "Klingelhöfer Testament"; letters to and from Gustav Klingelhöfer; Gustav Dahrendorf's remarks to the KPD meeting of June 12, 1945; and the materials for the Soviet response to Grotewohl's speech of November 11.

Neubecker Papers

These papers contain materials relating to the activities of the ZA and the SPD *Parteiausschuss* in January and February 1946.

Schulz Papers

Papers of Klaus-Peter Schulz dealing with the Berlin SPD Opposition in early 1946.

Thuringia Papers

This collection is in two parts: one consists of the papers of the late Hermann L. Brill and includes materials relating to the events in Buchenwald 1944–45, letters to and from Brill, speeches and articles by Brill, and his two letter-reports of December 1945 to Grotewohl on SPD relations with the KPD and the SMA. The second part consists of documents relating to the activities of the SPD in Thuringia and includes minutes and summaries of meetings of SPD bodies (particularly the *Landesvorstand*), reports from local organizations, and reports on confrontations between Social Democrats and the Soviet occupation authorities. These papers also include the complete file of the *Tribüne* and records of SPD and interparty meetings in Thuringia and Saxony.

3. Institutional Archives

Federal Republic of Germany, Governmental

Archiv für gesamtdeutsche Fragen (Archive for All-German Problems), Bonn.

This archive is an adjunct of the Federal Ministry of All-German Affairs and contains a variety of scattered materials relating to this topic.

Presse- und Informationsamt der Bundesregierung (Federal Government Press and Information Office), Bonn.

This office has scattered holdings of Soviet Zone newspapers from 1945–46.

City of [West] Berlin, Governmental

Landesarchiv Berlin-Abteilung Zeitgeschichte (Berlin *Land* Archive, Division of Current History), Berlin.

This archive contains a rich variety of materials on party developments in Berlin, including posters, proclamations, and rare numbers of newspapers. Especially noteworthy are a statement drawn up for the Archive by Karl J. Germer, Jr. (cited in this study as "Germer Statement"), and a copy of the letter from Deputy Mayor Karl Maron regarding licensing of political parties in June 1945.

Sozial Demokratische Partei Deutschlands (SPD) (Social Democratic Party of Germany)

Ostbüro (Eastern Bureau), Bonn.

The material in the files of this Bureau includes data on the organizational structure and membership of the SPD, voting figures for the Berlin Referendum of March 31, 1946, and a wide variety of reports, articles, clippings, texts of speeches, etc.

Aussenreferat (Foreign Department), Bonn.

Some additional materials were found in the files of this department.

Landesverband Berlin (Berlin organization of the SPD).

Due to the split in the Berlin SPD in 1946, there is not too much material on the early period in the files of this organization. The records of meetings of *Kreis* X (Wilmersdorf) of the SPD are included.

Freie Universität Berlin (Free University of Berlin)

Institut für politische Wissenschaften (Institute of Political Sciences).

The Institute's section on the DDR contains a varied and useful collection of materials on the period 1945–46.

Institut für Publizistik (Institute for Communications Media).

The Institute's files contain newspaper sources for the 1945–46 period.
Scattered material was also obtained from:

Archiv Telegraf, Berlin

Files of West Berlin, pro-SPD and antiunity newspaper (now defunct).
and the files of

Informationsbüro West (Information Bureau West), Berlin

National Archives (World War II Records Division), Alexandria, Va.

This division houses the records of the Allied Kommandatura Berlin.

Library of Congress, Newspaper Division

The Library has the best collection of Soviet Zone newspapers from 1945–46, including the *Tägliche Rundschau, Deutsche Volkszeitung,* and *Das Volk.*

Other Libraries

The Library of Congress, New York Public Library, the Library of the Free University of Berlin, other university libraries in the United States and in Germany, and especially the Columbia University Libraries provided useful material.

4. Memoranda

Gniffke Manuscript

As described in its first footnote citation, this is a manuscript prepared by Gniffke dealing with party developments in 1945–46. It formed the basis of the opening chapters of his later book, *Jahre mit Ulbricht*.

Gottfurcht Memorandum

Mr. Hans Gottfurcht's memorandum of his two trips to Germany in 1945–46 to observe German trade union developments for the British TUC.

Hurwitz Memorandum

Mr. Harold Hurwitz, formerly of the United States Military Government staff in Berlin, memorandum originally prepared for Professor W. Philips Davison.

Kriedemann Memorandum

Herbert Kriedemann's memorandum of the meeting in Brunswick on February 8, 1946, between Otto Grotewohl, Gustav Dahrendorf, Kurt Schumacher, and himself.

Schreiber Document

The ZA's memorandum of August 1945 on an "Eastern Orientation."

Professor Wolfgang Friedmann and Professor Philip E. Mosely, Letters

Letters clearing up some questions concerning British and American policy on the development of German party politics and on Allied occupation policies.

5. Newspapers

The newspapers listed below were consulted for the years 1944–47, except as otherwise cited in the notes. While only scattered copies were found for many Soviet Zone newspapers of 1945–46, almost complete files of the central SPD and KPD newspapers of the Soviet Zone in 1945–46 do exist. It should be noted that, for those newspapers especially, many by-lined articles by SPD and KPD officials have been cited.

Allgemeine Zeitung (American "overt" German-language newspaper)
Berliner Stimme (SPD weekly; cited for 1956)
Berliner Zeitung (official *Magistrat* newspaper in 1945–46)
Deutsche Volkszeitung (KPD central newspaper, 1945–46)
Freies Deutschland (newspaper of the "National Committee 'Free Germany' ")
Die Freie Gewerkschaft (FDGB newspaper in 1945–46)
Daily Herald (London)
Izvestiia (Soviet government newspaper)
Krasnaia Zvezda (Soviet army newspaper)
Der Kurier (French-licensed West Berlin newspaper, 1946)
London News Chronicle
Neues Deutschland (SED central party newspaper after April 1946)
The New York Times
Pravda (Soviet party newspaper)
Tägliche Rundschau (Soviet "overt" German-language newspaper)

Tagesspiegel (American-licensed newspaper in West Berlin 1945-)
Telegraf (British-licensed West Berlin newspaper, 1946-)
Thüringer Volkszeitung (KPD newspaper in Thuringia, 1945-46)
Tribüne (SPD newspaper in Thuringia, 1945-46)
Trud (Soviet trade union newspaper)
Das Volk (SPD central newspaper, Berlin, 1945-46)
Volkszeitung (KPD newspaper for Mecklenburg-Vorpommern, 1945-46)
Volks-Zeitung (KPD newspaper in Halle, *Provinz* Saxony, 1945-46)
Die Welt (Hamburg)
Westfalische Zeitung (Bielefeld, [West] Germany)
Die Zeit (weekly, Hamburg)

6. Records of Party Meetings

In addition to the materials (speeches, resolutions, etc.) of various party and interparty meetings cited in the footnotes, the following records of party meetings were available in full.

SPD (Social Democratic Party of Germany)

40. Parteitag der Sozialdemokratischen Partei Deutschlands am 19. und 20. April 1946 in Berlin. Berlin: Vorwärts, 1946.

Die Wiedergeburt der deutschen Sozialdemokratie. Bericht über Vorgeschichte und Verlauf der sozialdemokratischen Parteikonferenz von Hannover vom 5. bis 7. Oktober 1945. London: [Union of Social Democratic Organizations in Great Britain], 1945.

Protokoll der ersten Landeskonferenz der Sozialdemokratischen Partei Deutschlands, Berzirksverband Thüringen [July 1945]. (Unpublished.)

Protokoll vom Parteitag der Sozialdemokratischen Partei Deutschlands—Landesgruppe Sachsen:—Stenographischer Bericht über die Verhandlungen des Landesparteitages abgahalten am 7., 8. und 9. Oktober 1945 in Dresden-Freital. Dresden: Schrift und Kunst, [1945].

Sozialdemokratische Partei Deutschlands. Bezirksverband Berlin. Bezirksparteitag am Sonntag, dem 25. November 1945 vorm. 9 Uhr im "Prater," Berlin, Kastanienallee 7/8. (unpublished.)

Bezirksparteitag der SPD Gross-Berlins am 7.4.1946, nachm. 16 Uhr. (unpublished.)

KPD (Communist Party of Germany)

Bericht über die Verhandlungen des 15. Parteitages der Kommunistischen Partei Deutschlands 19. und 20. April 1946 in Berlin. Berlin: Neuer Weg, 1946.

Die nächsten Aufgaben beim Neuaufbau Deutschlands. Beschlüsse der Parteikonferenz der Kommunistischen Partei Deutschlands am 2. und 3. Marz 1946 in Berlin. Berlin: Neuer Weg, 1946.

Um die Erneuerung der deutschen Kultur. Erste zentrale Kulturtagung der Kommunistischen Partei Deutschlands vom 3. bis 5. Februar in Berlin (Stenographische Niederschrift). Berlin: Neuer Weg, 1946.

Joint Party Meetings

Stenographische Niederschrift über die gemeinsame Konferenz des Zentralkomitees der KPD und des Zentralausschusses der SPD mit den Vertretern der Bezirke am 20. und 21. 12. 1945 in Berlin, SPD-Haus, Behrenstrasse. (unpublished.)

Die Sozialistische Einheitspartei Deutschlands. Die Beschlüsse der gemeinsamen Konferenz der Parteileitungen der SPD und der KPD mit Vertretern der Bezirke am 26. Februar 1946 in Berlin. Berlin: Einheit, 1946.

Vorwärts und aufwärts auf dem Wege zur Einheit. Aufgaben der beiden Arbeiterparteien in der Provinz Brandenburg nach der gemeinsamen Bezirkskonferenz am 16. 2. 1946 in Potsdam. Potsdam: [BV, SPD] und [BL, KPD], n.d.

Unification Party Congresses

Protokoll des Vereinigungsparteitages der Sozialdemokratischen Partei Deutschlands (SPD) und der Kommunistischen Partei Deutschlands (KPD) am 21. und 22. April 1946 in der Staatsoper "Admiralspalast" in Berlin. Berlin: J. H. W. Dietz Nachf., 1946.

Einstimmig beschlossen: SED Gross-Berlin. Die Bildung der SED in der Hauptstadt Deutschlands. Der Bericht über die letzten Parteitäge der SPD und KPD am 13. 4. 1946 und der Vereinigungsparteitag am 14.4.1946. [Berlin]: n. p., [1946].

7. Select Bibliography of Books and Articles

NB. Beiträge zur Geschichte der deutschen Arbeiterbewegung—BzG Zeitschrift für Geschichtswissenschaft—ZfG

Abusch, Alexander et al., eds. *Walter Ulbricht: Schriftsteller, Kunstler, Wissenschaftler. und Pädagogen zu seinem siebzigsten Geburtstag.* Berlin: Aufbau, 1963.

Ackermann, Anton. *An die lernende und suchende deutsche Jugend.* Schriftenreihe der Freien Deutschen Jugend/Heft 1. Berlin and Leipzig: Volk und Wissen, 1946.

—— *Fragen und Antworten.* Berlin: Neuer Weg, 1946.

—— "Gibt es einen besonderen deutschen Weg zum Sozialismus?" *Einheit,* I, no. 1 (February 1946), 23–32.

Adler, H. G. "Selbstverwaltung und Widerstand in den Konzentrationslagern der SS." *Vierteljahrshefte für Zeitgeschichte,* 8, no. 3 (July 1960), 221–36.

Alperovitz, Gar. *Atomic Diplomacy: Hiroshima and Potsdam.* New York: Simon and Schuster, 1965.

—— *Cold War Essays.* Garden City, N.Y.: Doubleday Anchor, 1970.

An die Arbeit! Berlin: "Das Volk," n.d.

Anderle, A., et al., eds. *Zwei Jahrzehnte deutsch-sowjetische Beziehungen 1945–1965.* Berlin: Staatsverlag der Deutschen Demokratischen Republik, 1965.

Angress, Werner T. *Stillborn Revolution: The Communist Bid for Power in Germany 1921–1923.* Princeton: Princeton University Press, 1963.

Arnold, Wilhelm. "Zur Bedeutung und Verbreitung des Aufrufs des Zentralkomitees der Kommunistischen Partei Deutschlands vom 11. Juni 1945." *BzG,* 2, *Sonderheft* (1960), 111–28.

Avarian, V. "In Postwar Germany." *New Times,* no. 3 (February 1, 1946), 30–32.

Bader, William B. *Austria between East and West 1945–1955.* Stanford: Stanford University Press, 1966.

Bahne, Siegfried. " 'Sozialfaschismus' in Deutschland." *International Review of Social History,* 10, Part 2 (1965), 211–45.

Balfour, Michael and John Mair. *Four Power Control in Germany and Austria, 1945–1946.* Survey of International Affairs, 1939–1946, Vol. VIII. London: Oxford University Press, 1956.

Bartel, Walter. "Zum Tode Otto Grotewohls." *ZfG,* 12, no. 8 (1964), 1329–34.

Becher, Johannes. R. *Walter Ulbricht: ein deutscher Arbeitersohn.* 8th ed. Berlin: Dietz, 1964.

Befreites Leuna (1945–1950). Vol. II. 2d ed. Berlin: *Tribüne,* 1959.

Befehle des Obersten Chefs der Sowjetischen Militärverwaltung in Deutschland. Vol. I. Berlin: SWA-Verlag, 1946.

Benser, Gunther. "Bemerkenswerte Eingeständnisse." *BzG,* 3, *Sonderheft* (1961), 139–48.

—— "Klarheit über die Entstehung der Sozialistischen Einheitspartei Deutschlands—eine wichtige Voraussetzung für die Verwirklichung der Aktionseinheit der deutschen Arbeiterklasse." *BzG, 2, Sonderheft* (1960), 150–69.

—— "Probleme der Bündnispolitik der KPD und SED von 1945 bis 1949." *BzG,* 6, no. 1 (1964), 22–38.

—— "Uber den friedlichen Charakter der revolutionären Umwältzung in Ostdeutschland." *BzG,* 7, no. 2 (1965), 189–200.

Berlau, A. Joseph. *The German Social Democratic Party, 1914–1921.* New York: Columbia University Press, 1950.

Bernstein, Barton J., ed. *Politics and Policies of the Truman Administration.* Chicago: Quadrangle, 1970.

Berthold, Lothar. "Der Kampf gegen das Hitlerregime—der Kampf für ein neues Deutschland." *BzG,* 6, no. 6 (1964), 1007–22.

Birke, Ernst et al. *Die Sowjetisierung Ost-Mitteleuropas.* Frankfurt/Main-Berlin: Alfred Metzner, 1959.

Black, Cyril E. and Thomas P. Thornton. *Communism and Revolution: The Strategic Uses of Political Violence.* Princeton: Princeton University Press, 1964.

Blank, A. S. *Kommunisticheskaia Partiia Germanii v bor'be protiv fashistskoi diktatury (1933–1945).* Moscow: Mysl', 1964.

—— *Natsional'nyi Komitet "Svobodnaia Germaniia"—Tsentr antifashistskoi bor'by nemetskikh patriotov (1943–1945 gg).* Vologda: Vologodskoe Knizhnoe Izdatel'stvo, 1963.

Bohn, Helmut. "Die patriotische Karte in der sowjetischen Deutschlandpolitik." *Ost-Probleme,* 7, no. 38, 40, 42 [*Sonderdruck*].

Bolten, Seymour R. "Military Government and the German Political Parties." *The Annals of the American Academy of Political and Social Science,* Vol. 267 (January 1950), 55–67.

Borkenau, Franz. *World Communism.* Ann Arbor: University of Michigan Press, 1962.

Brandt, Heinz. *Ein Traum, der nicht entführbar ist.* Munich: Paul List, 1967.

Brandt, Willy. *Draussen: Schriften während der Emigration.* Günter Struve, ed. Munich: Kindler, 1966.

—— and Richard Löwenthal. *Ernst Reuter—ein Leben für die Freiheit.* Munich: Kindler, 1957.

Brill, Hermann L. *Gegen den Strom.* Offenbach am Main: Bollwerk-Verlag, 1946.

Brown, John Mason. "Government, Administration, and Politics in East Germany: A Selected Bibliography." *American Political Science Review,* 53, no. 2 (June 1959), 507–23.

Brzezinski, Zbigniew K. *The Soviet Bloc: Unity and Conflict.* Revised and enlarged ed. Cambridge: Harvard University Press, 1967.

Buber-Neumann, Margarete. *Als Gefangene bei Hitler und Stalin.* Stuttgart: Deutsche Verlags-Anstalt, 1958.

—— *Von Potsdam nach Moskau.* Stuttgart: W. Kohlhammer, 1957.

Buchwitz, Otto. *Brüder, in eins nun die Hände.* Berlin: Dietz, 1956.

—— "Lehren aus der Vergangenheit." *BzG*, 5, no. 2 (1963), 271–73.

Burmeister, Alfred [pseud.]. *Dissolution and Aftermath of the Comintern: Experiences and Observations, 1943–1947.* New York: Research Program on the USSR, 1955.

Clay, Lucius D. *Decision in Germany.* Garden City, N.Y.: Doubleday, 1950.

Control Council for Germany. *Official Gazette.* Berlin: Allied Secretariat, 1945–

Control Council, British Element. *British Zone Review,* 1945–

Corresponcence between the Chairman of the Council of Ministers of the USSR and the Presidents of the United States and the Prime Ministers of Great Britain during the Great Patriotic War of 1941–1945. 2 vols. Moscow: Foreign Languages Publishing House, 1957.

Croan, Melvin. "Dependent Totalitarianism." Dissertation, Harvard University, 1960.

—— "Soviet Uses of the Doctrine of the 'Parliamentary Road' to Socialism: East Germany, 1945–1946." *American Slavic and East European Review,* 17, no. 3 (October 1958), 302–315.

—— and Carl J. Friedrich. "The East German Regime and Soviet Policy in Germany." *The Journal of Politics,* 20, no. 1 (February 1958), 44–63.

Dahl, Hans F. "Behind the Fronts: Norway." *Journal of Contemporary History,* 5, no. 3 (1970), 37–50.

Dahrendorf, Gustav. *Der Mensch das Mass aller Dinge: Reden und Schriften zur deutschen Politik 1945–1954,* ed. Ralf Dahrendorf. Hamburg: Verlagsgesellschaft deutscher Konsumgenossenschaften, 1955.

[Dahrendorf, Gustav] "V.F." "Beiträge zur Vorgeschichte der Vereinigung von SPD und KPD in der Sowjetzone zur SED." *PZ-Archiv.* 1, no. 1 (September 1950)– no. 5 (November 1950) (pages various).

Dallin, Alexander. "Soviet Foreign Policy and Domestic Politics: A Framework for Analysis," in *The Conduct of Soviet Foreign Policy.* Erik P. Hoffmann and Frederic J. Fleron, Jr., eds. Chicago: Aldine, Atherton, 1971.

—— "The Soviet Stake in Eastern Europe." *The Annals of the American Academy of Political and Social Science,* 317 (May 1958), 138–145.

—— "Vlasov and Separate Peace: A Note." *Journal of Central European Affairs,* 26, no. 4 (January 1957), 294–296.

Degras, Jane, ed. *The Communist International 1919–1943: Documents.* III, 1929–43. London: Oxford University Press, 1965.

Delwig, Christoph. "Hoher Kommissar in Karlshorst." *SBZ-Archiv.* 4, no. 11 (June 1953), 161–62.

Deutscher, Isaac. *Stalin.* London: Oxford University Press, 1949.

Dimitroff, Georgi. *The United Front: The Struggle against Fascism and War.* New York: International Publishers, 1938.

[Dimitrov, G.] "Ein interessanter Brief Georgi Dimitroffs zur Vorbereitung des VII. Weltkongresses der Kommunistischen Internationale." *BzG*, 5, no. 2 (1963), 282–84.

Djilas, Milovan. *Conversations with Stalin.* New York: Harcourt, 1962.

Doernberg, Stefan. *Die Geburt eines neuen Deutschland 1945–1949.* Berlin: Rütten and Loening, 1959.

——, ed. *Beiträge zur Geschichte der Sozialistischen Einheitspartei Deutschlands.* Berlin: Dietz, 1961.

—— "Die Gründung der Sozialistische Einheitspartei Deutschlands und ihre historische Bedeutung." *ZfG*, 4, no. 2 (1956), 213–29.

Dokumente aus den Jahren 1945–1949: Um ein antifaschistisch-demokratisches Deutschland. Berlin: Staatsverlag der Deutschen Demokratischen Republik, 1968.

Dokumente der Kommunistischen Partei Deutschlands, 1945–1956. Berlin: Dietz, 1965.

Dokumente und Materialien zur Geschichte der deutschen Arbeiterbewegung. Series 3, vol. 1. Berlin: Dietz, 1959.

Dorn, Walter L. "The Debate over American Occupation Policy in Germany in 1944–1945." *Political Science Quarterly,* 72, no. 4 (December 1957), 481–501.

Drakhovitch, Milorad M. and Branko Lazitch, eds. *The Comintern: Historical Highlights—Essays, Recollections, Documents.* New York: Praeger (for the Hoover Institution on War, Revolution, and Peace), 1966.

Drobisch, Klaus. "Der Kampf um die Einheitspartei der Arbeiterklasse in Leipzig 1945–1946." *BzG,* 2, *Sonderheft* (1960), 129–49.

Duhnke, Horst. *Die KPD von 1933 bis 1945.* Cologne: Kiepenheuer and Witsch, 1972.

—— *Stalinismus in Deutschland.* [Cologne]: Verlag für Politik und Wirtschaft, [1955].

—— "German Communism in the Nazi Era." Dissertation, University of California (Berkeley), 1964.

Dziewanowski, M. K. *The Communist Party of Poland.* Cambridge: Harvard University Press, 1959.

Edinger, Lewis J. *German Exile Politics.* Berkeley: University of California Press, 1956.

—— *Kurt Schumacher: A Study in Personality and Political Behavior.* Stanford: Stanford University Press, 1965.

Ehrenburg, Ilya. *The War 1941–1945.* Vol. V: *Men, Years, Life.* trans. Tatiana Shebunina and Yvonne Kapp. London: Macgibbon and Kee, 1964.

Einheitsfront der antifaschistisch-demokratischen Parteien. Berlin: Der Neue Weg, n.d.

von Einsiedel, Heinrich Graf. *Tagebuch der Versuchung.* Berlin: Pontes, 1950.

Eliasberg, Vera Franke. "Political Party Development," in *The Struggle for Democracy in Germany,* Gabriel A. Almond, ed. Chapel Hill, N.C.: University of North Carolina Press, 1949.

Enactments and Approved Papers of the Control Council and Coordinating Committee. Berlin: OMGUS Legal Division, 1945–

"Ercoli" [Palmiro Togliatti]. "Die antifaschistische Einheitsfront und die nächsten Aufgaben der KPD." *Kommunistische Internationale,* 16, no. 20 (November 30, 1935), 1741–55.

"Ex-Insider." "Moscow-Berlin 1933." *Survey,* no. 44–45 (October 1962), 153–64.

Fechner, Max. *Einheit tut not! Rede auf der Versammlung der Zentralverwaltung für Industrie in Berlin am 12. März 1946.* Berlin: Einheit, 1946.

Feis, Herbert. *Between War and Peace: The Potsdam Conference.* Princeton: Princeton University Press, 1960.

—— *From Trust to Terror: The Onset of the Cold War 1945–1950.* New York: Norton, 1970.

—— *Roosevelt, Churchill, Stalin.* Princeton: Princeton University Press, 1957.

Findeisen, Otto. "Zu den Einheitsfrontverhandlungen am 23. November 1935 in Prag." *BzG,* 8, no. 3 (1966), 676–94.

Fischer-Galati, Stephen, ed. *Romania.* New York: Praeger, 1956.

Flechtheim, Ossip K., ed. *Dokumente zur Parteipolitischen Entwicklung in Deutschland seit 1945.* 5 vols. Berlin: Dokumenten Verlag-Dr. Herbert Wendler and Co., 1962.

—— *Die Kommunistische Partei in der Weimarer Republik.* Offenbach am Main: Bollwerk-Verlag Karl Drott, 1948.

Florin, Wilhelm. "Unser Verhältnis zur Sozialdemokratie und zu den sozialdemokratischen Massen." *Kommunistische Internationale*, 16, no. 20 (November 30, 1965), 1769–76.

Footman, David, ed. *International Communism*. St. Antony's Papers, No. 9, London: Chatto and Windus, 1960.

Friedmann, W. *The Allied Military Government of Germany*. London: Stevens, 1947.

Friedrich, Carl J. "Military Government and Dictatorship." *The Annals of the American Academy of Political and Social Science*, Vol. 267 (January 1950), 1–7.

Furbotn, Peder. *Kampen for Norges Suverenitet*. Oslo: Norsk Forlag Ny Dag, 1948.

Gaddis, John Lewis. *The United States and the Origins of the Cold War 1941–1947*. New York: Columbia University Press, 1972.

Galkin, A. A. and Mel'nikov, D. E. *SSSR, zapadnye derzhavy i germanskii vopros (1945–1965)*. Moscow: Nauka, 1966.

Gay, Peter. *The Dilemma of Democratic Socialism*. New York: Columbia University Press, 1952.

Gimbel, John. *The American Occupation of Germany: Politics and the Military 1945–1949*. Stanford: Stanford University Press, 1968.

—— *A German Community under American Occupation: Marburg, 1945–1952*. Stanford: Stanford University Press, 1961.

—— "Cold War: German Front." *The Maryland Historian*, 2 (Spring 1972), 41–45.

—— "On the Implementation of the Potsdam Agreement: An Essay on U.S. Postwar German Policy." *Political Science Quarterly*, 87, no. 2 (June 1972), 242–69.

Geschichte der deutschen Arbeiterbewegung in 15 Kapiteln: Kapitel 12, Periode von Mai 1945 bis 1949. Berlin: Dietz, 1968.

Zur Geschichte der Kommunistischen Partei Deutschlands: Eine Auswahl von Materialien und Dokumenten aus den Jahren 1914–1946. Berlin: Dietz, 1955.

Gniffke, Erich W. *Jahre mit Ulbricht*. Cologne: Verlag Wissenschaft und Politik, 1966.

Gorbatov, A. V. *Years Off my Life*. Trans. by Gordon Clough and Anthony Cash. New York: Norton, 1965.

Gottlieb, Manuel. *The German Peace Settlement and the Berlin Crisis*. New York: Paine-Whitman, 1960.

Griffith, William E., ed. *Communism in Europe: Continuity, Change, and the Sino-Soviet Dispute*. 2 vols. Cambridge: M.I.T. Press, 1964.

Gross, Babette L. "Die Volksfrontpolitik in den dreissiger Jahren: Ein Beitrag zum Verständnis der kommunistischen Taktik." *Aus Politik und Zeitgeschichte*. (Beilage zur Wochenzeitung "Das Parlament.") October 24, 1963.

Grotewohl, Otto. *Auf dem Wege zu einem friedlichen, demokratischen und sozialistischen Deutschland*. Berlin: VEB Deutscher Zentral-verlag, 1959.

—— *Im Kampf um die einige Deutsche Demokratische Republik. Reden und Aufsätze— Auswahl aus den Jahren 1945–1953*. Vol. I. Berlin: Dietz, 1954.

—— *Im Kampf um Deutschland. Reden und Aufsätze*. 2 vols. in one: Vol. I, 1945–1947; Vol. II, 1947–1948. Berlin: Dietz, 1948.

—— *Wo stehen wir, wohin gehen wir? Weg und Ziel der deutschen Sozialdemokratie*. Berlin: "Das Volk," 1945.

Grundriss der Geschichte der deutschen Arbeiterbewegung. Berlin: Dietz, 1963.

Gruber, Helmut. "Willi Münzenberg: Propagandist for and against the Comintern." *International Review of Social History*, 10, Part 2 (1965), 188–210.

Gulin, V. I. "Bor'ba sotsialisticheskoi edinoi partii Germanii za vybornye organy vlasti osen'iu 1946." *Vestnik M. G. U., Seriia 10*, no. 4 (1963), 15–33.

Gyptner, Richard. "Aktivisten der ersten Stunde." *BzG*, 1, no. 4 (1959), 745–51.

Harrell, Edwin. J. "Berlin: Rebirth, Reconstruction and Division, 1945–1948: A Study of Allied Cooperation and Conflict." Dissertation, Florida State University, 1965.

Heidelmeyer, Wolfgang and Guenter Hindrichs, eds. *Dokumente zur Berlin-Frage 1944–1962.* 2nd ed. Munich: R. Oldenbourg, 1962.

Herting, Günther and Günther Auruch, eds. *Wir sind die Stäkste der Parteien! Eine Bibliographie zum 15. Jahrestag der Gründung der Sozialistischen Einheitspartei Deutschlands.* Leipzig: VEB Verlag für Buch und Bibliothekswesen, 1961.

Hilger, Gustav and Alfred G. Meyer. *The Incompatible Allies: A Memoir-History of German-Soviet Relations 1918–1941.* New York: Macmillan, 1953.

Horn, Werner. "Zu einigen Problemen der Entwicklung Deutschlands nach dem zweiten Weltkrieg." *BzG*, 1, no 1 (1959), 439–58.

Howley, Frank. *Berlin Command.* New York: Putnam, 1950.

Iakovlev, L. "Novaia nemetskaia idilliia!" *Voina i Rabochii Klass*, no. 8 (1945), 10–15.

Ierusalimskii, V. P. *Gody stanovleniia i bor'by.* Moscow: Nauka, 1970.

Inozemtsev, N. *Amerikanskii imperializm i Germanskii vopros (1945–1954).* Moscow: Gospolizdat, 1954.

Ionescu, Ghita. *Communism in Rumania 1944–1962.* London: Oxford University Press, 1964.

"Istoricheskie resheniia Berlinskoi Konferentsii trekh derzhav (Peredovaia)." *Bol'shevik*, no. 15 (August 1945), 1–11.

Ivanov, S. "O roli sotsialisticheskikh partiakh posle vtoroi mirovoi voiny." *Bol'shevik*, no. 17–18 (September 1946), 50–65.

Iwanow, S. *Über die Rolle der sozialistischen Parteien nach dem zweiten Weltkriege.* Berlin: SWA-Verlag, 1947.

Kaden, Albrecht. *Einheit oder Freiheit. Die Wiedergründung der SPD 1945/1946.* Hanover: J. H. W. Dietz Nachf., 1964.

—— "Entscheidung in Wennigsen: Die Wiedergründung der SPD in 1945 und die 'Einheit der Arbeiterklasse.' " *Die neue Gesellschaft*, no. 6 (1960), 486–95.

—— "Die Wiedergründung der Sozialdemokratischen Partei Deutschlands 1945–1946." Dissertation, Universität Hamburg, 1960.

Kantorowicz, Alfred. *Deutsches Tagebuch.* 2 vols. Munich: Kindler, 1959.

—— " 'Free Germany' in Moscow: A Weapon of Psychological Warfare." *Free World*, 7, no. 2 (February 1944), 149–56.

Kautsky, Benedikt. *Teufel und Verdammte.* 2nd ed. Vienna: Verlag der Wiener Volksbuchhandlung, 1961.

Kelly, Matthew A. "The Reconstitution of the German Trade Union Movement." *Political Science Quarterly*, 44, no. 1 (March 1949), 24–49.

Kertesz, Stephen D. *Diplomacy in a Whirlpool.* South Bend, Ind.: University of Notre Dame Press, 1953.

Kleist, Peter. *Zwischen Hitler und Stalin, 1939–1945.* Bonn: Athenäum, 1950.

Klimow, Gregory. *Berliner Kreml.* Cologne: Kiepenheuer and Witsch, [1951].

Kluth, Hans. *Die KPD in der Bundesrepublik. Ihre politische Tätigkeit und Organisation 1945–1956.* Cologne: Westdeutscher Verlag, 1959.

Knittel, Fritz. "Die KPD—die einzige führende und organisierte Kraft des antifaschistischen Widerstandkampfes in Deutschland 1933–1945." *Zfg*, 6, *Sonderheft* (1958), 190–202.

Knoll, Regina. "Die Hilfe der Sowjetunion für die demokratischen Kräfte des deutschen Volkes (Mai/Juni 1945)." *BzG*, 2, *Sonderheft* (1960), 97–110.

Kogon, Eugon. *Der SS Staat*. 2d ed. Frankfurt: Verlag Frankfurter Hefte, 1947.

Kolko, Gabriel. *The Politics of War. The World and United States Foreign Policy 1943–1945*. New York: Random House, 1969.

Allied Kommandatura Berlin. *Documents*. Berlin, 1945– .

Kommunistische Partei Deutschlands. Zentralkomitee. Abteilung Kultur und Volksbildung. *Vortragsdisposition*.
No. *1/1945*: "Der Sieg des Faschismus in Deutschland und seine Lehren für unseren gegenwärtigen Kampf."
No. 2/1945: "Der Klassencharakter des Faschismus und die Probleme der Einheits- und Volksfront."

Korbonski, Andrzej. "The Polish Communist Party 1938–1942." *Slavic Review*, 16, no. 3 (September 1967), 430–44.

Korfes, Otto, "Zur Geschichte des Nationalkomitees 'Freies Deutschland.' " *ZfG*, 6, no. 6 (1958), 1284–97.

Korol'kov, Iu. *V Germanii posle voiny*. Moscow: Sovetskii Pisatel', 1951.

Korotkevich, G. and P. Poliakov. "Sozdanie sotsialisticheskoi edinoi partii Germanii." *Bol'shevik*, no. 13–14 (July 1946), 53–64.

Korsunskii, A. "Bor'ba za edinstvo rabochego klassa v Germanii." *Mirovoe khoziaistvo i mirovaia politika*, no. 12 (December 1946), 69–80.

Kotowski, Georg. "Der Kampf um die Selbstverwaltung in Berlin: Ein Beitrag zur Vorgeschichte der Spaltung der Stadt." *Das Hauptstadtproblem in der Geschichte*. Tübingen: Max Niemeyer, 1952.

Krieger, Leonard. "The Inter-Regnum in Germany: May–August 1945." *Political Science Quarterly*, 44, no. 4 (December 1949), 507–32.

Krippendorf, Ekkehart. *Die Liberal-Demokratische Partei Deutschlands in der sowjetischen Besatzungszone 1945/1948*. Dusseldorf: Droste, n.d.

—— "Die Gründung der Liberal-Demokratischen Partei in der sowjetischen Besatzungszone 1945." *Vierteljahrshefte für Zeitgeschichte*, 8, no. 3 (July 1960), 291–309.

LaFeber, Walter. *America, Russia, and the Cold War 1945–1966*. New York: Wiley, 1967.

Lampe, Albrecht, ed. *Berlin. Kampf um Freiheit und Selbstverwaltung 1945–1946*. 2d ed. Berlin: Heinz Spitzig, 1961.

Landesbildstelle Berlin. Tonband Archiv. "Berlin nach der Kapitulation," Tonband No. 684.

Lapus, Joseph. "Das Leipziger Nationalkomitee Freies Deutschland—ein Opfer des Faschismus und des Stalinismus." *Der dritte Weg*, 1, no. 7 (November 1959), n.p.

Laqueur, Walter. *Russia and Germany, a Century of Conflict*. London: Weidenfeld and Nicolson, 1965.

Laschitza, Horst. *Kämpferische Demokratie gegen Faschismus*. Berlin: Deutscher Militärverlag, 1969.

—— "Über Inhalt und Programm eines Blockes der kämpferischen Demokratie." *BzG*, 6, no. 6 (1964), 1037–41.

—— "Zwei Dokumente der KPD aus den Jahren 1944 und 1945 für das neue, demokratische Deutschland." *BzG*, 7, no. 2 (1965), 258–68.

Lebedev, N. M. "20 let sotsialisticheskoi edinoi partii Germanii (ob'edinennaia nauchnaia sessiia." *Novaia i Noveishaia Istoriia*, no. 4 (1966), 191–92.

Lederer, Ivo. J., ed. *Russian Foreign Policy: Essays in Historical Perspective.* New Haven: Yale University Press, 1962.

Lehmann, Helmut. "Von der Demokratie zum Sozialismus." *Einheit* 1, no. 1 (February 1946), 20–23.

Leibzon, B. M. and K. K. Shirinia. *Povorot v politike Kominterna (K 30-letiiu VII Kongressa).* Moscow: Mysl', 1965.

Leithäuser, Joachim G. *Wilhelm Leuschner: ein Leben für die Republik.* Cologne: Bund Verlag, 1952.

Lemin, I. "Berlinskaia Konferentsiia triokh derzhav." *Mirovoe khoziaistvo i mirovaia politika,* no. 9 (September 1945), 14–23.

Leonhard, Wolfgang. *Die Revolution entlässt ihre Kinder.* Cologne: Kiepenheuer and Witsch, 1955.

Lerche, Charles O., Jr. *The Cold War . . . and After.* Englewood Cliffs, N.J.: Prentice-Hall, 1965.

Lidtke, Vernon L. *The Outlawed Party. Social Democracy in Germany, 1878–1890.* Princeton: Princeton University Press, 1966.

Link, Werner, ed. *Mit dem Gesicht nach Deutschland: Eine Dokumentation über die sozialdemokratische Emigration, aus dem Nachlass von Friedrich Stampfer ergänzt durch andere Überlieferungen.* Düsseldorf: Droste, 1968.

Lipski, Horst. "Zum Kampf um die Verwirklichung der Beschlüsse der 'ersten Konferenz der Sechzig' im Januar und Februar 1946." *BzG,* 5, no. 2 (1963), 213–27.

Litchfield, Edward H. et al. *Governing Post-War Germany.* Ithaca, N.Y.: Cornell University Press, 1953.

Löbe, Paul. *Der Weg war Lang.* 2d ed. Berlin-Grunewald: Arani, 1954.

McCagg, William O. "Communism in Hungary." Dissertation, Columbia University, 1965.

McKenzie, Kermit E. *Comintern and World Revolution 1928–1943: The Shaping of Doctrine.* New York: Columbia University Press, 1964.

—— "The Soviet Union, the Comintern and World Revolution: 1935." *Political Science Quarterly,* 45, no. 2 (June 1950), 214–37.

McNeill, William Hardy. *American, Britain, and Russia. Their Cooperation and Conflict 1941–1946.* Survey of International Affairs, 1939–1946, Vol. III. London: Oxford University Press, 1953.

Mammach, Klaus. "Die Berner Konferenz der KPD." [I] *BzG,* 7, no. 6 (1965), 971–989.

—— "Die Berner Konferenz der KPD." [II] *BzG,* 8, no. 2 (1966), 227–240.

Matern, Hermann. "Die führende Rolle der Kommunistischen Partei Deutschlands in der antifaschistischen Bewegung 'Freies Deutschland.' " *Einheit,* 18, no. 5 (May 1963), 17–31.

Matthias, Erich. *Die deutsche Sozialdemokratie und der Osten, 1914–1945.* Tübingen: Arbeitsgemeinschaft für Osteuropaforschung, 1954.

—— *Sozialdemokratie und Nation.* Stuttgart: Deutsche Verlags Anstalt, 1952.

—— and Rudolf Morsey, eds. *Das Ende der Parteien 1933.* Düsseldorf: Droste, 1960.

Meissner, Boris. *Russland, die Westmächte und Deutschland (Die sowjetische Deutschlandpolitik 1943–1953).* Hamburg: H. H. Nölke, 1953.

Mel'nikov, D. [E.]. *Bor'ba za edinuiu, nezavisimuiu, demokraticheskuiu, miroliubivuiu Germaniiu.* Moscow: Gospolizdat, 1951.

—— "God posle porazheniia Germanii." *Mirovoe khoziaistvo i mirovaia politika,* no. 6 (1946), 69–80.

—— "Vnutripoliticheskoe polozhenie Germanii." *Mirovoe khoziaistvo i mirovaia politika*, no. 1–2 (1946), 56–67.

Molotov, V. M. *Problems of Foreign Policy. Speeches and Statements, April 1945–November 1948.* Moscow: Foreign Languages Publishing House, 1949.

Monin, D. "Chekhoslovakiia na novykh putakh." *Bol'shevik*, no. 10 (May 1946), 49–65.

Montgomery, John D. *Forced to be Free: The Artificial Revolution in Germany and Japan.* Chicago: University of Chicago Press, 1957.

Mosely, Philip E. *The Kremlin and World Politics.* New York: Vintage Books, 1960.

——, ed. *The Soviet Union, 1922–1962. A Foreign Affairs Reader.* New York: Praeger, 1963.

Müller, Walter. "Die Aktionsgemeinschaft zwischen KPD und SPD in München 1945/1946." *BzG*, 3, *Sonderheft* (1961), 117–38.

Nabokov, Nicolas. *Old Friends and New Music.* Boston: Little, Brown, 1951.

Nettl, J. P. *The Eastern Zone and Soviet Policy in Germany 1945–1950.* London: Oxford University Press, 1951.

Neumann, Franz L. "Soviet Policy in Germany." *The Annals of the American Academy of Political and Social Science*, 263 (May 1949), 165–79.

Neumann, Sigmund. *Die Parteien der Weimarer Republik.* 2nd ed. Stuttgart: W. Kohlhammer, 1965.

Nikolaev, P. A. *Politika SShA, Anglii i Frantsii v Germanskom Voprose 1945–1954.* Moscow: Nauka, 1964.

—— *Politika Sovetskogo Soiuza v Germanskom voprose 1945–1964.* Moscow: Nauka, 1966.

Nitzsche, Gerhard. "Zum 25. Jahrestag der Berner Konferenz der Kommunistischen Partei Deutschlands." *BzG*, 6, no. 1 (1964), 87–98.

Oschilewski, Walter G. *Gustav Dahrendorf.* Berlin-Grunewald: Arani, 1955.

—— and Arno Scholz. *Franz Neumann: ein Kämpfer für die Freiheit.* Berlin-Grunewald: Arani, 1954.

Pfefferkorn, O. "Hermann Matern." *SBZ-Archiv.*, 4, no. 3 (February 5, 1953), 39.

—— "Franz Dahlem." *SBZ-Archiv*, 4, no. 6 (March 20, 1953), 85–86.

—— "Walter Ulbricht." *SBZ-Archiv*, 4, no. 13 (July 5, 1953).

—— "Otto Grotewohl." *SBZ-Archiv*, 4, no. 16 (August 20, 1953), 253–54.

Pfeiffer, Gerd and Hans-Georg Strickert, eds. *KPD-Prozess.* 3 vols. Karlsruhe: C. F. Müller, 1955.

Pieck, Wilhelm. *Der neue Weg zum gemeinsamen Kampf für den Sturz der Hitlerdiktatur.* Strasbourg: Editions Promethee, n.d.

—— *Probleme der Vereinigung von KPD und SPD.* Berlin: Neuer Weg, 1946.

—— "Die Einheit der Arbeiterklasse und die Einheit der Nation." *Einheit*, 1, no. 1 (February 1946), 1–5.

—— "Zu einigen Problemen der Geschichte der KPD." *BzG*, 3, no. 1 (1961), 3–20.

Plener, Ulla. "Kurt Schumachers Konzeption der demokratischen Republik—die Grundlage seiner antikommunistischen Politik (1945/1946)." *BzG*, 8, no. 5 (1966), 802–21.

—— "Zum ideologisch-politischen Klärüngsprozess in der SPD der sowjetischen Besatzungszone 1945," *BzG*, 14, no. 1 (1972), 35–59.

"Propagandistenkonferenz zur Vereinigung von KPD und SPD in Mecklenburg-Vorpommern." *BzG*, 8, no. 3 (1966), 882–84.

Price, Arnold H., ed. *East Germany: A Selected Bibliography.* Washington: The Library of Congress, 1967.

von Puttkamer, Jesco. *Irrtum und Schuld; Geschichte des Nationalkomitess "Freies Deutschland."* Neuwied-Berlin: Michael, 1948.

Regler, Gustav. *The Owl of Minerva.* Trans. by Norman Denny. New York: Farrar, Straus and Cudahy, 1959.

Richardson, James L. "Cold War Revisionism: A Critique." *World Politics,* 24, no. 4 (July 1972), 579–612.

Richert, Ernst. *Das zweite Deutschland: Ein Staat der nicht sein darf.* Gütersloh: Sigbert Mohn, 1964.

Rieber, Alfred J. *Stalin and the French Communist Party 1941–1947.* New York: Columbia University Press, 1962.

Roberts, Henry L. *Rumania: Political Problems of an Agrarian State.* New Haven: Yale University Press, 1951.

Rosner, Fanny, Ilse Schiel, and Dr. Heinz Vosske, eds. *Vereint sind wir Alles. Erinnerungen an die Gründung der SED.* Berlin: Dietz, 1966.

Ruhm von Oppen, Beate, ed. *Documents on Germany under Occupation 1945–1954.* London: Oxford University Press, 1955.

Schenk, Fritz. *Im Vorzimmer der Diktatur.* Cologne: Kiepenheuer and Witsch, 1962.

Scheurig, Bodo. *Freies Deutschland. Das Nationalkomitee und der Bund deutscher Offiziere in der Sowjetunion 1943–1945.* Munich: Nymphenburger Verlagshandlung, 1960.

——, ed. *Verrat hinter Stacheldraht?* Munich: Deutscher Taschenbuch Verlag, 1965.

Schmidt, Walter A. *Damit Deutschland lebe.* Berlin: Kongress-Verlag, 1959.

Scholz, Arno. *Berlin ist eine freie Stadt.* Berlin-Grunewald: Arani, 1962.

—— *Berlin im Würgegriff.* Berlin-Grunewald: Arani, 1953.

Schorske, Carl. *German Social Democracy 1905–1917. The Development of the Great Schism.* Cambridge: Harvard University Press, 1955.

Schulz, Klaus-Peter. *Auftakt zum Kalten Krieg; Der Freiheitskampf der SPD in Berlin 1945/46.* Berlin: Colloquium, 1965.

—— *Berlin zwischen Freiheit und Diktatur.* Berlin: Ernst Staneck, 1963.

Schütz, Klaus. "Die Sozialdemokratie im Nachkriegsdeutschland," M. G. Lange, G. Schulz, K. Schutz, et al., eds. *Parteien in der Bundesrepublik.* Stuttgart: Ring, 1955.

Schutzler, Horst. "Die Unterstützung der Sowjetunion für die demokratischen Kräfte Berlins in den ersten Nachkriegsmonaten." *ZfG,* 13, no. 3 (1965), 396–418.

Seabury, Paul. *The Rise and Decline of the Cold War.* New York: Basic Books, 1967.

—— "Cold War Origins, I." *Journal of Contemporary History,* 3, no. 1 (January 1968), 169–83.

[SED, Politburo.] "Die Gründung der SED—ein historischer Sieg des Marxismus-Leninismus. Thesen des Politbüros des ZK zum 15. Jahrestag der Vereinigung von KPD und SPD." *BzG,* 3, *Sonderheft* (1961), 3–27.

Selbmann, Fritz. *Alternative-Bilanz-Credo.* Halle/Saale: Mitteldeutscher Verlag, 1969.

Seton-Watson, Hugh. *The East European Revolution.* 2d ed., rev. London: Methuen, 1950.

—— *From Lenin to Khrushchev: A History of World Communism.* New York: Praeger, 1960.

—— "Differences in the Communist Parties." *The Annals of the American Academy of Political and Social Science,* vol. 317 (May 1958), 1–7.

Shell, Kurt L. "The Austrian Socialist Party since 1945: Socialism in the 'Age of Fulfillment!' " Dissertation, Columbia University, 1955.

Shulman, Marshall D. *Stalin's Foreign Policy Reappraised.* Cambridge: Harvard University Press, 1963.

Slusser, Robert, ed. *Soviet Economic Policy in Postwar Germany*. New York: Research Program on the USSR, 1953.

Sokolov, A. "K voprosu o demokratii." *Voina i rabochii klass*, no. 8 (1945), 10–15.

Soviet Foreign Policy During the Patriotic War: Documents and Materials. trans. Andrew Rothstein. Vol. I, 22 June 1941 to 31 December 1943. London: Hutchinson, n.d.

Sparring, Ake, ed. *Kommunisten im Norden*. Cologne: Wissenschaft und Politik, 1967.

Stalin, J. V. *Speech to Electors . . . February 9, 1946*. Washington: Embassy of the USSR, March 1946.

—— *Works*. 13 vols. Moscow: Foreign Languages Publishing House, 1953–1955.

Stern, Carola. *Porträt einer bolschewistischen Partei. Entwicklung, Funktion, und Situation der SED*. Cologne: Verlag für Politik und Wirtschaft, 1957.

—— *Ulbricht: Eine politische Biographie*. Cologne: Kiepenheuer and Witsch, 1964.

—— "Otto Grotewohl." *SBZ-Archiv*, 15, no. 19/20 (October 1964), 305.

—— "Ulbricht und die Volksfront." *SBZ-Archiv*, 14, no. 10 (May 1963, 2d half), 148–53.

Starobin, Joseph R. "Origins of the Cold War: The Communist Dimension." *Foreign Affairs*, 47, no. 4 (July 1969), 681–96.

Taborsky, Edward. *Communism in Czechoslovakia 1948–1960*. Princeton: Princeton University Press, 1961.

Tegeran, Ialta, Potsdam: Sbornik dokumentov. Moscow: Mezhdunarodnye otnosheniia, 1967.

Theoharis, Athan. "Roosevelt and Truman on Yalta: The Origins of the Cold War." *Political Science Quarterly*, 87, no. 2 (June 1972), 210–41.

Thomas, Siegfried. *Entscheidung in Berlin*. 2d ed. Berlin: Akademie-Verlag, 1966.

—— "Der Kampf um die Vereinigung von KPD und SPD in Berlin." *ZfG*, 10, *Sonderheft* (1962), 127–45.

—— "Der Wiederbeginn des politischen Lebens in Berlin und die Aktionseinheit der Arbeiterparteien (Mai–Juni 1945)." *ZfG*, 8, no. 6 (1960), 1310–41.

Thoms, Liselotte and Hans Vieillard. *Ein guter Deutscher: Walter Ulbricht—eine biographische Skizze aus seinem Leben*. Berlin: Staatsverlag der Deutschen Demokratischen Republic, 1963.

Tjulpanov, Sergej Ivanovic. "Gedanken über den Vereinigungsparteitag der SED 1946." *ZfG*, 18, no. 5 (1970), 617–25.

—— [Tiul'panov, S. I.]. "Die Rolle der SMAD bei der Demokratisierung Deutschlands." *ZfG*, 15, no. 2 (1967), 240–52.

Tulpanov, S. [Tiul'panov, S. I.]. A New Study of the German Question." *International Affairs* [Moscow], no. 3 (March 1965), 100–2.

Tulpanow, S. I. [Tiul'panov, S. I.]. "Der Kampf der SED für den proletarischen Internationalismus." *BzG*, 8, no. 5 (1966), 788–92.

Tupolev, G. M. "Vosstanovlenie politicheskoi zhizni v Berline posle krakha fashizma." *Voprosy Istorii*, no. 5 (May 1961), 190–91.

Ulam, Adam. *The Rivals: America and Russia since World War II*. New York: Viking, 1971.

Ulbricht, Walter. *Die Entwicklung des deutschen volksdemokratischen Staates 1945–1948*. Berlin: Dietz, 1958.

—— *Die historische Mission der Sozialistischen Einheitspartei Deutschlands*. Berlin: Dietz, 1971.

—— *Zur Geschichte der deutschen Arbeiterbewegung. Aus Reden und Aufsätzen*. II, 1933–46. Berlin: Dietz, 1955. Supplement 1, 1966. Supplement 2, 1968.

—— "Die Grosse Sozialistische Oktoberrevolution und der Kampf der deutschen Arbeiterklasse für den Sozialismus." *Einheit,* 12, no. 11 (November 1957), 1345–50.

—— "Die grosse Vereinigung der Arbeiterschaft ganz Deutschlands wird kommen." *BzG,* 3, no. 3 (1961), 523–46.

—— "Referat zum Entwurf 'Grundriss der Geschichte der deutschen Arbeiterbewegung.' " *BzG,* 4, no. 3 (1962), 547–610.

—— "Zum 20. Jahrestag der Vereinigung von KPD und SPD." *BzG,* 8, no. 1 (1966), 3–8.

[Ulbricht, Walter.] "Die Bedeutung marxistisch-leninistische Theorie für die Entwicklung der Politik der SED (Interview mit Genossen Walter Ulbricht . . .)." *Einheit,* 21, no. 2 (February 1966), 150–67.

[Ulbricht, Walter.] "Walter." "Der Weg zum Sturz des Hitler-faschismus." *Kommunistische Internationale,* 16, no. [?], (August 20, 1935), 1318–40.

[Ulbricht, Walter.] "Zwei richtungsweisende Beiträge Walter Ulbrichts zur Entwicklung der Strategie und Taktik der KPD in den Jahren 1935–1937." *BzG,* 5, no. 1 (1963), 75–84.

U.S. Department of State. *Foreign Relations of the United States, 1945.* Vol. III. Washington: Government Printing Office, 1968.

—— *Foreign Relations of the United States: The Conference of Berlin (The Potsdam Conference) 1945.* 2 vols. Washington: Government Printing Office, 1955.

—— *Foreign Relations of the United States: The Conferences at Malta and Yalta, 1945.* Washington: Government Printing Office, 1955.

—— *Occupation of Germany: Policy and Progress, 1945–1946.* Washington: Government Printing Office, 1947.

U.S. Office of Military Government. *Monthly Report of the Military Governor, 1945–*

—— *Weekly Information Bulletin,* 1945–

U.S. Senate. Committee on Foreign Relations. *Documents on Germany, 1944–1961.* Washington: Government Printing Office, 1961.

Urban, Karl. "Der Kampf um die Wiedervereinigung der Arbeiterbewegung in der Provinz Brandenburg (Mai 1945 bis April 1946)." *ZfG,* 7, no. 7 (1959), 1544–76.

Varga, E. "Osobennosti vnutrennei i vneshnei politiki kapitalisticheskikh stran v epokhu obshchego krizisa kapitalizma." *Mirovoe khoziaistvo i mirovaia politika,* no. 6 (June 1946), 8–18.

Vietzke, Siegfried. *Die KPD auf dem Wege zur Brüsseler Konferenz.* Berlin: Dietz, 1966.

—— "Einige Probleme des Kampfes um die Demokratie in den Beschlüssen der Brüsseler Konferenz der KPD." *BzG,* 3, *Sonderheft* (1961), 55–76.

Vneshniaia Politika Sovetskogo Soiuza v Period Otchestevennoi Voiny, Dokumenty i Materialy. Vol. I, 22 June 1941–31 December 1943. Moscow: OGIZ (Gospolizdat), 1944.

Vosske, Heinz. "Über die Initiativsgruppe der ZK der KPD in Mecklenburg-Vorpommern (Mai bis Juli 1945)." *BzG,* 6, no. 3 (1964), 424–37.

—— "Über die politisch-ideologische Hilfe der KPdSU, der Sowjetregierung und der SMAD für die deutsche Arbeiterklasse in den ersten Nachkriegsjahren 1945 bis 1949," *BzG,* 14, no. 5 (1972), 725–39.

—— "Über die Struktur und die Bestände des Archivs des Instituts für Marxismus-Leninismus beim ZK der SED." *BzG,* 5, no. 1 (1963), 105–11.

Vysotskii, V. N. *Zapadnyi Berlin i ego mesto v sisteme sovremennykh mezhdunarodnykh otnoshenii.* Moscow: Mysl', 1971.

Weber, Hermann, ed. *Der deutsche Kommunismus Dokumente.* Cologne: Kiepenheuer and Witsch, 1963.

—— *Die Sozialistische Einheitspartei Deutschlands 1946–1971.* Hannover: Verlag für Literatur und Zeitgeschehen, 1971.

—— *Von Rosa Luxemburg zu Walter Ulbricht: Wandlungen des Kommunismus in Deutschland.* Hannover: Verlag für Literatur und Zeitgeschehen, 1961.

—— "Ulbricht—ein neuer Mensch." *SBZ-Archiv,* 14, no. 10 (May 1963, 2d half), 153–56.

Wehner, Helfried. "Dokumente internationalistischer, wegweisender Hilfe." *BzG,* 9, *Sonderheft* (1967), 139–40.

Weinert, Erich. *Das Nationalkomitee "Freies Deutschland" 1943–1945.* Berlin: Rütten and Loening, 1957.

Weisenborn, Gunther, ed. *Der lautlose Aufstand. Bericht über die Widerstandsbewegung des deutschen Volkes 1933–1945.* Hamburg: Rowolt, 1953.

Werth, Alexander. *Russia at War 1941–1945.* New York: Dutton, 1964.

Wesemann, Fried. *Kurt Schumacher: ein Leben für Deutschland.* Frankfurt-Main: Herkul Verlagsanstalt, 1952.

Willis, F. Roy. *The French in Germany.* Stanford: Stanford University Press, 1962.

Wohlgemuth, Franz. "Vor dem Einzug der Westmächte im Juli 1945 bestand in ganz Berlin eine antifaschistisch-demokratische Ordnung." *Beiträge, Dokumente, Informationen des Archivs der Hauptstadt der Deutscshen Demokratischen Republik* [BDI], 1, no. 1 (1964), 3–34.

Zahlen zeigen Zeitgeschichte: Berlin 1945–1947. Berlin: Hauptamt für Statistik von Gross-Berlin, 1947.

Zaslavskii, D. "Okkupatsiia Germanii v osveschenii lorda vansittarta." *Bol'shevik,* no. 17–18 (September 1946), 83–87.

Zinner, Paul E. *Communist Strategy and Tactics in Czechoslovakia, 1918–48.* New York: Praeger, 1963.

Zwerenz, Gerhard. *Walter Ulbricht.* Munich: Scherz, 1966.

Index

Studies of the Russian Institute

ALFRED ERICH SENN, *The Emergence of Modern Lithuania*
ERNEST J. SIMMONS, editor, *Through the Glass of Soviet Literature: Views of Russian Society*
THEODORE K. VON LAUE, *Sergei Witte and the Industrialization of Russia*
ALLEN S. WHITING, *Soviet Policies in China, 1917–1924*

PUBLISHED BY TEACHERS COLLEGE PRESS

HAROLD J. NOAH, *Financing Soviet Schools*

PUBLISHED BY PRINCETON UNIVERSITY PRESS

PAUL AVRICH, *The Russian Anarchists*
PAUL AVRICH, *Kronstadt 1921*
EDWARD J. BROWN, *Mayakovsky: A Poet in the Revolution*
MILTON EHRE, *Oblomov and His Creator: The Life and Art of Ivan Goncharov*
LOREN R. GRAHAM, *The Soviet Academy of Sciences and the Communist Party, 1927–1932*
PATRICIA K. GRIMSTED, *Archives and Manuscript Repositories in the USSR: Moscow and Leningrad*
ROBERT A. MAGUIRE, *Red Virgin Soil: Soviet Literature in the 1920's*
T. H. RIGBY, *Communist Party Membership in the U.S.S.R., 1917–1967*
RONALD G. SUNY, *The Baku Commune, 1917–1918*
JOHN M. THOMPSON, *Russia, Bolshevism, and the Versailles Peace*
WILLIAM ZIMMERMAN, *Soviet Perspectives on International Relations, 1956–1967*

PUBLISHED BY CAMBRIDGE UNIVERSITY PRESS

JONATHAN FRANKEL, *Vladimir Akimov on the Dilemmas of Russian Marxism, 1895–1903*
EZRA MENDELSOHN, *Class Struggle in the Pale: The Formative Years of the Jewish Workers' Movement in Tsarist Russia*

PUBLISHED BY THE UNIVERSITY OF MICHIGAN PRESS

RICHARD T. DE GEORGE, *Soviet Ethics and Morality*

PUBLISHED BY THE FREE PRESS

HENRY W. MORTON and RUDOLF L. TŐKÉS, editors, *Soviet Politics and Society in the 1970's*

DATE DUE

GAYLORD   PRINTED IN U.S.A.